SCIENCE AND INFORMATION THEORY

SCIENCE AND INFORMATION THEORY

LEON BRILLOUIN

Adjunct Professor of Physics, Columbia University

Member of the National Academy of Sciences

ACADEMIC PRESS INC. • PUBLISHERS • NEW YORK

1956

ACADEMIC PRESS INC.
125 East 23rd Street
New York 10, N. Y.

Library of Congress Catalog Card Number: 56—6601

Dedicated to my Wife, Whose Faithful Devotion and Love Have Been a Constant Inspiration

PREFACE

A new scientific theory has been born during the last few years, the theory of information. It immediately attracted a great deal of interest and has expanded very rapidly. This new theory was initially the result of a very practical and utilitarian discussion of certain basic problems: How is it possible to define the quantity of information contained in a message or telegram to be transmitted? How does one measure the amount of information communicated by a system of telegraphic signals? How does one compare these two quantities and discuss the efficiency of coding devices? All of these problems, and many similar ones, are of concern to the telecommunication engineer and can now be discussed quantitively.

From these discussions there emerged a new theory of both mathematical and practical character. This theory is based on probability considerations. Once stated in a precise way, it can be used for many fundamental scientific discussions. It enables one to solve the problem of Maxwell's demon and to show a very direct connection between information and entropy. The thermodynamical entropy measures the lack of information about a certain physical system. Whenever an experiment is performed in the laboratory, it is paid for by an increase of entropy, and a generalized Carnot Principle states that the price paid in increase of entropy must always be larger than the amount of information gained. Information corresponds to negative entropy, a quantity for which the author coined the word negentropy. The generalized Carnot Principle may also be called the negentropy principle of information. This principle imposes a new limitation on physical experiments and is independent of the well-known uncertainty relations of quantum mechanics.

The present book is based on lectures delivered before engineers of the International Business Machine Corporation at Poughkeepsie and Endicott, N. Y., and later on at different universities, especially at the University of California at Berkeley.

It is a very pleasant duty for the author to thank the National Science Foundation for a grant which made the completion of this book possible. The scholarly and scientific atmosphere of Columbia University have aided greatly in this task. The author is also greatly indebted to Mrs. Mary H. Payne for her help and for many helpful criticisms.

January, 1956.

Leon Brillouin

INTRODUCTION

A new territory was conquered for science when the theory of information was recently developed. This discovery opened a new field for investigation and immediately attracted pioneers and explorers. It is an interesting phenomenon to watch, in the history of science, and such a sudden expansion of the domain of scientific research deserves closer consideration. How did it happen? How far does it reach? And where can it still expand? Does it mean an invasion of science into a territory traditionally belonging to philosophy, or is it a discovery of a new country, of some "no man's land," which has escaped previous exploration? All of these questions should be examined and carefully answered.

First of all, what is "Information"? Let us look at Webster's dictionary: "Communication or reception of knowledge or intelligence. Facts, ready for communication, as distinguished from those incorporated in a body of thought or knowledge. Data, news, intelligence, knowledge obtained from study or observation..." We may state that information is the raw material and consists of a mere collection of data, while knowledge supposes a certain amount of thinking and a discussion organizing the data by comparison and classification. Another further step leads to scientific knowledge and the formulation of scientific laws.

How is it possible to formulate a scientific theory of information? The first requirement is to start from a precise definition. Science begins when the meaning of the words is strictly delimited. Words may be selected from the existing vocabulary or new words may be coined, but they all are given a new definition, which prevents misunderstandings and ambiguities within the chapter of science where they are used. It may happen that the same word is used with different meanings in two different branches of scientific research: The word "root" has one clearly defined meaning for the student of algebra and another equally specific meaning for the botanist. There is, however, little danger of confusion in such widely separated fields. The "roots" of algebra do not grow, and the botanist's "roots" are never imaginary! This uniqueness of the meaning of words is characteristic of the scientific method. Since similar definitions have been introduced by scientists of every country, translation is made easy by a "one-to-one" correspondence between scientific vocabularies. If such a situation prevailed in everyday usage, international understanding would be very much easier!

The layman has an uneasy feeling when common words are used with a new scientific definition, and he may be inclined to call such usage "scientific jargon."

But "jargons" are the rule in every specialized field — in theology or even in philosophy — as well as in engineering. The lay reader cannot understand the language of the specialists because he does not know enough about the matters under discussion.

The precise definition of words in the scientific language is usually based on two distinct methods: In mathematics, definitions start with a certain number of carefully selected and stated postulates, and more complex entities are derived from, and defined in terms of, these initial postulates. The new definitions amount to a verbal translation of formulas given symbolically and based on postulates. Experimental sciences have introduced another type of definition, often called "operational." Force, mass, velocity, etc., are defined by a short description of the type of experiment required for the measurement of these quantities. The operational point of view in the experimental sciences has been strongly recommended by many prominent scientists, and the name of P. W. Bridgman is often quoted in this connection. As a rule it has been found advisable to introduce into the scientific language only those quantities which can be defined operationally. Words not susceptible of an operational definition have, usually, eventually been found untrustworthy, and have been eliminated from the scientific vocabulary. For example, remember the "ether," and how relativity theory rendered the term meaningless.

Returning to information theory, we must start with a precise definition of the word "information." We consider a problem involving a certain number of possible answers, if we have no special information on the actual situation. When we happen to be in possession of some information on the problem, the number of possible answers is reduced, and complete information may even leave us with only one possible answer. Information is a function of the ratio of the number of possible answers before and after, and we choose a logarithmic law in order to insure additivity of the information contained in independent situations. These problems and definitions are discussed in Chapter I, and constitute the basis of the new theory.

The methods of this theory can be successfully applied to all technical problems concerning information: coding, telecommunication, mechanical computers, etc. In all of these problems we are actually processing information or transmitting it from one place to another, and the present theory is extremely useful in setting up rules and stating exact limits for what can and cannot be done. But we are in no position to investigate the process of thought, and we cannot, for the moment, introduce into our theory any element involving the human value of the information. This elimination of the human element is a very serious limitation, but this is the price we have so far had to pay for being able to set up this body of scientific knowledge. The restrictions that we have introduced enable us to give a quantitative definition of information and to treat information as a physically measurable quantity. This definition cannot distinguish between information of great importance and a piece of news of no great value for the person who receives it.

The definition may look artificial at first sight, but it is actually practical and scientific. It is based on a collection of statistical data on each problem to be discussed, and these data, once available, are the same for all observers. Hence our definition of information is an absolute objective definition, independent of the observer. The "value" of the information, on the other hand, is obviously a subjective element, relative to the observer. The information contained in a sentence may be very important to me and completely irrelevant for my neighbor. An item from a newspaper may be read with some interest by many readers, but a theorem of Einstein is of no value to the layman, while it will attract a great deal of attention from a physicist.

All these elements of human value are ignored by the present theory. This does not mean that they will have to be ignored forever, but, for the moment, they have not yet been carefully investigated and classified. These problems will probably be next on the program of scientific investigation, and it is to be hoped that they can be discussed along scientific lines.

The present theory extends over the "no man's land" of absolute information, problems that neither scientists nor philosophers ever discussed before. If we reach into the problems of value, we shall begin to invade a territory reserved for philosophy. Shall we ever be able to cross this border and push the limits of science in this direction? This is for the future to answer.

The definition of absolute information is of great practical importance. The elimination of the human element is just the way to answer a variety of questions. The engineer who designs a telephone system does not care whether this link is going to be used for transmission of gossip, for stock exchange quotations, or for diplomatic messages. The technical problem is always the same: to transmit the information accurately and correctly, whatever it may be. The designer of a calculating machine does not know whether it will be used for astronomical tables or for the computation of pay checks. Ignoring the human value of the information is just the way to discuss it scientifically, without being influenced by prejudices and emotional considerations.

Physics enters the picture when we discover a remarkable likeness between information and entropy. This similarity was noticed long ago by L. Szilard, in an old paper of 1929, which was the forerunner of the present theory. In this paper, Szilard was really pioneering in the unknown territory which we are now exploring in all directions. He investigated the problem of Maxwell's demon, and this is one of the important subjects discussed in this book. The connection between information and entropy was rediscovered by C. Shannon in a different class of problems, and we devote many chapters to this comparison. We prove that information must be considered as a negative term in the entropy of a system; in short, information is negentropy. The entropy of a physical system has often been described as a measure of randomness in the structure of the system. We can now state this result in a slightly different way:

Every physical system is incompletely defined. We only know the values of some macroscopic variables, and we are unable to specify the exact positions and velocities of all the molecules contained in a system. We have only scanty, partial information on the system, and most of the information on the detailed structure is missing. Entropy measures the lack of information; it gives us the total amount of missing information on the ultramicroscopic structure of the system.

This point of view is defined as the negentropy principle of information, and it leads directly to a generalization of the second principle of thermodynamics, since entropy and information must be discussed together and cannot be treated separately. This negentropy principle of information will be justified by a variety of examples ranging from theoretical physics to everyday life. The essential point is to show that any observation or experiment made on a physical system automatically results in an increase of the entropy of the laboratory. It is then possible to compare the loss of negentropy (increase of entropy) with the amount of information obtained. The efficiency of an experiment can be defined as the ratio of information obtained to the associated increase in entropy. This efficiency is always smaller than unity, according to the generalized Carnot principle. Examples show that the efficiency can be nearly unity in some special examples, but may also be extremely low in other cases.

This line of discussion is very useful in a comparison of fundamental experiments used in science, more particularly in physics. It leads to a new investigation of the efficiency of different methods of observation, as well as their accuracy and reliability.

An interesting outcome of this discussion is the conclusion that the measurement of extremely small distances is physically impossible. The mathematician defines the infinitely small, but the physicist is absolutely unable to measure it, and it represents a pure abstraction with no physical meaning. If we adopt the operational viewpoint, we should decide to eliminate the infinitely small from physical theories, but, unfortunately, we have no idea how to achieve such a program.

Altogether we do hope that the scientific theory of information marks just the beginning of a new and important chapter of scientific investigation especially in physics and also in biology.

Table of Contents

Preface vii

Introduction ix

Chapter 1. The Definition of Information 1
1. Definition of Information 1
2. Unit Systems 2
3. Generalization and Examples 3
4. Information Using the Alphabet 4
5. Information Content in a Set of Symbols with Different *a priori* Probabilities 5
6. General Remarks 8

Chapter 2. Application of the Definitions and General Discussion 11
1. Definitions 11
2. Property A 12
3. Property B 13
4. Property C 14
5. Joint Events 17
6. Conditional Information 19

Chapter 3. Redundancy in the English Language 21
1. Correlation and Joint Events 21
2. Correlation in Language 22
3. Redundancy in Language 23
4. Some Typical Experiments 25
5. Coding Devices 26

Chapter 4. Principles of Coding, Discussion of the Capacity of a Channel 28
1. Introduction 28
2. Definition of a Channel and its Capacity 28
3. Symbols, Words, and Messages in Sequential Coding 30
4. Discussion 32
5. Examples 34
6. Computation of the Capacity of a Channel 37
7. Matching a Code with a Channel 38
8. General Problem: Symbols with Different Lengths 41
9. The Matching Problem 44
10. Problems of Word Statistics (Mandelbrot) 44
11. Solving the Matching Problem 47

Appendix 49

Chapter 5. Coding Problems 51

1. Alphabetic Coding, Binary System 51
2. Alphabetic Coding, Ternary System 53
3. Alphabet and Numbers 54
4. Binary Coding by Words 55
5. Alphabetic Coding by Words 58
6. Coding Based on Letter Groups and on Correlation 58

Chapter 6. Error Detecting and Correcting Codes 62

1. Error Detecting Codes 62
2. Single Error Detecting Codes 63
3. Single Error Correcting and Double Error Correcting Codes . . . 66
4. Efficiency of Self-Correcting Codes 67
5. The Capacity of a Binary Channel with Noise 69

Chapter 7. Applications to Some Special Problems 71

1. The Problem of Filing Using a Miscellaneous Cell 71
2. Filing with Cross Referencing 73
3. The Most Favorable Number of Signals per Elementary Cell . . . 75

Chapter 8. The Analysis of Signals: Fourier Method and Sampling Procedure 78

1. Fourier Series 78
2. The Gibbs' Phenomenon and Convergence of Fourier Series . . . 80
3. Fourier Integrals 83
4. The Role of Finite Frequency Band Width 87
5. The Uncertainty Relation for Time and Frequency 89
6. Degrees of Freedom of a Message 93
7. Shannon's Sampling Method 97
8. Gabor's Information Cells 99
9. Autocorrelation and Spectrum; the Wiener-Khintchine Formula . 101
10. Linear Transformations and Filters 103
11. Fourier Analysis and the Sampling Method in Three Dimensions . 105
12. Crystal Analysis by X-Rays 111

Appendix. Schwarz' Inequality 113

Chapter 9. Summary of Thermodynamics 114

1. Introduction 114
2. The Two Principles of Thermodynamics; Entropy and Negentropy . 114
3. Impossibility of Perpetual Motion; Thermal Engines 117
4. Statistical Interpretation of Entropy 119
5. Examples of Statistical Discussions 121
6. Energy Fluctuations; Gibbs Formula 122
7. Quantized Oscillator 124
8. Fluctuations 125

Chapter 10. THERMAL AGITATION AND BROWNIAN MOTION 128
1. Thermal Agitation 128
2. Random Walk 129
3. Shot Effect 132
4. Brownian Motion 134
5. Thermal Agitation in an Electric Circuit 137
Appendix 139

Chapter 11. THERMAL NOISE IN AN ELECTRIC CIRCUIT; NYQUIST'S FORMULA 141
1. Random Impulses Model 141
2. The Nyquist Method 143
3. Discussion and Applications 145
4. Generalizations of Nyquist's Formula 146
5. Thermal Agitation in a Rectifier 148

Chapter 12. THE NEGENTROPY PRINCIPLE OF INFORMATION 152
1. The Relation between Information and Entropy 152
2. The Negentropy Principle of Information; Generalization of Carnot's Principle 153
3. Some Typical Physical Examples 156
4. Some General Remarks 159

Chapter 13. MAXWELL'S DEMON AND THE NEGENTROPY PRINCIPLE OF INFORMATION 162
1. Maxwell's Demon: Historical Survey 162
2. The Demon Exorcised 164
3. Discussion 166
4. The Demon's Operation as a Transformation of Information into Negative Entropy 168
5. The Negentropy Required in the Observation 172
6. Szilard's Problem: The Well-Informed Heat Engine 176
7. Gabor's Discussion 179
Appendix I 182
Appendix II 183

Chapter 14. THE NEGENTROPY PRINCIPLE OF INFORMATION IN GENERAL PHYSICS 184
1. The Problem of Measurements in Physics 184
2. Observations Made on an Oscillator 185
3. High-Frequency Resonator and the Cost of an Observation . . . 188
4. Experiments Requiring Many Simultaneous Observations at Low Frequencies 190
5. Problems Requiring High Reliability 194
6. A More Accurate Discussion of Experiments Using High Frequencies 196
7. An Example Showing the Minimum Negentropy Required in an Observation 198

Chapter 15. OBSERVATION AND INFORMATION 202
1. Experimental Errors and Information 202
2. Length Measurements with Low Accuracy 204
3. Length Measurements with High Accuracy 206
4. Efficiency of an Observation 209
5. Measurement of a Distance with an Interferometer 210
6. Another Scheme for Measuring Distance 213
7. The Measurement of Time Intervals 217
8. Observation under a Microscope 219
9. Discussion of the Focus in a Wave Guide 223
10. Examples and Discussion 226
11. Summary 228

Chapter 16. INFORMATION THEORY, THE UNCERTAINTY PRINCIPLE, AND PHYSICAL LIMITS OF OBSERVATION 229
1. General Remarks 229
2. An Observation is an Irreversible Process 231
3. General Limitations in the Accuracy of Physical Measurements . . 232
4. The Limits of Euclidean Geometry 235
5. Possible Use of Heavy Particles Instead of Photons 236
6. Uncertainty Relations in the Microscope Experiment 238
7. Measurement of Momentum 241
8. Uncertainty in Field Measurements 243

Chapter 17. THE NEGENTROPY PRINCIPLE OF INFORMATION IN TELECOMMUNICATIONS 245
1. The Analysis of Signals with Finite Band Width 245
2. Signals and Thermal Noise: Representation in Hyperspace . . . 246
3. The Capacity of a Channel with Noise 247
4. Discussion of the Tuller-Shannon Formula 248
5. A Practical Example 252
6. The Negentropy Principle Applied to the Channel with Noise . . 254
7. Gabor's Modified Formula and the Role of Beats 257

Chapter 18. WRITING, PRINTING, AND READING 259
1. The Transmission of Information: Live Information 259
2. The Problem of Reading and Writing 260
3. Dead Information and How to Bring it Back to Life 261
4. Writing and Printing 263
5. Discussion of a Special Example 264
6. New Information and Redundancy 265

Chapter 19. THE PROBLEM OF COMPUTING 267
1. Computing Machines 267
2. The Computer as a Mathematical Element 269
3. The Computer as a Circuit Element, Sampling and Desampling (Linvill and Salzer) 273

4. Computing on Sampled Data at Time t 275
5. The Transfer Function for a Computer 277
6. Circuits Containing a Computer, The Problem of Stability 279
7. Discussion of the Stability of a Program 281
8. A Few Examples 283

Chapter 20. INFORMATION, ORGANIZATION, AND OTHER PROBLEMS 287
1. Information and Organization 287
2. Information Contained in a Physical Law 289
3. Information Contained in a Numerical Table 291
4. General Remarks 293
5. Examples of Problems Beyond the Present Theory 294
6. Problems of Semantic Information 297

Author Index 302

Subject Index 304

CHAPTER 1

THE DEFINITION OF INFORMATION

1. Definition of Information

A theory of information has been developed in recent years, and has found wide application in different fields: telecommunications, computing, pure physics, and discussion of the fundamental process of scientific observation. A certain expression can be defined to measure the amount of information in a given operation, and we shall prove that the quantity thus introduced is very closely related to the physical entropy of thermodynamics.

The definition of information is derived from statistical considerations. First we discuss a very simple example:

Let us consider a situation in which P_0 different possible things might happen, but with the condition that these P_0 possible outcomes are equally probable *a priori*. This is the initial situation, when we have no special information about the system under consideration. If we obtain more information about the problem, we may be able to specify that only one out of the P_0 outcomes is actually realized. The greater the uncertainty in the initial problem is, the greater P_0 will be, and the larger will be the amount of information required to make the selection. Summarizing, we have:

Initial situation: $I_0 = 0$ with P_0 equally probable outcomes;

Final situation: $I_1 \neq 0$ with $P_1 = 1$, i. e. one single outcome selected.

The symbol I denotes information, and the definition of the information is

$$I_1 = K \ln P_0, \tag{1.1}$$

where K is a constant and "ln" means the natural logarithm to the base e.

The use of a logarithm in formula (1.1) is justified by the fact that we want the information to have an additive property. For let us consider two independent problems, the first one possessing P_{01} *a priori* equally probable solutions, and the second one P_{02}. Each solution of the first problem can be coupled with any solution of the second one. Hence the total number of initial cases is

$$P_0 = P_{01} \cdot P_{02},$$

giving

$$I_1 = K \ln (P_{01} \cdot P_{02}) = I_{11} + I_{12}, \tag{1.2}$$

where

$$I_{11} = K \ln P_{01} \qquad \text{and} \qquad I_{12} = K \ln P_{02}.$$

The total amount of information required for solving both of the problems is just the sum of the two separate informations I_{11} and I_{12}.

2. Unit Systems

The question of *units* must be discussed before proceeding. It has become customary, in information theory, to consider the information I as a dimensionless quantity (a pure number), and hence the constant K is a pure number. The most convenient unit system is based on binary digits (abbreviated "bits"). Let us illustrate with an example. We consider a problem with n different independent selections, each of them corresponding to a binary choice: 0 or 1. The total number of possibilities is

$$P = 2^n$$

and from Eq. (1.1) we obtain the information

$$I = K \ln P = K n \ln 2.$$

We want to identify I with n, the number of binary digits, and we take

$$K = 1/(\ln 2) = \log_2 e. \tag{1.3 a}$$

We thus obtain the information I in bits:

$$I = \log_2 P. \tag{1.3 b}$$

As an example, consider a pack of 32 different cards, of which one is to be selected. From. Eq. (1.3 b) we say that

$$I = 5 \text{ bits}, \qquad \text{since } 32 = 2^5.$$

But now consider two separate packs of cards, each containing 32 different cards. If we now select two cards, one from each pack, we would like to be able to say that we have twice as much information. The total number P of possibilities is

$$P = P_1 \cdot P_2 \qquad \text{with} \qquad P_1 = P_2 = 32 = 2^5,$$

and hence

$$P = 2^{10}.$$

Now, from Eq. (1.1),

$$I = K \ln P = K \ln(P_1 \cdot P_2) = K \ln P_1 + K \ln P_2.$$

Therefore

$$I = 10 \text{ bits.}$$

Thus, the logarithmic definition of information seems reasonable.

Another unit system will be introduced when we compare "information" with thermodynamical "entropy" and decide to measure both quantities with the same units. Entropy (see Chapter 9) has the dimensions of energy divided by temperature. In the c. g. s. and centigrade degree unit system, entropy is measured in ergs per degree. Also there is for entropy a formula very similar to Eq. (1.1), the Boltzmann formula, which contains a coefficient

$$k = 1.38 \times 10^{-16} \text{ ergs per degree centigrade.} \tag{1.4}$$

This constant k is known as the Boltzmann constant [Eq. (9.15)]. If we use this k instead of K in Eq. (1.1), we measure information in entropy units.

We may go one step further, and decide to choose our units in such a way tha both entropy and information will be dimensionless and represent pure numbers.[1] This can be done by measuring the temperature in energy units. The usual centigrade scale applies when k has the numerical value given by Eq. (1.4) and is considered as a pure number. When this is done the ratio between the units of our two systems is a pure number:

$$k/K = k \ln 2 \approx 10^{-16}. \tag{1.4 a}$$

This numerical value plays an important role in all the applications of the theory.

3. Generalization and Examples

The definition of the measure of information can be generalized to cover the case when P_0 possibilities exist in the initial situation, while the final situation still contains P_1 possibilities:

Initially: $I_0 = 0$ with P_0 equally probable cases;

Finally: $I_1 \neq 0$ with P_1 equally probable cases.

In such a case we take

$$I_1 = K \ln(P_0/P_1) = K \ln P_0 - K \ln P_1. \tag{1.5}$$

This definition [Eq. (1.5)] reduces to Eq. (1.1) when $P_1 = 1$ and represents an obvious generalization of Eq. (1.1).

Let us consider a numerical case, in which we shall assume that all the digits are equally probable. We shall consider a number G of digits, with base N. In general

$$I = K \ln N^G = K G \ln N. \tag{1.6}$$

---

[1] D. E. Bell, *J. Appl. Phys.* **23**, 372 (1952).

We may write Eq. (1.6) in terms of bits:

$$I = G \log_2 N \tag{1.7}$$

since

$$(\log_2 N)(\ln 2) = \ln N, \qquad \text{and} \qquad K = 1/(\ln 2).$$

Thus, if $N = 2$, we will have 2^G different possibilities, and

$$I = G \text{ bits of information.} \tag{1.8}$$

It is easy to prove that we obtain the same value for the information when we change the base N and adjust accordingly the number of digits. Let us, for instance, choose a base $N' = 8$. Then the number under consideration will require only $G' = G/3$ digits for its representation, and

$$I = G' \log_2 N' = (G/3) \cdot 3 = G, \tag{1.9}$$

which agrees with Eq. (1.8).

In a decimal system let us consider a number with G_{10} digits:

$$N = 10, \qquad \text{and} \qquad I = G_{10} \log_2 10 = G_{10} \cdot 3.32 \text{ bits.} \tag{1.10}$$

One decimal digit yields 3.32 bits of information, and a binary representation of a number requires 3.32 more digits than does a decimal representation.

4. Information Using the Alphabet

Most of the information we use is communicated by means of the language. In the spoken language the elementary symbols are the fundamental sounds (often called phonemes) and the written language consists of words spelled out in letters. Let us consider the problem of a written sentence and compute the amount of information contained in this sentence. This is an intricate problem of great practical importance, and it has been very carefully discussed by C. E. Shannon[1] and many other authors. As we shall see, a complete and rigorous solution has not yet been obtained, because of a lack of complete statistical data about the language.

We may consider the letters as the symbols which we have to select in order to build up a sentence. A complete alphabet actually contains 27 symbols: the usual 26 letters plus the "blank" or spacing between words. If these 27 symbols were equally probable *a priori*, we would say that the information contained in a sentence of G letters would be

$$I = G \log_2 27 \text{ bits,} \tag{1.11}$$

[1] C. E. Shannon and W. Weaver, "The Mathematical Theory of Communication." U. of Illinois Press, Urbana, Ill., 1949.

or

$$i = \log_2 27 = 4.76 \text{ bits per letter.}$$

This corresponds to a direct application of formula (1.7). The solution thus obtained is, however, not satisfactory, since the different letters do not occur with equal *a priori* probabilities in the language. A table of these probabilities for the English language has been constructed and is given in Table 1.1.

TABLE 1.1

The Probability of Occurrence p and Values of $-\log_{10} p$ for the Letters of the English Language

Symbol	Probability, p	$-\log_{10} p$	Symbol	Probability, p	$-\log_{10} p$
Word space, or "blank"	0.2	0.699	*L*	0.029	1.54
E	0.105	0.979	*C*	0.023	1.64
T	0.072	1.143	*FU*	0.0225	1.65
O	0.0654	1.184	*M*	0.021	1.68
A	0.063	1.2	*P*	0.0175	1.76
N	0.059	1.23	*YW*	0.012	1.92
I	0.055	1.26	*G*	0.011	1.96
R	0.054	1.27	*B*	0.0105	1.98
S	0.052	1.28	*V*	0.008	2.1
H	0.047	1.33	*K*	0.003	2.52
D	0.035	1.46	*X*	0.002	2.7
			JQZ	0.001	3.0

Let p_j be the *a priori* probability of the j-th letter ($j = 1, 2, \ldots, 27$) as specified in Table 1.1. The average information per letter can, according to Shannon, be written as

$$i = -K \sum_{j=1}^{27} p_j \ln p_j. \tag{1.12}$$

We shall now discuss the validity of this formula.

5. Information Content in a Set of Symbols with Different *a priori* Probabilities

We now assume that we are using M different symbols, $1, 2, \ldots, j, \ldots, M$, which have, respectively, *a priori* probabilities of $p_1, p_2, \ldots, p_j, \ldots, p_M$, no other conditions or constraints being introduced about the use of these symbols.

We want to derive Shannon's equation [Eq. (1.12)], which says that a sentence containing G symbols should have an information content

$$I = G \cdot i = -GK \sum_{j=1}^{j=M} p_j \ln p_j, \tag{1.13}$$

where i is the average information per symbol, and

$$\sum_{j=1}^{j=M} p_j = 1.$$

We shall start with a simple problem, which will be easy to generalize afterwards.

Let us consider an alphabet of two "letters," dot and dash as in telegraphy, or 0 and 1. Consider G cells and assume that N_0 of the cells contain 0 and N_1 contain 1, so that $N_0 + N_1 = G$. Thus, all of the cells will be filled. Then the probability of a cell containing 0 would be

$$p_0 = N_0/G, \tag{1.14}$$

and the probability that it contains 1 is

$$p_1 = N_1/G \tag{1.15}$$

with

$$p_0 + p_1 = 1, \tag{1.16}$$

since the probability that it contains either 0 or 1 is unity.

Now, let us find the number of ways of filling each of the G cells with either 0 or 1, but never with both. This is exactly the same as a problem in Fermi statistics. The number of ways we can fill the G cells will be equal to the number of ways we can fill N_0 of the cells with 0, since once we have distributed N_0 0's the remaining N_1 cells must each contain 1. But the number of ways we can fill N_0 of the cells with 0 is just the number of combinations of G things taken N_0 at a time:

$$P = G!/N_0!\,N_1!. \tag{1.17}$$

This is the number of "messages" of G symbols, consisting of one symbol of a two letter alphabet used N_0 times and the other used N_1 times. If we select one of these messages, we can, by Eq. (1.1), write the information

$$I = K \ln P = K\,[\ln G! - \ln N_0! - \ln N_1!]. \tag{1.18}$$

If the message is a long one, and G, N_0, and N_1 are sufficiently large, the logarithms of the factorials may be approximated by means of Stirling's formula:

$$\ln Q! \approx Q(\ln Q - 1). \tag{1.19}$$

This formula is known to give a very good approximation for $Q > 100$. So if $G \gg 1$, $N_0 \gg 1$, and $N_1 \gg 1$, then

$$I \approx K\,[G(\ln G - 1) - N_0(\ln N_0 - 1) - N_1(\ln N_1 - 1)],$$

or, recalling that $G = N_0 + N_1$, we have

$$I \approx K\,[G \ln G - N_0 \ln N_0 - N_1 \ln N_1]. \tag{1.20}$$

Again using $G = N_0 + N_1$, we may rewrite Eq. (1.20) as

$$I \approx -KG\left[\frac{N_0}{G}\ln\frac{N_0}{G} + \frac{N_1}{G}\ln\frac{N_1}{G}\right]. \tag{1.21}$$

If we insert Eqs. (1.14) and (1.15), and divide by G, Eq. (1.21) becomes

$$i = I/G \approx -K\,[p_0 \ln p_0 + p_1 \ln p_1], \tag{1.22}$$

where i is the information per symbol of the message. This is exactly Shannon's formula (1.13) for a problem with just two symbols. Note that since p_0 and p_1 are each less than unity, their logarithms are negative, and therefore formula (1.22) yields a positive value for i.

The generalization for more than two symbols is easy. We specify the numbers $N_1, N_2, \ldots, N_j, \ldots, N_M$ of symbols of M different types to be used, and we select a number of cells

$$G = \sum_{j=1}^{j=M} N_j. \tag{1.23}$$

We then define the probabilities:

$$p_j = N_j/G \quad \text{for the } j\text{-th symbol}. \tag{1.24}$$

Hence

$$\sum_{j=1}^{j=M} p_j = 1. \tag{1.25}$$

The total number P of messages that can be obtained by distributing the symbols at random on the G cells (with never more than one symbol per cell) is

$$P = G! \Big/ \prod_{j=1}^{j=M} N_j!, \tag{1.26}$$

a formula which is a direct generalization of Eq. (1.17). We then obtain for the information contained in one special message:

$$I = K \ln P = K\left[\ln(G!) - \sum_{j=1}^{j=M} \ln(N_j!)\right]$$
$$\approx K\left[G \ln G - \sum_{j=1}^{j=M} N_j \ln N_j\right]. \tag{1.27}$$

The equalities in Eq. (1.27) correspond to Eqs. (1.18), (1.19), and (1.20), assuming, again, that the G and N_j's are large enough numbers so that Stirling's formula may be used. The method used to obtain Eqs. (1.21) and (1.22) yields here

$$I \approx -KG \sum_{j=1}^{j=M} (N_j/G) \ln(N_j/G) = -KG \sum_{j=1}^{j=M} p_j \ln p_j, \tag{1.28}$$

and this is the original Shannon formula.

As an example, consider a 10,000 letter message constructed from letters of the 27 letter alphabet by selecting them at random with equal *a priori* probabilities. Then

$$G = 10{,}000, \text{ and } I = 10{,}000 \log_2 27 = 47{,}600 \text{ bits}, \tag{1.29}$$

and

$$i = I/10{,}000 = 4.76 \text{ bits per letter.} \tag{1.29 a}$$

If, however, we select letters for a message of the same length, but take the *a priori* probabilities of the individual letters into account, then Eq. (1.28) must be used:

$$i = I/G = I/10{,}000 \approx -K \sum_{j=1}^{j=27} p_j \ln p_j = 4.03. \tag{1.30}$$

This last value can easily be computed from the data of Table 1.1.

A more careful analysis of the structure of the language will be given in the following sections. It will show that the above value is still an upper limit, and that the actual amount of information per letter is much lower than 4, probably somewhere between one and two bits per letter.

6. General Remarks

A general remark can immediately be made: Every type of constraint, every additional condition imposed on the possible freedom of choice immediately results in a decrease of information. Let us discuss a system which exhibits P different possibilities when all variables are free. When we impose constraints restricting the freedom of choice on the variables, these conditions will eliminate some of the possibilities which previously were acceptable. The new number P' of possibilities, with constraints, must obviously be smaller than the original P, and hence we must have a new measure of information $I' < I$:

$$\begin{aligned} &\text{with no constraint: } P \text{ cases and } I = K \ln P \\ &\text{with constraints: } P' \text{ cases with } P' < P \text{ and} \\ &\qquad I' = K \ln P' < I. \end{aligned} \tag{1.31}$$

The example in the preceding section on the use of letters illustrates this. When letters are used freely (equal *a priori* probabilities), the information is 4.76 bits per letter. If we impose the constraints corresponding to Table 1.1, and take into account the *a priori* probabilities of the different letters, the information per letter drops to 4.03 bits. Additional constraints will reduce it still further. Another way of explaining this general result is to say that the constraint represents a certain advance information I_c that we have about the message to be selected; hence

$$I' = I - I_c$$

is the amount of information still to be obtained after I_c is known.

A few words are now needed in order to explain more completely our procedure and to show its limitations. We have selected in Eq. (1.1) a statistical definition of the word information. This mathematical definition will be very useful in the discussion of many scientific and technical problems. It will enable us to draw some general conclusions of real practical value and great generality. But this very precise definition is a limitation. In order to obtain it we must exclude and ignore many of the usual connotations of the word "information."

We define "information" as the result of a choice; we do not consider "information" as a basis for a prediction, as a result that could be used for making another choice. We completely ignore the human value of the information. A selection of 100 letters is given a certain information value, and we do not investigate whether it makes sense in English, and, if so, whether the meaning of the sentence is of any practical importance. According to our definition, a set of 100 letters selected at random (according to the rules of Table 1.1), a sentence of 100 letters from a newspaper, a piece of Shakespeare or a theorem of Einstein are given exactly the same information value. In other words, we define "information" as distinct from "knowledge," for which we have no numerical measure.

We make no distinction between useful and useless information, and we choose to ignore completely the value of the information. Our statistical definition of information is based only on scarcity. If a situation is scarce, it contains information. Whether this information is valuable or worthless does not concern us. The idea of "value" refers to the possible use by a living observer. This is beyond the reach of our theory, and we are unable to discuss the process of thinking or any other problem about the use of the information by living creatures.

Our definition of information is, nevertheless, extremely useful and very practical. It corresponds exactly to the problem of a communications engineer who must be able to transmit all the information contained in a given telegram, without paying any attention to the value of this information for the person receiving the telegram.

Information is an absolute quantity which has the same numerical value for any observer. The human value of the information, on the other hand, would necessarily be a relative quantity, and would have different values for different observers, according to the possibility of their understanding it and using it later. A theorem from Einstein would probably have much greater value for a mathematician than an item from a newspaper. For a lay reader, on the other hand, the news item might or might not have value, while the theorem would almost certainly not have value.

To take a more trivial example, the information obtained by selecting a card from a pack of 32 cards is 5 bits (see Section 2). It is always measured by this number of 5 bits, whether the card be an ace, a seven, or a king. The values of these cards will, however, depend upon the rules of the game to be played.

According to our definition, information is always measured by a positive quantity. The value of the information can, and must in certain cases, be regarded as negative. A professor gives a long lecture, then suddenly discovers that he made a mistake, and concludes, "Excuse me, this was all wrong." This last sentence has a negative value, and destroys all the value of the preceding information.

These examples clearly show the limitations of the present theory, and they should be kept in mind in any application of this theory.

CHAPTER 2

APPLICATION OF THE DEFINITIONS AND GENERAL DISCUSSION

1. Definitions

In the first chapter it was shown that the measure of information as the amount of uncertainty which existed before a choice was made, was precise, but necessarily restrictive. Thus, for example, the "value" of the information could not be included in such a measure.

It was also shown that if unequal *a priori* probabilities existed for the possible choices, then these *a priori* probabilities may be interpreted as being "constraints" on our choice, the end result being a decrease in the amount of information.

Thus, if the *a priori* probabilities are $p_1, p_2, \ldots, p_j, \ldots$ for symbols (1), (2), ..., (*j*), ..., respectively, then the amount of information per symbol was shown to be [Eq. (1.12)]:

$$I/\text{symbol} = -K \sum_j p_j \ln p_j. \tag{2.1}$$

This equation was obtained, in effect, from the formula for information per symbol, when the choice had no constraints:

$$I/\text{symbol} = (K/G) \ln m^G = K \ln m \tag{2.2}$$

for m different equally probable symbols, where G is the total number of symbols used (we have replaced M of Section 5 of Chapter 1 by m). Thus, we used Eq. (2.2) as a starting point, and derived from it Eq. (2.1). Eq. (2.1) has, however, been used as a starting point by several authors, notably Shannon, and Eq. (2.2) follows from it immediately. For suppose that we have m different symbols, each with the same *a priori* probability. Then

$$p_1 = p_2 = \ldots = p_j = \ldots = p_m = 1/m, \tag{2.3}$$

and from Eq. (2.1), we have

$$I/\text{symbol} = -K \sum_{m\,terms} (1/m) \ln(1/m) = -K \ln(1/m) = K \ln m, \tag{2.4}$$

which is Eq. (2.2).

We shall now consider some of the properties of Eq. (2.1).

2. Property *A*

If a choice is broken down into two successive choices, then the original information should be the weighted sum of the individual informations. We consider an example. The probability of going from point O to point A is $1/2$, from O to B is $1/3$, and from O to C is $1/6$, as illustrated schematically in Fig. 2.1. Let us, however, consider the diagram of Fig. 2.2. In Fig. 2.2, an intermediate point M is chosen, such that the probability of going from O to M is also $1/2$.

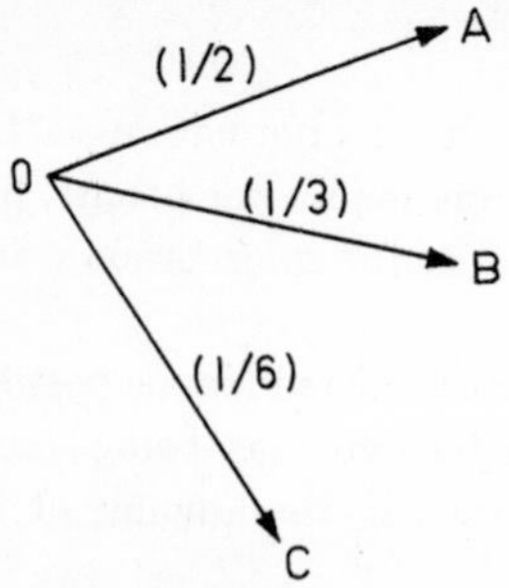

FIG. 2.1. Probabilities of going from point O to points A, B, and C.

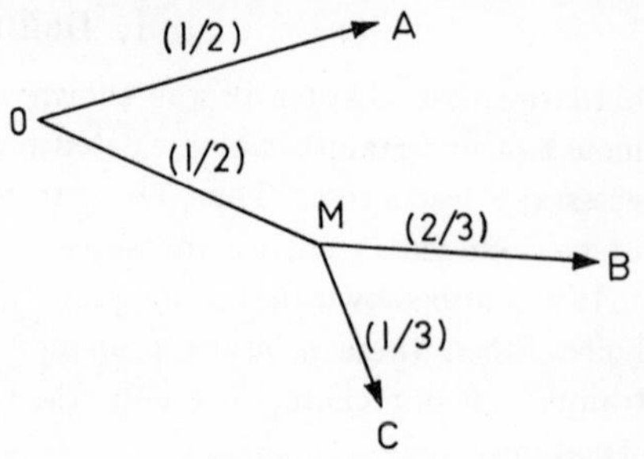

FIG. 2.2. Probabilities of going from point O to points A, B, and C, with an intermediate point M between point O and the points B and C.

This means that the probability of going from M to B must be $2/3$ since the original probability of going from O to B is $1/3$. Similarly, the probability of going from M to C is $1/3$.

We denote the information corresponding to Fig. 2.1 by $I\left(\frac{1}{2}, \frac{1}{3}, \frac{1}{6}\right)$. For Fig. 2.2 the information for the paths OA, OM is $I\left(\frac{1}{2}, \frac{1}{2}\right)$, and the information for paths MB, MC is $I\left(\frac{2}{3}, \frac{1}{3}\right)$.

The total information for Figs. 2.1 and 2.2 must be the same: $I\left(\frac{1}{2}, \frac{1}{3}, \frac{1}{6}\right)$. From Fig. 2.1 we have

$$I\left(\frac{1}{2}, \frac{1}{3}, \frac{1}{6}\right) = -K\left[\frac{1}{2}\ln\frac{1}{2} + \frac{1}{3}\ln\frac{1}{3} + \frac{1}{6}\ln\frac{1}{6}\right], \tag{2.5}$$

which becomes, on factoring:

$$I\left(\frac{1}{2}, \frac{1}{3}, \frac{1}{6}\right) = -K\left[\frac{1}{2}\ln\frac{1}{2} + \frac{1}{2}\cdot\frac{2}{3}\ln\left(\frac{1}{2}\cdot\frac{2}{3}\right) + \frac{1}{2}\cdot\frac{1}{3}\ln\left(\frac{1}{2}\cdot\frac{1}{3}\right)\right]. \tag{2.6}$$

Expanding, and regrouping, we obtain

$$I\left(\frac{1}{2},\frac{1}{3},\frac{1}{6}\right)=-K\left[\left\{\frac{1}{2}\ln\frac{1}{2}+\frac{1}{2}\ln\frac{1}{2}\right\}+\frac{1}{2}\left\{\frac{2}{3}\ln\frac{2}{3}+\frac{1}{3}\ln\frac{1}{3}\right\}\right]$$

$$=-K\left[\frac{1}{2}\ln\frac{1}{2}+\frac{1}{2}\ln\frac{1}{2}\right]+\frac{1}{2}\left[-K\left\{\frac{2}{3}\ln\frac{2}{3}+\frac{1}{3}\ln\frac{1}{3}\right\}\right]$$

$$=I\left(\frac{1}{2},\frac{1}{2}\right)+\frac{1}{2}I\left(\frac{2}{3},\frac{1}{3}\right). \tag{2.7}$$

This last expression corresponds to Fig. 2.2, for which the total information should be the weighted sum of the informations for paths OA, OM and MB, MC. This is a general result which is a consequence of the fact that information is a logarithmic function.

3. Property *B*

Property B is an inequality for which we shall later have use. To obtain the inequality, we consider the function

$$\Psi=\sum_j p_j \ln q_j,$$

where p_j is the probability of the j-th choice, and the q_j's may be regarded as another set of probabilities, so that

$$\sum_j p_j=\sum_j q_j=1. \tag{2.8}$$

Let us write

$$q_j=p_j+u_j=p_j(1+u_j/p_j).$$

Then the u_j's satisfy the condition that

$$\sum_j u_j=0. \tag{2.9}$$

Now, replacing q_j in Ψ, we have

$$\Psi=\sum_j p_j \ln\,[p_j(1+u_j/p_j)]$$

$$=\sum_j p_j \ln p_j+\sum_j p_j \ln(1+u_j/p_j). \tag{2.10}$$

If we compare the graphs of $\ln(1 + u/p)$ and u/p (Fig. 2.3), we see that

$$u/p \geqslant \ln(1 + u/p) \tag{2.11}$$

wherever $\ln(1 + u/p)$ is defined. Applying Eq. (2.11) to Eq. (2.10), we obtain

$$\sum_j p_j \ln p_j + \sum_j p_j \ln(1 + u_j/p_j) \leqslant \sum_j p_j \ln p_j + \sum_j p_j(u_j/p_j). \tag{2.12}$$

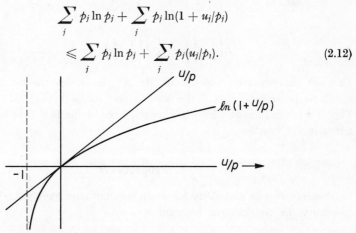

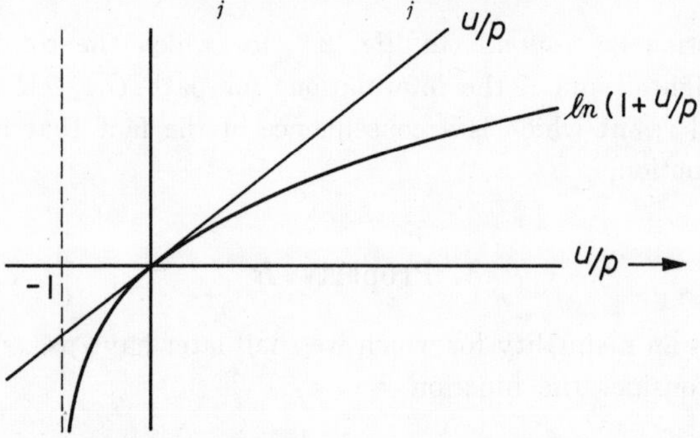

FIG. 2.3. The graphs of u/p and $\ln(1 + u/p)$ plotted as functions of u/p.

Therefore, from Eq. (2.9), it follows that

$$\sum_j p_j \ln q_j \leqslant \sum_j p_j \ln p_j. \tag{2.13}$$

Or, on multiplying Eq. (2.13) through by $-K$, we obtain Property B:

$$-K \sum_j p_j \ln q_j \geqslant -K \sum_j p_j \ln p_j. \tag{2.14}$$

4. Property C

The information I is a maximum when all m of the probabilities are equal:

$$p_1 = p_2 = \ldots = p_j = \ldots = p_m = 1/m. \tag{2.15}$$

To prove this, we first note that the information is a function of only $(m-1)$ independent variables since

$$\sum_{j=1}^{j=m} p_j = 1, \qquad \text{or} \qquad p_m = 1 - \sum_{j=1}^{j=m-1} p_j. \tag{2.16}$$

We shall take as the $(m-1)$ independent variables $p_1, p_2, \ldots, p_{m-1}$. The conditions[1] that the information $I(p_1, p_2, \ldots, p_{m-1})$ shall be a maximum are, first, that each of the first order partial derivatives of I shall be zero. To obtain the second condition, we construct the determinant of the second derivatives of I evaluated at the point determined by the first condition:

$$\begin{vmatrix} I_{11} & I_{12} & \ldots I_{1(m-1)} \\ I_{12} & I_{22} & \ldots I_{2(m-1)} \\ \cdots & \cdots & \cdots \\ I_{1(m-1)} & I_{2(m-1)} & \ldots I_{(m-1)\,(m-1)} \end{vmatrix} \tag{2.17}$$

where

$$I_{ij} = \partial^2 I / \partial p_i \, \partial p_j = I_{ji}, \quad \text{evaluated at the extremum.}$$

The second condition for I to be a maximum is that I_{11} and the determinants of order 2, 3, ..., $(m-1)$ obtained by successively including the next row and column of (2.17) shall alternate in sign.

From the second form of Eq. (2.16), we have

$$\partial p_m / \partial p_j = -1,$$

and therefore

$$\partial I / \partial p_j = -K(\ln p_j + 1 - \ln p_m - 1) = -K \ln(p_j / p_m).$$

Applying the first condition, we find that in order to obtain a maximum we must have

$$p_j = p_m \qquad \text{for} \qquad j = 1, 2, \ldots, (m-1),$$

and hence, using Eq. (2.16),

$$p_j = 1/m, \qquad j = 1, 2, \ldots, m.$$

The second derivatives of I evaluated at this point are

$$\partial^2 I / \partial p_j{}^2 = -K \left[\frac{1}{p_j} + \frac{1}{p_m} \right] = -2\,K\,m,$$

$$\partial^2 I / \partial p_i \, \partial p_j = -K(1/p_m) = -K\,m,$$

and the second condition requires that determinants of the form

$$\begin{vmatrix} -2\,K\,m & -K\,m & \ldots & -K\,m \\ -K\,m & -2\,K\,m & \ldots & -K\,m \\ \cdots & \cdots & \cdots & \cdots \\ -K\,m & -K\,m & \ldots & -2\,K\,m \end{vmatrix}$$

[1] See, for example, W. F. Osgood, "Differential and Integral Calculus," p. 342. Macmillan, New York, 1911.

of order 1, 2, . . ., $(m - 1)$ shall alternate in sign as the order increases. This is indeed the case, since the value of such a determinant of order n is readily shown to be

$$(-K\,m)^n\,(n+1),$$

and hence Property C is proved.

Property C can be demonstrated graphically in simple cases. For the case of two possibilities with $p_1 + p_2 = 1$, we have

$$I = -K\,[p_1 \ln p_1 + p_2 \ln p_2]. \tag{2.18}$$

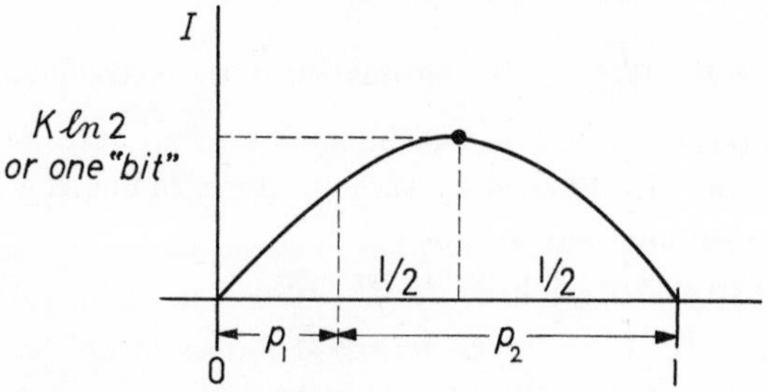

FIG. 2.4. The information as a function of $p_1 = 1 - p_2$. The maximum occurs for $p_1 = p_2 = \frac{1}{2}$, and is $K \ln 2 = 1$ bit.

In Fig. 2.4 we plot I as a function of p_1 (or p_2). I must be zero for $p_1 = 0$ and $p_1 = 1$. Hence, by symmetry, I must be a maximum at $p_1 = \frac{1}{2} = p_2$, and this maximum value is

$$I = -K\left[\frac{1}{2}\ln\frac{1}{2} + \frac{1}{2}\ln\frac{1}{2}\right] = -\left(\frac{1}{\ln 2}\right)\cdot(-\ln 2) = 1 \text{ bit}.$$

For three possibilities,

$$p_1 + p_2 + p_3 = 1, \tag{2.19}$$

$$\text{with } I = -K\,[p_1 \ln p_1 + p_2 \ln p_2 + p_3 \ln p_3],$$

we construct the two-dimensional diagram shown in Fig. 2.5. Two dimensions are sufficient since only two of p_1, p_2, p_3 are independent. In a plane we take three directions making angles of $2\pi/3$ with one another. We take a length p_1 in the first direction, p_2 along the second, and p_3 in the third direction, and thus obtain a point M. Condition (2.19) requires that the point M must remain within the equilateral triangle $A_1 A_2 A_3$. Point A_1, for example, is obtained when $p_1 = 1$, $p_2 = p_3 = 0$. The line $A_1 A_2$ corresponds to $p_1 + p_2 = 1$, $p_3 = 0$. This is easily seen by using rectangular coordinates in the plane, and projecting the contour $O\,p_1\,p_2\,p_3\,M$ first on the x-axis and then on the y-axis. The coordinates of M are:

$$x = \sqrt{3}\,(-p_1 + p_2)/2,$$
$$y = -(p_1 + p_2)/2 + p_3 = (3\,p_3 - 1)/2. \tag{2.20}$$

The equation of $A_1 A_2$ is $y = -\frac{1}{2}$ which, by Eq. (2.20), gives $p_3 = 0$, and hence $p_1 + p_2 = 1$. Similar results apply, by symmetry, to the other sides of the triangle.

We may thus use the triangle $A_1 A_2 A_3$ as a base. Each point within the triangle corresponds to a set of numbers p_1, p_2, and p_3 satisfying Eq. (2.19). We plot the information vertically in a direction perpendicular to the plane of the triangle and obtain the surface shown, in perspective, in Fig. 2.6. Along each side of the triangle, we obtain a curve similar to that of Fig. 2.4. The maximum of the surface occurs when $p_1 = p_2 = p_3 = 1/3$, that is, at the center of triangle $A_1 A_2 A_3$.

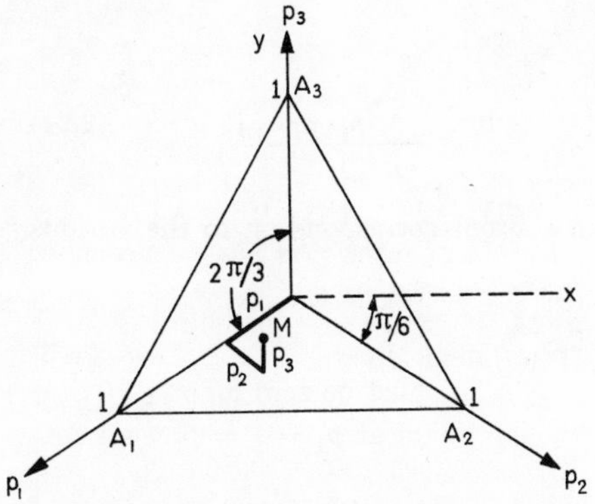

FIG. 2.5. Representation of p_1, p_2, and p_3 on a two-dimensional diagram. This is possible since only two of these three probabilities are independent: $p_1 + p_2 + p_3 = 1$.

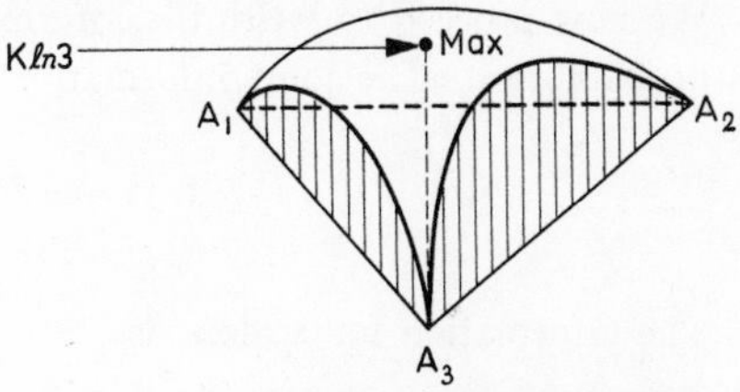

FIG. 2.6. The surface of I (information) plotted as a function of p_1, p_2, p_3, with $p_1 + p_2 + p_3 = 1$. The maximum value of I occurs at $p_1 = p_2 = p_3 = {}^1/_3$, and is $K \ln 3 = (\ln 3)/(\ln 2)$ bits.

5. Joint Events

We now consider the problem of "joint events." Suppose that we have two variables, x and y, which can take on the values:

$$x = 1, 2, 3, \ldots, i, \ldots, m,$$
$$y = 1, 2, 3, \ldots, j, \ldots, n$$

and that at a given instant we select a value for each of the two variables. Thus we might have $x = i$ and $y = j$ at time t. We define $p(i, j)$ as the probability that $x = i$ and $y = j$ at the same time. Then

$$\sum_{i,j} p(i,j) = 1. \tag{2.21}$$

If p_i is the probability that $x = i$ (without regard to the value of y), then

$$p_i = \sum_{j=1}^{j=n} p(i,j). \tag{2.22}$$

Similarly, the probability that $y = j$, without considering x, is

$$p_j = \sum_{i=1}^{i=m} p(i,j). \tag{2.23}$$

We have the following relations:

$$\sum_{i=1}^{m} p_i = 1, \qquad \sum_{j=1}^{n} p_j = 1, \qquad \text{and} \qquad \sum_{i,j} p_i \cdot p_j = 1. \tag{2.24}$$

We now proceed to write the information content corresponding to the various probabilities. The joint information is:

$$I(x, y) = -K \sum_{i,j} p(i,j) \ln p(i,j). \tag{2.25}$$

The information for x alone is

$$I(x) = -K \sum_{i=1}^{i=m} p_i \ln p_i = -K \sum_{i,j} p(i,j) \ln p_i, \tag{2.26}$$

and for y alone is

$$I(y) = -K \sum_{j=1}^{n} p_j \ln p_j = -K \sum_{i,j} p(i,j) \ln p_j. \tag{2.27}$$

We wish to compare the sum $I(x) + I(y)$ with $I(x, y)$. From Eqs. (2.26) and (2.27), we have

$$I(x) + I(y) = -K \sum_{i,j} p(i,j) \ln (p_i \cdot p_j). \tag{2.28}$$

We can easily prove, using Property B, that

$$I(x, y) \leqslant I(x) + I(y). \tag{2.29}$$

For, if we replace q_j of Eq. (2.14) by $p_i \cdot p_j$, we have

$$I(x, y) = -K \sum_{i,j} p(i, j) \ln p(i, j)$$

$$\leqslant -K \sum_{i,j} p(i, j) \ln(p_i \cdot p_j) = I(x) + I(y).$$

It is clear that the existence of a probability $p(i, j)$ of the joint event implies a constraint, which, as was discussed in the first chapter, has the effect of reducing the information content. The equality will hold only if $p(i, j) = p_i \cdot p_j$, which means that the events are independent.

6. Conditional Information

In an attempt to set up an equality, Shannon uses the concept of "conditional information" by introducing another probability $p_i(j)$, which is the probability that $y = j$, when it is already known that $x = i$. We call $p_i(j)$ the "conditional probability." It is clear that

$$p_i \cdot p_i(j) = p(i, j), \qquad \text{or} \qquad p_i(j) = p(i, j)/p_i. \tag{2.30}$$

The conditional information is the information associated with the probability $p_i(j)$, and is symbolized $I_x(y)$, and defined as

$$I_x(y) = -K \sum_{i,j} p(i, j) \ln p_i(j). \tag{2.31}$$

We can readily show that $I(x, y) = I(x) + I_x(y)$, for on expanding the right hand side of this equation, we have

$$I(x) + I_x(y) = -K \left\{ \sum_{i,j} p(i, j) \ln p_i + \sum_{i,j} p(i, j) \ln p_i(j) \right\}$$

$$= -K \sum_{i,j} p(i, j) \ln (p_i \cdot p_i(j)) = I(x, y) \tag{2.32}$$

from Eq. (2.30).

Now, combining Eqs. (2.29) and (2.32), we obtain

$$I(x) + I(y) \geqslant I(x, y) = I(x) + I_x(y),$$

or

$$I_x(y) \leqslant I(y). \tag{2.33}$$

The conditional information $I_x(y)$ is information about y, with x already known. This knowledge of x imposes a constraint, which decreases the information content on selecting y. The equality will hold only if x and y are independent events.

CHAPTER 3

REDUNDANCY IN THE ENGLISH LANGUAGE

1. Correlation and Joint Events

In order to introduce the subject of correlation, we shall review some of the considerations applying to joint events.

We considered two variables x and y, which, for example, can take on the values

$$x = 1, 2, 3, \ldots, i, \ldots, m,$$
$$y = 6, 9, 8, \ldots, j, \ldots, n$$

and defined $p(i, j)$ as the probability that $x = i$ and $y = j$ at a given time t. Associated with this, we have the information $I(x, y)$. We also defined other probabilities.

$$p_i = \sum_{\text{all } j} p(i, j) = \text{probability of } x = i \text{ for any value of } y.$$

This probability has the information $I(x)$ associated with it.

$$p_j = \sum_{\text{all } i} p(i, j) = \text{probability of } y = j \text{ for any value of } x.$$

The information associated with this probability is $I(y)$.

It was found in the previous chapter that

$$I(x) + I(y) \geqslant I(x, y).$$

This inequality resulted from the fact that the information content of a system is reduced when a constraint is applied to the system.

To create an equality, we introduced a "conditional probability," $p_i(j)$, the probability that $y = j$ when we already know that $x = i$. Associated with this probability is the conditional information $I_x(y)$.

The relation among the probabilities was found to be

$$p_i \cdot p_i(j) = p(i, j),$$

and when the conditional information was defined as

$$I_x(y) = -K \sum_{i, j} p(i, j) \ln p_i(j),$$

the following equality was obtained:

$$I(x) + I_x(y) = I(x, y).$$

2. Correlation in Language

Correlation is present in all languages,[1] for if a certain letter occurs the probability that certain others will follow is not the same as the *a priori* probabilities that these letters occur. Thus, in the English language, if the letter "*t*" is given, the probability that "*h*" will follow immediately is much greater than the probability that "*n*" will follow. Similarly, given the complex "tio," the probability that *n* will follow is extremely high. Correlation of this type is defined as "redundancy" by Shannon.[2, 3]

We may now apply the equations of the preceding section to the analysis of the information content of a message. These equations will apply if there is correlation between nearest neighbors only. For each pair of letters we associate the variable x with the first one and y with the second one. Then the average information per symbol (or letter) will be the conditional information

$$\begin{aligned} I_x(y) &= -K \sum_{i,j} p(i,j) \ln p_i(j) \\ &= -K \sum_{i,j} p_i \cdot p_i(j) \ln p_i(j). \end{aligned} \tag{3.1}$$

We assume that conditions are stationary, and that the probabilities do not change in the course of time.

If no correlation exists between letters, then, since $p_i(j) = p_j$ and $\sum_i p_i = 1$, Eq. (3.1) reduces to the usual formula

$$I(y) = -K \sum_j p_j \ln p_j. \tag{3.2}$$

---

[1] In addition to the specific references mentioned later, the following books should also be noted.

Fletcher Pratt, "Secret and Urgent," Blue Ribbon Books, New York, 1939, 1942 (contains probability data on the English Language); G. Dewey, "Relative Frequency of English Speech Sounds," Harvard U. P., Cambridge, Mass., 1923; G. K. Zipf, "Human Behavior and the Principle of Least Effort," Addison-Wesley, Cambridge, Mass., 1949. (In this book and other publications, Zipf has a variety of curves of the type plotted in Fig. (3.1), for all sorts of languages.)

[2] C. E. Shannon and W. Weaver, "The Mathematical Theory of Communication," pp. 3–28. U. of Illinois Press, Urbana, Ill., 1949. Shannon's "entropy of information" must be identified with our "information measure," and not with the physical entropy. As we shall see later, "information measure" will be shown to be related to "negative entropy."

[3] C. E. Shannon, Prediction and Entropy of Printed English, *Bell System Tech. J.* **30**, 50–64 (1951).

Consideration of correlation between single letters can be readily extended to "blocks of letters" or letter complexes such as "tio" mentioned above. We denote a complex of $(N-1)$ letters by the symbol $b_i(N-1)$, and we represent the probability that this block of $(N-1)$ letters will appear by $p(b_i(N-1))$. We now want to discuss the probability that this block will be followed by a certain letter j, thus making a new block of N letters

$$b_{ij}(N) = (b_i(N-1), j).$$

We denote the probability of occurrence of this new block, taken as a whole, by

$$p(b_i(N-1), j).$$

The conditional probability $p_{b_i(N-1)}(j)$ is the probability that j follows a given block of $(N-1)$ letters $b_i(N-1)$. This definition is similar to the one used in the previous section, and we have a similar relation among the probabilities:

$$p(b_i(N-1), j) = p(b_i(N-1)) \cdot p_{b_i(N-1)}(j). \tag{3.3}$$

We now define the "average information per symbol" in a series where correlation up to distance N is taken into account

$$F_N = -K \sum_{i,j} p(b_i(N-1), j) \ln p_{b_i(N-1)}(j), \tag{3.4}$$

a formula similar to Eq. (3.1). The sum over i is extended over all possible letter complexes consisting of $(N-1)$ letters.

3. Redundancy in Language

Applying our definition to a typical example, the English language, we should be able to obtain an exact value for the average information per letter. It would be given by the limit

$$I = \lim_{N\to\infty} F_N. \tag{3.5}$$

When N is increased, more constraints are taken into consideration, hence the information is decreased. The F_N sequence must, then, decrease monotonically, and its final limit is the actual average information per letter.

The probabilities for single letters, as well as groups of two and three letters have been established for the English language, but insufficient data exist on larger groups. The existing data are tabulated below, where the F's denote the information in terms of bits per letter:

1. all letters equally probable (27 letters, including blank) $F_0 = 4.76$ bits/letter
2. using probabilities of individual letters $F_1 = 4.03$ bits/letter
3. using data on groups of two letters $F_2 = 3.32$ bits/letter
4. using data on groups of three letters $F_3 = 3.1$ bits/letter

Redundancy is defined in terms of the F's:

$$R = 1 - F_{\text{lim}}/F_0. \tag{3.6}$$

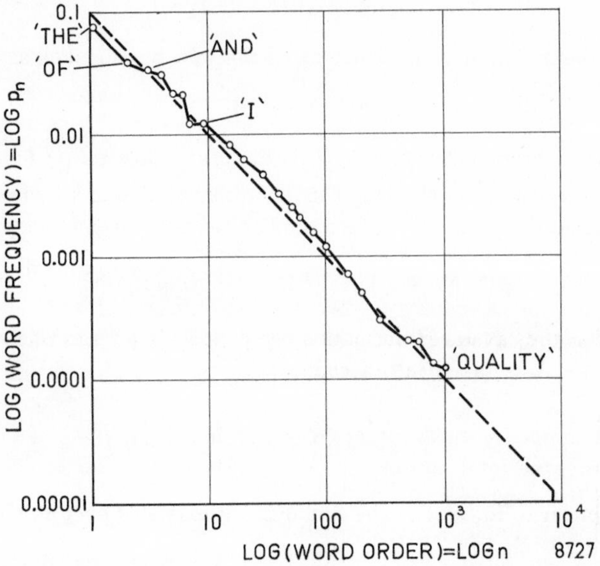

FIG. 3.1. The log-log plot of word frequency against word order for the first 8727 words. [Reproduced by courtesy of C. E. Shannon, *Bell System Tech. J.* **30**, 50 (1951).]

However, F_{lim} is unknown since very few data exist on letter complexes of more than three letters. For a clue to the value of F_{lim}, we can look to another set of statistics, that of frequency of occurrence of words. These have been compiled both for use in coding, and also for efficiency in learning a new language.

The "word order" of a word is the number of its position in an ordering according to frequency of occurrence. Fig. 3.1 graphs the log of word frequency against the log of word order, starting with "the" and cutting off at the 8727th word in order to normalize the sum of word frequencies to unity. As can be seen, this graph is, remarkably, a straight line (on log-log plot), and can be well represented by the empirical formula

$$p_n \approx \frac{0.1}{n}. \tag{3.7}$$

Using Eq. (3.7), we find that

$$-K \sum_n p_n \ln p_n = 11.82 \text{ bits/word.} \tag{3.8}$$

Furthermore, if we assume that the average English word (including blanks) contains 5.5 letters, then we obtain as a limiting value, $F_{\text{word}} = 2.14$ bits/letter. This cannot be identified as F_{lim}, because there are additional constraints imposed, such as connections between successive words.

4. Some Typical Experiments

In order to obtain more data, a game is proposed: a sentence is selected, and then an individual with no previous information about the sentence is selected, and required to guess the letters (including blanks) starting with the first. After each guess he is given the answer yes or no, and proceeds further. The number of guesses for each letter is recorded, summed, and then divided by the total number of letters in the sentence. This yields the number of bits per letter, since every guess answered by yes or no represents just one bit of information.

Some examples of this type were published by Shannon.[4] In one sentence of 102 letters, the total number of guesses required to reconstruct the sentence was 198. This indicates 1.94 bits per letter.

In another example, the game was played differently. After each guess the answer was "yes" for a correct guess, but if the guess was wrong, the correct letter was given. In a sentence of 129 letters, 89 were guessed correctly and 40 had to be given. Using the information F_1 of 4 bits per letter (as previously indicated), we obtain a total number of bits

$$89 + 40 \times 4 = 249$$

or

1.93 bits per letter.

A third example gives about 1.9 bits per letter. The number 1.9 should be considered an upper value, however, since in many cases the letters to be guessed were almost obvious, and the correct guess, followed by an affirmative answer, could hardly be counted as one real bit of information.

---

[4] C. E. Shannon, *Bell System Tech. J.* **30**, 54–58 (1951).

Figure 3.2 reproduces a graph by Shannon, plotting bits per letter as a function of the number of letters, out to 15 letters, with an extrapolation out to 100 letters. If we accept the extrapolated value of 1.4 bits per letter, as compared with $F_0 = 4.76$ bits per letter, we observe that the English language has a large redundancy content. Apparently, a reduction by a factor of three could be accomplished, perhaps making the language more precise. Other considerations may, however, also enter, such as the intelligibility of speech, and the extraction of intelligible speech in the presence of noise.

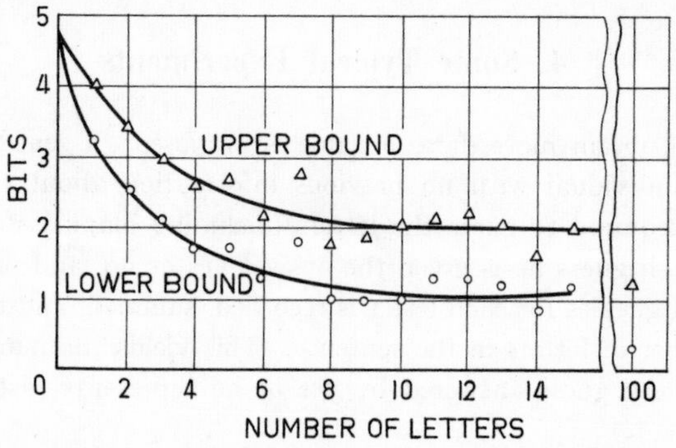

FIG. 3.2. The number of bits per letter plotted as a function of the number of letters out to 15 letters, with an extrapolation out to 100 letters. [Reproduced courtesy of C. E. Shannon, *Bell System Tech. J.* **30**, 50 (1951).]

5. Coding Devices

The considerations of the preceding sections lead naturally to problems of coding and coding devices. Thus, for example, the coding device must have a memory in order to reduce the redundancy of the incoming letters; i. e., the coder must "remember" the preceding letter in order to create the code for the next incoming letter. If we let

$$\alpha_n = \text{state of memory at a given instant,}$$

and let

$$x_n = \text{next letter,}$$

$$y_n = f(x_n, \alpha_n) = \text{code for the letter } x_n,$$

then the memory must change its state to a new value which will also depend on x_n and α_n:

$$\alpha_{n+1} = g(x_n, \alpha_n).$$

A result of our probability arguments concerning joint events is stated succinctly in Shannon's theorem 7:[5]

"The coding system can decrease or at best
maintain the information measure"

We shall discuss methods of coding in the next chapter.

A reversible coding device that can be used for either coding or decoding keeps the information measure a constant. This information content can be taken for a whole sentence, or can be computed "per unit time" if the message is emitted continuously from a certain source. Shannon's result is similar to the situation in thermodynamics, where a reversible process involves no change in entropy, while the entropy always increases in an irreversible process.

---

[5] See p. 27 in ref. 2.

CHAPTER 4

PRINCIPLES OF CODING

DISCUSSION OF THE CAPACITY OF A CHANNEL

1. Introduction

In the preceding chapters, we have defined the information content of a certain message, and we have discussed the role of redundancy, which results in decreasing the actual amount of information per letter in a written message. If i is the average information per letter, and if a source is emitting letters at the rate of m letters per second, the rate of emission of information is

$$I' = m\,i \quad \text{bits per second.} \tag{4.1}$$

We may find it convenient to replace the alphabet by a different set of symbols, in order to reduce the redundancy and to decrease the number of symbols to be transmitted per second. The general procedure to be applied for such an encoding operation was described at the end of the preceding chapter. If the transducer used is reversible, it maintains a constant rate of flow of information I', and no information is lost in the procedure. A similar transducer (working backward) can be used to decode the coded message and retranslate it into printed English. If our transducer is not reversible it may lose some of the information and introduce errors or misunderstandings. Hence the first requirement on a transducer is that it must be reversible.

How shall we design our transducer for best efficiency? There is no general answer to the question; it depends upon the use we intend to make of the coded signals. We have to discuss first the properties of the "channel" on which the signals are to be transmitted (in a problem of telecommunication) or stored (if we think of a memory device for a computing machine).

The best coding method will be the one that matches efficiently the rate of flow of information with the capacity of the channel. Let us first discuss the problem of the channel and its capacity.

2. Definition of a Channel and Its Capacity

If we want to transmit information or to store it in a memory device, we first select a physical medium, a cable, a radio link, a mercury line, a magnetic tape, etc., and we have to study the physical limitations of this medium. For instance, if we use a cable with a band width $\Delta \nu$, the shortest signals that can be transmitted have a duration Δt such that (see Chapter 8)

$$\Delta t \cdot \Delta \nu = 1. \tag{4.2}$$

Next comes the technical problem of devising a set of symbols, adapted to the physical medium, and enabling us to use it for communication: dots, dashes, and spaces, signals of different intensities or polarity, etc. Once this choice is made, we have defined a communication channel. For our statistical discussion the only consideration is the set of n discrete symbols $S_1, S_2, \ldots, S_j, \ldots, S_n$ to be used, and the lengths (or durations) $t_1, t_2, \ldots, t_j, \ldots t_n$ of these symbols. From here on we may forget the physical structure of the transmission device, and the technical or practical reasons which lead to the choice of the different symbols S_j and of their durations t_j. The "channel" from now on, and for all theoretical and practical discussions, is simply defined by the set of symbols S_j of duration t_j. We can ignore the physical structure of the symbols; only their durations will play a role in the discussion. Of course, we do not introduce any restriction on these durations, and we may have any number of symbols with the same duration.

We assume that the symbols S_j are completely independent of each other and have been defined in a way which does not imply any kind of correlation. An arbitrary succession of symbols is assumed capable of representing a certain message. The total duration T of a message is simply the sum of the individual durations t_j of the elementary symbols contained in this message.

Let us consider all the possible distinct messages having a total duration T. These messages will correspond to all the possible combinations of symbols S_j whose total duration is T. Let us call $N(T)$ the number of such distinct messages, which will differ in the order of the symbols used, and in the selection of symbols. We assume absolutely no restriction, no constraint, no correlation in the use of the different symbols. All of the N messages of total duration T are to be considered as equally probable *a priori*. Then when we select one of these messages, we obtain information

$$I = K \ln N$$

according to Eq. (1.1), where the choice of units depends on the choice of the constant K. The rate at which information is transmitted on the channel is I/T. This rate varies with the total duration T, but it can be shown that, in all practical cases, it approaches a limit as T becomes larger and larger. Shannon[1] selects this limit as the definition of the capacity of the channel

$$C = K \lim_{T \to \infty} \frac{\ln N(T)}{T}. \tag{4.3}$$

[1] C. E. Shannon and W. Weaver, "The Mathematical Theory of Communication," p. 7. U. of Illinois Press, Urbana, Ill., 1949.

If we use entropy units, we take $K = k$, Boltzmann's constant. In most information problems, we shall measure the information in bits. This is obtained by taking

$$K = \log_2 e, \tag{4.4}$$

or

$$C = \lim_{T \to \infty} (\log_2 N(T))/T \tag{4.5}$$

and the capacity is given in bits per second, if T is measured in seconds.

In the following sections of this chapter, we will discuss the validity of this definition, and the condition for the existence of the limit C. Then we will show that the capacity of the channel corresponds to the maximum average rate of flow of information on the channel, when all possible combinations of symbols are permitted. Finally we shall investigate how to code messages so that we use the full capacity of the channel. This will raise the problem of coding in a practical way: Given a set of messages written in a certain language with a certain alphabet, the problem is to match the language with the channel and to approach as nearly as possible a rate of transmission of information corresponding to the capacity C of the channel. We shall prove that this problem can be solved, and discuss some general conditions which must be fulfilled by the code in order to reach the theoretical limit.

3. Symbols, Words, and Messages in Sequential Coding

Let us assume that we have made a choice of symbols, and that we want to use combinations of these symbols to build up words or messages. This represents a typical case of sequential coding. Our symbols may correspond to letters, which can be combined into words, or they may represent digits whose sequence gives a certain number. A more general problem includes the case of digits or letters used to represent whole sentences. In the case of speech, each word is represented by a combination of elementary sounds, or phonemes, which play the role of symbols.

Each symbol has a certain "cost," and the way to compute these costs depends upon the physical system of transmission. In our first problems, we shall assume that the cost corresponds to the time duration of the signal representing the symbol. This is really the main problem for telecommunications, where the power required is small, while the real problem is to transmit as many messages as possible in a certain time T. Each symbol S_j has a certain duration t_j, and many symbols may have the same duration: this happens, for instance, if we use pulses of variable intensity or different frequencies. This is also the case for teletype signals, which consist of combinations of dots and blanks, each having the same total length.

We assume that no restrictions or constraints are imposed on the possible sequences of symbols. If we use letters, this means accepting sequences impossible to pronounce, and having no meaning in any language. Among our symbols we may select a special one to represent a blank, or we may use some combination of symbols for that purpose. Let us now sort our symbols according to their cost (or duration). We have

$$\begin{array}{l} a_1 \text{ symbols of duration } t_1, \\ a_2 \text{ symbols of duration } t_2, \\ a_j \text{ symbols of duration } t_j, \\ a_m \text{ symbols of duration } t_m = \sigma, \end{array} \qquad a_j \geqslant 0. \tag{4.6}$$

If σ represents the duration of the longest possible symbol, and n is the total number of symbols, we have

$$\sum_j a_j = n \qquad \text{and} \qquad 1 \leqslant t_1 < t_2 < \ldots < t_j < \ldots < t_m = \sigma. \tag{4.7}$$

The a_j's are non-negative integers, and we may assume the durations t_j to be integers. This represents a practical assumption, since these durations will always be defined only to within a certain error.

Following the program outlined in Section 2, we now want to compute the number $N(t)$ of distinct messages of total duration t. This number N satisfies a relation

$$N(t) = a_1 N(t-t_1) + a_2 N(t-t_2) + \ldots + a_m N(t-t_m) = \sum_{j=1}^{j=m} a_j N(t-t_j), \tag{4.8}$$

which states that messages of duration $(t-t_1)$ can be completed by any one of the a_1 symbols of duration t_1 to build up a message of total length t, and similarly for $t_2, t_3, \ldots, t_m$.

Equation (4.8) is a linear equation with finite differences. It has σ independent solutions[2] of the type

$$N_k(t) = X_k{}^t, \qquad k = 1, 2, \ldots, \sigma, \tag{4.9}$$

and the general solution is a linear combination

$$N(t) = \sum_{k=1}^{k=\sigma} A_k X_k{}^t, \tag{4.10}$$

[2] See the appendix at the end of this chapter.

with constant coefficients A_k. Substituting the particular solution $N(t) = X^t$ into Eq. (4.8), we see that the X_k's are the roots of an equation

$$X^t - \sum_{j=1}^{j=m} a_j X^{t-t_j} = 0,$$

or

$$1 - \sum_{j=1}^{j=m} a_j X^{-t_j} = 0. \tag{4.11}$$

This is called the characteristic equation of Eq. (4.8). We may multiply by X^σ, in order to eliminate the negative powers of X, and we obtain an algebraic equation of degree σ:

$$X^\sigma - \sum_{j=1}^{j=m} a_j X^{\sigma-t_j} = 0, \qquad a_j \geqslant 0. \tag{4.12}$$

There is only one variation in sign and hence, by Descartes' rule, there is just one positive root. Furthermore, the polynomial is negative for $X = 1$, since our problem requires at least two symbols, so that

$$\sum_{j=1}^{j=m} a_j \geqslant 2.$$

The polynomial becomes positive for very large X. We thus have

$$\begin{cases} \text{one real positive root, greater than 1: } X_1 > 1 \\ \sigma - 1 \text{ negative or complex roots: } X_2, X_3, \ldots X_\sigma. \end{cases} \tag{4.13}$$

4. Discussion

The preceding statement of the problem was first given by Shannon[3], and a careful discussion is found in Mandelbrot's thesis[4].

We have a general solution (4.10) containing σ constant coefficients A_k. These coefficients are determined by the initial boundary conditions, which we shall now discuss. Let us consider Eq. (4.8) for small values of t. One of the terms will correspond to

$$t_j = t \qquad \text{or} \qquad t - t_j = 0,$$

[3] See p. 5 in ref. 1.

[4] B. Mandelbrot, "Contribution à la théorie mathématique des jeux de communication," Ph. D. thesis, Paris, December 16, 1952. Publ. de l'Inst. de Statistique de l'Univ. de Paris, Vol. 2, fasc. 1, 2, pp. 80–102, 1953; also see *Trans. I. R. E.* (*P. G. I. T.*) **3**, 124 (1954).

and we must take $N(0) = 1$, since it is obvious that we can use the a_j symbols of duration t_j to represent some of the messages of total duration $t = t_j$. The larger values $t_{j+1}, t_{j+2}, \ldots, t_m$ cannot be used. These statements hold for all values of j. We satisfy these conditions by taking

$$N(0) = 1,$$
$$N(-1) = N(-2) = \ldots = N(-\sigma + 1) = 0. \tag{4.14}$$

We thus obtain σ initial conditions that determine our σ arbitrary coefficients A_k. The values of the function $N(t)$ for $t = -\sigma, -\sigma - 1, \ldots$ can never appear in Eq. (4.8), and they play no role in our problem.

Let us isolate the positive root X_1 and write

$$N(t) = A_1 X_1^t + \sum_{k=2}^{k=\sigma} A_k X_k^t. \tag{4.15}$$

The first term increases exponentially with t, and is the dominant term. The other terms oscillate. If a root X_k is negative, it gives alternately positive and negative terms X_k^t as t increases unit by unit (t is always an integer). If X_k is a complex root, its complex conjugate X_k^* is also a root, and these two roots together give oscillations as t increases.

The solution (4.15) is stable if all these oscillating terms decrease in amplitude, and unstable if the amplitude of the oscillations increases. We say that our solution exhibits

$$\begin{aligned} &\text{absolute stability for} && |X_j| < 1, \quad j \geqslant 2, \\ &\text{relative stability for} && |X_j| < X_1, \quad j \geqslant 2, \\ &\text{instability for} && |X_j| \geqslant X_1 \text{ for at least one } j \geqslant 2. \end{aligned} \tag{4.16}$$

In the first case, the amplitude of the oscillations decreases; in the second case, the amplitude of the oscillations increases at a slower rate than the dominant term.

The initial condition (4.14) gives

$$N(0) = A_1 + A_2 + \ldots + A_\sigma = 1. \tag{4.17}$$

In the first two cases (absolute or relative stability), we may, for many problems, ignore the oscillations, and retain only the dominant term of Eq. (4.15):

$$N'(t) = A_1 X_1^t = A_1 e^{\beta t}, \qquad \text{with} \qquad \beta = \ln X_1. \tag{4.18}$$

Now $N(t)$ represents the number of messages of total length t. We shall also be interested in the number $N_1(t)$ of messages of length smaller than t or equal to t. Recalling that t is always an integer, we have

$$N_1(t) = \sum_{s=1}^{s=t} N(s) = \sum_{s=1}^{s=t} \sum_{k=1}^{k=\sigma} A_k X_k^s = \sum_{k=1}^{k=\sigma} A_k \left(\sum_{s=1}^{s=t} X_k^s \right). \tag{4.19}$$

We have not included $s = 0$ in the sum since a message of length zero has no significance. Making use of

$$\sum_{s=1}^{s=t} X_k^s = X_k(1 + X_k + X_k^2 + \ldots + X_k^{t-1}) = X_k \frac{1 - X_k^t}{1 - X_k}, \tag{4.20}$$

we have

$$N_1(t) = \sum_{k=1}^{k=\sigma} A_k X_k \frac{1 - X_k^t}{1 - X_k} = \sum_{k=1}^{k=\sigma} B_k(X_k^t - 1), \tag{4.21}$$

with

$$B_k = A_k X_k/(X_k - 1) = A_k/(1 - X_k^{-1}).$$

We may rewrite this result in the following way:

$$N_1(t) = B_1 X_1^t + \sum_{k=2}^{k=\sigma} B_k X_k^t - B_0, \tag{4.22}$$

where

$$B_0 = \sum_{k=1}^{k=\sigma} B_k.$$

The number N_1 of messages of duration shorter than t or equal to t contains a dominant term in X_1^t, oscillating terms $(k = 2, 3, \ldots, \sigma)$ and a constant B_0. Ignoring the oscillations, we have

$$N_1'(t) = B_1 X_1^t - B_0 = B_1 e^{\beta t} - B_0, \tag{4.23}$$

and this will be a good approximation for large t in the stable cases. We thus obtain

$$t = \frac{1}{\beta} \ln \frac{N_1' + B_0}{B_1} = t_0 + \frac{1}{\beta} \ln (N_1' + B_0) \tag{4.24}$$

with

$$t_0 = -\frac{1}{\beta} \ln B_1.$$

5. Examples

We present a few examples to show how the method works.

A. All Symbols Having Equal Length

Here we take $a_1 = n$, the total number of symbols of length $t_1 = \sigma = 1$. Equation (4.12) yields

$$X - n = 0. \tag{4.25}$$

We have just one real positive root $X = n$, and hence

$$N = n^t \qquad \text{and} \qquad N_1 = (n^t - 1)/(1 - n^{-1}).$$

This channel yields absolute stability with no oscillations at all.

B. Symbols with Two Different Lengths: 1 *and* σ

The degree of the characteristic equation is equal to σ. In the general case, we have

$$X^\sigma - a_1 X^{\sigma-1} - a_\sigma = 0. \tag{4.26}$$

B. 2 The simplest case occurs for $\sigma = 2$:

$$X^2 - a_1 X - a_2 = 0. \tag{4.27}$$

The roots of this equation are

$$\left.\begin{matrix} X_1 \\ X_2 \end{matrix}\right\} = \tfrac{1}{2}\left(a_1 \pm \sqrt{a_1^2 + 4a_2}\right). \tag{4.28}$$

Since $|X_2| < X_1$, we are certain to have relative stability. Absolute stability requires

$$|X_2| = -X_2 < 1 \qquad \text{or} \qquad a_1 > a_2 - 1. \tag{4.29}$$

This condition is satisfied, for example, by a channel with just two symbols:

$$a_1 = a_2 = 1, \quad X_1 = \frac{1 + \sqrt{5}}{2} = 1.62,$$

$$X_2 = \frac{1 - \sqrt{5}}{2} = -0.62. \tag{4.30}$$

B. 3 Let us consider the case when the long signals are three times the short ones:

$$t_1 = 1, \quad t_2 = 2, \quad t_3 = 3, \quad \sigma = 3,$$

$$a_1 > 0, \quad a_2 = 0, \quad a_3 > 0.$$

The characteristic equation is

$$X^3 - a_1 X^2 - a_3 = 0. \tag{4.31}$$

We take

$$Y = X^{-1},$$

and obtain

$$Y^3 + pY + q = 0, \qquad \text{where} \quad p = a_1/a_3 \quad \text{and} \quad q = -1/a_3. \tag{4.32}$$

This is a well known equation.[5] Since the quantity $27\,q^2 + 4\,p^3$ is positive, we have one positive and two complex roots:

$$Y_1 = A + B, \qquad Y_2 = \omega A + \tilde{\omega} B, \qquad Y_3 = \tilde{\omega} A + \omega B, \tag{4.33}$$

where

$$\omega = (-1 + \sqrt{3}\,i)/2, \qquad \tilde{\omega} = (-1 - \sqrt{3}\,i)/2, \qquad \omega^2 = \tilde{\omega},$$

$$A^3 = \frac{1}{2}\left(-q + \sqrt{q^2 + \frac{4\,p^3}{27}}\right), \qquad B^3 = \frac{1}{2}\left(-q - \sqrt{q^2 + \frac{4\,p^3}{27}}\right).$$

We choose for A and B the real cube roots so that Y_1 is real while Y_2 and Y_3 are complex conjugates.

Relative stability occurs if

$$|X_2| = |X_3| < X_1 \qquad \text{or} \qquad |Y_2| = |Y_3| > Y_1. \tag{4.34}$$

One may easily compute

$$|Y_2|^2 = Y_2\,\tilde{Y}_2 = Y_2\,Y_3 = A^2 + B^2 - A\,B$$

$$Y_1{}^2 = A^2 + B^2 + 2\,A\,B.$$

But

$$A\,B = -p/3 < 0,$$

and hence condition (4.34) for relative stability is satisfied. Absolute stability requires that

$$|Y_2|^2 = |Y_3|^2 > 1, \tag{4.35}$$

a condition satisfied when $|A|$ and $|B|$ are not too small. One has

$$A^3 + B^3 = (A + B)\,(A^2 + B^2 - A\,B) = -q = 1/a_3;$$

hence

$$Y_1\,|Y_2|^2 = 1/a_3.$$

But Y_1 is smaller than 1 ($X_1 > 1$), so that condition (4.35) requires

$$a_3\,Y_1 < 1, \tag{4.36}$$

a condition easily satisfied.

C. One symbol per length

In this case, we have

$$a_1 = a_2 = \ldots = a_\sigma = 1$$

---

[5] I. S. Sokolnikoff and E. S. Sokolnikoff, "Higher Mathematics for Engineers and Physicists," p. 86. McGraw-Hill, New York, 1941.

corresponding to

$$t_1 = 1, \quad t_2 = 2, \ldots, t_\sigma = \sigma.$$

The characteristic equation (4.12) reads

$$X^\sigma - X^{\sigma-1} - X^{\sigma-2} - \ldots - X - 1 = 0, \tag{4.37}$$

or

$$X^\sigma - \frac{X^\sigma - 1}{X - 1} = 0.$$

Multiplying by $(X - 1)$, we obtain

$$X^{\sigma+1} - 2X^\sigma + 1 = 0. \tag{4.38}$$

This Eq. (4.38) has an extraneous root $X = 1$. Equation (4.37) has only one positive root somewhere between 1.62 [case $\sigma = 2$, see Eq. (4.30)] and 2 (for $\sigma \to \infty$). Starting from Eq. (4.38), we write

$$1.62 \leqslant X_1 \leqslant 2, \qquad X_1 = 2 - \frac{1}{X_1^\sigma}. \tag{4.39}$$

There is one negative root when σ is even and no negative root for odd σ. This is readily seen by applying Descartes' rule of signs to Eq. (4.38):

$$X' = -X \quad \begin{cases} \sigma \text{ even: } -X'^{\sigma+1} - 2X'^\sigma + 1 = 0, \text{ one change of sign} \\ \sigma \text{ odd: } \;\; X'^{\sigma+1} + 2X'^\sigma + 1 = 0, \text{ no change of sign.} \end{cases} \tag{4.40}$$

All the remaining roots are complex. When σ is even, the negative root is somewhere between $X' = 0$ and $X' = 1$ (corresponding to $X = -1$), and hence it will not affect the stability of the solution. For large values of σ, the complex roots are not far from the σ-th roots of unity: let us write

$$X = e^{\frac{2n\pi i}{\sigma} + \varepsilon} \qquad \text{with } n \text{ an integer and } \varepsilon \text{ small.} \tag{4.41}$$

This value of X satisfies Eq. (4.38) if ε is given approximately by

$$e^{\sigma\varepsilon} \approx 1/(2 - e^{2n\pi i/\sigma}), \qquad \sigma \gg 1.$$

This gives a small value for ε when σ is large. The complex roots will then have absolute values not far from unity, and hence relative stability is certain.

6. Computation of the Capacity of a Channel

We are now in a position to find the capacity of a channel, given by Eq. (4.3). We consider the case of sequential coding (see Section 3) and assume that the system is stable. For very long T the solution reduces to the dominant term (4.18)

$$N(T) \to A_1 X_1^T = A_1 e^{\beta T} \qquad \text{as} \qquad T \to \infty \tag{4.42}$$

and hence

$$\ln N \to \beta T + \ln A_1 \qquad \text{with} \qquad \beta = \ln X_1.$$

Now using Eq. (4.3), we obtain for the capacity of the channel

$$C = \lim_{T\to\infty} \left(K\beta + \frac{K \ln A_1}{T} \right) = K\beta. \tag{4.43}$$

Shannon also discusses problems with restrictions imposed on the possible sequences of symbols S_i, but we shall restrict our present discussion to the preceding problem with no restrictions or constraints.

After thus defining the capacity of a channel, Shannon introduces his definition of the measure of information which we discussed in the previous chapters. He then proves a fundamental theorem[6] for a noiseless channel:

If the channel has a capacity of C bits per second and accepts messages from a source of information at the rate of i bits per symbol, then the best possible coding system will enable us to use the channel at the rate of $R = C/i$ symbols per second.

The proof of this theorem will result from the discussion of the following sections.

7. Matching a Code with a Channel

We intend to discuss more precisely the physical meaning of Shannon's very important theorem, and to specify the properties of the coding systems enabling one to use the channel to full capacity. It will be shown that the best codings are the ones yielding the most probable distribution of symbols, and specific rules will be given for finding these optimum coding systems.

Let us first rewrite here some of the results of the preceding chapters. We assumed that we were using n different symbols in our communication system, and we computed the total number of messages or different combinations of such symbols when the numbers $N_1, N_2, \ldots, N_j, \ldots, N_n$ of the different symbols used in the messages were given in advance. Let

$$G_0 = N_1 + N_2 + \ldots + N_n = \sum_{j=1}^{j=n} N_j \tag{4.44}$$

[6] See p. 28, Section 9, in ref. 1.

be the total number of symbols in the messages and let

$$p_j = N_j/G_0, \qquad \text{with} \sum_{j=1}^{j=n} p_j = 1 \tag{4.45}$$

represent the relative density of the j-th symbol. The total number of different messages of this type is given by [Eq. (1.26)]

$$P = G_0!/\prod_j N_j!.$$

Using Stirling's formula, we have, approximately,

$$\ln P = -G_0 \sum_{j=1}^{j=n} p_j \ln p_j. \tag{4.46}$$

This formula was used to define the amount of information obtained when one special message is selected out of the P possibilities [Eq. (1.28)], and the information i per symbol was

$$i = I/G_0 = -K \sum_{j=1}^{j=n} p_j \ln p_j. \tag{4.47}$$

A. Symbols of equal length.

Let us consider first a simple example, assuming all symbols to have an equal length t_1. A long time interval T contains

$$G = T/t_1$$

positions (or cells) for different symbols. For each cell we can dispose of n different symbols, and so the total number of possible messages is

$$N(T) = n^G = n^{T/t_1}. \tag{4.48}$$

Our definition (4.3) now yields for the channel capacity

$$C = (K \ln n)/t_1. \tag{4.48 a}$$

In the problem of channel capacity, no assumption is made about the *a priori* density of the n different symbols. When we defined "information," we assumed that we knew the *a priori* densities of the different symbols, $p_1, p_2, \ldots, p_j, \ldots, p_n$, and we obtained the information density (per symbol) given in Eq. (4.47). The information density is a maximum when all the p_j's are equal:

$$p_1 = p_2 = \ldots = p_j = \ldots = p_n = 1/n,$$

and this maximum value is

$$i_{max.} = -K \sum_{j=1}^{j=n} \frac{1}{n} \ln \frac{1}{n} = K \ln n,$$

since we have n equal terms in the sum. This is the information per symbol when all the symbols are equally probable. Each symbol has a duration t_1, and the rate at which information is transmitted is

$$i/t_1 = (K \ln n)/t_1 \text{ bits per second.} \tag{4.49}$$

This is identical with Eq. (4.48 a) for the channel capacity. The similarity between Eqs. (4.48 a) and (4.49) is striking. In the computation of channel capacity we used all possible distributions of symbols. In the case of Eq. (4.49) we assumed an arbitrary *a priori* set of densities, which we adjusted later (taking $p_j = 1/n$) in order to maximize the information, and we obtain identical results.

Shannon's relation yields a rate of transmission

$$R = C/i = 1/t_1 \tag{4.50}$$

from Eqs. (4.48 a) and (4.49), and we certainly cannot transmit more than $1/t_1$ symbols of duration t_1 (seconds) per second. Hence, in our simplified problem, the best coding is the one using all symbols in equal proportion, in accordance with Shannon's theorem.

We may note that the condition for maximum information yields the most probable distribution. For $N(t)$ is the total number of possible messages, and P, with

$$\ln P = -\sum_{j=1}^{j=n} p_j \ln p_j = i/K$$

is the number of messages possible with a distribution of symbols defined by the probabilities p_j. Maximizing $\ln P$ (or information) is the same as maximizing P. But P/N (where N is regarded as constant) is the probability that the distribution P (defined by p_j) occurs, and if P is a maximum, then we have the most probable distribution.

In the simplified case of this section (all symbols of equal length), then, we have the result that the most probable distribution yields maximum information. Furthermore, we can say that this distribution is an asymptotic distribution because of Eq. (4.48 a) which was derived without reference to the *a priori* distribution. This asymptotic distribution may be thought of as an average distribution in the sense that, in an average taken over a long period of time, the asymptotic distribution is the only one of importance. We shall see in the next section that these remarks apply also to the case where the symbols do not all have the same duration.

8. General Problem: Symbols with Different Lengths

We now want to discuss the general problem, with symbols of different lengths, and we shall prove that our preceding result still applies: The most efficient coding is the one yielding for the different symbols the most probable *a priori* density distribution. Furthermore, we are going to derive this most probable distribution and to see a connection between it and Eqs. (4.11) and (4.12).

The discussion is slightly more involved for symbols of different lengths than for symbols of equal length. We start with the assumption of a message of total duration T, and we specify that we are using $N_1, N_2, \ldots, N_j, \ldots, N_n$ symbols respectively of types $1, 2, \ldots, j, \ldots, n$. The total duration of the message is

$$T = \sum_{j=1}^{j=n} N_j t_j. \tag{4.51}$$

We introduce the total number of symbols G_0 and the relative proportions p_j:

$$G_0 = \sum_{j=1}^{j=n} N_j, \qquad p_j = N_j/G_0, \tag{4.52}$$

and hence

$$\sum_{j=1}^{j=n} p_j = 1. \tag{4.53}$$

We can rewrite Eq. (4.51) in the following way:

$$T = G_0 \sum_{j=1}^{j=n} p_j t_j. \tag{4.54}$$

The logarithm of the total number P of different messages that we can construct by interchanging the positions of the different symbols is still given by Eq. (4.46):

$$\ln P = -G_0 \sum_{j=1}^{j=n} p_j \ln p_j. \tag{4.55}$$

The information obtained by selecting one of these P messages is given by $K \ln P$ according to our definition (1.1). All these messages have the same duration T since they use the same numbers $N_1, N_2, \ldots, N_n$ of the different symbols, and they are to be considered equally probable *a priori*. Now we want to obtain the most probable distribution, which is the same as maximizing the information per message. That is, we maximize $\ln P$, while taking into account the two conditions (4.53) and (4.54). This is done by the method of Lagrange's multipliers. We simply write the condition[7]

$$d(\ln P) - \alpha\, d\left(\sum_{j=1}^{j=n} p_j\right) - \beta\, dT = 0 \tag{4.56}$$

with the two arbitrary multipliers α and β to be determined later. The variables are $G_0, p_1, p_2, \ldots, p_j, \ldots, p_n$. Differentiating Eq. (4.55), we obtain

$$d(\ln P) = -(dG_0)\sum_{j=1}^{j=n} p_j \ln p_j - G_0 \sum_{j=1}^{j=n} (1 + \ln p_j)\, dp_j.$$

If we substitute this expression into Eq. (4.56), we obtain

$$-dG_0\left[\sum_{j=1}^{j=n} p_j \ln p_j + \beta \sum_{j=1}^{j=n} p_j t_j\right] + \sum_{j=1}^{j=n} dp_j\,[-\alpha - \beta G_0 t_j - G_0(1 + \ln p_j)] = 0. \tag{4.57}$$

We must now regard the dG_0 and dp_j's as arbitrary independent quantities. The total differential can be zero only if all the brackets are zero:

$$\sum_{j=1}^{j=n} p_j(\ln p_j + \beta t_j) = 0, \tag{4.58}$$

$$\ln p_j = -1 - \beta t_j - \alpha/G_0. \tag{4.59}$$

Substitution of Eq. (4.59) into Eq. (4.58) yields

$$\sum_{j=1}^{j=n} p_j(-1 - \alpha/G_0) = 0,$$

We also have condition (4.53), and hence we must choose

$$1 + \alpha/G_0 = 0 \qquad \text{or} \qquad \alpha = -G_0, \tag{4.60}$$

and now Eq. (4.59) reduces to

$$\ln p_j = -\beta t_j \qquad \text{or} \qquad p_j = e^{-\beta t_j}. \tag{4.61}$$

The arbitrary constant β is determined by the condition (4.53):

$$\sum_{j=1}^{j=n} p_j = \sum_{j=1}^{j=n} e^{-\beta t_j} = 1. \tag{4.62}$$

---

[7] Condition (4.56) specifies that $\ln P$ is an extremum, but it does not actually prove that the extremum is a maximum. The proof that it actually is a maximum can be carried out by the method used in the proof of Property C, Chapter 2, Section 3.

Let us write

$$X = e^{\beta}$$

and remember that we may have more than one symbol with a certain duration. Let us say there are a_j symbols of duration t_j. Then Eq. (4.62) reads

$$\sum_{j=1}^{j=n} a_j X^{-t_j} = 1, \tag{4.63}$$

and this is identical with Eq. (4.11) of Section 3. When we consider infinitely long messages, we have again the identity between the asymptotic distribution of Section 3 and the distribution for maximum information, which, by the arguments of Section 7, is also the most probable distribution as well as the average distribution. The distribution (4.61) yields a number of messages (4.55):

$$\ln P = -G_0 \sum_{j=1}^{j=n} p_j \ln p_j = G_0 \sum_{j=1}^{j=n} \beta\, t_j\, e^{-\beta t_j} = G_0 \beta \sum_{j=1}^{j=n} t_j\, p_j \tag{4.64}$$

or

$$\ln P = \beta\, T \qquad \text{or} \qquad P = e^{\beta T} = X^T$$

according to Eq. (4.54) and the definition of X. Our P (most probable distribution) is again identical with Shannon's $N(T)$ corresponding to all possible distributions, and the channel capacity, according to formula (4.43) is

$$C = K \ln X = K\, \beta. \tag{4.65}$$

For long messages, the most probable distribution is so much more probable than any other one, that all other possible distributions can simply be omitted. The best coding is the one that achieves this most efficient distribution of symbols, namely

$$(\ln p_j)/t_j = -\beta \quad \text{(a constant)} \tag{4.66}$$

according to Eq. (4.61). The largest real root β of Eq. (4.62) corresponds to the largest X solution of Eq. (4.12) and yields, according to Eq. (4.64), the utmost probable distribution, with the largest value for P.

If we use the most efficient code and a distribution of symbols corresponding to the most probable one, we have a density of information per symbol

$$i = -K \sum_{j=1}^{j=n} p_j \ln p_j = -K\, \beta \sum_{j=1}^{j=n} t_j\, p_j = -K\, \beta\, \bar{t}, \tag{4.67}$$

where $\bar{t}$ is the average duration of a symbol, when the probability of the different symbols is given by (4.61). The rate of transmission, by Eqs. (4.65) and (4.67)

$$R = C/i = 1/\bar{t} \tag{4.68}$$

a formula very similar to Eq. (4.50).

9. The Matching Problem

The condition (4.61) or (4.66) corresponds to the coding system that matches the channel most efficiently. It is just as important in coding problems as the condition of matching characteristic impedances in circuit problems. Shannon uses, in a special problem, a procedure that leads to a very similar rule.[8] We have proved here that the result is absolutely general and applies to all coding problems. Special applications and examples will be discussed in the next chapter.

Let us note, in concluding, that the coincidence of average and most probable distributions is a well known result for extremely large numbers of events. This rule plays a most important role in statistical thermodynamics, where it explains the coincidence between different definitions of entropy given by J. W. Gibbs, Maxwell, Boltzmann, and Planck. This point is very clearly discussed in H. A. Lorentz's *Leçons au College de France* (*Les theories statistiques en thermodynamique,* Teubner, Leipzig, 1916).

10. Problems of Word Statistics (Mandelbrot)

The results of Sections 3, 4, 7, and 8 have been applied by Mandelbrot[4] to the problem of word statistics which was discussed in the preceding chapter from an empirical point of view. What is the role of a word in the language? The meaning of the word can be found in a dictionary. It represents a sort of special message. This message is coded in letters in writing. It is coded in phonemes in speech. How is it coded in the brain? This is obviously an open question, but we may assume some sort of coding based on elementary symbols or signals, each of which should be characterized by a certain cost. This assumption allows us to use the preceding analysis, where we shall simply substitute "cost" for "duration." We shall further assume that the coding is practically matched with the word frequencies, that is with their relative probabilities of use in the language. These assumptions have been applied by Mandelbrot to an analysis of the situation.

[8] See pp. 29 and 30 in ref. 1.

Let $S_1, S_2, \ldots, S_j, \ldots, S_n$ be the fundamental symbols or signals of the code, and $t_1, t_2, \ldots, t_j, \ldots, t_n$ their relative costs. The number $N(t)$ of words of cost t is given by Eq. (4.15), and, if the coding is stable, we may use the simplified expression (4.18). The number of words of cost smaller than t or equal to t is given by $N_1(t)$ of Eq. (4.22), which for a stable code simplifies to Eq. (4.23)

$$N_1'(t) = B_1 e^{\beta t} - B_0. \tag{4.23}$$

Let us now sort all the words of the vocabulary according to increasing cost t. N_1' will represent the word's rank or order in this classification. Equation (4.24) should represent the average relation between cost t and rank N_1'

$$t = t_0 + \frac{1}{\beta} \ln(N_1' + B_0). \tag{4.24}$$

We now discuss the frequency of use (or probability) of the word. There might be no relation between cost and probability, but this is not our assumption. We assumed that the word's probability and cost are properly matched, which means long costly coding for rare words and short inexpensive coding for the most usual words.

We discussed the matching problem in Sections 8 and 9, and considered specifically how to select the best probability rule for symbols of varying costs t_j. The result was summarized in Eq. (4.61):

$$\ln p_j = -\beta_1 t_j \qquad \text{or} \qquad p_j = e^{-\beta_1 t_j}. \tag{4.61}$$

We now want to apply a similar analysis to words instead of letters or symbols. The word numbered N_1' has a cost $t_{N_1'}$, the two quantities being related by Eqs. (4.23) and (4.24). Our new condition of good matching requires that the probability $p_{N_1'}$ of the word be related to its cost $t_{N_1'}$ by a condition of the general type (4.61), containing a new arbitrary constant β_1. Comparing these formulas, we can eliminate the cost $t_{N_1'}$ and connect directly the rank N_1' of the word with its probability $p_{N_1'}$:

$$-\beta_1 t_{N1'} = \ln p_{N1'} = -\beta_1 t_0 - \frac{\beta_1}{\beta} \ln (N_1' + B) \tag{4.69}$$

and hence

$$p_{N1'} = P(N_1' + B)^{-\gamma} \qquad \text{with} \qquad P = e^{-\beta_1 t_0}, \qquad \gamma = \beta_1/\beta. \tag{4.70}$$

The idea of some sort of coding of the words in the brain, and the notion of the cost of such codings were necessary for obtaining relations (4.23) and (4.24), but we have managed to eliminate the unknown costs with the assumption of good matching.

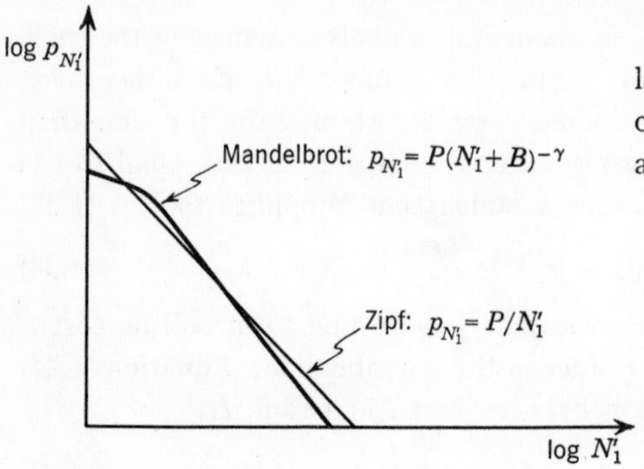

FIG. 4.1. Comparison of Mandelbrot's distribution of word frequency as a function of word order with Zipf's distribution. [Reproduced by courtesy of B. Mandelbrot, "Jeux de communication". Publ. de l'Inst. de Statistique de l'Univ. de Paris, 1953.]

Formula (4.70) corresponds to a law proposed by Mandelbrot. It contains the law suggested by Zipf as a special case:

$$p_{N_1'} = P/N_1', \qquad P \approx 1/10,$$

$$B = 0, \qquad \gamma = 1, \qquad (\beta_1 = \beta). \tag{4.71}$$

Another important quantity to consider is the total number of words in the vocabulary. If we use a dictionary of R words, we have

$$1 \leqslant N_1' \leqslant R$$

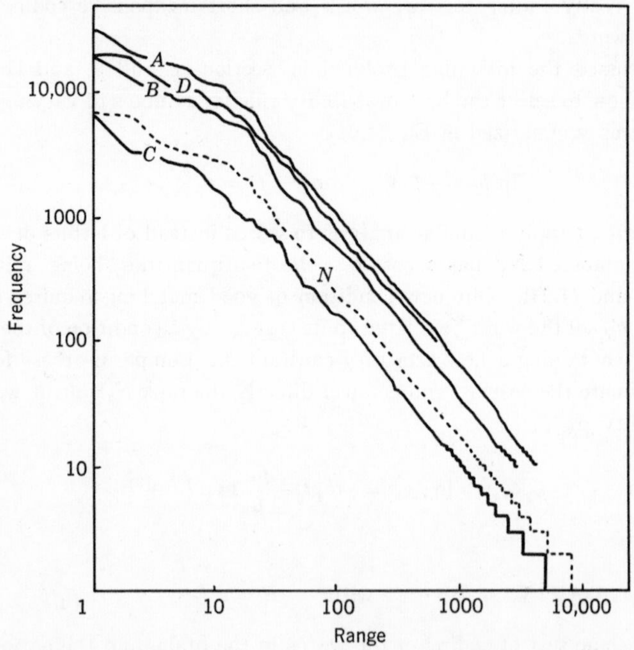

FIG. 4.2. Experimental curves of word frequency plotted against word order. Curves A, B, C, and D are for Norwegian, and curve N is for German. [Reproduced by courtesy of B. Mandelbrot, "Jeux de communication". Publ. de l'Inst. de Statistique de l'Univ. de Paris, 1953.]

and the sum of the probabilities must be unity:

$$\sum_{N_1'=1}^{N_1'=R} p_{N_1'} = P \sum_{N_1'=1}^{N_1'=R} (N_1' + B)^{-\gamma} = 1\,. \tag{4.72}$$

This equation determines P. Or if P is given (Zipf takes $P = 1/10$) it determines the total number of words to be used. This is how Shannon computed 8727 words in a dictionary according to Zipf. Most languages give $1 \leqslant \gamma \leqslant 1.2$, although γ may, in exceptional cases, reach 1.6, as, for example, in children's talk.

Many examples of applications were given by Mandelbrot in the two papers quoted previously,[4] where some other properties of languages are also discussed. Figure 4.1 shows a comparison between the laws proposed by Zipf and those proposed by Mandelbrot. Figure 4.2 represents some experimental curves computed by Zipf.

11. Solving the Matching Problem

We emphasized in Section 9 the need for a coding system that would match the channel with the language used in the transmission. We found in Eq. (4.61) the condition for good matching. The problem now is to show how this result can be obtained practically.

In Section 4, we started with a discussion of the properties of the channel. We assumed that we had n symbols $S_1, \ldots, S_j, \ldots, S_n$ on the channel, and that their respective durations were $t_1, \ldots, t_j, \ldots, t_n$. We found that the average information per symbol was maximum (see Section 8) when the probability p_j of the symbol S_j was related to its duration by Eq. (4.61):

$$p_j = e^{-\beta t_j}, \qquad \beta \text{ a constant.} \tag{4.61}$$

Now let us consider a message written in a language using a certain number ν of signs Σ_λ, where a sign may be a letter, a group of letters, a word, etc. In Chinese, for instance, each sign corresponds to a word. In order to simplify the problem, we shall assume that each sign Σ_λ has a certain probability π_λ, which is independent of any other signs preceding it. In other words, we omit correlation between signs in order to avoid complications in the problem.

We may first consider the simplest possible code, using ν symbols (or groups of symbols, if $n < \nu$) and giving the shortest symbols to the most probable signs. This will usually not satisfy condition (4.61), and the matching will be poor.

We may obtain a much better solution by coding groups of signs into groups of symbols, but the discussion of such a system requires first an investigation into the probabilities of groups of signs. We have

$$\nu \text{ signs: } \Sigma_1, \Sigma_2, \ldots, \Sigma_\lambda, \ldots \Sigma_\nu, \qquad \text{probabilities: } \pi_1, \pi_2, \ldots, \pi_\lambda, \ldots, \pi_\nu. \tag{4.73}$$

Let us define probability exponents θ_λ:

$$\pi_\lambda = e^{-\theta_\lambda}. \tag{4.74}$$

A group of signs $\Sigma_1 \Sigma_2 \ldots \Sigma_\lambda$ has a probability

$$\pi = \pi_1 \pi_2 \ldots \pi_\lambda = e^{-(\theta_1 + \theta_2 + \ldots + \theta_\lambda)} = e^{-\Theta}. \tag{4.75}$$

We thus have a law of additivity for the probability exponents θ. We may now investigate the number $\mathfrak{N}(\Theta)$ of groups of signs corresponding to a certain probability $\pi = e^{-\Theta}$. The problem is exactly similar to the one discussed in Section 3, where we simply have to replace the durations t_j and T by the probability exponents θ_λ and Θ. For long groups of signs, we transcribe the results obtained in Eqs. (4.18) and (4.23):

$$\mathfrak{N}(\Theta) = a_1 e^{\gamma\Theta}, \tag{4.76}$$

where $\mathfrak{N}(\Theta)$ is the average number of groups of signs with $\Sigma\,\theta = \Theta$, with a coefficient γ replacing our previous β. Also

$$\mathfrak{N}_1(\Theta) = b_1 e^{\gamma\Theta} - b_0, \tag{4.77}$$

where $\mathfrak{N}_1(\Theta)$ is the average number of groups of signs with $\Sigma\,\theta \leqslant \Theta$.

We may now compare the statistical properties of the groups of signs and the groups of symbols. We decide to code the $\mathfrak{N}_1(\Theta)$ groups of signs with the shortest $N_1(t)$ groups of symbols, thus using the shortest coding for the most frequent groups of signs. We equate $\mathfrak{N}_1(\Theta)$ and $N_1(t)$, and make use of Eqs. (4.77) and (4.23):

$$\mathfrak{N}_1(\Theta) = b_1 e^{\gamma\Theta} - b_0 = B_1 e^{\beta t} - B_0 = N_1(t). \tag{4.78}$$

The groups of signs and symbols must be long in order for these simplified formulas to apply. Hence the exponentials in Eq. (4.78) will be much larger than the constants b_0 and B_0, which we may ignore. The condition, for practical purposes, reads

$$b_1 e^{\gamma\Theta} = B_1 e^{\beta t}, \qquad \gamma\Theta = \beta t + \ln(B_1/b_1). \tag{4.79}$$

Since Θ and t are large, we may ignore the last term and write

$$\Theta = \beta t/\gamma. \tag{4.80}$$

This condition gives the ratio of the two scales, the probability exponent Θ being proportional to the duration t.

In such a coding, a symbols S_j of duration t_j will have an average probability

$$p_j = e^{-\theta_j} = e^{-\beta t_j/\gamma}, \tag{4.81}$$

and this is exactly the exponential law (4.61) required for optimum coding. The condition (4.78) leaves us with a great degree of freedom in the selection of the special type of coding, but we have been able to prove the possibility of satisfying our conditions for matching the language with the channel. A good matching requires coding for long groups of signs and symbols, and this means a delay in the coding procedure at the transmitter and in the decoding at the receiver.

More complicated problems involving correlation between successive signs (and redundancy) could be solved by a method similar to the one used in our simplified problem.

Returning to condition (4.78), we have assumed long groups of symbols for rare groups of signs and short groups of symbols for frequent groups of signs. A difficulty in using groups of symbols of variable length is the need for a special symbol indicating the interval between code groups. This can be avoided by taking groups of symbols all of equal length. At first sight this solution may appear uneconomical. Nevertheless, it can be shown to be as satisfactory as the coding discussed above. We replace condition (4.78) by

$$\mathfrak{N}_1(\Theta) = b_1\, e^{\gamma\Theta} - b_0 = A_1\, e^{\beta t} = N(t). \tag{4.82}$$

Since Θ and t are long, we may again ignore the constant b_0, and we obtain

$$\gamma\,\Theta = \beta\, t + \ln(A_1/B_1) \tag{4.83}$$

where we may drop the last term, so that we arrive again at condition (4.80). This exemplifies the great variety of possible coding methods giving good matching.

Appendix

A homogeneous linear difference equation with constant coefficients can be written[9]

$$P\big(u(x)\big) = u(x+n) + p_{n-1}\,u(x+n-1) + \ldots + p_1\,u(x+1) + p_0\,u(x) = 0, \tag{A.1}$$

where the p's are constants. The equation is linear in the unknown function $u(x)$ and x proceeds by unit increment. This equation has n particular solutions

[9] L. M. Milne-Thomson, "The Calculus of Finite Differences", Chapters 12, 13. Macmillan, London, 1951.

$u_1(x), \ldots, u_n(x)$, which are independent when no linear relation exists among them. These solutions can be found by putting

$$u(x) = \rho^x. \tag{A.2}$$

Substitution in (A.1) yields

$$\rho^x f(\rho) = 0,$$

$$f(\rho) = \rho^n + p_{n-1}\rho^{n-1} + \ldots + p_1\rho + p_0 = 0, \tag{A.3}$$

and we obtain a solution of (A.1) if ρ be a root of the characteristic equation (A.3). Let $\rho_1 \rho_2 \ldots \rho_n$ be these roots which we suppose to be all different. One can prove that these solutions are independent, and the general solution is

$$u(x) = \sum_{k=1}^{n} A_k \rho_k^x \tag{A.4}$$

with n arbitrary coefficients A_k. The case of a multiple root ρ_i of degree ν is solved by taking

$$\rho_i^x, x\rho_i^x, \ldots, x^{\nu-1}\rho_i^x$$

for the independent solutions.

Equations with right-hand terms can also be discussed.

The problem is to find the roots of the algebraic equation (A.3). Let us recall some fundamental results[10] about an algebraic equation with real coefficients

$$f(x) = a_0 x^n + a_1 x^{n-1} + \ldots + a_n = 0: \tag{A.5}$$

A. If $f(\alpha)$ and $f(\beta)$ are of opposite signs, there is at least one root between α and β. The number of such roots is odd.

B. Descartes' rule. The number of positive real roots of Eq. (A.5) is either equal to the number of variations in sign of $f(x)$, or less than that number by a positive even integer. The number of negative real roots is similarly related to the number of variations of $f(x')$, where $x' = -x$.

C. The total number of roots is n. When a root is complex, $(a + i\,b)$, then the complex conjugate $(a - i\,b)$ is also a root.

[10] See p. 27 in ref. 5; also see H. B. Fine, "College Algebra," p. 425 Ginn, New York, 1904; L. E. Dickson, "First Course in the Theory of Equations," Chapter 2. Wiley, New York, 1939.

CHAPTER 5

CODING PROBLEMS

1. Alphabetic Coding, Binary System

We have discussed, in the preceding chapters, conditions for the most efficient coding, and we reached the conclusion that ideal coding procedures should satisfy the relation

$$-\log p_j = \beta t_j, \tag{5.1}$$

where p_j is the *a priori* probability of symbol S_j, t_j is the duration or length of this symbol, and β is a constant.

Condition (5.1) can easily be explained: Most probable symbols have a p_j relatively close to unity, and hence $(-\log p_j)$ will be a relatively small positive number, and the corresponding signals, according to Eq. (5.1) should have a relatively short duration. In other words, most probable signals must be short, while improbable signals may be long. The result is almost obvious, and Eq. (5.1) specifies the ideal condition that should be approximated as closely as possible. This condition can be applied to alphabetic codes, if we use the well known probabilities of the different letters in the English language. Table 5.1, which is the same as Table 1.1, gives these probabilities p_j and their negative logarithms. It does not matter here which kind of logarithm we use; a change of base of the logarithm simply multiplies the constant β by a constant factor.

We note in Table 5.1 that the logarithms of the probabilities for the letters of the alphabet range from 0.7 to 3. We can obtain a corresponding variation in the length of the signals in a binary code. This would apply to a channel capable of transmitting only one type of pulse: no pulse means 0 and one pulse means 1. Since our composite signals have different lengths we must provide some means for recognizing the end of one signal. The double, triple, or quadruple 0 may characterize the termination of the pulse system representing a letter. This means that we must keep only single 0's in the signal proper. Table 5.2 is such an example.

The length varies from 3 to 8 per letter, which gives an over all ratio of reasonable value. In a long message, the average duration per letter is obtained by multiplying the duration t_j of the letter by its probability p_j and adding. The computation gives

$$\bar{t} = \sum_{j=1}^{j=27} p_j t_j = 4.65 \tag{5.2}$$

TABLE 5.1
The Probability of Occurrence p and Values of $-\log_{10} p$ for the Letters of The English Language

Symbol	Probability, p	$-\log_{10} p$	Symbol	Probability, p	$-\log_{10} p$
Word space, or "blank"	0.2	0.699	*L*	0.029	1.54
E	0.105	0.979	*C*	0.023	1.64
T	0.072	1.143	*FU*	0.0225	1.65
O	0.0654	1.184	*M*	0.021	1.68
A	0.063	1.2	*P*	0.0175	1.76
N	0.059	1.23	*YW*	0.012	1.92
I	0.055	1.26	*G*	0.011	1.96
R	0.054	1.27	*B*	0.0105	1.98
S	0.052	1.28	*V*	0.008	2.1
H	0.047	1.33	*K*	0.003	2.52
D	0.035	1.46	*X*	0.002	2.7
			JQZ	0.001	3.0

TABLE 5.2
A Possible Binary Code for the Letters of the English Language

Letter	Code	Letter	Code	Letter	Code
Word space or "blank"	000	*H*	101100	*W*	1101000
E	100	*D*	110000	*G*	1101100
T	1000	*L*	110100	*B*	1110000
O	1100	*C*	111000	*V*	1110100
A	10000	*F*	111100	*K*	1111000
N	10100	*U*	1010000	*X*	1111100
I	11000	*M*	1010100	*J*	10101000
R	11100	*P*	1011000	*Q*	10101100
S	101000	*Y*	1011100	*Z*	10110000

with the p_j values of Table 5.1. The value 4.65 is also the average number of symbols per letter, and, since we are using a binary system, we have

$$I/\text{letter} = (I/\text{symbol}) \times (\text{symbols/letter}) = 4.65 \times \log_2 2 = 4.65.$$

In order to discuss this result, let us compare it with some other codings. If we take symbols of equal lengths, we need five binary digits to obtain 32 combinations, out of which we may select 27 for the alphabet. Symbols of equal length 5 are a little worse than our system of variable lengths. Our final value is, however, still too large since it exceeds the theoretical value of 4.03 bits per letter given by Eq. (1.30). The code shown in Table 5.2 is much better than the usual Morse côde used in telegraphy.

Table 5.3
A Possible Ternary Code for the Letters of the English Language

Letter	Code	Letter	Code	Letter	Code
Word space or "blank"	1,–1	*H*	011,–1	*W*	0100,–1
E	0,–1	*D*	100,–1	*G*	0101,–1
T	00,–1	*L*	101,–1	*B*	0110,–1
O	01,–1	*C*	110,–1	*V*	0111,–1
A	10,–1	*F*	111,–1	*K*	1000,–1
N	11,–1	*U*	0000,–1	*X*	1001,–1
I	000,–1	*M*	0001,–1	*J*	1010,–1
R	001,–1	*P*	0010,–1	*Q*	1011,–1
S	010,–1	*Y*	0011,–1	*Z*	1100,–1

2. Alphabetic Coding, Ternary System

Many experimental devices give the possibility of using positive or negative pulses, in addition to no pulse. This is the case for magnetic tape and for telegraphic systems using positive and negative current. These systems lead to the consideration of a ternary code, based on $-1, 0, +1$. We give an example (and probably not the most favorable one) of such a coding in Table 5.3. We may use one of the three signals (-1, for instance) for the letter space. This leaves us with a binary coding for the letters.

This code gives an average number of 3.3 symbols per letter, as can easily be computed with the probabilities of Table 5.1. The number of bits per letter is

$$3.3 \log_2 3 = 5.25, \tag{5.3}$$

a result which is definitely higher than with the codes of the preceding section. The difficulty in all codes with variable length is the price to be paid for the special signals indicating the termination of a letter code. The code of Table 5.3 is not exactly balanced since the symbol -1 is less frequent than 0 and 1. A more elaborate coding could improve on this point and slightly decrease the number of bits per symbol.

We shall discuss, at the end of this chapter, the problem of coding by words instead of coding by letters, and we shall show that it can be much more economical.

3. Alphabet and Numbers

Another problem is that of coding numbers in addition to all the letters of the alphabet. The solution will depend on the purpose of the coding. On a typewriter we may assume that letters are used more frequently than numbers. On a computing or accounting machine the reverse is true. Here are a few examples:

A. Use an *IBM* code with 6 binary digits (check mark not included), letters and the ten decimal digits having the same lengths. This gives an average probability ratio of

$$\frac{\text{probability of a letter}}{\text{probability of a decimal digit}} = \frac{27}{10} = 2.7, \tag{5.4}$$

which is a suitable ratio for a typewriter. The code is, however, inefficient because it uses only 37 out of a possible 64 combinations, thus leaving 27 unused code signals.

B. Use 7 binary digits, giving 128 combinations, and code all the numbers from 0 to 99, plus 27 letters. One combination will be unused. This is a very efficient coding, giving an average of 3.5 bits per number (the optimum is 3.32). We think of each of these 100 numbers as a two decimal digit number (the number 7, for example, is thought of as 07), so that there are, altogether, 200 decimal digits occurring in the numbers. Hence we have

$$\frac{\text{probability of a letter}}{\text{probability of a decimal digit}} = \frac{27}{200} = 0.135. \tag{5.5}$$

This ratio is reasonable for an accounting machine.

C. Use 10 binary digits, giving 1024 combinations and code all numbers from 0 to 999 plus 24 letters. This leaves two uncoded letters. We may use the same code for 0 and zero, and also for 1 and *L*. Here we have 3.33 bits per number, practically the best possible value. There are 1000 three decimal digit numbers, and hence 3000 decimal digits altogether, and so the ratio is

$$\frac{\text{probability of a letter}}{\text{probability of a decimal digit}} = \frac{26}{3000} = 0.00866. \tag{5.6}$$

This code would be suitable for a computing machine, with letters used only occasionally.

In the codes B and C the complements to 99 or 999 would play the role of the usual 9 complement, and could easily be obtained by using an "excess 14" or "excess 12" coding, respectively. The important point is that, before selecting a code, one must know the relative probability of digits and letters.

4. Binary Coding by Words

We discussed, in Chapter 3, Shannon's work on redundancy in the English language. In one of his examples, Shannon considered the frequency of different words in the language and indicated a law

$$p_m = 1/10\,m \tag{5.7}$$

for the probability of occurrence of the word of rank m in a classification from most frequent to less frequent words. This law cannot apply indefinitely, because the sum would diverge, and Shannon assumed that one would use only 8727 words, this number being chosen in such a way as to make the sum equal to unity:[1]

$$\sum_{m=1}^{m=8727} p_m = 1. \tag{5.8}$$

Under such assumptions, the average information per word was computed

$$\begin{aligned} I &= 11.82 \text{ bits per word,} \\ i &= \ \ 2.14 \text{ bits per letter,} \end{aligned} \tag{5.9}$$

since an average word requires 5.5 letters in a 27 letter alphabet (26 letters plus word space). The figure 2.14 bits per letter represents a great saving over ordinary alphabetical coding, which requires about 5 bits per letter.

Let us now see how one could take advantage of this situation. We may first consider signals all having the same length. If we use binary digits 0 and 1 and

[1] In computing the limit, 8727, Shannon used the experimental probabilities for the most frequent words, and turned to formula (5.7) only for large values of m ($m > 100$). If formula (5.7) were applied throughout, the limit would be materially higher that 8727, and close to 12000.

take a constant length of 13 digits, we obtain $2^{13} = 8192$ different signals that can be used to code 8192 words, representing an adequate vocabulary for many purposes. This very simple coding results in 13 bits per word, or 2.36 bits per average letter, a result already close to the theoretical limit of Eq. (5.9).

A better result can be obtained by a method similar to the one discussed in the first section of this chapter, and exemplified in Table 5.2. We eliminate multiple zeros in the main signal, and use them only in the termination. Every signal starts with a 1 and ends with 00, 000, 0000, ... The first such combinations are shown in Table 5. 4

Table 5. 4

I	II	III	IV	V
1.00	10.00	100.00	1000.00	10000.00
	11.00	101.00	1010.00	10100.00
		110.00	1011.00	10101.00
		111.00	1100.00	10110.00
			1101.00	10111.00
			1110.00	11000.00
			1111.00	11010.00
				11011.00
				11100.00
				11101.00
				11110.00
				11111.00

In the fourth column, the combination 1001 has been omitted because of the two zeros in succession. For the same reason we have omitted 10001.00, 10010.00, 10011.00, and 11001.00 from the fifth column.

In the following discussion we shall omit the last two zeros, which appear at the end of every signal. Let us suppose that we have found all the signals of a certain column (for instance, the seven signals of column IV, with four digits in the main part of each signal). Let

n be the rank of the column,
$N_{n,1}$ be the number of signals ending with 1,
$N_{n,0}$ be the number of signals ending with a single 0, and
$N_{n,00}$ be the number of signals ending with a series of zeros.

For instance, in the case of column IV (ignoring the last two zeros after the point),

$$n = 4, \qquad N_{4,1} = 3, \qquad N_{4,0} = 2, \qquad N_{4,00} = 2.$$

We now want to compute the numbers $N_{n+1,1}$, $N_{n+1,0}$, and $N_{n+1,00}$ for signals with $n+1$ digits in the main part. The $N_{n,0}$ and $N_{n,1}$ signals can be completed with either 0 or 1. The $N_{n,00}$ can be completed only with 0, and hence we have the following relations:

$$\begin{aligned} N_{n+1,1} &= N_{n,1} + N_{n,0}, \\ N_{n+1,0} &= N_{n,1}, \\ N_{n+1,00} &= N_{n,0} + N_{n,00}. \end{aligned} \tag{5.10}$$

These relations yield, step by step, the results shown in Table 5.5.

If we use 1 to 17 columns for the main part, the number of binary digits will vary from 3 to 19 (including the two zeros to be added to the end of each signal) and this would cover a dictionary of about 11,000 words. A computation of the average number of bits per word can be made without great difficulty, assuming Shannon's results for the probability of successive words. It leads to a result of nearly 12 bits per word, very close to the theoretical limit of 11.82. This type of coding seems to be the most economical that can be obtained practically.

For any practical application, the code should be completed with a letter code. Letters would still be needed for all the words not in the dictionary, especially names, surnames, names of cities, counties, rivers, etc. If such words are infrequent, one might keep the last 27 symbols of the code for the alphabet. If the special words occur very frequently, the coding by word will become impractical.

We can use the relations (5.10) to compute the relative probabilities p_{n1}, p_{n0}, p_{n00} of signals whose main part ends with 1, 0, or 00.

$$\begin{gathered} N_{n1} = N_n \cdot p_{n1}, \qquad N_{n0} = N_n \cdot p_{n0}, \qquad N_{n00} = N_n \cdot p_{n00}, \\ N_n = N_{n1} + N_{n0} + N_{n00}. \end{gathered} \tag{5.11}$$

Equations (5.10) and (5.11) together determine the successive values of the p's. When n is large ($n > 10$, for instance), these probabilities p become independent of n and one easily obtains

$$p_1 \approx p_{00} = \tfrac{1}{2}(3 - \sqrt{5}) = 0.382, \qquad p_0 = 0.236, \tag{5.12}$$

and Eqs. (5.10) result in

$$N_{n+1} = N_n(2p_1 + 2p_0 + p_{00}) = 1.618\, N_n; \tag{5.13}$$

hence

$$\begin{gathered} N_n = D_0(1.618)^n \qquad \text{with} \qquad D_0 = 1.163, \\ N_1 + N_2 + \ldots + N_n = D_1(1.618)^n \qquad \text{with} \qquad D_1 \approx 3. \end{gathered} \tag{5.14}$$

These approximate relations can be checked with the exact figures of Table 5.5 and are found to represent a good approximation for $n > 10$. These formulas could be used for a more detailed discussion of the code proposed in this section.

TABLE 5.5
Binary Coding of Words

	Column number, n																		
	1	2	3	4	5	6	7	8	9	10	11	12	13	14	15	16	17	18	19
N_{n1}	1	1	2	3	5	8	13	21	34	55	89	144	233	377	610	987	1597	2584	4181
N_{n0}	0	1	1	2	3	5	8	13	21	34	55	89	144	233	377	610	987	1597	2584
N_{n00}	0	0	1	2	4	7	12	20	33	54	88	143	232	376	609	986	1596	2583	4180
ΣN	1	2	4	7	12	20	33	54	88	143	232	376	609	986	1596	2583	4180	6764	10945
Total number of words coded	1	3	7	14	26	46	79	133	221	364	596	972	1581	2567	4163	6746	10926	17690	28635

5. Alphabetic Coding by Words

Another way of coding by words could be based on the use of letters. If we use coded words of two letters: *aa, ab, ac, . . ., zz,* we may code $(26)^2$ or 676 words, with a bit content of $2 \times 4.7 = 9.4$ per word, since an alphabet of 26 letters yields 4.7 bits per letter. This would correspond to a dictionary of basic English. For greater flexibility in the language, we may use code words containing three letters, giving $(26)^3$ or 17576 words, a very large dictionary, without any redundancy, yielding an information content of $3 \times 4.7 = 14.1$ bits per word. Both examples show the amount of redundancy in the usual spelling of words, where 5.5 letters per word are used on the average, instead of 2 or 3 letters, as in these new codes. Of course, the coded words will usually be impossible to pronounce!

A less radical code, of about 10,000 words, was designed by P. Luhn, of the IBM Corporation, using pronounceable words of three and four letters, ending in such a way as to make the "word space" unnecessary. This makes a practical code of about 3.8 letters per word instead of 5.5, as in English.

6. Coding Based on Letter Groups and on Correlation

We discussed, at the end of Chapter 3, a general type of coding procedure, proposed by Shannon. The method is based on a mechanism with a memory device, and the use of known correlation relations in the coding of successive letters. This procedure is a direct application of the mathematical discussion of Chapter 3, but it can be used only for a language where the probabilities of digrams and trigrams (groups of 2, 3, or more letters) are known from a previous detailed statistical study of the language.

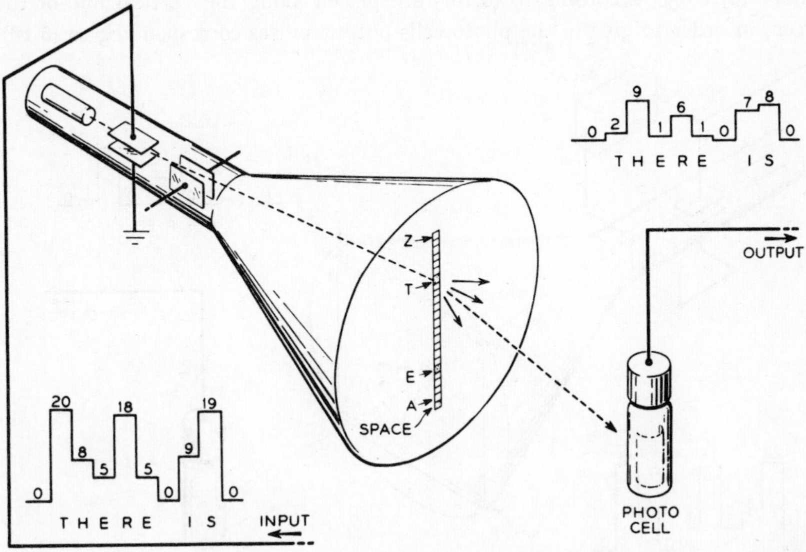

FIG. 5.1. Oliver's "Monogrammer" for coding single letters. [Reproduced by courtesy of B. M. Oliver, *Bell System Tech. J.* **31**, 724 (1952).]

B. M. Oliver[2] recently discussed practical methods of this nature. He assumed that the transmission system used 27 pulses of intensities 0, 1, 2, . . ., 27, and investigated the possibility of reducing to a minimum the average power used on the channel. The first possibility is to use our quantized pulses in alphabetical order:

symbol:	space	*A*	*B*	*C*	*D*	*E*	. . .	(5.15)
pulse height:	0	1	2	3	4	5	. . .	

This is obviously a poor solution. A better coding can be based on the probabilities of Table 5.1:

symbol:	space	*E*	*T*	*O*	*A*	*N*	. . .	(5.16)
pulse height:	0	1	2	3	4	5	. . .	

[2] B. M. Oliver, Efficient coding, *Bell System Tech. J.* **31**, 724 (1952).

This is certainly more efficient, since most probable letters now correspond to low intensity pulses.

A practical way to do this was designed by Oliver, and is represented in Fig. 5.1. Pulses are used to deflect the beam of a cathode ray tube, and masks of variable opacity [according to (5.16)] are placed along the vertical line of the screen, in order to give in the photo cells output pulses corresponding to (5.16).

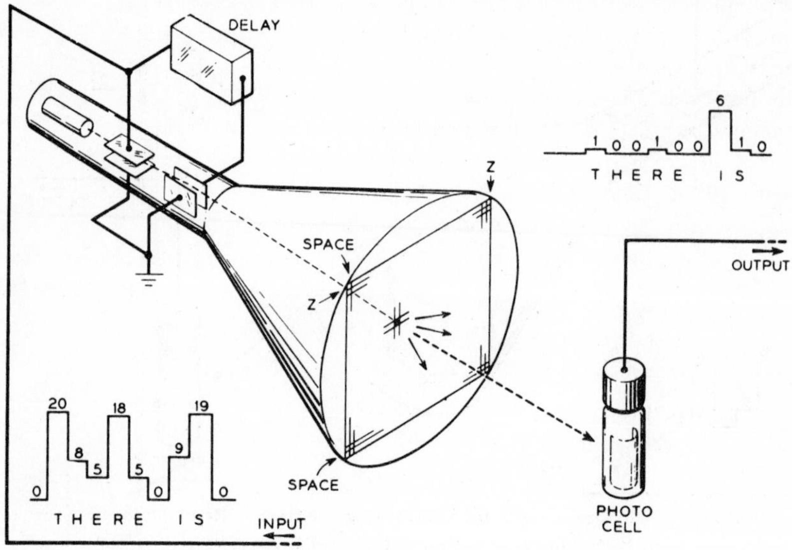

FIG. 5.2. Oliver's "Digrammer" for coding pairs of letters. [Reproduced by courtesy of B. M. Oliver, *Bell System Tech. J.* **31**, 724 (1952).]

This system is called the "monogrammer." A "digrammer" is shown in Fig. 5.2, also taken from Oliver's original paper. The device uses both deflection plates of a cathode ray tube. One set of plates is actuated by the preceding letter, and the other set of plates by the incoming letter. Each group of letters (i, j) corresponds to a point on the screen, and the opacity of the masks, in front of each screen position, is computed from the $p(i, j)$ probabilities. This could provide an additional saving in the average power required for transmission. Devices based on trigrams and tetragrams are discussed, but do not seem to be very practical.

Another method of coding has been proposed by various authors.[3] It can be best described for a problem in telephony: a continuous curve is to be trans-

[3] P. Elias, Harvard University thesis, *Proc. I.R.E.* **39**, 839 (1951); E. R. Kretzmer, *Bell System Tech. J.* **31**, 751 (1952); C. W. Harrison, *ibid.* p. 764.

mitted, and we have statistical data on the type of curves being used. Using this information and some of the preceding values already transmitted, we can predict the most probable next value, and transmit only the correction or departure from this predicted value. The power of the method is that it can be applied to two dimensions (television) provided the corresponding statistical data have been obtained. In the case of television, let us consider a system using $64 = 2^6$ quantized intensity levels. If all levels are equally probable, we would require 6 bits per sample point. Different levels have, however, different probabilities and this simple condition immediately reduces the information to 5 bits per point. Using correlation between adjacent points makes it possible to compute a value of 2.4 to 2.6 bits per point. This represents a potential possible saving of about two to one in the channel capacity required for television transmission. As in other similar problems we must note, however, that such transmission, with negligible redundancy, is much more vulnerable to interference, since the elimination of redundancy also eliminates the possibility for prediction and error correction in the receiver.

CHAPTER 6

ERROR DETECTING AND CORRECTING CODES

1. Error Detecting Codes

In the preceding chapters, we have discussed the methods according to which one should be able to eliminate redundancy, and to design codes using the smallest possible number of bits per letter. The method can be used for any type of symbols, instead of letters, in more general problems of the theory of information.

Now the question must be raised whether redundancy cannot be beneficial in many practical problems. If we store information on a device that has a high noise level, some errors may be introduced by spurious noise signals, and a certain amount of redundancy will be very useful in helping to detect, or even to correct, errors. This is what we do automatically when we read a book containing some misprints or when we receive a telegram in which some of the letters have been incorrectly transmitted. Instead of taking advantage of the very high redundancy in the English language for detecting errors, we may devise a checking mechanism to be used in conjunction with a code of low redundancy. This will be much more effective than the redundancy of the language, which cannot be used to detect errors in spelling surnames, names of cities, countries, etc.

A parity check is the simplest method of checking when a binary code is used. We may, for instance, under certain experimental conditions, feel reasonably sure that there cannot be more than one error in a certain number (say, $n = 6$) of binary signals. To obtain a parity check, we arrange our signals in groups of six each, and add to each group a seventh signal, so chosen that the total number of ones is even. For example:

signals: 101100, checking signal 1,

signals: 100010, checking signal 0.

This will enable the receiver to detect immediately a single error on the main signal, though it would not tell him which signal was in error. A double error would not be detected.

2. Single Error Detecting Codes

We may go one step further, and investigate the possibility of checking methods that would enable the receiver to detect the exact location of an error, and to correct it immediately.

In a very interesting paper, R. W. Hamming[1] discussed the problem of codes enabling one to detect the position of an error and to correct it. This is done by using several parity checks, and Hamming gives a few practical examples of his method.

We consider a set of n binary digits and assume that there can never be more than one error in these n positions. Out of these n positions, we select m positions for information and use the remaining k positions for checks. Our k binary digits used in the checking positions represent 2^k different binary numbers that must indicate the following:

1. either there is no error or
2. if there is an error, the position of this error.

Altogether there are $n + 1$ indications, and hence we have the condition

$$2^k \geqslant n + 1. \tag{6.1}$$

The checking is most efficient if the equality holds in Eq. (6.1). In Table 6.1, we have given the maximum number of symbols which can be checked for various values of k.

The second case in Table 6.1 corresponds to the assumption that there can never be more than one error in a sequence of three binary digits. One of these digits is used for information and the other two as checks, according to Table 6.2. The checking digits B and C are to be chosen so that

$$(A + B) \text{ is even,} \qquad \text{and} \qquad (A + C) \text{ is even.}$$

The receiver of the message computes the two sums; if only one of them fails, the checking signal in that one is wrong. If for instance, $(A + B)$ is odd, while $(A + C)$ is even, then signal B is wrong. If A is wrong, then both sums will be odd. Hence, it is obvious which signal must be corrected.

The third case is a four out of seven code: four binary digits for information and three for checks. Errors can be detected and located under the assumption that there can never be more than one error in seven binary digits. The checks can be used as indicated in Table 6.3.

---

[1] R. W. Hamming, *Bell System Tech. J.* **29**, 147 (1950).

TABLE 6.1
Maximum Number of Symbols Which Can be Checked Using One to Five Checking Symbols

Checks k	Total n	Information $m = k - n$
1	1	0
2	3	1
3	7	4
4	15	11
5	31	26

TABLE 6.2
Scheme for a Code Using One Binary Digit for Information and Two for Checking*

Information	Checks	
A	B	C
x	x	
x		x

* Checks are to be chosen so that the symbols "x" along each row add to an even number.

TABLE 6.3
A Code Using Four Binary Digits for Information and Three for Checking*

Information				Checks		
A	B	C	D	E	F	G
x—	x—	x		x		
x—	x		x		x	
x		x—	x			x

* Checks are to be chosen so that the symbols "x" along each row add to an even number.

The signals A, B, C, and D may be either 0 or 1. The check signals are to be so chosen that

$$\left.\begin{aligned} A + B + C + E &= \text{even}, \\ A + B + D + F &= \text{even}, \\ A + C + D + G &= \text{even}. \end{aligned}\right\} \qquad (6.2)$$

The receiver of the message immediately compiles these three sums:

If they are all even, there is no error, because we have assumed that there is never more than one error in seven signals.

If just one of the sums is odd, the error is in the checking signal in that sum. If, for instance, only the first sum is odd, this means that the signal E is wrong.

If exactly two sums fail, the error is in the signal common to them, but not in the third. If, for instance, the first two fail, the error must be in B.

If all three sums are odd, the error is in A.

The method used here is slightly different from the one selected by Hamming, but it leads to exactly similar results.

Let us consider the fourth case of Table 6.1, and assume that there cannot be more than one error in 15 binary digits. This means

$$m = 11 \quad \text{information positions,}$$

$$k = 4 \quad \text{checking positions.}$$

The checking system is as shown in Table 6.4.

TABLE 6.4

A Code Using Eleven Binary Digits for Information and Four for Checking*

	Information											Checks			
Positions	A	B	C	D	E	F	G	H	I	J	K	L	M	N	O
	x—	x—	x—	x		x—	x—	x				x			
	x—	x—	x		x—	x			x—	x			x		
	x—	x		x—	x		x		x		x			x	
	x		x—	x—	x			x		x—	x				x

* Checks are to be chosen so that the symbols "x" along each row add to an even number.

This means that the checks are to be chosen so that:

$$\begin{aligned} A + B + C + D + F + G + H + L &= \text{even}, \\ A + B + C + E + F + I + J + M &= \text{even}, \\ A + B + D + E + G + I + K + N &= \text{even}, \\ A + C + D + E + H + J + K + O &= \text{even}. \end{aligned} \tag{6.3}$$

A single failure among these sums means that the checking signal is wrong. Errors in the information signals result in 2, 3, or 4 failures in the checking sums.

The general method used in these examples is now obvious. If we have k checking positions and a certain number m of information signals $A, B, C, D, \ldots$, we include A in all k of the checking sums. Each of the next k signals occurs in $(k-1)$ of the k checking sums. Next we use $(k-2)$ out of the k checking sums for the following $\frac{1}{2}k(k-1)$ signals, etc. Each checking sum contains just one checking signal, and a given checking signal occurs just once. Hence, in general, k checking positions will yield

$$m = 1 + k + \frac{k(k-1)}{2} + \frac{k(k-1)(k-2)}{2 \cdot 3} + \ldots + \frac{k(k-1)}{2} = 2^k - k - 1 \qquad (6.4)$$

checking possibilities, and this is the maximum number m of information signals which can be checked. Single errors appear for the k checking positions and the case of no error gives one more possibility. Thus

$$2^k = m + k + 1 = n + 1$$

in agreement with Eq. (6.1), so that the method is general.

If we have a problem with 6 information positions, as in an *IBM* code, we still need four checking positions (see Table 6.1), and we may select at random 6 of the 11 positions A to K of Table 6.4.

3. Single Error Correcting and Double Error Detecting Codes

We may extend our preceding schemes in order to detect double errors. Let us start with a single error correcting code. To this code we may add one additional position for checking all the previous positions, using a parity check. We then have the following cases:

A. No errors, all parity checks satisfied.

B. One single error. Some of the original checks fail and indicate the location of the error. The last check fails also.

C. Two errors. The last parity check is satisfied, and some of the previous ones are not, indicating trouble somewhere. The method is general and can be used on any of the examples discussed in the preceding sections. Hamming has indicated a geometrical discussion, using representation in a multidimensional space. It gives a very elegant proof of the general validity of the preceding methods.

New developments of the theory of self-correcting codes can be found in a paper by E. N. Gilbert.[2] A great many discussions of codes for multiple

[2] E. N. Gilbert, *Bell System Tech. J.* **31**, 504 (1952).

error correction can be found in the Transactions of the I. R. E. Professional Group on Information Theory.[3]

4. Efficiency of Self-Correcting Codes

The self-correcting codes discussed in the preceding sections can be used in the following way. We select, as a specific example, the 4 out of 7 code of Table 6.3. We start with a message coded in binary digits, say

$$0000100010100100, \tag{6.5}$$

and we split it into groups of four digits each:

$$0000, \quad 1000, \quad 1010, \quad 0100. \tag{6.6}$$

Next we complete each of these groups of four digits with the three digits corresponding to the parity checks of Eqs. (6.2):

$$0000000, \quad 1000111, \quad 1010010, \quad 0100110. \tag{6.7}$$

This message is transmitted, and the receiver uses the parity tests for corrections, then he erases the unnecessary last three digits in each group of seven, and recovers the original message given in Eqs. (6.6) and (6.5).

The method is satisfactory if we never have more that one error per n digits ($n = 7$ in our example). This condition will never be exactly realized. What usually happens is that there is a set of random errors with an average probability p. We want to show that the error correcting code may considerably reduce the number of errors, and yield a small probability P of uncorrected errors. We call p the probability of one error in a certain digit. This means that a 0 will be changed to a 1, or a 1 into a 0. We use a (k, n, m) code with k checks, n total binary positions, and m information positions, as defined in Table 6.1. In a given sequence of n binary digits, we obtain the following probabilities:

$$\begin{aligned}
&\pi_0 = (1-p)^n && \text{probability of no error,}\\
&\pi_1 = n\,p(1-p)^{n-1} && \text{probability of one error,}\\
&\pi_2 = \frac{n(n-1)}{2}\,p^2(1-p)^{n-2} && \text{probability of two errors in two different positions,}\\
&\pi_l = \frac{n!}{l!(n-l)!}\,p^l\,(1-p)^{n-l} && \text{probability of } l \text{ errors in } l \text{ different positions.}
\end{aligned} \tag{6.8}$$

---

[3] *Trans. I. R. E.* (*P. G. I. T.*) **1–4**; see especially, in Vol. **4**, the papers by Golay, Elias, Reed, Silverman, Balser, and others. See, also, the Convention Record of the I. R. E. National Convention, 1954.

Let us discuss the case of one error to show how the π_l's are obtained. In this case we have $(n-1)$ correct digits, with a probability of $(1-p)^{n-1}$, and one wrong digit (with a probability of p) which can be in any one of the n different positions. This yields the value given for π_1.

The other probabilities are computed under the assumption that errors always occur in different positions. This is justified by the fact that two superimposed errors compensate each other, and yield no visible error: if we have a 1, then one error changes it into 0, and a second error changes it back to 1. Superimposed errors thus always appear, finally, as giving a smaller number of visible errors.

The π_l coefficients are real probabilities since their sum is unity:

$$\sum_{l=0}^{l=n} \pi_l = \sum_{l=0}^{l=n} \frac{n!}{l!(n-l)!} p^l (1-p)^{n-l} = [(1-p)+p]^n = 1^n = 1, \qquad (6.9)$$

by the binomial formula.

If we have no error, or just one error, in one sequence, the message will be received correctly, but if we happen to have $2, 3, \ldots, l, \ldots$ errors, the final sequence will be incorrect. The probability of an incorrect sequence is thus

$$P = \pi_2 + \pi_3 + \ldots + \pi_n = 1 - \pi_0 - \pi_1. \qquad (6.10)$$

Let us assume that p is small, and neglect terms in $p^3, p^4, \ldots$. The dominant term in P comes from π_2:

$$P \approx \pi_2 \approx \tfrac{1}{2} n(n-1) p^2, \qquad (6.11)$$

and this must be compared to the number of errors to be expected if we were using no corrective checks. This would mean using only m information positions with a chance

$$1-(1-p)^m = mp - \tfrac{1}{2} m(m-1) p^2 \ldots \approx mp$$

of errors. The ratio mp/P can be used as a figure of merit of the code. We can also define $p' = P/m$, which represents the new probability of error per original digit, after correction. In Table 6.5 we give the mp, P, mp/P, and p' values for several different codes.

As an example, let us assume a probability p of 10^{-2}, or an average of one error in 100 digits in the uncorrected code. The four out of seven code gives $P = 21 \cdot 10^{-4}$ or approximately 1/475, one error in a sequence of 475 digits, after correction. The figure of merit is $4 \cdot 10^2/21 = 19$. The probability p' of error per original digit is $p' = 5.25 \cdot 10^{-4}$.

Table 6.5
Various Checking Codes and Their Characteristics

Code			mp	P	mp/P	p'
k	n	m				
2	3	1	p	$3p^2$	$\frac{1}{3p}$	$3p^2$
3	7	4	$4p$	$21p^2$	$\frac{4}{21p}$	$\frac{21}{4}p^2$
4	15	11	$11p$	$105p^2$	$\frac{11}{105p}$	$\frac{105}{11}p^2$
5	31	26	$26p$	$465p^2$	$\frac{26}{465p}$	$\frac{465}{26}p^2$

5. The Capacity of a Binary Channel with Noise

We may compare these results with a theoretical formula of Shannon.[4] This author discusses the general problem of a discrete channel with noise, and in the simple case of a binary channel, he obtains

$$C = 1 + p \log_2 p + (1-p) \log_2(1-p). \tag{6.12}$$

C is the capacity of the noisy channel in bits per digit, and p is the probability of an error in one binary digit. This formula can be justified in an elementary way. We transmit a message of N binary digits, and there will be Np digits transmitted incorrectly. All we need in order to make a correction is the position of the wrong digits. If a wrong digit was received as a 1, we simply change it into 0, and vice versa. The information on the position of the errors is transmitted by including extra signals in a binary code (1 for incorrect, 0 for correct) with a probability p for 1 and $(1-p)$ for 0. These additional signals require a channel of capacity

$$-p \log_2 p - (1-p) \log_2(1-p)$$

in bits per digit. This additional information must be sent over our channel and decreases its capacity. The original channel without noise had $C = 1$, and the noisy channel, therefore, has a capacity given by Eq. (6.12). Theoretically, one should be able to find a coding method operating at this rate.

---

[4] C. E. Shannon and W. Weaver, "The Mathematical Theory of Communication," p. 38. U. of Illinois Press, Urbana, Ill., 1949.

In our previous example with $p = 10^{-2}$, formula (6.12) indicates a capacity of the order of 0.92, which proves that only one additional binary digit per nine original digits should be enough for the corrections. Our four out of seven code does not correct completely and requires seven digits per original four digits of information, which is an increase of 3/4 instead of 1/9.

We are still very far from the optimum theoretical limit. E. N. Gilbert[2] comes to similar conclusions without offering any practical solution. His paper contains many interesting discussions on the performance of a great variety of signaling alphabets and their relative efficiencies.

The problem of error correcting procedures is most important for telecommunications and many papers have recently been written on the question. The Hamming method of Section 2 is designed for correcting automatically the symbol in error. A more economical method was proposed by C. A. Wagner of the Massachusetts Institute of Technology. Its principle is to determine, by probability computations, the symbol which has the greatest chance of being wrong, and to correct it. This method was discussed by Silverman and Balser[5] and appears very promising. In order to discover the symbol which has the greatest chance of being in error, the authors use some advance knowledge of the laws of correlation in the transmitted message. Correlation, however, means redundancy, and indicates that the number of symbols used in the transmission is too high. The computations made by Silverman and Balser on the number of symbols required in their method and in Hamming's method seem to overlook this point. The general idea is, however, very promising, and further discussions of the different methods of correction should be watched carefully.

[5] Silverman and Balser, *Proc, I. R. E.* **42**, 1428 (1954); *Trans. I. R. E. (P. G. I. T.)* **4**, 50 (1954).

CHAPTER 7

APPLICATIONS TO SOME SPECIAL PROBLEMS

1. The Problem of Filing Using a Miscellaneous Cell

If we wish to classify data (letters, faults, plants, etc.) in a set of cells or files, we have to discuss the optimum size of the cells: if the cell-size is too small relative to the size of the elements, an uncertainty will occur; if the size is too large, the filing is not very efficient. We shall consider this problem and investigate the role of different possible filing instructions. We may use a "miscellaneous" cell for elements not clearly belonging to one well defined cell, or we may use "cross-referencing." It is interesting to compare the two methods for efficiency.[1] Our discussion is based on the fundamental formula given in Eq. (1.13):

$$I = -K \sum_j p_j \ln p_j, \tag{7.1}$$

which gives the information content per symbol in a problem where a selection is made out of a certain number of cases $a, b, \ldots, j, \ldots$ having *a priori* probabilities $p_a, p_b, \ldots, p_j, \ldots$. If we use binary digits

$$K = \log_2 e,$$

$$I = -\sum_j p_j \log_2 p_j, \tag{7.1 a}$$

and the information is measured in bits.

As a simplified model of such a problem, we consider filing an element of given length l on a line of total length L, and we assume that $L \gg l$ so that we may neglect end effects. This line L is divided into N contiguous segments of length m, so that

$$N m = L. \tag{7.2}$$

The length m represents the file size, and we seek the optimum length m, that is the length m yielding the greatest information content. This model is shown

---

[1] This problem was first stated and discussed by D. K. C. MacDonald, *J. Appl. Phys.* **23**, 529 (1952).

in Fig. 7.1. Let us locate, at random, on the line L, a segment AB of length l. CD is one of the filing cells of length m. If point A falls between C and E, the whole segment $A\ B$ is within the cell. If A falls between E and D, the segment lies across the junction D between two filing cells. We have

$$CD = m, \qquad ED = l, \qquad CE = m - l. \tag{7.3}$$

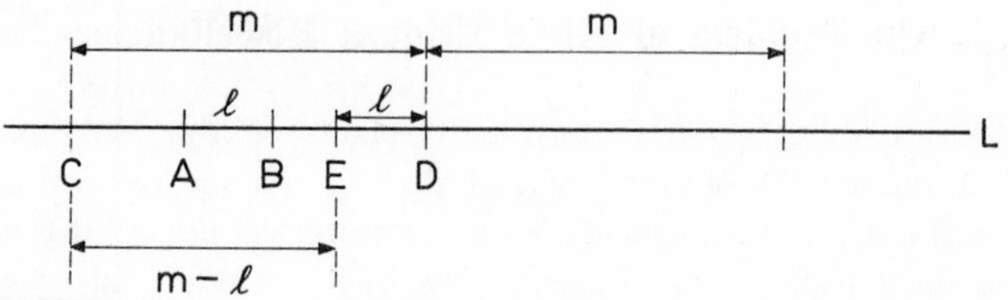

FIG. 7.1. Model for a file, with cells of length $m = CD$ and elements, to be filed, of length $l = AB$.

We assume that the different cells have equal probabilities of receiving AB. Accordingly, the probability that it falls completely inside one cell, say the i-th, is

$$p_i = (m - l)/L. \tag{7.4}$$

(This, of course, reduces to $p_i = m/L$ for "point" elements.) The total probability that AB will fall completely inside *some* cell is

$$P = \sum_{i=1}^{i=N} (m - l)/L = N(m - l)/L = 1 - l/m. \tag{7.5}$$

The case $m = 0$ is trivial, and we do not consider it, so the m in the denominator cannot lead to trouble.

The complementary probability that AB crosses a boundary between cells, and hence that it will have to be placed in an (extra) "miscellaneous" cell, is clearly

$$1 - P \equiv q = l/m. \tag{7.6}$$

The information content (per element of data) is given by formula (7.1):

$$\begin{aligned} I/K &= -\left\{ \sum_{i=1}^{i=N} p_i \ln p_i + q \ln q \right\} \\ &= -\left\{ N\left(\frac{m-l}{L}\right) \ln \left(\frac{m-l}{L}\right) + \frac{l}{m} \ln \frac{l}{m} \right\} \\ &= -\left\{ (1 - l/m) \ln \left(\frac{m-l}{L}\right) + \frac{l}{m} \ln \frac{l}{m} \right\}. \end{aligned} \tag{7.7}$$

We want to obtain the maximum information, hence we equate the derivative of I with respect to m to zero:

$$\frac{I}{K}\frac{dI}{dm} = \frac{-l}{m^2}\ln\left(\frac{m-l}{L}\right) - \left(1-\frac{l}{m}\right)\left(\frac{1}{m-l}\right) + \frac{l}{m^2}\cdot\ln\frac{l}{m} + \frac{l}{m^2} = 0,$$

or

$$-\frac{l}{m}\ln\left(\frac{m-l}{L}\right) - 1 + \frac{l}{m}\ln\frac{l}{m} + \frac{l}{m} = 0,$$

yielding a maximum for I when

$$\frac{l}{m}\left(1 + \ln\left\{\frac{l}{m}\left(\frac{L}{m-l}\right)\right\}\right) = 1,$$

or

$$m = l\left(1 + \ln\frac{lL}{m(m-l)}\right). \tag{7.8}$$

It is clear then that, generally, m is optimally of the same order of magnitude as l, but the exact solution depends (rather uncritically, as we might expect, because of the logarithmic dependence) on the choice of L; or, rather, on the "length" of the whole filing system relative to the basic data element l. Thus, let us take $L = e^5\, l$; that is $L \approx 150\, l$, which means in terms of a structure liable to faults that the "typical" fault involves something less than 1% of the entire structure. Then writing $x = m/l$, we have

$$x = 6 - \ln\{x(x-1)\}, \tag{7.9 a}$$

which has a solution $x \approx 3.7$: that is, the basic file-segment should be about four times the length of the data element.

If, however, $L = e^{10}\, l$ (i. e. $L \approx 22{,}000\, l$, so that the typical fault occupies about (1/200)% of the whole file system), we then have

$$x = 11 - \ln\{x(x-1)\}, \tag{7.9 b}$$

yielding $x \approx 8.0$ in this case.

2. Filing with Cross Referencing

Let us now consider a model representative of cross referencing for data elements which are found not to lie wholly within any *one* filing cell. In the first place we shall assume (as might well be the case in a structure liable to localized faults) that an element can only overlap two neighboring cells. Our analysis will now depend on the type of action we take on finding an overlap, and on how we interpret it.

If we were concerned, say, with a letter filing system, a simple cross reference in the adjacent file would simply mean that the letter had now been assigned a broader location in filing space. In terms of the model of Section 1, we would have a length $(2m - l)$ in which A could fall. Thus we should now have (again neglecting "end effects")

$$I/K = -\left\{\left[\sum_{i=1}^{i=N} \frac{m-l}{L} \ln \left(\frac{m-l}{L}\right)\right] + \frac{l}{m} \ln \left(\frac{2m-l}{L}\right)\right\}. \tag{7.10}$$

It should be observed that in the second term the multiplying factor has remained unchanged, on the assumption that the *a priori* probability l/m of an overlap is unaltered, while the amount of information resulting from the operation of cross referencing, $\ln(2m - l)/L$, is now, of course, different. Maximizing I with respect to m, and writing $m/l = x$, as before, we find the optimal condition

$$x = \frac{2x-1}{2x+1} \ln \frac{2x-1}{x-1}. \tag{7.11}$$

This yields $x \approx 1.06$, and it is interesting to note that this value is independent of L.

In the case, however, that we are concerned in our classification system with the direct accumulation of statistical information, an overlap may enable us to locate an element.

This then leads to

$$I/K = -\left\{\left(1 - \frac{l}{m}\right) \ln \frac{m-l}{L} + \frac{l}{m} \ln \frac{l}{L}\right\}, \tag{7.12}$$

and now the optimal equation is

$$x = -\ln(x-1) \tag{7.13}$$

yielding $x \approx 1.28$, again independent of L.

We now wish to compare the information gain per element under these various filing methods, used optimally in each case. In the first double filing case, we have, on using the optimal value of m/l:

$$\left(\frac{I}{K}\right)_{\text{opt}} = \ln \frac{L}{l} + \ln \left(\frac{l}{m-l}\right) - \frac{2m+l}{2m-l}, \tag{7.14}$$

or

$$(I/K)_{\text{opt}} = \ln(L/l) + .03, \tag{7.14 a}$$

while in the second case:

$$(I/K)_{\text{opt}} = \ln(L/l) + .28. \tag{7.15}$$

Comparison of this latter value with the case of the "miscellaneous" file, treated in Section 1, shows that the double filing system is always better, as we might expect, so long as

$$\frac{m-l}{l} + \ln \frac{m-l}{l} \geqslant -.28,$$

that is, if

$$L/l \geqslant 1.11, \tag{7.16}$$

and this value of L is so low anyway as to render filing almost meaningless.

Finally, we may mention that there is no difficulty in considering a system where the elements of data have some statistical distribution in length. Thus, if the distribution density function of l is $p(l)$, then for a "miscellaneous" file system [Eq. (7.7)], for example:

$$I/K = -\int_0^\infty \left\{\left(1 - \frac{l}{m}\right) \ln \left[\left(1 - \frac{l}{m}\right) \frac{m}{L}\right] + \frac{l}{m} \ln \frac{l}{m}\right\} p(l)\, dl. \tag{7.17}$$

If we take

$$p(l) = \begin{cases} 1/l_0 & \text{when} \quad 0 \leqslant l \leqslant l_0 \\ 0 & \text{when} \quad l > l_0, \end{cases}$$

then we obtain, after some reduction, the condition for maximum information content:

$$m/l_0 = 1 + \ln \left(\frac{L\, l_0}{m(m-l_0)}\right) - \left(\frac{m}{l_0}\right)^2 \cdot \ln \left(\frac{m}{m-l_0}\right),$$

which, for the case of $L/l_0 = e^5$ considered earlier, yields

$$m/l_0 = 2.2. \tag{7.18}$$

All these examples deal with elements that can be classified along a line, in one dimension. Similar considerations should be extended to elements depending on 2, 3, or more variables, which should be classified on a surface, in space or in a many dimensional space. These conditions would modify very seriously the situation with respect to overlapping since one single element might now overlap on many different cells.

3. The Most Favorable Number of Signals per Elementary Cell

Different answers can be given to this question, depending upon the line of approach. Let us take the point of view of a physicist, using circuits having certain definite time constants, and trying to reach maximum efficiency. The following discussion is due to Mr. R. M. Walker (IBM, Watson Laboratory).

We assume noiseless circuits. Noise problems will be discussed separately in the following chapters. Our lines, circuits, and components possess a certain time constant τ. If excited to an energy E_n, the circuit will decay according to an exponential law

$$E = E_n e^{-t/\tau}. \tag{7.19}$$

Let us now assume that we use n equidistant energy levels

$$O, E_0, 2E_0, \ldots, E_n = (n-1) E_0. \tag{7.20}$$

If the highest energy level E_n has been excited, and decays according to Eq. (7.19), we must certainly wait until E has dropped below $E_0/2$ before we can read the next energy step, which might be 0 or E_0. This leads to the condition

$$E_0/2 = (n-1) E_0 e^{-t/\tau},$$

$$t/\tau = -\ln \frac{1}{2(n-1)} = \ln 2(n-1). \tag{7.21}$$

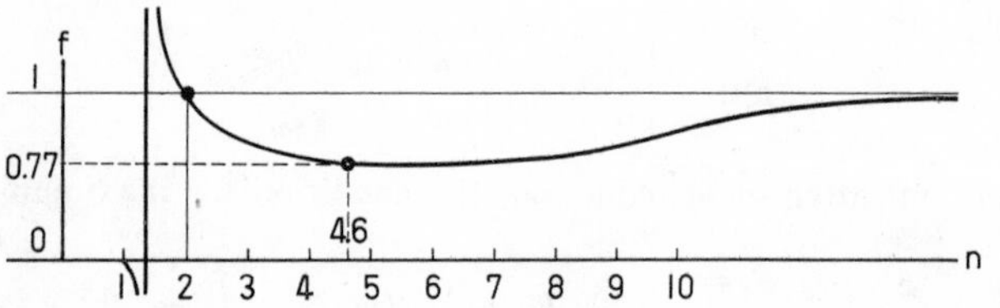

FIG. 7.2. Plot of $f(n) = (\ln n)/(\ln 2(n-1))$ as a function of n.

The time t defined by Eq. (7.21) certainly represents the shortest time interval between two successive pulses, if we want to distinguish between pulses of the type (7.20).

For a long time T, we have a total number of signals

$$G = T/t = T/(\tau \ln 2(n-1)). \tag{7.22}$$

Assuming that all of the pulses have equal *a priori* probabilities, we obtain the maximum possible information content [Eq. (1.6)]:

$$I = KG \ln n = (K\, T/\tau)\, f(n), \tag{7.23}$$

where

$$f(n) = (\ln n)/(\ln 2(n-1)). \tag{7.24}$$

We can plot the curve of $f(n)$ as a function of the integer n, ranging from 2 (binary code) to ∞ (continuous variation), and this curve is shown in Fig. 7.2. The function is unity for $n = 2$, reaches a minimum of 0.77 at $n = 4.6$, and increases to 1 again for very large values of n.

This proves that the amount of information transmitted in a given time is maximum for a binary telegraphic code, or for telephonic communication with continuous variation.

CHAPTER 8

THE ANALYSIS OF SIGNALS: FOURIER METHOD AND SAMPLING PROCEDURES

1. Fourier Series

We shall need, in the following chapters, a certain number of mathematical results on the analysis of different kinds of signals. The present chapter will be devoted to a systematic discussion of these mathematical methods and of their interrelations.

We start with the Fourier analysis of periodic functions.[1] Let $f(t)$ be a periodic function of period τ. It can be analyzed as a sum of harmonic terms. We choose the complex exponential form

$$f(t) = \sum_{n=-\infty}^{+\infty} C_n\, e^{in\omega_0 t}, \qquad \omega_0 = \frac{2\pi}{\tau}, \tag{8.1}$$

with

$$C_n = \frac{1}{\tau} \int_0^\tau f(t)\, e^{-in\omega_0 t}\, dt. \tag{8.2}$$

If $f(t)$ is a real function, one has the condition

$$C_{-n} = C_n^*, \tag{8.3}$$

where the star means "complex conjugate." Many practical methods have been proposed for the computation of the integrals (8.2). Let us discuss the method of finite intervals, on account of its close relationship with many problems to be discussed later on. We select N equidistant points on the interval $[0, \tau]$ corresponding to one period

$$t_m = m\,\theta, \qquad \theta = \frac{\tau}{N}, \qquad \text{where } m \text{ is an integer,} \tag{8.4}$$

[1] A clear, concise, and rigorous development of the fundamental theory of Fourier series is given in H. Bohr, "Almost Periodic Functions," Chapter 1. Chelsea, New York, 1947.

and we compute, instead of the integral (8.2), a discrete sum

$$\gamma_{n'} = \frac{1}{N} \sum_{m=1}^{N} f(t_m)\, e^{-in'\omega_0 t_m}. \tag{8.5}$$

Replacing $f(t_m)$ by the Fourier Series (8.1), we have

$$\gamma_{n'} = \frac{1}{N} \sum_{m=1}^{N} \sum_{n=-\infty}^{+\infty} C_n\, e^{i(n-n')m\omega_0\theta}, \qquad \omega_0\,\theta = \frac{2\pi}{N}. \tag{8.6}$$

But we have the following result:

$$\sum_{m=1}^{N} e^{ipm\frac{2\pi}{N}} = \begin{cases} N & \text{when} \quad p = q\,N, \\ 0 & \text{when} \quad p \neq q\,N, \end{cases} \quad q \text{ is an integer,} \tag{8.7}$$

since, in the second case, we sum on a series of angles $p\,m\,2\pi/N$ equally distributed between 0 and $2\,p\,\pi$. The non-zero terms in the sum (8.6) correspond to

$$p = n - n' = q\,N,$$

where q is a positive, or negative (or zero) integer, hence

$$\gamma_{n'} = \sum C_n = \sum_q C_{n'+qN}. \tag{8.8}$$

The coefficient $\gamma_{n'}$, computed from the discrete sum (8.5) is the sum of the C_n coefficients with indices $n = n' + q\,N$. Furthermore, the $\gamma_{n'}$ coefficients are periodic in n' with the period N. These relations represent a special example of a general result.[2]

An interesting case occurs for a real function when the upper harmonics of the Fourier series become negligible beyond a certain limit n_M:

$$C_n = 0 \quad \text{when} \quad |n| > n_M \qquad C_{-n} = C_n^*, \tag{8.9}$$

We may then take

$$N = 2\,n_M + 1, \tag{8.10}$$

and we find

$$\gamma_n = C_n, \qquad \text{if} \quad |n| \leqslant n_M. \tag{8.11}$$

The first N terms γ_n give correctly the first C_n Fourier coefficients, and higher γ_n terms simply repeat these C_n coefficients, with the period N (see Fig. 8.1) in the upper frequency bands.

---

[2] L. Brillouin, "Wave Propagation in Periodic Structures," 1st ed. McGraw-Hill, New York, 1946, 2nd ed., Dover Publications, New York, 1952: see, for instance, Chapter 1, p. 7.

A very important result is known as the *Parseval relation*, which applies whenever the function $f(t)$ is real, bounded, and integrable in the interval $[0, \tau]$ corresponding to one period:

$$\frac{1}{\tau}\int_0^\tau f^2\,dt = \sum_{n=-\infty}^{+\infty} |C_n|^2. \tag{8.12}$$

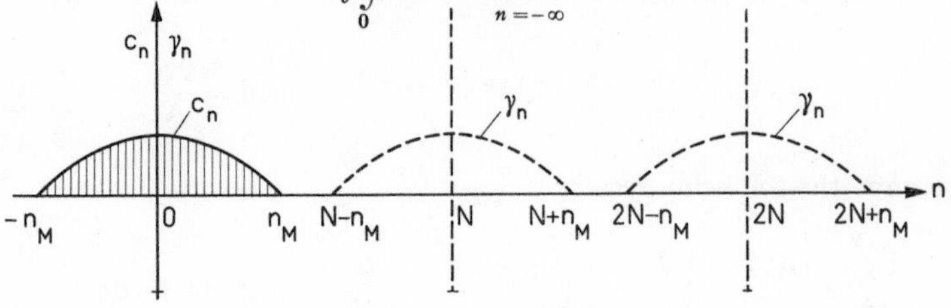

FIG. 8.1. Diagram showing the equality of the Fourier coefficients C_n with the γ_n of the finite sum for $-n_M \leqslant n \leqslant n_M$, and the periodicity of the γ_n as a function of n for higher values of n.

This formula is easily proved by replacing one of the $f(t)$'s, in the first integral, by its Fourier expansion (8.1):

$$\frac{1}{\tau}\int_0^\tau f^2\,dt = \frac{1}{\tau}\int_0^\tau f\sum_n C_n e^{in\omega_0 t}\,dt = \sum_n C_n C_n^* = \sum_n |C_n|^2.$$

In many applications, the quantities appearing in Eq. (8.12) represent energy and thus the Parseval relation shows that the energy, per period τ, can be computed either from the integral of f^2 or from the sum of the energies of the Fourier components.

2. The Gibbs' Phenomenon and Convergence of Fourier Series

The conditions of convergence of Fourier series have been discussed in many text books.[3] The Fourier expansion can be used for functions having a finite number of discontinuities within a period τ. Let us assume a discontinuity at a point t_0, with right and left hand values $f(t_0 - 0)$ and $f(t_0 + 0)$, and right and left hand derivatives at t_0. The Fourier series, for $t = t_0$, converges to the value

$$\tfrac{1}{2}[f(t_0 - 0) + f(t_0 + 0)]. \tag{8.13}$$

[3] R. V. Churchill, "Fourier Series and Boundary Value Problems," McGraw-Hill, New York, 1941; I. S. Sokolnikoff and E. S. Sokolnikoff, "Higher Mathematics for Engineers and Physicists," p. 68. McGraw-Hill, New York, 1941.

The best way to visualize this curious result is to examine a special but very typical example. Let us consider a function with period 2π and discontinuities at $t = \pm\pi, \pm 3\pi, \ldots$ (Fig. 8.2):

$$f(t) = t, \qquad -\pi < t < +\pi; \tag{8.14}$$

the discontinuity of the function at $t = \pi$ is -2π. The corresponding Fourier series is

$$f(t) = 2\left(\frac{\sin t}{1} - \frac{\sin 2t}{2} + \frac{\sin 3t}{3} \cdots\right). \tag{8.15}$$

Let us now take the sum S_p of the first p terms and compare it to the original function. The difference Δ is

$$\Delta = f(t) - S_p = 2\sum_{n=p+1}^{\infty}(-1)^{n+1}\frac{\sin nt}{n}. \tag{8.16}$$

We want to investigate the situation in the neighborhood of the discontinuity at $t = \pi$. We take

$$t = \pi - \theta, \qquad \sin nt = (-1)^{n+1}\sin n\theta;$$

hence

$$\Delta = f - S_p = 2\sum_{n=p+1}^{\infty}\frac{\sin n\theta}{n}.$$

The successive values of n differ by $\Delta n = 1$, and θ is supposed to be very small. Let us introduce a new variable

$$\eta = n\theta, \qquad \Delta\eta = \theta, \qquad \theta \ll 1.$$

We may, by the fundamental theorem of calculus, replace the discrete sum by an integral, and write

$$\Delta = 2\int_{\eta=(p+1)\theta}^{\infty}\frac{\sin\eta}{\eta}\,d\eta = -2\,\mathrm{si}(p+1)\,\theta, \tag{8.17}$$

where $\mathrm{si}(x)$ represents the "sine-integral," according to the usual definition.[4] The si function has the value $-\pi/2$ at $x = 0$, and exhibits damped oscillations until it reaches zero for x infinite. The first maxima and minima occur for

$$\frac{(p+1)\,\theta}{\pi} = \frac{x}{\pi} = \begin{cases} 1 \\ 2 \\ 3 \\ 4 \end{cases} \qquad \mathrm{si}(x) = \begin{cases} +\,0.281 \\ -\,0.153 \\ +\,0.104 \\ -\,0.079 \end{cases} \tag{8.18}$$

[4] Jahnke-Emde, "Tables of Functions," p. 9. Dover Publications, New York, 1945.

The behavior of the successive approximations is shown on Fig. 8.2. We note the following points:

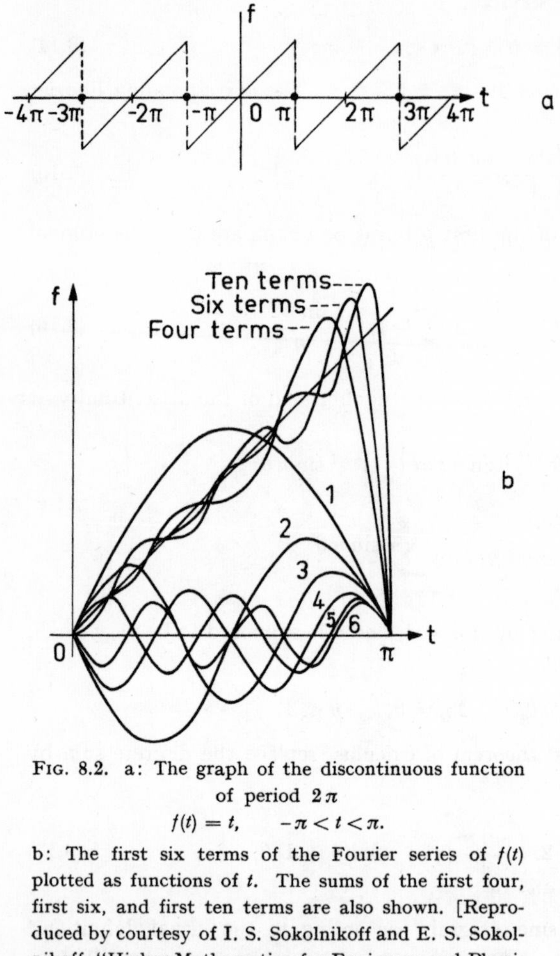

FIG. 8.2. a: The graph of the discontinuous function of period 2π

$$f(t) = t, \qquad -\pi < t < \pi.$$

b: The first six terms of the Fourier series of $f(t)$ plotted as functions of t. The sums of the first four, first six, and first ten terms are also shown. [Reproduced by courtesy of I. S. Sokolnikoff and E. S. Sokolnikoff, "Higher Mathematics for Engineers and Physicists." MrGraw-Hill, New York, 1941.]

A. All the partial sums S_p are represented by curves going through the point $t = \pi$, $S_p = 0$. Hence the point in the middle of the discontinuity is a point of convergence, a result which agrees with condition (8.13).

B. The partial sums exhibit large spurious oscillations in the neighborhood of the discontinuity. When the number p of terms in the partial sum is large enough, these oscillations are represented by a standard curve Δ [Eq. (8.17)]. The oscillations always have the same magnitude, with maxima and minima given by Eq. (8.18). The partial sum first overshoots at $\theta = \pi/p$ and is in excess of the actual function by 0.281, giving a relative error

$$\frac{\Delta}{f} = \frac{\Delta}{\pi} = \frac{2}{\pi}(0.281)$$
$$= 18\%. \tag{8.19}$$

When the number p of terms kept in the partial sum is increased, the result is to decrease the length of the perturbed region, but the maxima and minima retain the same amplitude. This is known as the "Gibbs' Phenomenon." It is easy to note on Fig. 8.2 that the height of the overshot is always 18%, when 4, 6, or 10 terms are kept in the partial sum.

The results obtained for this special example are general, and apply to any function with discontinuities. Let us consider a function $F(t)$, with period 2π, exhibiting discontinuities $D_1, D_2, D_3 \ldots$ at $t_1, t_2, t_3 \ldots$. We may build a continuous function

$$G = F + \frac{D_1}{2\pi} f(t - t_1 + \pi) + \frac{D_2}{2\pi} f(t - t_2 + \pi) \ldots$$

by adding to the function F a certain number of functions (8.14) multiplied by convenient coefficients. The Fourier Series of the continuous function G converges rapidly, with coefficients decreasing in $1/n^2$ or faster. The discontinuities in the f functions give coefficients decreasing only in $1/n$ [Eq. (8.15)] and the behavior of the Fourier series of F near the discontinuities is overwhelmingly represented by these slowly converging terms, which reproduce the features discussed in the preceding problem.

Another point of importance should be emphasized: the partial sum S_p represents the best possible approximation to the original function, giving the least mean square deviation.[1]

3. Fourier Integrals

We shall discuss Fourier Integrals for a simplified example corresponding very closely to practical problems of pulse technique. We consider a pulse of duration θ, repeated periodically (period τ). We analyze this pulse system in Fourier Series, according to Eqs. (8.1) and (8.2) (see Fig. 8.3):

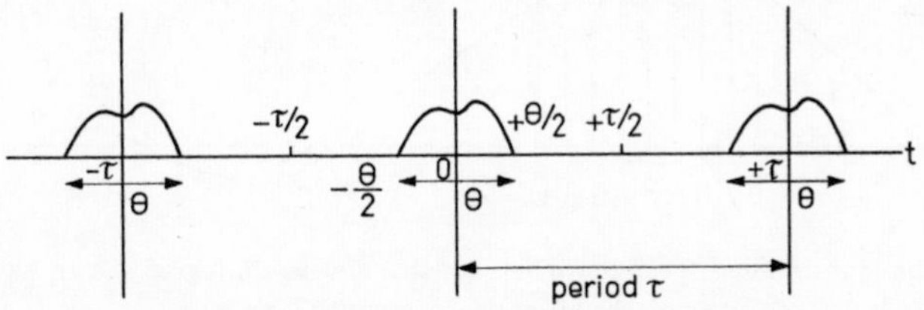

FIG. 8.3. A pulse of duration θ repeated periodically at intervals τ.

$$f(t) = \sum_{n=-\infty}^{+\infty} C_n e^{in\omega_0}, \qquad \omega_0 = 2\pi\nu_0 = \frac{2\pi}{\tau},$$

$$C_n = \frac{1}{\tau} \int_{-\tau/2}^{\tau/2} f(t)\, e^{-in\omega_0 t}\, dt, \qquad C_{-n} = C_n{}^*, \tag{8.20}$$

where $f(t)$ is a real function. The pulse being zero, outside the short interval θ, the limits of integration for C_n can be taken at $\pm\, \theta/2$. We now assume that we progressively increase the distance τ between successive pulses and go to the limit $\tau \to \infty$. The discrete sum in $f(t)$ can be written

$$f(t) = \sum_{-\infty}^{\infty} C_n e^{i\,2\pi \nu_n t} \Delta\, n = \sum_{-\infty}^{\infty} C_n \tau\, e^{i\,2\pi \nu t} \Delta\, \nu, \qquad \nu_n = n\, \nu_0,$$

$$\Delta\, n = 1, \qquad \Delta\, \nu = \nu_0 = 1/\tau.$$

When τ is very large, the sum becomes an integral:

$$\tau \to \infty: \qquad f(t) = \int_{\nu=-\infty}^{\infty} C(\nu)\, e^{i\,2\pi\nu t}\, d\nu, \tag{8.21}$$

and

$$\lim_{\tau \to \infty} (C_n \tau) = C(\nu) = \int_{t=-\infty}^{\infty} f(t)\, e^{-i\,2\pi\nu t}\, dt = C^*(-\,\nu). \tag{8.22}$$

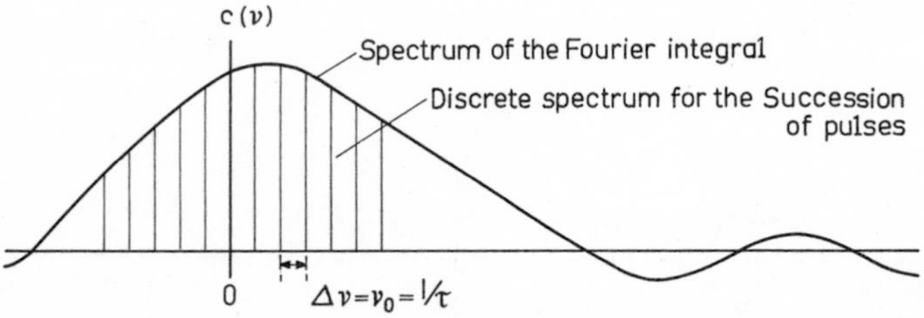

FIG. 8.4. The continuous spectrum $C(\nu)$ of the Fourier integral shown as the envelop of the discrete spectrum $C_n\, \tau$.

In the second integral (8.22), the integration actually covers an interval θ, corresponding to a single pulse, since $f(t) \neq 0$ only for $-\,\theta/2 < t < \theta/2$.

For large τ, we obtain for $C_n\, \tau$ a discrete spectrum, the envelope of which is given by the continuous spectrum of the Fourier integral. The longer τ is, the shorter will be the interval $\Delta\, \nu = 1/\tau$ of the discrete spectrum (see Fig. 8.4). Equations (8.21) and (8.22) show the complete reciprocity between the t and ν variables: If a pulse $f(t)$ has a spectrum $C(\nu)$, then a pulse $C(t)$ has a spectrum $f(\nu)$.

When the pulse is symmetrical, the spectrum is also symmetrical:

$$f(t) = f(-t) = \int_{\nu=-\infty}^{\infty} C(\nu) \cos 2\pi \nu t \, d\nu, \tag{8.23}$$

$$C(\nu) = C(-\nu) = \int_{t=-\infty}^{\infty} f(t) \cos 2\pi \nu t \, dt. \tag{8.24}$$

These are the fundamental formulas required for our discussion. Now we give a few examples:

Rectangular Pulse — Spectrum

$$f(t) = \begin{cases} 1 & |t| < (\tfrac{1}{2})\,\theta_1 \\ 0 & |t| > (\tfrac{1}{2})\,\theta_1 \end{cases} \qquad C(\nu) = \theta_1 \frac{\operatorname{Sin} \pi \nu \theta_1}{\pi \nu \theta_1} \tag{8.25}$$

Rounded Pulse — Rectangular Spectrum

$$f(t) = 2\,\nu_M \frac{\operatorname{Sin} 2\pi \nu_M t}{2\pi \nu_M t} \qquad C(\nu) = \begin{cases} 1 & |\nu| < \nu_M \\ 0 & |\nu| > \nu_M \end{cases}. \tag{8.26}$$

Triangular Pulse

$$f(t) = \begin{cases} \left(1 - \dfrac{|t|}{\theta_1}\right) & |t| < \theta_1 \\ 0 & |t| > \theta_1 \end{cases} \qquad C(\nu) = \theta_1 \left(\frac{\operatorname{Sin} \pi \nu \theta_1}{\pi \nu \theta_1}\right)^2. \tag{8.27}$$

Gaussian Pulse — Gaussian Spectrum

$$f(t) = e^{-\pi (t/\theta_1)^2} \qquad C(\nu) = \theta_1 \, e^{-\pi (\nu \theta_1)^2}. \tag{8.28}$$

The corresponding curves have been drawn on Fig. 8.5. The first two cases are an example of inverse functions and exhibit the t, ν symmetry in Eqs. (8.23) and (8.24).

We have for the Fourier integral a *Parseval relation*, similar to Eq. (8.12) for the Fouier series. We derive it in a simple way

$$\int |f|^2 \, dt = \int f^* f \, dt = \int f^* \, dt \int C(\nu) \, e^{i 2\pi \nu t} d\nu,$$

where we replaced $f(t)$ by its Fourier integral (8.21). Integrating in t, we note

$$\int f^*(t) \, e^{i 2\pi \nu t} d\nu = C^*(\nu),$$

and we obtain

$$\int_{-\infty}^{+\infty} |f(t)|^2 \, dt = \int_{-\infty}^{+\infty} |C(\nu)|^2 \, d\nu = E. \tag{8.29}$$

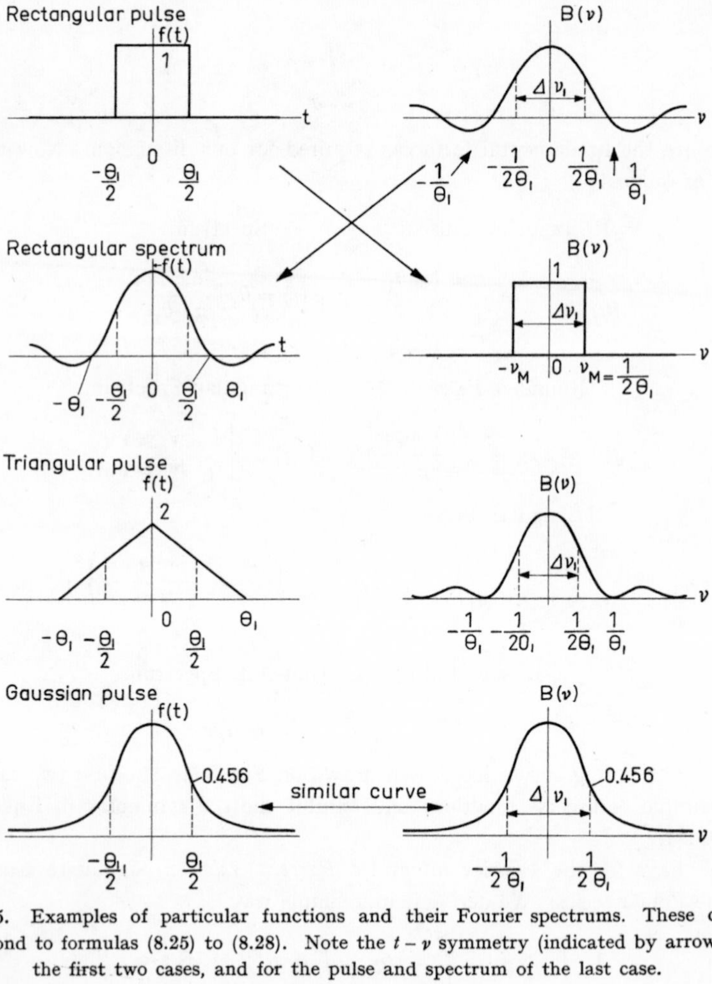

FIG. 8.5. Examples of particular functions and their Fourier spectrums. These curves correspond to formulas (8.25) to (8.28). Note the $t-\nu$ symmetry (indicated by arrows) for the first two cases, and for the pulse and spectrum of the last case.

For many physical problems, the above integral will represent the total energy associated with a wave of amplitude $f(t)$, and the quantity E can be computed either from the wave $f(t)$ itself, or from its Fourier spectrum.

4. The Role of Finite Frequency Band Width

One of the important characteristics of any system of telecommunication is the fact that it always uses a finite range of frequencies. The system may be of the "low-pass" type, using all frequencies from zero up to a certain maximum ν_M, or it may belong to the "band-pass" type, allowing for frequencies between two limits ν_1 and ν_2. The so-called "high-pass" type is purely hypothetical, since there is no physical system without an upper frequency limit. The analysis of a band-pass system can be reduced to the case of low-pass acting as modulation on a carrier frequency. We can therefore limit our discussion to the *low-pass* problem. The question is: Given a certain upper frequency ν_M, what sort of signals can we transmit? Or in other words: What are the characteristics of functions $f(t)$ whose Fourier spectrum does not extend beyond ν_M?

This condition means that we use the frequency band $\Delta \nu_1$:

$$|\nu| \leqslant \nu_M, \qquad -\nu_M \leqslant \nu \leqslant \nu_M, \qquad \Delta \nu_1 = 2\nu_M. \tag{8.30}$$

The first point which we want to make clear is that a signal of duration θ_1 requires, for its representation, a spectrum

$$\Delta \nu_1 \geqslant \frac{1}{\theta_1}, \qquad \Delta \nu_1 \cdot \theta_1 \geqslant 1. \tag{8.30 a}$$

The frequency band is, in practice, not sharply defined. For frequencies inside the band $C(\nu)$ is large compared with its value for frequencies outside of the band. In a similar way, the function $f(t)$ will represent a signal of relatively large intensity for a duration θ_1 and relatively small intensity at other times. The product $\Delta \nu_1 \cdot \theta_1$ has a lower bound. This can be seen qualitatively from examples (8.25) to (8.28), where the more sharply defined signals clearly have much larger frequency bands.

The problem of defining quantitatively the width of the frequency band and the duration of the signal appears to be empirical. The following experiment, from television, yields a basis for selecting quantitative definitions. It has been found that a band width of about 6 megacycles is required for transmitting signals which will cover 525 lines on a screen, repeated 30 times per second, with 360 pulses per line. This gives a pulse length

$$\theta_1 = \frac{1}{525 \times 30 \times 360} = \frac{1}{5.7} \times 10^{-6},$$

and

$$\Delta \nu_1 \cdot \theta_1 = 6 \cdot 10^6 \cdot \frac{1}{5.7} \cdot 10^{-6} = 1.05.$$

This example suggests that the band width and signal duration should satisfy the inequality

$$\Delta \nu_1 \cdot \theta_1 \geqslant 1. \tag{8.30 a}$$

Let us now consider the examples (8.25) to (8.28) introduced in the preceding section. These are short symmetrical pulses with maximum amplitude at $t = 0$, maximum spectral intensity at $\nu = 0$, and real amplitude $C(\nu)$ in the Fourier spectrum. The following definitions for $\Delta \nu_1$ and θ_1 will be seen to be consistent with Eq. (8.30 a).[5]

$$f(0) \cdot \theta_1 = \int_{-\infty}^{+\infty} f(t)\, dt, \qquad \theta_1, \text{ nominal duration,} \tag{8.31}$$

$$C(0) \cdot \Delta \nu_1 = \int_{-\infty}^{+\infty} C(\nu)\, d\nu, \qquad \Delta \nu_1, \text{ nominal band width.} \tag{8.32}$$

But the integral in (8.31) is equal to $C(0)$ in Eq. (8.24). Similarly, the integral in (8.32) represents $f(0)$ in (8.23), hence

$$\theta_1 = \frac{C(0)}{f(0)}, \qquad \Delta \nu_1 = \frac{f(0)}{C(0)}, \qquad \theta_1 \Delta \nu_1 = 1. \tag{8.33}$$

These definitions give an equality instead of the inequality of Eq. (8.30). They can be easily checked on our previous examples. These special examples, however, do not correspond to the general situation, and conditions (8.31) and (8.32) cannot be used for a practical and general definition of signal duration or band width. In the computation of the duration θ_1 of a signal, for instance, negative values of f should come in with a positive contribution, whereas in Eq. (8.31) they appear with a negative sign. We may thus try the following modified definitions, based on absolute values:

$$|f(0)|\, \theta_2 = \int_{-\infty}^{\infty} |f(t)| dt \geqslant \left| \int_{-\infty}^{\infty} f(t)\, dt \right| = |C(0)|, \tag{8.34}$$

and similarly

$$|C(0)|\, \Delta \nu_2 = \int_{-\infty}^{\infty} |C(\nu)| d\nu \geqslant \left| \int_{-\infty}^{\infty} C(\nu)\, d\nu \right| = |f(0)|. \tag{8.35}$$

---

[5] H. A. Wheeler, *Proc. I. R. E.* **27**, 359 (1939); P. LeCorbeiller, "Electronic Circuits and Tubes," pp. 586–590. McGraw-Hill, New York, 1947.

These definitions give

$$\theta_2 \geqslant \theta_1, \qquad \Delta\nu_2 \geqslant \Delta\nu_1, \qquad \theta_2\Delta\nu_2 \geqslant \theta_1\Delta\nu_1 = 1. \tag{8.36}$$

which is the condition (8.30 a) which we want to satisfy. Fig. 8.6 illustrates the method: A length θ_2 is chosen so as to give a rectangle whose area $|f(0)|\,\theta_2$ is equal to the area below the rectified $|f(t)|$ curve. The situation is similar with the band width. The duration θ_2 can be decreased by chosing the origin of time at a point where $|f|$ is maximum. In a similar way, the band width $\Delta\nu_2$ can be reduced by a proper choice of the origin of frequencies, which can be obtained by multiplying the spectrum by a factor $e^{2\pi i\nu t}$. This operation is simply a "demodulation" of the signal. But even these new θ_2' and $\Delta\nu_2'$ will always satisfy the general condition (8.36).

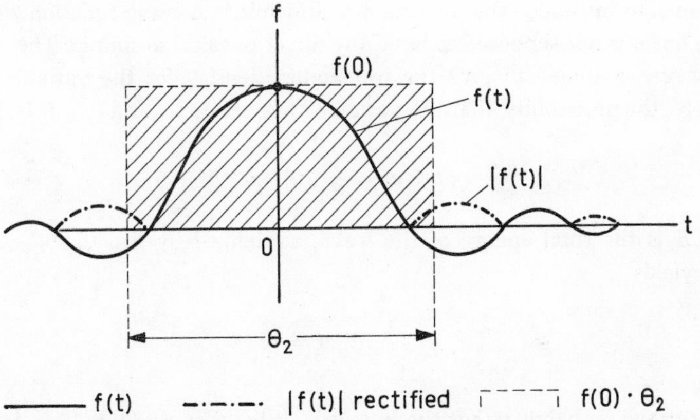

FIG. 8.6. The duration θ_2 of a pulse is obtained by equating $f(0)\cdot\theta_2$ to the area between the rectified curve $|f(t)|$ and the t axis.

5. The Uncertainty Relation for Time and Frequency

Our general condition (8.30 a) is a special case of the uncertainty principle of quantum mechanics. This principle states that a variable q and its "conjugate momentum" p cannot be measured simultaneously with arbitrary accuracy, but that there is a relation between the error Δq in q and the error Δp in p. This relation is

$$\Delta q \cdot \Delta p \geqslant \alpha, \tag{8.37}$$

where α is sometimes taken as h, Planck's constant, and sometimes as $h/2\pi = \hbar$, Dirac's constant. Both values are so small that either is acceptable from the experimental point of view.

It is well known that, in mechanics, the energy E is the momentum conjugate to the time variable t, so that according to Eq. (8.37)

$$\Delta E \cdot \Delta t \geqslant \alpha. \tag{8.38}$$

The energy associated with oscillations of frequency ν is $h\nu$ and therefore

$$\Delta E = h \Delta \nu,$$

and, if we make use of the empirical condition (8.30 a), we have

$$\Delta E \cdot \Delta t = h \Delta \nu \cdot \Delta t \geqslant h. \tag{8.39}$$

Therefore we should take $\alpha = h$, rather than $\alpha = \hbar$. We shall discuss this point further, at the end of the section.

First, however, we wish to present the line of reasoning used in wave mechanics to introduce the uncertainty principle.[6] A wave function $f(t)$ is computed, but it is not supposed to have any direct physical meaning. The square $|f|^2$ is, however, assumed to give the probability density for the variable t. More precisely, the probability that the variable t lies between t and $t + dt$ is defined as

$$p(t)\, dt = \frac{1}{E} |f(t)|^2\, dt, \tag{8.40}$$

where E is the total energy of the wave, as defined by Eq. (8.29). Condition (8.29) yields

$$\int_{-\infty}^{\infty} p(t)\, dt = 1. \tag{8.40 a}$$

Similarly, the probability that the frequency is between ν and $\nu + d\nu$ is given by

$$P(\nu)\, d\nu = \frac{1}{E} |C(\nu)|^2\, d\nu, \tag{8.41}$$

and

$$\int_{-\infty}^{\infty} P(\nu)\, d\nu = 1. \tag{8.41 a}$$

Now the average time t_0 of the occurrence of the signal is

$$t_0 = \int_{-\infty}^{\infty} t\, p(t)\, dt, \tag{8.42}$$

[6] See, for example, D. Gabor, M. I. T. Lectures, 1951.

and the average frequency is

$$\nu_0 = \int_{-\infty}^{\infty} \nu\, P(\nu)\, d\nu. \tag{8.43}$$

The deviations t_1 and ν_1 from these averages are given by

$$t = t_0 + t_1, \qquad \nu = \nu_0 + \nu_1.$$

We compute the averages of the squares of these deviations:

$$\overline{t_1^{\,2}} = \int_{-\infty}^{\infty} t_1^{\,2}\, p(t)\, dt, \qquad \overline{\nu_1^{\,2}} = \int_{-\infty}^{\infty} \nu_1^{\,2}\, P(\nu)\, d\nu. \tag{8.44}$$

We define the average errors Δt in time and $\Delta \nu$ in frequency as

$$\Delta t = \sqrt{a\, \overline{t_1^{\,2}}}, \qquad \Delta \nu = \sqrt{a\, \overline{\nu_1^{\,2}}}, \tag{8.45}$$

and determine the constant a so that the condition (8.30 a) shall be satisfied. That is we wish to determine a so that

$$\Delta t \cdot \Delta \nu = \sqrt{a^2\, \overline{t_1^{\,2}}\, \overline{\nu_1^{\,2}}} \geqslant 1, \qquad \text{or} \qquad a^2\, \overline{t_1^{\,2}}\, \overline{\nu_1^{\,2}} \geqslant 1. \tag{8.45 a}$$

If we make use of Eqs. (8.40), (8.41), and (8.44), we may replace Eq. (8.45 a) by

$$a^2 \int_{t=-\infty}^{\infty} t_1^{\,2} f^*(t)\, f(t)\, dt \int_{\nu=-\infty}^{\infty} \nu_1^{\,2}\, C^*(\nu)\, C(\nu)\, d\nu \geqslant E^2. \tag{8.46}$$

We may assume, without loss of generality, that $t_0 = 0$ and $\nu_0 = 0$; then $t_1 = t$ and $\nu_1 = \nu$.

The first step in the determination of a is to prove the identity

$$\int_{\nu=-\infty}^{\infty} \nu^2\, C^*(\nu)\, C(\nu)\, d\nu = -\frac{1}{4\pi^2} \int_{t=-\infty}^{\infty} f^*(t)\, \frac{d^2 f}{dt^2}\, dt, \tag{8.47}$$

and this can be done provided that $f(t)$ and $C(\nu)$ are both differentiable and vanish fast enough at infinity. The Fourier integral (8.21) yields:

$$\frac{d^2 f}{dt^2} = \int_{\nu=-\infty}^{\infty} C(\nu)\, (-4\pi^2 \nu^2)\, e^{2\pi i \nu t}\, d\nu,$$

and so

$$\int_{t=-\infty}^{\infty} f^* \frac{d^2 f}{dt^2} dt = -4\pi^2 \int_{\nu=-\infty}^{\infty} \nu^2 C(\nu)\, d\nu \int_{t=-\infty}^{\infty} f^* e^{2\pi i \nu t} dt.$$

The integral in t is just $C^*(\nu)$, according to Eq. (8.22), and this proves the identity (8.47).

Using Eq. (8.47), we may rewrite Eq. (8.46) as

$$-\frac{a^2}{4\pi^2} \int_{t=-\infty}^{\infty} t^2 f^* f\, dt \int_{t=-\infty}^{\infty} f^* \frac{d^2 f}{dt^2} dt \geqslant \left| \int_{t=-\infty}^{\infty} f^* f\, dt \right|^2. \qquad (8.48)$$

To proceed, we make use of Schwarz's inequality:[7]

$$4 \int F^* F\, dt \int G^* G\, dt \geqslant \left| \int (F^* G + F G^*)\, dt \right|^2 \qquad (8.49)$$

with

$$F = t f \qquad \text{and} \qquad G = df/dt.$$

We integrate the second integral by parts, and recall that f vanishes at infinity:

$$\int_{-\infty}^{\infty} G^* G\, dt = \int_{-\infty}^{\infty} \frac{df^*}{dt} \frac{df}{dt} dt = f^* \frac{df}{dt}\bigg|_{-\infty}^{\infty} - \int_{-\infty}^{\infty} f^* \frac{d^2 f}{dt^2} dt = -\int_{-\infty}^{\infty} f^* \frac{d^2 f}{dt^2} dt. \qquad (8.50)$$

We also integrate the right hand side of Schwarz's inequality by parts:

$$\int_{-\infty}^{\infty} t \left(f^* \frac{df}{dt} + f \frac{df^*}{dt} \right) dt = (t\, |f|^2) \bigg|_{-\infty}^{\infty} - \int_{-\infty}^{\infty} |f|^2\, dt = -E$$

and the Schwarz inequality now becomes

$$-4 \int_{-\infty}^{\infty} t^2 f f^*\, dt \int_{-\infty}^{\infty} f^* \frac{d^2 f}{dt^2} dt \geqslant E^2.$$

Comparison with Eq. (8.48) shows that we should take

$$a^2 = 16\pi^2, \qquad \text{or} \qquad a = 4\pi;$$

that is, we define

$$\Delta t = \sqrt{4\pi\, \overline{t_1^{\,2}}}, \qquad \Delta \nu = \sqrt{4\pi\, \overline{\nu_1^{\,2}}}.$$

---

[7] A proof of the Schwarz inequality is given in the appendix at the end of this chapter.

A comparison of these definitions with the ones used in Eqs. (8.31) and (8.32) is interesting. In the preceding section we had a duration θ_1 and a band width $1/\theta_1$ for examples (8.25), (8.27), and (8.28). The new definitions yield the following:

$$(8.25):\quad E = \theta_1,\quad \Delta t = \sqrt{\frac{\pi}{3}}\,\theta_1,\quad \Delta\nu = \infty,\quad \Delta t\,\Delta\nu = \infty,$$

$$(8.27):\quad E = \frac{2}{3}\,\theta_1,\quad \Delta t = \sqrt{\frac{2\pi}{5}}\,\theta_1,\quad \Delta\nu = \frac{1}{\theta_1}\sqrt{\frac{3}{\pi}},\quad \Delta t\,\Delta\nu = \sqrt{\frac{6}{5}},$$

$$(8.28):\quad E = \frac{\theta_1}{\sqrt{2}},\quad \Delta t = \sqrt{2}\,\theta_1,\quad \Delta\nu = \frac{1}{\theta_1}\sqrt{2},\quad \Delta t\,\Delta\nu = 2.$$

The calculations of E, $\Delta\nu$, and Δt for these examples are left for the reader. Some of the integrals involved are:

$$\int_{-\infty}^{\infty}\left(\frac{\operatorname{Sin} x}{x}\right)^2 dx = \pi,\qquad \int_{-\infty}^{\infty}\frac{\operatorname{Sin}^4 x}{x^2}\,dx = \frac{\pi}{2},\qquad \int_{-\infty}^{\infty} x^2 e^{-x^2}\,dx = \sqrt{\pi}.$$

Many original papers and textbooks on quantum mechanics use the value 2 for a. Then

$$\Delta_1 t = \sqrt{2\,\overline{t_1^{\,2}}} = \frac{\Delta t}{\sqrt{2\pi}},\qquad \Delta_1\nu = \frac{\Delta\nu}{\sqrt{2\pi}},$$

which results in

$$\Delta_1 t\cdot\Delta_1\nu \geqslant \frac{1}{2\pi}\cdot$$

If similar definitions are used for $\Delta_1 q$ and $\Delta_1 p$, the uncertainty relation takes the form

$$\Delta_1 q\cdot\Delta_1 p \geqslant \hbar.$$

These definitions seem unrealistic in view of the preceding discussion. They divide the lower bound of $\Delta\nu\cdot\Delta t$ by 2π which, in the case of the television problem outlined in the preceding section, would mean that a band of about 1 megacycle should be sufficient. Needless to say, the television broadcasters would replace each six megacycle band by six 1-megacycle bands if this were feasible.

6. Degrees of Freedom of a Message

We want to consider now the following problem: A certain function of time $f(t)$ has a spectrum containing no frequencies above a certain limit ν_M, and it extends over a time interval τ. How many parameters (or degrees of freedom) are required to define such a function? We shall prove that there are only

$$N = 2\,\nu_M\,\tau\ (\text{assuming } \nu_M\,\tau \gg 1) \tag{8.51}$$

independent parameters for such a function, and we intend to discuss different possible choices of these parameters, as well as some general properties of the functions involved.

First of all, we must note that the function is not completely defined when we only give its value over a finite interval, $0 < t < \tau$ for instance. In order to state the problem correctly we must specify the value of the function before 0 and after τ. This must be done without adding anything to the information contained in the message $f(t)$. Two different definitions can be used:

A. A *periodic function* $f(t)$ repeating indefinitely the behavior of f between 0 and τ

$$f(t + q\tau) = f(t), \qquad q \text{ is an integer.} \tag{8.52}$$

B. A *single message* function, with

$$f(t) = 0 \qquad \text{for} \qquad t < 0 \qquad \text{or} \qquad t > \tau. \tag{8.53}$$

This last example is the one considered by Shannon.

We start with the definition A and investigate a periodic function of period τ. The periodic function is expanded in Fourier series:

$$f(t) = \frac{1}{2} a_0 + \sum_{n=1}^{n_M} (a_n \cos n\phi + b_n \sin n\phi), \tag{8.54}$$

with

$$\phi = \frac{2\pi t}{\tau} = 2\pi \nu_0 t, \qquad \nu_0 = \frac{1}{\tau}\cdot \tag{8.55}$$

We assume that the maximum frequency ν_M corresponds exactly to one of the harmonics of ν_0:

$$n_M = \nu_M \tau \qquad \text{or} \qquad n_M \nu_0 = \nu_M. \tag{8.56}$$

The Fourier series contains a finite number of terms extending up to the integer n_M. For each proper frequency we have two components a_n, b_n, hence a total of

$$N = 2n_M + 1 = 2\nu_M \tau + 1 \tag{8.57}$$

components, including the constant term a_0. If the duration τ of the signal is large enough, formula (8.57) practically reduces to (8.51). The a_n and b_n coefficients represent one possible choice of parameters. Instead of the real Fourier series (8.54) we may use the complex Fourier series as in Eqs. (8.1) and (8.2):

$$f(t) = \sum_{n=-n_M}^{+n_M} c_n e^{in\omega_0 t}, \qquad \omega_0 = 2\pi \nu_0 = \frac{2\pi}{\tau}, \tag{8.58}$$

$$c_n = \frac{1}{2}(a_n - i\,b_n) = \frac{1}{\tau}\int_0^\tau f(t')\,e^{-in\omega_0 t'}\,dt' = c^*_{-n},$$

where the star means "complex conjugate."

Instead of the Fourier series, we may use a sampling method on our periodic functions $f(t)$. We select N equidistant sampling points along the period τ, for instance

$$t_m = m\,\theta, \qquad \theta = \frac{\tau}{N} = \frac{1}{2\,\nu_M + \nu_0}, \tag{8.59}$$

with

$$N = 2\,n_M + 1 = \tau(2\,\nu_M + \nu_0) = 2\,\nu_M\,\tau + 1,$$

and we call the sampled value f_m:

$$f_m = f(m\,\theta), \tag{8.59 a}$$

$$f_{m+qN} = f_m, \qquad q \text{ integer},$$

according to the periodicity condition (8.52).

We can rebuild our original function $f(t)$ when we know the $2\,n_M + 1$ sampled values over a period τ. We write

$$f(t) = \sum_{m=1}^{N} f_m\,g(t - m\,\theta), \tag{8.60}$$

where $g(t)$ represents a pulse function, centered on the instant of time $t = 0$ and repeated for periodicity on $t = q\,\tau$. We choose for this pulse function the following specifications:

$$g(t) = 1 \quad \text{for} \quad t = 0 \quad \text{or} \quad t = q\,\tau, \quad q \text{ integer},$$

$$g(t) = 0 \quad \text{for} \quad t = m\,\theta, \quad m \neq q\,N.$$

The pulse function is zero on all other sampling points along the period τ. Such a function is not difficult to build with a finite spectrum never exceeding ν_M. The answer is contained in Lagrange's identity

$$\frac{1}{2} + \sum_{n=1}^{n_M} \cos n\,\phi = \frac{1}{2}\sum_{n=-n_M}^{+n_M} e^{in\phi} = \frac{\sin\,(n_M + \frac{1}{2})\,\phi}{2\sin\,(\phi/2)}, \tag{8.61}$$

where we take $\phi = \omega_0\,t$.

This function is equal to $n_M + \frac{1}{2}$ at $t = 0$, or $t = q\tau$, when the denominator is zero. It oscillates and is zero at the points

$$(n_M + \tfrac{1}{2})\, \omega_0 t = \pi, 2\pi, \ldots m\pi,$$

$$t = \frac{\tau}{N}, \ \frac{2\tau}{N} \ldots \frac{m\tau}{N}, \qquad m \neq q N,$$

as long as m is not an integer multiple of N.

We can take for our impulse function $g(t)$ the expression

$$g(t) = \frac{\sin\left(N \dfrac{\omega_0 t}{2}\right)}{N \sin\left(\dfrac{\omega_0 t}{2}\right)} = \frac{1}{N} \sum_{-n_M}^{+n_M} e^{i n \omega_0 t}. \tag{8.62}$$

Comparing now Eqs. (8.60), (8.62), and (8.58) we obtain

$$f(t) = \frac{1}{N} \sum_{-n_M}^{+n_M} \sum_{m=1}^{N} f_m\, e^{i n \omega_0 (t - m\theta)},$$

hence

$$c_n = \frac{1}{N} \sum_{m=1}^{N} f_m\, e^{-i n m \omega_0 \theta}, \tag{8,63}$$

an equation which directly relates the Fourier coefficients[8] c_n to the sampled values f_m. The reverse relation is obtained from Eq. (8.58):

$$f_m = f(m\theta) = \sum_{n' = -n_M}^{+n_M} c_{n'}\, e^{i n' m \omega_0 \theta}. \tag{8.63 a}$$

In the complex Fourier series we have $N = 2 n_M + 1$ complex amplitudes c_n, which are complex conjugate for $\pm n$. Altogether, this gives N independent real variables and our N sampling points provide an equal number of degrees of freedom. A direct check of Eqs. (8.63) and (8.63 a) is easily obtained:

$$\left.\begin{aligned} c_n &= \frac{1}{N} \sum_{m=1}^{N} \sum_{n'=-n_M}^{n_M} c_{n'}\, e^{i(n'-n) m \omega_0 \theta}\,; \\ &\text{but} \\ \frac{1}{N} \sum_{m=1}^{N} e^{i p m \omega_0 \theta} &= \begin{cases} 1 & \text{for } p = 0 \\ 0 & \text{for } p \neq 0 \text{ (integer)}, \end{cases} \end{aligned}\right\} \tag{8.63 b}$$

[8] Eq. (8.63) is identical with our previous Eqs. (8.5) and (8.11) because we are dealing here with a function having a finite band width as in Eq. (8.9).

since for $p = 0$ we have N terms of value 1 in the sum, while for $p \neq 0$ the N harmonic terms have phases uniformly distributed from 0 to 2π, giving a zero resultant. Altogether

$$c_n = \sum c_{n'}\,\delta(n - n'), \qquad \text{Q.E.D.}$$

Instead of sampling at the instants of time $m\,\theta$ one might use the instants of time $m\,\theta + \theta'$ with a constant time $\theta' < \theta$ added. This would give a different set of sampled values $f'_m = f(m\,\theta + \theta')$ which could be used instead of the f_m. Eqs. (8.63) and (8.63 a) would be replaced by

$$c_n = \frac{1}{N} \sum_m f'_m\, e^{-in\omega_0(m\theta + \theta')}, \qquad f'_m = \sum_{n'} c_{n'}\, e^{in'\omega_0(m\theta + \theta')}.$$

There would also be a set of N linear relations between the f_m and f'_m.

7. Shannon's Sampling Method

Shannon uses the sampling method in connection with the problem B [Eq. (8.53)] of a single message function, assumed to be zero for $t < 0$ or $t > \tau$. We can solve this problem through the following procedure: We take a periodic function with a long period $\tau_1 > \tau$ and assume that $f(\tau)$ has its original values from 0 to τ and is zero from τ to τ_1. This supposes, of course, a smooth junction with the zero line at both ends, 0 and τ, in order not to introduce any frequencies above the limit ν_M. The new function is sampled over the new interval τ_1 at N_1 equidistant points according to the procedure developed in Eqs. (8.59) and (8.62). The new sampling interval θ_1 is similar to (8.59):

$$\theta_1 = \frac{1}{2\,\nu_M + \nu_1}, \qquad \nu_1 = \frac{1}{\tau_1}, \qquad \omega_1 = \frac{2\pi}{\tau_1}; \tag{8.64}$$

when τ and τ_1 are both large, ν_0 and ν_1 are negligible compared to the maximum frequency ν_M and we have

$$\theta_0 \approx \theta_1 \approx \frac{1}{2\,\nu_M}.$$

The total number of sampling points is now

$$N_1 = 2\,\nu_M \tau_1 + 1. \tag{8.65}$$

Out of these N_1 sampling points, we have N points falling into the original interval $0 < t < \tau$ and $N_1 - N$ in the interval $\tau < t < \tau_1$. The first set of points give non zero sampled values

$$f_m = f(m\,\theta_1) \neq 0, \qquad 0 \leq m < N, \tag{8.66}$$

and the other points give zero:

$$f_m = f(m\,\theta_1) = 0, \qquad N < m < N_1.$$

Our impulse function $g(t)$ of Eq. (8.62) becomes

$$g(t) = \frac{\sin\left(N_1 \dfrac{\omega_1 t}{2}\right)}{N_1 \sin\left(\dfrac{\omega_1 t}{2}\right)}. \tag{8.67}$$

We now let τ_1 go to infinity and ν_1 go to zero which gives, in the limit, a sampling interval

$$\theta_{\text{lim}} = \frac{1}{2\,\nu_M},$$

and we have an infinite number of sampled values f_m equal to zero. The only non zero samples correspond to

$$0 < m\,\theta_{\text{lim}} < \tau.$$

Their number is

$$N_{\text{lim}} = \tau/\theta_{\text{lim}} = 2\,\nu_M\,\tau, \tag{8.68}$$

a result which agrees with Eq. (8.51), while the impulse function $g(t)$ reduces to

$$g(t) \approx \frac{\sin\left(N_1 \dfrac{\omega_1 t}{2}\right)}{N_1 \dfrac{\omega_1 t}{2}} \approx \frac{\sin 2\pi\,\nu_M\,t}{2\pi\,\nu_M\,t,}, \tag{8.69}$$

since

$$N_1\,\omega_1 = (2\,\nu_M\,\tau_1 + 1)\,\frac{2\pi}{\tau_1} = 4\pi\,\nu_M + \frac{2\pi}{\tau_1} \approx 4\pi\nu_M.$$

The function is thus represented, in the limit, by Eq. (8.60) which takes the form

$$f(t) = \sum_m f_m \frac{\sin\pi\,(2\,\nu_M\,t - m)}{\pi\,(2\,\nu_M\,t - m)}. \tag{8.70}$$

It is easy to prove that the expansion (8.70) takes the values f_m at all our sampling points. For instance, let us consider the point q:

$$t_q = \frac{q}{2\,\nu_M}.$$

The term $m = q$ in the sum (8.70) yields a contribution f_q and all other terms are zero:

$$m \neq q: \qquad \sin \pi(q - m) = 0.$$

The sum (8.70) does not give exactly $f(t) = 0$ for $t < 0$ and $t > \tau$, but it indicates a function dying out very rapidly on both sides, with small oscillations of frequency ν_M. This type of representation is the one used by Shannon.

The *single message* function $f(t)$ defined according to (8.53) has only N degrees of freedom, as shown by the preceding sampling method. When this function is analyzed with the Fourier method it leads to a Fourier integral instead of a Fourier series. The number of terms in the Fourier analysis is infinite, but they contain only the N independent variables f_m. We can check this result readily since our $g(t)$ function is identical with the rounded pulse of Eq. (8.26) and has a spectrum:

$$B(\nu) = \begin{cases} \dfrac{1}{2\,\nu_M} & \text{for} \quad |\nu| < \nu_M \\ 0 & \text{for} \quad |\nu| > \nu_M \end{cases} \tag{8.70 a}$$

hence,

$$g(t) = \frac{1}{2\,\nu_M} \int_{\nu = -\nu_M}^{+\nu_M} \cos 2\pi\,\nu\,t\,d\nu = \frac{1}{2\,\nu_M} \int_{\nu = -\nu_M}^{+\nu_M} e^{i\,2\pi\nu t}\,d\nu, \tag{8.71}$$

and

$$f(t) = \sum_m \frac{f_m}{2\,\nu_M} \int_{-\nu_M}^{+\nu_M} e^{i\,2\pi\,\nu(t - m\theta)}\,d\nu, \quad \text{with} \quad \theta = \frac{1}{2\,\nu_M}. \tag{8.72}$$

The general principle of the problem was discovered independently by a number of scientists. The first idea seems to go back to Whittaker in 1915.[9] Further details and applications will be found in Chapter 17, Sections 6 and 7.

8. Gabor's Information Cells

The two representations just discussed are two special cases of a more general method, discussed by D. Gabor.[10] In the ν, t plane, the region occupied by the function is a rectangle $\nu_m\,\tau$ (see Fig. 8.7). This rectangle can be divided into elementary cells of unit area

$$\Delta\nu \cdot \Delta t = 1, \tag{8.73}$$

---

[9] E. T. Whittaker, *Proc. Roy. Soc. Edinburgh* **35**, 181 (1915).

[10] D. Gabor, Theory of communication, *J. Inst. Elec. Engrs.* **93**, III, 429 (1946); **94**, III, 369 (1947); also *Phil. Mag.* [7] **41**, 1161 (1950); "La Cybernetique," p. 115. Editions Revue d'optique, Paris 1951.

and for each cell the function has two components, a symmetrical one and an antisymmetrical one, namely the two elementary functions using a band width $\Delta\nu$ and a duration Δt. The amplitudes of both functions must be given, and define completely our function $f(t)$. The number of cells is

$$n = \nu_M \tau$$

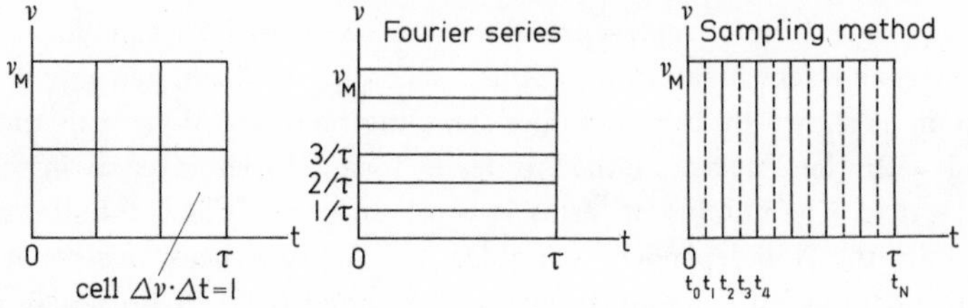

FIG. 8.7. Various ways of selecting cells of unit area in the $\nu - t$ plane.

The number of components is

$$N = 2n = 2\nu_M \tau, \tag{8.74}$$

as in Eq. (8.51). The shape of the cells does not matter, but only their area. The Fourier series [Eq. (8.58)] uses horizontal cells, and the sampling method [Eq. (8.61)] requires vertical cells. Gabor recommends the use of cosine type or sine type functions with Gaussian amplitude as plotted on Fig. 8.8.

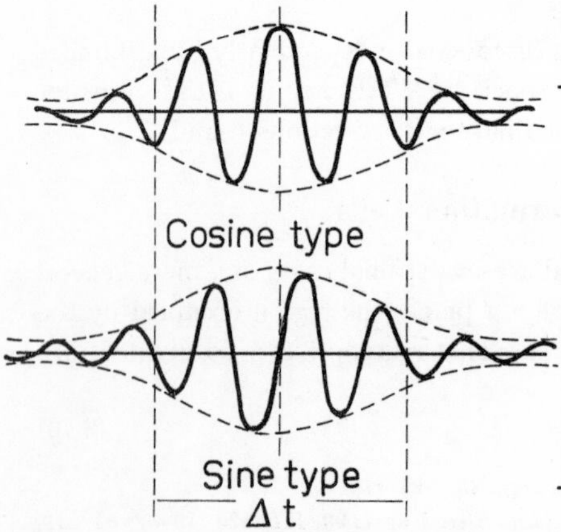

FIG. 8.8. Gabor's sine and cosine message functions.

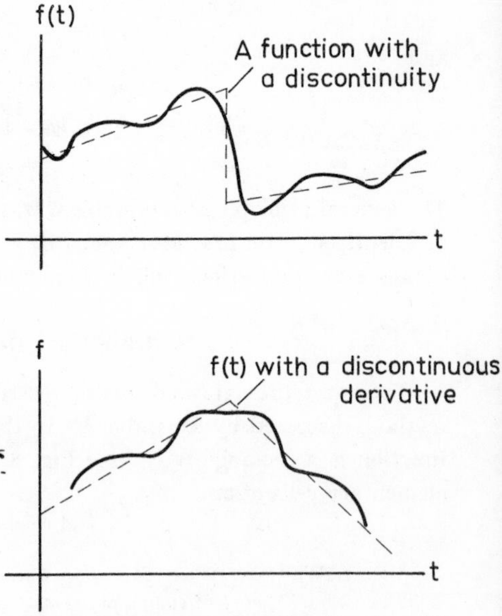

FIG. 8.9. Representation of a function with a finite band width.

The cells (8.73) correspond to the cells in quantum mechanics, where energy E and time t are two conjugate variables, and a cell is defined by

$$\Delta E \cdot \Delta t = h, \qquad \text{with} \qquad E = h\nu \qquad \text{and} \qquad \Delta \nu \cdot \Delta t = 1. \tag{8.75}$$

The functions defined with a finite band width are a very special type of functions. They can have no discontinuity, no sharp angle, but only rounded features as sketched in Fig. 8.9.

9. Autocorrelation and Spectrum; the Wiener-Khintchine Formula

Let us consider again the problem A of Section 6, with a real periodic function $f(t)$ of period τ [Eq. (8.52)], the spectrum of which contains no frequency above ν_M. We expand $f(t)$ in a complex Fourier series (8.1) and (8.58):

$$\begin{aligned} f(t) &= \sum_{-n_M}^{+n_M} C_n e^{in\omega_0 t}, \qquad \omega_0 = \frac{2\pi}{\tau} = 2\pi\nu_0, \\ C_{-n} &= C_n^*, \qquad n_M = \frac{\nu_M}{\nu_0} = \nu_M \tau. \end{aligned} \tag{8.76}$$

We define the autocorrelation function $R(t_0)$ for our function $f(t)$:

$$R(t_0) = \overline{f(t)\, f(t+t_0)} = \frac{1}{\tau}\int_0^\tau f(t)\, f(t+t_0)\, dt. \tag{8.77}$$

Replacing $f(t+t_0)$ by its Fourier expansion (8.76) we obtain

$$R(t_0) = \frac{1}{\tau}\sum_{-n_M}^{n_M} C_n e^{in\omega_0 t_0}\int_0^\tau f(t)\, e^{in\omega_0 t}\, dt = \sum_{-n_M}^{+n_M} C_n C_n^* e^{in\omega_0 t_0}, \tag{8.78}$$

since the integral is just C_n^* according to Eq. (8.2). We thus obtain the Fourier expansion of $R(t_0)$ and we note that it contains only the intensities

$$I_n = C_n C_n^* = |C_n|^2 = |C_{-n}|^2 = I_{-n} \tag{8.79}$$

of the Fourier coefficients of the original function $f(t)$. The phases dropped out in the averaging process (8.77) and (8.78). We can rewrite (8.78) in the following way [using the symmetry (8.79)]

$$R(t_0) = I_0 + 2\sum_{n=1}^{n_M} I_n \cos n\omega_0 t_0 = R(-t_0). \tag{8.80}$$

The autocorrelation function is an even function of the delay time t_0. It is also periodic with the same period τ as the original function, and has the same frequency limitation $|\nu| \leqslant \nu_M$. Equation (8.80) represents a special case of the Wiener-Khintchine formula[11] relating autocorrelation and Fourier spectrum. The original function $f(t)$ had a finite number N of degrees of freedom [Eq. (8.57)]

$$N = 2\,n_M + 1,$$

where we could distinguish

1	amplitude of the constant term,	$C_0 = \gamma_0$,
n_M	amplitudes of the oscillating terms	γ_n,
n_M	phases of the oscillating terms	ϕ_n,

$$C_n = \gamma_n\, e^{i\phi_n}, \qquad C_{-n} = \gamma_n\, e^{-i\phi_n}, \tag{8.81}$$

hence

$$I_n = \gamma_n^2, \qquad n = 0, 1, \ldots, n_M. \tag{8.82}$$

The new expansion (8.80) contains only $n_M + 1$ degrees of freedom, since we have lost the n_M phases.

From the Fourier expansion (8.78) and (8.80) of the autocorrelation function we can pass to a sampling procedure, similar to the one used in Eqs. (8.59) and (8.63). We select N equidistant sampling points along a full period τ extending from $-\tau/2$ to $+\tau/2$:

$$t_{0m} = m\,\theta, \qquad \theta = \frac{\tau}{N}, \qquad N = 2\,n_M + 1, \tag{8.83}$$

$$m = -n_M, -n_M + 1, \ldots, -1, 0, 1, \ldots, n_M - 1, n_M,$$

and we consider the sampled values

$$R_m = R(m\,\theta) = R_{-m}. \tag{8.84}$$

The symmetry condition (8.80) leaves us with $n_M + 1$ independent samples corresponding to

$$m = 0, 1, \ldots, n_M, \tag{8.85}$$

a result which agrees with our earlier discussion proving that the number of degrees of freedom is equal to $n_M + 1$. The function $R(t_0)$ can be rebuilt out of the sampled values, as in Eq. (8.60):

$$R(t_0) = \sum_{m=1}^{n_M} R_m\,[g(t_0 - m\,\theta) + g(t_0 + m\,\theta)] + R_0\, g(t_0) \tag{8.86}$$

with the function g defined in (8.62).

---

[11] N. Wiener, *Acta Math.* **55**, 117 (1930); A. Khintchine, *Math. Ann.* **109**, 604 (1934); Y. W. Lee, T. P. Cheatham, and J. B. Wiesner, M.I.T. Report, No. 141, 1949.

This procedure uses only $n_M + 1$ degrees of freedom of the original function, out of the $2\,n_M + 1$ total number. It applies with great success to all problems where the phases ϕ_n cannot be obtained, either because of their randomness (noise problems) or because the experimental procedure used in the measuring device cannot detect the phase angles (X-ray investigation of crystal structures, for instance). Instead of the complex Fourier series (8.76) of $f(t)$ we may use a real Fourier series (8.54):

$$f(t) = \frac{1}{2} A_0 + \sum_{n=1}^{n_M} A_n \cos (n\,\omega_0\,t + \phi_n),$$
$$A_0 = 2\,\gamma_0, \qquad A_n = 2\,\gamma_n, \qquad I_0 = \frac{A_0{}^2}{4}, \qquad I_n = \frac{A_n{}^2}{4}, \tag{8.87}$$

and, according to (8.80),

$$R(t_0) = \frac{1}{4} A_0{}^2 + \frac{1}{2} \sum_{n=1}^{n_M} A_n{}^2 \cos (n\,\omega_0\,t_0). \tag{8.88}$$

White (thermal) noise, for instance, yields constant $A_n{}^2$ values, independent of n.

10. Linear Transformations and Filters

A very powerful method for the analysis of functions can be based on linear transformations.[12] Let us consider a function and its Fourier integral

$$f(t) = \int c(\nu)\, e^{2\pi i \nu t} d\nu, \tag{8.89}$$

and a transformation function

$$\phi(\theta) = \int \gamma(\nu)\, e^{2\pi i \nu \theta}\, d\nu, \tag{8.90}$$

which vanishes fast enough at infinity. The transformed function is defined as

$$F(t) = \int f(t + \theta)\, \phi(\theta)\, d\theta, \tag{8.91}$$

[12] H. Labrouste and Y. Labrouste *Compt. rend.* **184**, 259 (1927); *Ann. Inst. phys. globe Univ. Paris* **7**, 190 (1929); **9**, 99 (1931); **11**, 93 (1933); *Terrestrial Magnetism and Atm. Elec.* **41**, 15, 105 (1936); H. Devé, "Tables numériques," Evreux, Paris, 1930; M. Levy, *Compt. rend.* **198**, 2222 (1934); **199**, 1031 (1934); **200**, 646 (1935); Ph. D. thesis, Paris, 1951.

H. Labrouste discussed more specifically the case of numerical computation using discrete values of the function. His general transformation is of the type

$$F(t) = \sum_n \varphi_n f(t + n\,\tau), \qquad n \text{ integer.}$$

M. Levy generalized the results for integral transformations of type (8.91).

and can be expanded in a Fourier integral

$$F(t) = \int C(\nu)\, e^{i2\pi\nu t}\, d\nu, \tag{8.92}$$

with

$$C(\nu) = \int F\, e^{-i2\pi\nu t}\, dt = \int f(t')\, e^{-i2\pi\nu t'}\, dt' \int \phi(\theta)\, e^{+i2\pi\nu\theta}\, d\theta,$$

using (8.91) and setting $t' = t + \theta$. The two integrals are $c(\nu)$ and $\gamma^*(\nu)$, hence

$$C(\nu) = c(\nu)\, \gamma^*(\nu). \tag{8.93}$$

The use of the transformation function ϕ is thus equivalent to filtering with a filter having a transfer function $\gamma(\nu)$. Labrouste and Levy discussed a variety of transformation functions enabling one to isolate sine terms in a complicated curve resulting from experimental data. The different pulses of Eqs. (8.25)—(8.28), for instance, yield transfer functions corresponding to their respective spectra, and can be used for transformation. The function (8.91) is simply the cross-correlation between the functions f and ϕ. When ϕ is identical with f, we obtain the autocorrelation for the function f, and Eqs. (8.91) and (8.93) are similar to Eqs. (8.77) and (8.79).

Let us take an example to show the connection between results obtained in different sections of this chapter. Suppose we want to discuss an experimental curve $f(t)$, about which we know that frequencies above a certain ν_M have not been recorded too reliably. We first want to cut off these higher frequencies and we may do it by using a transformation (8.91) with the transformation function (8.26), thus computing

$$F(t) = 2\,\nu_M \int f(t+\theta)\, \frac{\sin(2\pi\,\nu_M\,\theta)}{2\pi\,\nu_M\,\theta}\, d\theta. \tag{8.94}$$

This $\phi(\theta)$ function has a sharp cut off at ν_M, with a spectrum

$$\gamma(\nu) = \begin{cases} 1 & \text{when} \quad |\nu| \leqslant \nu_M \\ 0 & \text{when} \quad |\nu| > \nu_M \end{cases}.$$

The transformation represents an ideal low-pass filter, and suppresses all higher frequencies. It smoothes the experimental curve and eliminates sharp angles and discontinuities that may be spurious, and which we do not believe to be reliable. Our new function $F(t)$ has a well defined cut off at ν_M. If it has been observed over a time interval τ, it contains only

$$N = 2\,\nu_M\,\tau$$

degrees of freedom [Eq. (8.51)]. We consider it as a single message function (Section 6, B) and we decide to use Shannon's sampling method (Section 7), with a sampling interval (8.68)

$$\theta_{\text{lim}} = \frac{1}{2\,\nu_M}.$$

The sampling operation replaces the continuous curve by a system of pulses with the sampled amplitudes $F_M = F(m\,\theta_{\text{lim}})$. This pulse system now has a spectrum extending to infinity, as noted in Section 1, Eqs. (8.9), (8.11), and Fig. 8.1. The spectrum consists of the original spectrum $(|\nu| \leqslant \nu_M)$ repeated periodically along the ν scale, with a period $2\,\nu_M$.

The sampled values can be transmitted on a telecommunication system, with any one of the pulse techniques now in use. These values are rebuilt at the receiving station and the problem is to reconstruct the continuous curve $F(t)$. This can be done electrically by means of a bandpass filter selecting any one of the identical frequency bands of Fig. 8.1. The same operation can be performed numerically, by computing the sum (8.70)

$$F(t) = \sum_m F_m \frac{\sin \pi(2\,\nu_M\,t - m)}{\pi(2\,\nu_M\,t - m)}, \tag{8.94 a}$$

which corresponds again to a mathematical method representing an ideal low-pass filter. In order to compute the function at time t, we need, in principle, all the sampled values before and after t. If we want to rebuild $F(t)$ with an accuracy of 10^{-4} we need at least 10^4 terms before and after the time t, since our terms decrease very slowly, in m^{-1} or $(t' - t)^{-1}$ only. It seems, however, that the computation of the above sum will be the best way to reconstruct the curve when great accuracy is required.

11. Fourier Analysis and the Sampling Method in Three Dimensions

The methods discussed in the preceding sections can be extended from one dimension to two or three dimensions. We intend to investigate briefly these problems and to show the connection with the analysis of crystal structures by X-rays or neutron diffraction.

Periodicity in space is exhibited by crystal lattices, and can be characterized by three translations $\boldsymbol{d}_1, \boldsymbol{d}_2, \boldsymbol{d}_3$. A function $F(\boldsymbol{r})$, where $\boldsymbol{r}$ is the vector (x, y, z), exhibits these three periods if it has the following property:

$$F(\boldsymbol{r} + \rho_1 \boldsymbol{d}_1 + \rho_2 \boldsymbol{d}_2 + \rho_3 \boldsymbol{d}_3) = F(\boldsymbol{r}), \tag{8.95}$$

ρ_1, ρ_2, ρ_3 positive or negative integers.

The general case, with oblique vectors $\boldsymbol{d}_1, \boldsymbol{d}_2, \boldsymbol{d}_3$ introduces some complications which disappear for the case of *orthogonal vectors*. We shall limit our present discussion to this simpler problem, and take rectangular coordinates x_1, x_2, x_3, in the directions of $\boldsymbol{d}_1, \boldsymbol{d}_2$, and $\boldsymbol{d}_3$. The vectors have the following components (Fig. 8.10)

$$\begin{aligned} \boldsymbol{r}&: \quad (x_1\ x_2\ x_3), \\ \boldsymbol{d}_1&: \quad (d_1\ 0\ 0), \\ \boldsymbol{d}_2&: \quad (0\ d_2\ 0), \\ \boldsymbol{d}_3&: \quad (0\ 0\ d_3), \end{aligned} \tag{8.96}$$

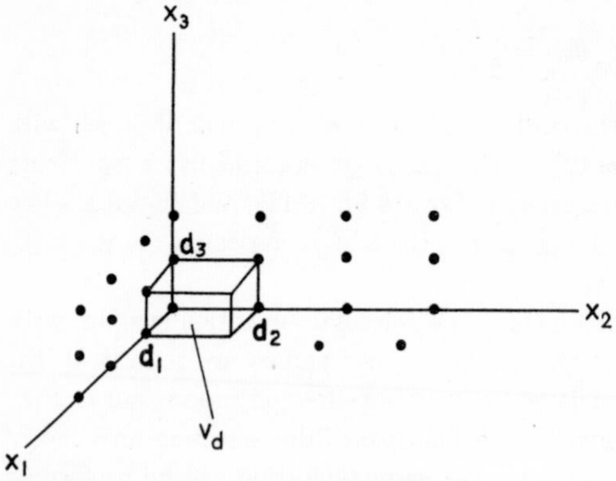

FIG. 8.10. A rectangular lattice defined by the orthogonal vectors $\boldsymbol{d}_1, \boldsymbol{d}_2, \boldsymbol{d}_3$.

and the periodicity (8.95) is

$$F(x_1 + \rho_1 d_1,\ x_2 + \rho_2 d_2,\ x_3 + \rho_3 d_3) = F(x_1, x_2, x_3). \tag{8.96 a}$$

The three vectors $\boldsymbol{d}_1, \boldsymbol{d}_2, \boldsymbol{d}_3$, define the fundamental cell of the lattice, with a volume

$$V_d = d_1\, d_2\, d_3.$$

The periodic function F can be expanded in triple Fourier series

$$F = \sum_{h_1 h_2 h_3} C_{h_1 h_2' h_3}\ e^{2\pi i (h_1 b_1 x_1 + h_2 b_2 x_2 + h_3 b_3 x_3)}, \tag{8.97}$$

$$b_1 = \frac{1}{d_1}, \qquad b_2 = \frac{1}{d_2}, \qquad b_3 = \frac{1}{d_3}, \qquad h_1\, h_2\, h_3 \text{ integers.}$$

The three reciprocal vectors $\boldsymbol{b}_1, \boldsymbol{b}_2, \boldsymbol{b}_3$ are again orthogonal and define the cell of the reciprocal lattice (Fig. 8.11):

$$V_b = b_1\, b_2\, b_3 = \frac{1}{V_d}.$$

A reciprocal lattice can be defined for oblique structures and its consideration leads to formulas very similar to the preceding ones. The Fourier coefficients $C_{h_1 h_2 h_3}$ are obtained by the following integrals

$$C_{h_1 h_2 h_3} = \frac{1}{V_d} \int_0^{d_1}\!\!\int_0^{d_2}\!\!\int_0^{d_3} F(x_1, x_2, x_3)\, e^{-2\pi i (h_1 b_1 x_1 + h_2 b_2 x_2 + h_3 b_3 x_3)}\, dx_1 dx_2 dx_3. \tag{8.98}$$

When the function F is real, one has

$$C_{-h_1,-h_2,-h_3} = C^*_{h_1,h_2,h_3}.$$

These formulas are the direct generalization of Eqs. (8.1), (8.2), and (8.3). The correspondence of notations is as follows

period τ:	d_1, d_2, d_3,
fundamental frequency ν_0:	b_1, b_2, b_3,
harmonic number n:	h_1, h_2, h_3.

We may have different sorts of frequency limitations in the three-dimensional spectrum:

A. Three Separate Limits in the Three Directions:

$$|h_1 b_1| \leqslant \rho_1, \qquad |h_2 b_2| \leqslant \rho_2, \qquad |h_3 b_3| \leqslant \rho_3; \tag{8.99}$$

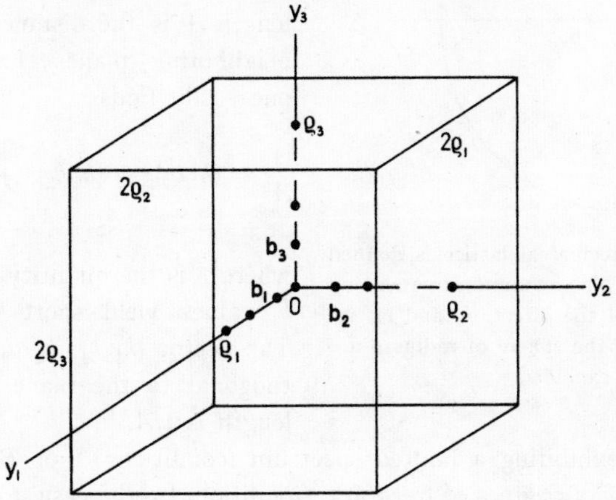

FIG. 8.11. The reciprocal lattice is defined by $\boldsymbol{b}_1, \boldsymbol{b}_2$, and $\boldsymbol{b}_3$. The lattice points are restricted to the parallelopiped shown if ρ_1, ρ_2, and ρ_3 are the maximum frequencies used in the three directions.

hence (Fig. 8.11):

$$|h_1| \leqslant \frac{\rho_1}{b_1} = \rho_1 d_1, \qquad |h_2| \leqslant \rho_2 d_2, \qquad |h_3| \leqslant \rho_3 d_3.$$

The three quantities $\rho_1 \rho_2 \rho_3$ represent the maximum frequencies in the 1, 2, 3 directions. This problem represents simply a superposition of three separate 1-dimensional problems, of the type A discussed in Section 6 of this chapter. In this example the correspondance of notation is:

$$\text{max frequency } \nu_M \ldots \rho_1 \rho_2 \rho_3.$$

B. We may have to consider a *single frequency limit* ρ, with a condition (Fig. 8.12)

$$h_1^2 b_1^2 + h_2^2 b_2^2 + h_3^2 b_3^2 \leqslant \rho^2. \tag{8.100}$$

This condition corresponds to a shortest wavelength $1/\rho$. Let us discuss its physical meaning more precisely: Each component $h_1\, h_2\, h_3$ in the expansion (8.97) represents a sinusoidal distribution in space. All points lying on the plane

$$h_1 b_1 x_1 + h_2 b_2 x_2 + h_3 b_3 x_3 = 0$$

have the same phase as the origin. Other parallel planes with the same phase are found at

$$h_1 b_1 x_1 + h_2 b_2 x_2 + h_3 b_3 x_3 = m,$$

where m is any integer. The wavelength Λ is the distance between two neighboring planes $\Delta m = \pm 1$, and one easily finds

$$\frac{1}{\Lambda^2} = (h_1 b_1)^2 + (h_2 b_2)^2 + (h_3 b_3)^2 \leqslant \rho^2, \tag{8.100 a}$$

where ρ is the quantity (8.100). Large h values yield short wave lengths. The vector $(h_1\, b_1,\, h_2\, b_2,\, h_3\, b_3)$ is orthogonal to the plane waves and its length is $1/\Lambda$.

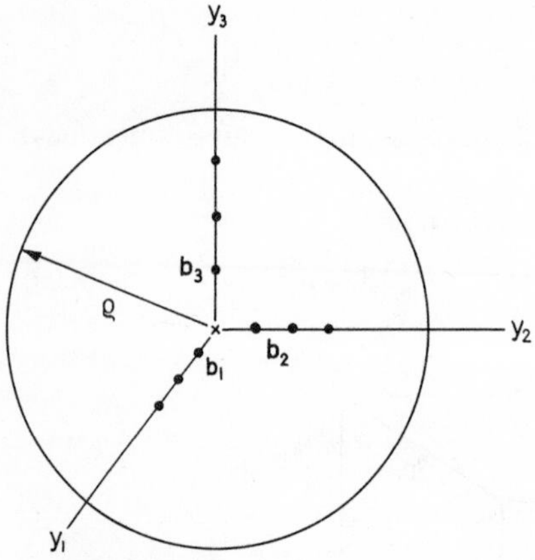

FIG. 8.12. The reciprocal lattice is defined by $\boldsymbol{b}_1, \boldsymbol{b}_2$, and $\boldsymbol{b}_3$. The maximum frequency ρ is independent of the direction, and lattice points outside of the sphere of radius ρ are excluded.

Functions exhibiting a limited spectrum (conditions *A* or *B*) possess only a finite number of degrees of freedom. Condition *A* is the easiest one to discuss, since it generalizes directly from problem *A* of Section 6. The analogue of Eq. (8.57) is

$$\begin{aligned} N_1 &= 2\rho_1 d_1 + 1, && \text{degrees of freedom along } x_1, \\ N_2 &= 2\rho_2 d_2 + 1, && \text{degrees of freedom along } x_2, \\ N_3 &= 2\rho_3 d_3 + 1, && \text{degrees of freedom along } x_3; \end{aligned} \tag{8.101}$$

hence a total number of degrees of freedom

$$N = N_1 N_2 N_3 \approx 8\, V_d\, \rho_1 \rho_2 \rho_3. \tag{8.102}$$

The last approximation is obtained when the limits $\rho_1\, \rho_2\, \rho_3$ are much larger than $b_1\, b_2\, b_3$:

$$\frac{\rho_1}{b_1} = \rho_1 d_1 \gg 1, \qquad \rho_2 d_2 \gg 1, \qquad \rho_3 d_3 \gg 1.$$

The sampling procedure developed in Section 6 [Eqs. (8.59) — (8.64)] is directly applicable, with a rectangular lattice of N sampling points within the periodicity cell $d_1 d_2 d_3$:

$$x_{1s} = m_1 \xi_1,$$
$$x_{2s} = m_2 \xi_2, \qquad \xi_i = \frac{d_i}{N_i} = \frac{1}{2\rho_i + b_i} \approx \frac{1}{2\rho_i}, \tag{8.103}$$
$$x_{3s} = m_3 \xi_3, \qquad 0 \leqslant m_i < N_i, \qquad i = 1, 2, 3.$$

The correspondance is here:

Sampling interval $\theta, \ldots, \xi_1, \xi_2, \xi_3$.

The original function can easily be rebuilt out of the sampled values, using a triple sum

$$F = \sum_{m_1 m_2 m_3} F_{m_1 m_2 m_3} g_1(x_1 - m_1 \xi_1)\, g_2(x_2 - m_2 \xi_2)\, g_3(x_3 - m_3 \xi_3), \tag{8.104}$$

with

$$F_{m_1 m_2 m_3} = F(m_1 \xi_1, m_2 \xi_2, m_3 \xi_3).$$

The g function was defined in Eq. (8.62):

$$g_i(x_i) = \frac{\sin(N_i \pi b_i x_i)}{N_i \operatorname{Sin}(\pi b_i x_i)}, \qquad i = 1, 2, 3, \tag{8.105}$$

if we take into account the correspondence of notations. This problem is thus completely solved, and the sampling method applies without any difficulty.

The second problem, B, with the single limit ρ, Eq. (8.100), is more complicated. We shall easily prove the finite number of degrees of freedom of the function, but the sampling method can only be sketched, and remains open for discussion.

The Fourier components $h_1 h_2 h_3$ in the expansion (8.97) can be visualized as corresponding to the points of a rectangular lattice

$$y_1 = h_1 b_1, \qquad y_2 = h_2 b_2, \qquad y_3 = h_3 b_3, \tag{8.106}$$

$h_1 h_2 h_3$ positive or negative integers. This lattice is known as the "reciprocal lattice." Each point $(h_1 h_2 h_3)$ of this reciprocal lattice corresponds to one Fourier component. The fundamental cell V_b of this lattice has a volume

$$V_b = b_1 b_2 b_3;$$

hence we obtain

$$\frac{1}{V_b} = V_d \tag{8.107}$$

points of the reciprocal lattice per unit volume. The limit (8.100) corresponds to a spherical boundary in the reciprocal lattice. It has a volume $(4/3)\,\pi\,\rho^3$ and contains a number of points

$$N \approx V_d \frac{4}{3} \pi \rho^3 \tag{8.108}$$

according to (8.107). This expression gives the number of Fourier components, hence the number of independent degrees of freedom of our function. The similarity between Eqs. (8.102) and (8.108) is obvious. The first one, (8.102), corresponds to a rectangular boundary in the reciprocal lattice, and the second one to a spherical boundary.

We should be able to develop a sampling procedure, using N sampling points in the elementary cell $d_1\, d_2\, d_3$ of the direct lattice, but this problem has, so far, not been properly discussed. A rectangular (or cubic) lattice of sampling points would not do since it does not exhibit the required spherical symmetry, and corresponds to a different problem [Eq. (8.99)]. One might think of a set of lattice points distributed as the centers of close packed spheres. This leads to a face-centered cubic lattice structure, since the other hexagonal type exhibits smaller symmetry.[13] Let us then consider a set of sampling points arranged in a face-centered cubic lattice (edge δ). The cube δ^3 contains four sampling points,[14] and hence a volume u per sampling point of

$$u = \tfrac{1}{4}\,\delta^3. \tag{8.109}$$

In the elementary cell V_d of the crystal lattice we obtain

$$N' = \frac{V_d}{u} = \frac{4\, V_d}{\delta^3} \tag{8.110}$$

sampling points. This number of sampling points should be equal to the number N of degrees of freedom [Eq. (8.108)], hence a relation

$$N' = N, \qquad \frac{4}{3} \pi \rho^3 = \frac{4}{\delta^3}, \qquad \rho\,\delta = \left(\frac{3}{\pi}\right)^{1/3}. \tag{8.111}$$

The distance between planes of sampling points parallel to the x_1, x_2, or x_3 axis is $\delta_1 = \delta/2$; the distance between planes perpendicular to the main diagonals is $\delta_2 = \delta/\sqrt{3}$. We have to compare these distances with the shortest wavelengths $\lambda = \rho^{-1}$. This gives

$$2\,\rho\,\delta_1' = \left(\frac{3}{\pi}\right)^{1/3} \approx 0.986, \qquad 2\,\rho\,\delta_2 = \left(\frac{3}{\pi}\right)^{1/3} \frac{2}{\sqrt{3}} \approx 1.14, \tag{8.112}$$

---

[13] L. Brillouin, p. 149 in ref. 2.

[14] See footnote 8, p. 135, in Brillouin, ref. 2.

instead of the condition

$$2\rho\xi = 1$$

in the 3 dimensional problem [Eq. (8.103)].

In order to carry out consistently the sampling method one should discuss the pulse function $g(r)$ corresponding to this problem. The pulse functions should contain only wavelengths larger than $1/\delta$. It remains to be seen whether, in three dimensions (or in two dimensions) such a condition would be consistent with the other assumption made about Eq. (8.60): that the pulse function $g(r)$ should be unity at $r = 0$ and zero at all other sampling points. If this second condition could not be maintained, it would complicate seriously the use of sampling values. The only practical solution, for the moment, would be to use a procedure similar to the one discussed at the end of Section 10, namely to introduce arbitrarily a cut off of type A [Eq. (8.99)] by a triple integration similar to (8.94) and then use the rectangular lattice of sampling points (8.103) and (8.104). This at least represents a consistent and practical method.

12. Crystal Analysis by X-Rays

The questions discussed in the preceding sections are closely related with the problem of the analysis of crystals by X-rays. A crystal is a three-dimensional periodic structure with a fundamental cell $\boldsymbol{d}_1, \boldsymbol{d}_2, \boldsymbol{d}_3$, and the periodic function $F(\boldsymbol{r})$ in this lattice is the electron density. The intensity of X-rays reflected in different directions measures the intensities $|C_{h_1 h_2 h_3}|^2$ of the Fourier coefficients in the triple expansion (8.97) but the corresponding phases cannot be obtained from experimental data.[15] Furthermore, there is a limit to the number of coefficients that can be obtained from experiments performed with X-rays of a given wavelength λ. A sinusoidal distribution of electron densities, with a wavelength Λ, reflects X-rays, incident at an angle ϕ, when Bragg's condition is satisfied:

$$\lambda = 2\Lambda\cos\phi. \tag{8.113}$$

When a crystal is examined under X-rays and rotated in the beam in all directions, it is possible to detect all Λ values larger than $\frac{1}{2}\lambda$

$$\Lambda \geqslant \frac{1}{2}\lambda = \frac{1}{\rho}. \tag{8.114}$$

The Debye-Scherrer method results in a similar limitation. We are thus led to the problem B of Section 11. The function F has, under such conditions, no more

---

[15] See for instance L. Brillouin, Chapters 6 and 7 in ref. 2; R. W. James, "The Optical Principles of the Diffraction of X-Rays," Chapter 7, G. Bell, London, 1950.

than N degrees of freedom [Eq. (8.108)] and we obtain only $N/2$ data from the experimental results on X-ray diffraction. A. L. Patterson[16] proposed consideration of the function

$$P(u_1, u_2, u_3) = \frac{1}{V_d} \int_0^{d_1}\int_0^{d_2}\int_0^{d_3} F(x_1 + u_1, x_2 + u_2, x_3 + u_3) F(x_1 x_2 x_3)\, dx_1\, dx_2 dx_3. \quad (8.115)$$

This is simply the autocorrelation function (8.77) in three dimensions. Replacing $F(x_1 + u_1 \ldots)$ in Eq. (8.115) by its Fourier expansion (8.97) one obtains

$$P(u_1, u_2, u_3) = \sum_{h_1 h_2 h_3} C_{h_1 h_2 h_3}\, e^{2\pi i \Sigma h_i b_i u_i} \frac{1}{V_d} \int_0^{d_1}\int_0^{d_2}\int_0^{d_3} F(x_1 x_2 x_3)\, e^{2\pi i \Sigma h_i b_i x_i} \cdot dx_1\, dx_2\, dx_3 \quad (8,116)$$

$$= \sum_{h_1 h_2 h_3} C_{h_1 h_2 h_3}\, C^*_{h_1 h_2 h_3}\, e^{2\pi i (h_1 b_1 u_1 + h_2 b_2 u_2 + h_3 b_3 u_3)},$$

a formula which is the direct generalization of Eq. (8.78) and contains only the intensities CC^* but no phases. The Patterson method, which was discovered independently, is thus the direct extension of Wiener's autocorrelation function. The symmetry relations, discussed in Section 9, apply directly here again, and the Patterson function contains only $\frac{1}{2} N$ independent parameters. If one chooses to use sampled values for the representation of the Patterson function, the symmetry makes it necessary to give only $\frac{1}{2} N$ sampled values over one half of the elementary crystal cell.

Another powerful method of discussion has been initiated by R. Pepinsky[17] under the name of "convolution." It corresponds practically to the transformations discussed in Section 10, generalized for three dimensions. The method has been found extremely useful in the discussion of complicated structures. We recommended, at the end of Section 10, the use of the pulses (8.25)—(8.28) as kernels for linear transformations. Pepinsky calls the function (8.26) "Dirichlet's kernel," and the inverse of function (8.27) "Fejer's kernel," with $C(t)$ for the function and $f(\nu)$ for the spectrum (f and C interchanged). Other types of kernels have been proposed by Pepinsky, and many important applications are discussed.

There, again, X-ray analysis of crystals appears as a three-dimensional problem, similar to signal analysis in one dimension.

---

[16] A. L. Patterson, *Phys. Rev.* **46**, 372 (1934); *Z. Krist.* **90**, 517 (1935); D. Harker, *J. Chem. Phys.* **4**, 381 (1936); R. W. James, ref. 15.

[17] R. Pepinsky, Report to the Office of Naval Research, Feb. 1, 1952.

Appendix

Schwarz's Inequality.

We want to prove the inequality (8.49) and we consider the integral

$$I = \int |F + cG|^2 \, dt = \int (F^* + cG^*)(F + cG)\, dt > 0, \qquad (8\,\text{A.1})$$

where c is a real constant. Expanding, we obtain

$$I = c^2 \int G^* G \, dt + c \int (F^* G + F G^*)\, dt + \int F^* F \, dt.$$

This is a relation in c

$$A c^2 + B c + C > 0, \qquad (8\,\text{A.2})$$

and there must be no real root c, hence

$$B^2 - 4AC \leqslant 0,$$

or

$$4AC \geqslant B^2, \qquad (8\,\text{A.3})$$

which is Schwarz's inequality.

CHAPTER 9

SUMMARY OF THERMODYNAMICS

1. Introduction

We have discussed in the preceding chapters how to obtain a mathematical definition of information, and to measure this quantity numerically. The limitations of such a definition were emphasized in the first chapter, while the following chapters were devoted to the development and applications of these general definitions.

A close connection has been discovered between information theory and thermodynamics; information appears to be related to entropy. In order to discuss this new aspect of the theory, we start with a short summary of thermodynamics and its principles.[1]

2. The Two Principles of Thermodynamics; Entropy and Negentropy

A. Conservation of energy.

B. Carnot's principle. According to Kelvin, this principle means "degradation of energy."

High grade energy is mechanical or electric energy.

Medium grade energy is chemical energy.

Low grade energy is heat.

The total quantity of energy remains constant, in a closed isolated system. Transformations or chemical reactions within the system will maintain the quality or grade constant for reversible transformations. Irreversible transformations result in a loss of grade.

Grade of energy can be exactly defined as corresponding to negative entropy ($-S$). The second principle states that entropy S must always increase or at least remain constant, hence the negative entropy always decreases.

---

[1] M. W. Zemansky, "Heat and Thermodynamics," 3rd ed. McGraw-Hill, New York, 1951; K. K. Darrow, The concept of entropy, *Am. J. Phys.* **12**, 183 (1944); Entropy and statistics, *Bell System Tech. J.* **21**, 51 (1942); **22**, 108, 362 (1943); L. Brillouin, "Quantenstatistik." Springer, Berlin, 1931; J. E. Mayer and M. G. Mayer, "Statistical Mechanics." Wiley, New York, 1940; R. C. Tolman and P. C. Fine, *Revs. Modern Phys.* **20**, 51 (1948).

Definition of Entropy

If a system receives a quantity of heat Δq, there corresponds an increase

$$\Delta S = \Delta q / T, \quad \Delta q = T \Delta S \tag{9.1}$$

of the entropy of the system; T is the absolute (Kelvin) temperature. In centigrade degrees:

$$T^0 \mathrm{K} = t^0 \mathrm{C} + 273.15.$$

A few typical cases will serve as examples. Let us consider two systems A and B in contact, and assume that they can exchange work and heat. We also assume that the system AB is isolated from its surroundings. A certain transformation results in the following conditions:

System	Temperature	Work *output*	Heat *input*	Entropy *input*
A	T_A	W_A	q_A	$\Delta S_A = q_A / T_A$
B	T_B	W_B	q_B	$\Delta S_B = q_B / T_B$

$$\left.\begin{aligned} &\text{First principle:} \quad W_A - q_A + W_B - q_B = 0. \\ &\text{Second principle:} \quad \Delta S_A + \Delta S_B \geqslant 0. \end{aligned}\right\} \tag{9.2}$$

There is no change in the total energy of the system AB.

Examples of Irreversible Transformation:

Heat flow from a hot to a cold body: $T_A > T_B$;
No work done: $W_A = 0, \quad W_B = 0$;
Heat transferred: $q_A = -q_B, \quad q_B > 0$,

$$\Delta S_A + \Delta S_B = q_B \left(\frac{1}{T_B} - \frac{1}{T_A} \right) > 0. \tag{9.3}$$

The total entropy is increased.

Friction, viscous damping: $T_A = T_B = T$ uniform temperature. There is work done by A and heat produced in B:

$$W_A > 0, \quad q_A = 0, \quad W_B = 0, \quad q_B > 0,$$
$$W_A - q_B = 0,$$

$$\Delta S_A + \Delta S_B = \frac{q_B}{T} = \frac{W_A}{T} > 0. \tag{9.4}$$

The total entropy is increased.

The *total energy content* of a system can be defined if we know how to build the system out of components (the energy of which is supposed to be known), and if we take into account the work output and heat input involved in building up the system. This total energy U is a function of all the physical and chemical parameters defining the system.

If the system can be built up by a succession of *reversible transformations*, the *total entropy* S of the system can be defined as,

$$S = S_1 + S_2 + \ldots S_n, \tag{9.5}$$

the sum of the entropies involved at each reversible step.

Negentropy ($N = -S$) represents the quality or grade of energy, and must always decrease. This is the meaning of Kelvin's principle of "degradation of energy," and it is no wonder that the importance of negentropy was recognized by a close friend of Kelvin, who wrote:[2]

"It is very desirable to have a word to express the *Availability* for work of the heat in a given magazine; a term for that possession, the waste of which is called *Dissipation*. Unfortunately the excellent word *Entropy*, which Clausius has introduced in this connection, is applied by him to the *negative* of the idea we most naturally wish to express. It would only confuse the student if we were to endeavour to invent another term for our purpose. But the necessity for some such term will be obvious from the beautiful examples which follow".

An isolated system contains *negentropy* if it reveals a possibility for doing mechanical or electrical work: If the system is not at a uniform temperature T, but consists of different parts at different temperatures, it contains a certain amount of negentropy. This negentropy can be used to obtain some mechanical work done by the system, or it can be simply dissipated and lost by thermal conduction. A difference in pressure between different parts of the system is another case of negentropy. A difference of electrical potential represents another example. A tank of compressed gas in a room at atmospheric pressure, a vacuum tank in a similar room, a charged battery, any device that can produce high grade energy (mechanical work) or be degraded by some irreversible process (thermal conduction, electrical resistivity, friction, viscosity) is a source of negentropy.

The importance of considering negative entropy was emphasized by E. Schrödinger in his most interesting book *What is Life?*[3] If a living organism needs food, it is only for the negentropy it can get from it, and which is needed

[2] P. G. Tait, "Sketch of Thermodynamics," p. 100. Edmonston & Douglas, Edinburgh, 1868.

[3] E. Schrödinger, "What is Life?" Cambridge U. P., N. Y. 1945.

to make up for the losses due to mechanical work done, or simple degradation processes in the living system. Energy contained in food does not really matter, since energy is conserved and never gets lost, but negentropy is the important factor.

3. Impossibility of Perpetual Motion; Thermal Engines

An engine using just *one* heat reservoir at one given temperature T cannot change heat into work, since this would be the reverse of our example of Eq. (9.4) and would yield a decrease of entropy.

An engine can do work if it uses two heat reservoirs A, B at two different temperatures

$$T_A > T_B.$$

The operation will consist of successive cycles involving

A. A quantity of heat q_A transferred from the heat reservoir A to the engine (heat input).

B. Work done by the engine W (work output).

C. A quantity of heat transferred from the engine to the heat reservoir at low temperature B. Since we count "heat input" as positive, we have here a negative heat input $q_B < 0$.

After completion of a full cycle of operation, the engine is back to its initial conditions. This means that its total energy has come back to the initial value

$$W - q_A - q_B = 0. \tag{9.6}$$

If the operation is reversible, there must be no final change either in the total entropy of the engine

$$\Delta S_A + \Delta S_B = 0, \tag{9.7}$$

hence

$$\frac{q_A}{T_A} + \frac{q_B}{T_B} = 0,$$

or

$$q_B = -\frac{T_B}{T_A} q_A; \tag{9.8}$$

q_B is a negative quantity, as explained before.

In other words, a certain quantity of entropy

$$\Delta S = +\Delta S_A = -\Delta S_B \tag{9.9}$$

has been falling from a high temperature T_A to a low temperature T_B. The heat inputs at the two temperatures were, correspondingly

$$q_A = + T_A \Delta S, \qquad q_B = - T_B \Delta S. \tag{9.10}$$

The total $q_A + q_B = (T_A - T_B) \Delta S > 0$ is positive. The engine received more heat from the high temperature source than it gave back at low temperature. The balance of energy appears as work done by the engine [Eq. (9.6)]. The *thermal efficiency* is defined by the ratio of work done to heat input q.

$$\frac{W}{q_A} = \frac{T_A - T_B}{T_A} < 1. \tag{9.11}$$

Examples:

Heat engine: heat flowing from a high temperature to a low temperature, work output.

The refrigerator is the inverse type of engine with a *work input* resulting in heat flowing from a low temperature to a high temperature.

The different grades of energy can easily be recognized in these examples. Work can always be entirely changed into heat [Eq. (9.4)]. Heat can only be partly changed back into work [Eq. (9.11)].

If we measure heat in energy units, q is given in ergs ($c\,g\,s$ system), not in calories. Taking the temperature in centigrade-Kelvin degrees, we obtain the entropy S in ergs per centigrade degree. The entropy S can be made a pure dimensionless number if the temperature T is considered as having the dimensions of energy (Chapter 1, Section 1). In such a case, the coefficient of transformation is

$$k = 1.38 \times 10^{-16}.$$

The quantity kT has the dimensions of energy, and k should be considered as a pure number.

Thermodynamics yields very important information on all problems involving heat and temperature. If reversible transformations only are considered, it is possible to define the total energy U of a certain physical system and its total entropy S. Both U and S are functions of the physical variables defining the state of the system.

As an example of the use of thermodynamical methods let us consider the case of a dielectric with a dielectric power $\varepsilon(T)$ depending upon temperature. For instance,

$$D = \varepsilon E, \qquad \varepsilon(T) = \varepsilon_0 + \frac{C}{T - \theta}, \tag{9.12}$$

D = electric displacement, E = electric field
C = Curie constant, θ = Curie temperature

Theoretical considerations reveal that the specific heat of a substance depends upon its polarization, hence upon the displacement D. A detailed discussion yields the relations between these different properties: The total energy U and the entropy S of the substance are given by

$$U(T, D) = U_0(T) + \frac{1}{2} D^2 \left(\frac{1}{\varepsilon} - T \frac{\partial}{\partial T} \left(\frac{1}{\varepsilon} \right) \right), \tag{9.13}$$

$$S(T, D) = S_0(T) - \frac{1}{2} D^2 \frac{\partial}{\partial T} \left(\frac{1}{\varepsilon} \right), \tag{9.14}$$

where U_0 and S_0 correspond to the unpolarized material ($D = 0$). The material is supposed to be an incompressible solid, and electrostriction is ignored. Similar formulas apply to the magnetic problem,[4] and these results have many important applications. They are the basis for the famous Debye-Giauque cooling method by demagnetization, which enables one to reach temperatures down to a fraction of an absolute degree.

4. Statistical Interpretation of Entropy

The quantity called "entropy" is formally defined by Eq. (9.1) and we have given a few examples to show how it corresponds to the reverse of "energy grade." The second principle states that entropy must always increase (in a closed system) while the energy always loses its quality or grade (Kelvin's degradation of energy).

A clear interpretation of these general features was given by J. W. Gibbs, J. C. Maxwell, L. Boltzmann, and completed by M. Planck. The basis for this explanation is found in the atomic structure of matter and in the quantum laws that provide for the stability of atoms, molecules, and crystals. Atoms are so small that there is a stupendous number of them in any piece of matter with which we experiment. A gram-atom of matter contains about 6×10^{23} actual atoms. Accordingly, we are completely unable to follow the motion of the individual atoms. The only properties that we can observe, in practice, are average values, obtained from statistical considerations. The statistical theory of thermodynamics is based on these general remarks and represents one of the most advanced chapters of physics. Entropy is shown to be related to probability. A closed isolated system may have been created artificially with a very improbable structure. When left to itself, it will progressively follow a normal evolution

---

[4] See, for instance, L. Brillouin and H. P. Iskenderian, *Elec. Commun.* **25**, 300 (1948).

toward a more probable structure. The probability has a natural tendency to increase, and so does the entropy. The exact relation is given by the famous Boltzmann-Planck formula:

$$S = k \ln P, \tag{9.15}$$

where $k = 1.38 \times 10^{-16}$ in ergs per centigrade degree (Boltzmann's constant), S is the entropy of the system under discussion, and P is the number of "elementary complexions." Let us first discuss the exact meaning of this number P in order to explain the connection with probability theory.

Quantum theory tells us that atoms or molecules can exist only with a finite number of distinct structures. There is no continuity at the atomic level but only discrete stable (or metastable) structures, and the atomic system suddenly jumps from one structure to another one, while absorbing or emitting energy. Each of these discrete configurations of the quantized physical system was called a "complexion" by Planck, and the word has remained in the scientific literature with this well-defined meaning.

Let us now consider a physical system: a piece of crystal, or a gas in a container, under specified conditions of volume, pressure, total energy, temperature, chemical constitution. *Macroscopic variables* are those quantities that we are able to measure in the laboratory. These do not suffice to define completely the state of the system. There is an enormous number of "microscopic variables" which we are completely unable to measure in detail: positions and velocities of all the individual atoms, quantum states of these atoms or of the molecular structures, etc. All these unknown quantities make it possible for the system to take a large variety of quantized structures, the so-called Planck's complexions. It is the total number P of these microscopic complexions that we use in Eq. (9.15) and connect with the entropy of the system. This number is extremely large but finite and Eq. (9.15) has a specific meaning.

Another important relation will be needed in our discussions; it is the famous relation between energy and frequency

$$E_1 - E_2 = h\nu; \tag{9.16}$$

where E_1 = initial energy and E_2 = final energy of a system emitting a vibration of frequency ν, and $h = 6.6 \cdot 10^{-27}$ c g s (Planck's constant). Radiation is emitted when a physical system loses energy, and absorbed when the system gains energy. Since energy levels are discrete, frequencies of emission (or absorption) build a discontinuous spectrum, typical of the atomic or molecular system under consideration.

5. Examples of Statistical Discussions

Some examples will show how our statistical definitions do correspond with experimental facts. Let us consider two bodies, A_1 and A_2, in contact so that they can exchange only heat. The $A_1 A_2$ system is contained in an insulating container V, as shown in Fig. 9.1. Under such conditions the total energy

$$E_1 + E_2 = E \qquad (9.17)$$

of the whole system remains constant, but we have to consider the possibility of a transfer of q calories from A_1 to A_2:

$$\Delta E_1 = -q, \qquad \Delta E_2 = +q. \qquad (9.18)$$

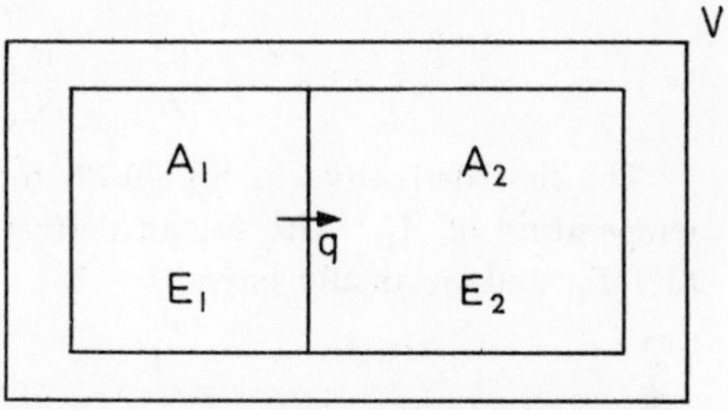

FIG. 9.1. Two bodies A_1 and A_2, containing energies E_1 and E_2, respectively, are in contact. They can exchange only heat. The $A_1 A_2$ system is contained in an insulating container V.

We want to find the most probable distribution of energy between A_1 and A_2. The number of complexions P_1 for A_1 is a function of E_1, and the number of complexions P_2 for A_2 is a function of E_2. The total number of complexions for the composite system is

$$P = P_1(E_1) \cdot P_2(E_2), \qquad (9.19)$$

since each complexion of A_1 can be associated with any one of the $P_2(E_2)$ complexions of A_2. The most probable energy distribution is the one for which P is a maximum. If P is a maximum, it will not change when a small quantity of heat q is transferred from A_1 to A_2 [Eq. (9.18)]. We assume that P_1 and P_2 can be considered as continuous functions of E_1 and E_2 respectively, and that they are differentiable. Then

$$\Delta P = \frac{dP}{dq} q = \left(-\frac{dP_1}{dE_1} P_2 + P_1 \frac{dP_2}{dE_2} \right) q = 0, \qquad (9.20)$$

when we take into account the signs in Eq. (9.18).

The preceding condition results in

$$\frac{1}{P_1} \frac{dP_1}{dE_1} = \frac{1}{P_2} \frac{dP_2}{dE_2}, \qquad (9.21)$$

or

$$\frac{d \ln P_1}{dE_1} = \frac{d \ln P_2}{dE_2}. \qquad (9.22)$$

We now use the Boltzmann-Planck Eq. (9.15) for the definition of the entropies $S_1\, S_2$ of the bodies $A_1\, A_2$ and obtain

$$\frac{1}{k}\frac{dS_1}{dE_1} = \frac{1}{k}\frac{dS_2}{dE_2}. \tag{9.23}$$

In our example, the only type of energy exchanged between A_1 and A_2 was heat, hence according to Eq. (9.1):

$$\frac{dS_1}{dE_1} = \frac{dS_1}{dQ_1} = \frac{1}{T_1}. \tag{9.24}$$

The first derivative in Eq. (9.23) represents the reciprocal of the absolute temperature of A_1. The second derivative in the same equation corresponds to $1/T_2$, and we finally have

$$\frac{1}{T_1} = \frac{1}{T_2}, \qquad \text{or} \qquad T_1 = T_2. \tag{9.25}$$

The most probable energy distribution between A_1 and A_2 corresponds to equalization of the temperatures.

Our system of formulas is consistent and checks with well-known empirical results.

The crucial point in this reasoning is the assumption that $P_1(E_1)$ and $P_2(E_2)$ are continuous functions with regular derivatives. This will be true only for large material systems, containing an enormous number of atoms, when the energies E_1 and E_2 are extremely large compared to the quantum discontinuities of energy.

6. Energy Fluctuations; Gibbs Formula

Let us consider such a very large body, assuming, for instance, that A_1 is a large tank full of water and very carefully insulated thermally from its surroundings. This corresponds to the physical structure known as a "thermostat" or apparatus maintaining practically a constant temperature. The temperature T_1 of the system is actually constant so long as the heat quantities q involved remain very small compared with the total energy E_1 of thermostat A_1.

For such a thermostat we have, from Eqs. (9.15) and (9.24):

$$\frac{d \ln P_1}{dE_1} = \frac{1}{k\,T_1}, \tag{9.26}$$

or, by direct integration

$$\ln P_1 = \frac{E_1}{k\,T_1} + C_1, \tag{9.27}$$

with an integration constant C_1, hence

$$P_1 = P_0 e^{\frac{E_1}{kT_1}}, \quad \text{with} \quad P_0 = e^{C_1}. \tag{9.28}$$

Such a relation between the number of complexions P_1 and the energy E_1 is typical of a thermostat.

In this thermostat A_1 let us now introduce a small piece of matter A_2, and discuss the state of this element A_2 maintained at a constant temperature T_1 by the thermostat. The most probable energy E_2 is given by our relations (9.21), (9.24), and (9.25), but other energy values may also occur, although they correspond to lower probabilities. The body A_2 will not stay permanently with its most probable energy but will exhibit *energy fluctuations*.

From condition (9.17) we derive

$$E_1 = E - E_2. \tag{9.29}$$

We use this value in Eq. (9.28) and write

$$P_1 = B_1 e^{\frac{-E_2}{kT_1}}, \qquad \text{with} \qquad B_1 = P_0 e^{\frac{E}{kT_1}}. \tag{9.30}$$

The number of complexions P for the whole system is still given by Eq. (9.19), hence

$$P = P_2(E_2)\, B_1 e^{\frac{-E_2}{kT_1}}. \tag{9.31}$$

This shows that, in a thermostat at *temperature* T_1, each of the P_2 complexions of A_2, corresponding to a certain energy E_2, has *a probability* coefficient

$$p(T) = B_1 e^{\frac{-E_2}{kT_1}}. \tag{9.32}$$

This last formula is typical of the definition originally introduced by Gibbs. As a matter of fact, instead of starting from Eq. (9.15), as Boltzmann did, Gibbs used a formula of the type of Eq. (9.32) for the definition of the state of a body A_2 maintained at a temperature T_1. It can be proved that the two lines of reasoning are equivalent. We shall have to use Gibbs' formula (9.32) for the discussion of many problems where fluctuations are of importance.

This discussion illustrates the use of statistical considerations in the explanation of thermodynamics. A body at temperature T is in a state of perpetual agitation. In the case of a gas, molecules travel back and forth across the container, and collide very frequently. The average kinetic energy of the molecules is

$$\overline{E}_{\text{Kin}} = \tfrac{1}{2} k T \text{ per degree of freedom,} \tag{9.33}$$

and this *thermal agitation* represents the energy content of the gas at a temperature T.

In a crystal, atoms are bound to fixed positions in space and build up a regular lattice which constitutes the crystal. Thermal agitation results in vibrations of the atoms about their equilibrium positions. As long as the frequency of these vibrations is low, the kinetic energy of the vibration is still given by Eq. (9.33) and the average total energy of each oscillator is easily computed as the sum of kinetic and potential energies

$$\overline{E}_{\text{total}} = \overline{E}_{\text{kin}} + \overline{E}_{\text{pot}}, \qquad \overline{E}_{\text{pot}} = \overline{E}_{\text{kin}} = \tfrac{1}{2} k\,T, \tag{9.34}$$

$$\overline{E}_{\text{total}} = k\,T, \tag{9.35}$$

for a low frequency oscillator.

7. Quantized Oscillator

These simple formulas cease to apply for oscillators of higher frequency, when the quantum $h\,\nu$ is no longer a small quantity compared to $k\,T$. In such a case we have to take into account the fact that the quantized oscillator can have only discrete energy values:

$$E = 0, h\,\nu, 2\,h\,\nu, 3\,h\,\nu, \ldots, n\,h\,\nu, \ldots. \tag{9.36}$$

These energy levels, in a thermostat T, have probabilities defined by Eq. (9.32):

$$p_0 = B, \qquad p_1 = B\,e^{-\frac{h\nu}{kT}}, \qquad p_2 = B\,e^{-\frac{2h\nu}{kT}}, \ldots, p_n = B\,e^{-\frac{nh\nu}{kT}} \ldots. \tag{9.37}$$

The coefficient B is determined by the condition that the sum of all these probabilities must be unity:

$$1 = \sum_{i=0}^{\infty} p_i = B(1 + e^{-x} + e^{-2x} + \ldots + e^{-nx} + \ldots) = \frac{B}{1-e^{-x}}, \tag{9.38}$$

$$\text{with } x = \frac{h\,\nu}{kT}. \tag{9.39}$$

Hence

$$B = 1 - e^{-x}, \tag{9.40}$$

a result which yields

$$p_0 = 1 - e^{-x}, p_1 = e^{-x} - e^{-2x}, \ldots, p_n = e^{-nx} - e^{-(n+1)x} \ldots. \tag{9.41}$$

A very simple expression is obtained for the sum of the probabilities of the energies above a certain limit:

$$E \geqslant m\,h\,\nu, \qquad n \geqslant m,$$

$$\sum_{n=m}^{\infty} p_n = p_m + p_{m+1} + p_{m+2} + \ldots = e^{-mx}, \tag{9.42}$$

as is easily computed from Eq. (9.41).

Having obtained the probabilities p_n of the discrete energy levels, we can proceed and compute the average energy $\overline{E}$ of the quantized resonator

$$\overline{E} = \overline{n}\, h\, \nu, \qquad \overline{n} = \text{average number of quanta};$$

$$\overline{n} = \sum_{n=0}^{\infty} n\, p_n = B(0 + e^{-x} + 2\, e^{-2x} + \ldots + n\, e^{-nx} + \ldots) = B \frac{e^{-x}}{(1 - e^{-x})^2}. \quad (9.43)$$

The sum is computed by noting that it is the x derivative of

$$-\sum_{n=0}^{\infty} e^{-nx} = -1/(1 - e^{-x}).$$

Replacing B by its value given in Eq. (9.40), we find

$$\overline{n} = 1/(e^x - 1) \qquad \text{with} \qquad x = h\nu/kT, \quad (9.44)$$

so that

$$\overline{E} = h\nu/(e^{h\nu/kT} - 1). \quad (9.45)$$

This is the well known Planck formula, which is the basis of the theory of "black body" radiation.

We may recognize, in the problem of a single quantized resonator [Eqs. (9.38) —(9.44)], the difference between:

The most probable state, corresponding to the greatest p value $p_0 = B$, $n = 0$.

The average quantum number $\overline{n}$ [Eq. (9.44)].

For very small values of x:

$$x \ll 1, \qquad h\nu \ll kT, \qquad \frac{1}{e^x - 1} \approx \frac{1}{x},$$

we have

$$\overline{E} = h\nu/x = kT. \quad (9.46)$$

This is the case of low frequencies, and this result agrees with the earlier one obtained in Eq. (9.35).

8. Fluctuations

We shall need these formulas in our discussions on the accuracy of physical measurements. At any given temperature T, thermal agitation of all the pieces of apparatus results in disordered motions that make it impossible to measure any quantity with unlimited accuracy.

Thermal agitation is the origin of Brownian motion, noise in electric circuits, background noise in acoustics, etc. All these effects will be considered in connection with the application of information theory to actual physical problems. They will indicate a very interesting connection between information and entropy, and lead us to a systematic discussion of the fundamental limitations encountered in physical experiments.

Thermal energy would be no obstacle to the accuracy of measurements, if it remained constant. What makes observations difficult is the perpetual state of fluctuation, where the actual energy of a system, at a given instant of time, cannot be predicted, and may differ greatly from the average value.

We noted, in the last section, the distinction between most probable and average energy values. Let us investigate the fluctuation problem for a quantized oscillator.

At a certain instant of time, the system has

$$n = \bar{n} + m \qquad \text{quanta} \tag{9.47}$$

with a "fluctuation" m above the average value $\bar{n}$. We shall compute the average value $\overline{n^2}$ of n^2,

$$n^2 = (\bar{n} + m)^2 = (\bar{n})^2 + 2\,\bar{n}\,m + m^2. \tag{9.48}$$

Taking the average, we remember that $\bar{m} = 0$ because $\bar{n}$ is the average value of n, hence

$$\overline{n^2} = (\bar{n})^2 + \overline{m^2}. \tag{9.49}$$

If we know $\overline{n^2}$ we can easily obtain the average square fluctuation $\overline{m^2}$ from Eq. (9.49). Computing $\overline{n^2}$ is easy enough, since we know the probabilities [Eq. (9.37)] of all quantized states. We simply write

$$\overline{n^2} = \sum_{n=0}^{\infty} n^2 p_n = B \sum_{n=0}^{\infty} n^2 e^{-nx} = -B\frac{d}{dx}\sum_{n=0}^{\infty} n\, e^{-nx} = -B\frac{d}{dx}\,[e^{-x}/(1-e^{-x})^2], \tag{9.50}$$

where we have made use of Eq. (9.43). Performing the differentiation and using the value of B from Eq. (9.40), we obtain:

$$\overline{n^2} = B\frac{e^{-x} + e^{-2x}}{(1-e^{-x})^3} = \frac{e^{-x} + e^{-2x}}{(1-e^{-x})^2} = \frac{e^x + 1}{(e^x - 1)^2}, \tag{9.51}$$

using the B value from Eq. (9.40).

Comparing Eqs. (9.49) and (9.51), we obtain

$$\overline{m^2} = \overline{n^2} - (\bar{n})^2 = \frac{e^x + 1 - 1}{(e^x - 1)^2} = (\bar{n})^2 + \bar{n}, \tag{9.52}$$

using expression (9.44).

This is a famous result, first discovered by Planck and Einstein, relating fluctuations to average values.

For a *low frequency oscillator* ($h\nu \ll kT$) the average number of quanta $\bar{n}$ is very large and the result simplifies into

$$\overline{m^2} = (\bar{n})^2. \tag{9.53}$$

This can be translated into energy fluctuations ε:

$$E = \bar{E} + \varepsilon, \qquad \overline{\varepsilon^2} = \overline{m^2}(h\nu)^2 = (\bar{E})^2, \tag{9.54}$$

where $\bar{E} = \bar{n}\,h\nu$ is the average energy of the oscillator.

Low frequencies:

$$h\nu \ll kT \qquad \text{and} \qquad (\overline{\varepsilon^2})^{\frac{1}{2}} = \bar{E} = kT. \tag{9.55}$$

For low frequencies, the square root of the average squared fluctuations is equal to the average energy, or, roughly speaking, fluctuations are of the order of magnitude of the average energy.

For *high frequencies* ($h\nu \gg kT$) the average $\bar{n}$ is small, and $(\bar{n})^2$ is still smaller, hence

$$\overline{m^2} \approx \bar{n} \ll 1, \tag{9.56}$$

or

$$\overline{\varepsilon^2} \approx \bar{n}(h\nu)^2 = \bar{E}\,h\nu. \tag{9.57}$$

The average energy fluctuations are much larger for high frequencies, since $\bar{E}$ is smaller than $h\nu$, hence

$$\bar{E}\,h\nu \gg \bar{E}^2. \tag{9.58}$$

Fluctuations at high frequencies [Eq. (9.57)] are comparatively larger than fluctuations at low frequencies [Eq. (9. 54)]. This result is typical of quantum effects.

Let us now consider a system of N harmonic oscillators with low frequencies. The total average energy $\bar{E}_t$ is

$$\bar{E}_t = N\bar{E} = NkT, \tag{9.59}$$

and we observe fluctuations ε_t

$$E_t = \bar{E}_t + \varepsilon_t. \tag{9.60}$$

Fluctuations in the N oscillators are independent, and hence

$$\overline{\varepsilon_t{}^2} = N\overline{\varepsilon^2} = N(kT)^2, \tag{9.61}$$

according to Eqs. (9.54) and (9.55).

CHAPTER 10

THERMAL AGITATION AND BROWNIAN MOTION

1. Thermal Agitation

We recall one of the important conclusions of the previous chapter, namely, $E_{kin} = kT/2$ for each degree of freedom of low frequency, and proceed to a discussion of some practical applications.

Brownian Motion

If we consider small particles immersed in a liquid and examine them under a microscope, we find that they move continually with a random type of motion. While early investigators first thought that these particles were alive, it was quickly established that their motion was due entirely to the random bombardment on all sides by the molecules of the liquid. This was first successfully explained by Einstein (in 1905), and verified experimentally by Perrin. Perrin's experiments, furthermore, enabled him to obtain a value for the absolute size of atoms since he could determine directly Avogadro's number A, the number of atoms or molecules in one mole of a substance.

Ultimate Accuracy of Measurements

Consider the problem of measuring current by means of an ammeter. The needle is pivoted at a point and hence has one degree of freedom, as indicated in Fig. 10.1. Thus the kinetic energy of the random oscillations of the needle, $E_{kin} = kT/2$, and their magnitude can readily be computed. We can reduce their amplitude by cooling the instrument, which would only reduce it in part; we must also cool the rest of the circuit if we want to obtain a steady state of low agitation.

The problem of noise (in resistors, for example) has been extensively investigated, Nyquist being one of the early workers in the field. If we consider the series $L\,R\,C$ circuit shown in Fig. 10.2 with the elements of the circuit all at same temperature T, we observe that we have one degree of freedom (the current I through the network) and hence we have

$$\tfrac{1}{2}kT = E_{kin} = \tfrac{1}{2}LI^2. \tag{10.1}$$

We therefore have disordered currents of magnitude determined by the above equation. The only way these currents can be reduced, again, is by cooling the entire circuit. The frequency distribution of these noise currents can be investigated and will be discussed later.

FIG. 10.1. The needle of an ammeter is pivoted at a point, and hence has one degree of freedom.

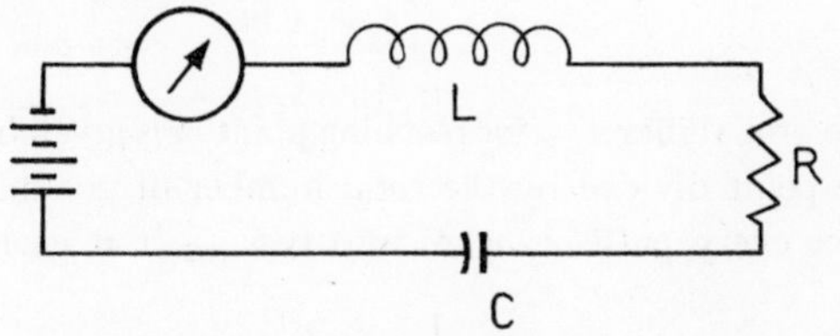

FIG. 10.2. A series circuit containing a source of emf, an ammeter, an inductance L, a resistance R, and a capacitance C. Noise is generated in the resistance.

2. Random Walk

Let us start with a statistical problem of great importance in connection with all these examples of disordered agitation. A particle can move along a line and take equal steps, either to the right or to the left, at equal intervals of time.

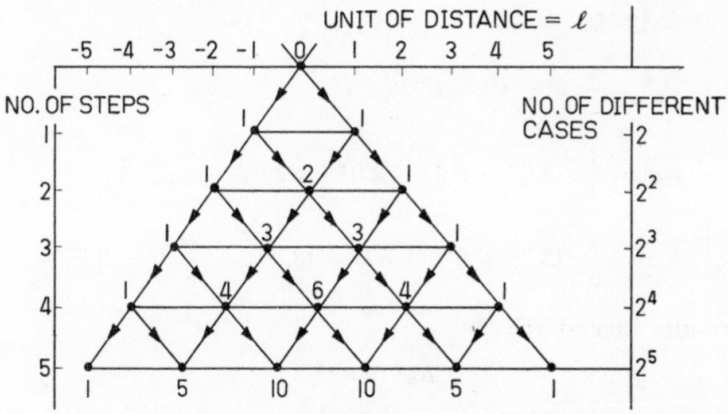

FIG. 10.3. Random walk with steps of equal length, which obviously reproduces Pascal's triangle for binomial coefficients. The numbers represent the number of paths reaching a certain point. The total number of cases is 2^n.

We shall consider the units of displacement to be l, and the units of time in which the displacement occurs to be 1, 2, 3, etc. Fig. 10.3 gives the general scheme. The whole diagram reproduces the well known Pascal triangle, and the number of distinct paths reaching a point after n steps is $\frac{n!}{q!\,(n-q)!}$ when the distance of the point from the origin is

$$m = -n + 2q,$$

$$q = \frac{n+m}{2}, \qquad n-q = \frac{n-m}{2}. \tag{10.2}$$

The probability $\pi_{n,m}$ for reaching point m is given by the number of paths reaching the point divided by the total number of possible paths, which is obviously 2^n, since every path branches into two ($\pm l$) at each step

$$\pi_{n,m} = \frac{1}{2^n} \cdot \frac{n!}{q!\,(n-q)!} = \frac{n!}{2^n \left(\frac{n+m}{2}\right)!\left(\frac{n-m}{2}\right)!}. \tag{10.3}$$

The points m that can be reached after n steps have the same parity as n, on account of condition (10.2). The average displacement $\overline{R_n}$ after n steps is obviously zero, since the chances of moving to the right or to the left are equal. The average $\overline{R_n^2}$ of the square displacement increases with the number of steps. The schematic drawing of Fig. 10.3 yields:

$$\overline{R_n^2} = \overline{m^2}\,l^2 = l^2 \sum_{m=-n}^{+n} m^2 \pi_{n,m}; \tag{10.4}$$

$$\left.\begin{aligned}
\overline{R_0^2} &= 0,\\
\overline{R_1^2} &= \frac{1}{2}\,(l^2 + l^2) = l^2,\\
\overline{R_2^2} &= \frac{1}{4}\,[(2\,l)^2 + 2\cdot 0 + (2\,l)^2] = 2\,l^2,\\
\overline{R_3^2} &= \frac{1}{8}\,[(3\,l)^2 + 3\,l^2 + 3\,l^2 + (3\,l)^2] = \frac{24}{8}\,l^2 = 3\,l^2.
\end{aligned}\right\} \tag{10.5}$$

These results suggest the law

$$\overline{R_n^2} = n\,l^2, \tag{10.6}$$

which we can prove by induction; that is we show that if

$$\overline{m_n^2} = \sum_{m=-n}^{m=n} \pi_{n,m}\, m^2 = n, \tag{10,7}$$

it follows that

$$\overline{m_{n+1}^2} = \sum_{m=-n-1}^{m=n+1} \pi_{n+1,m}\, m^2 = n + 1. \tag{10.7 a}$$

To do this, we first note that if position $m < n + 1$ is reached in $n + 1$ steps, the position after n steps must have been either $m + 1$ or $m - 1$, and that these two possibilities are equally probable. Therefore

$$\pi_{n+1,m} = \tfrac{1}{2}(\pi_{n,m+1} + \pi_{n,m-1}), \qquad m < n + 1. \tag{10.8}$$

Also

$$\pi_{n+1,n+1} = \pi_{n+1,-n-1} = \frac{1}{2^{n+1}}. \tag{10.8 a}$$

We recall that the two subscripts of the $\pi_{n,m}$ have the same parity, so that only alternate values of a subscript contribute to a sum over that subscript. Using this fact and Eqs. (10.8) and (10.8 a), we obtain for the sum in Eq. (10.7 a):

$$\overline{m_{n+1}{}^2} = 2\,\frac{(n+1)^2}{2^{n+1}} + \tfrac{1}{2}\sum_{m=-n+1}^{m=n-1}(\pi_{n,m+1} + \pi_{n,m-1})\,m^2$$

$$= \frac{(n+1)^2}{2^n} + \tfrac{1}{2}\sum_{m=-n+1}^{m=n-1}\pi_{n,m+1}\,m^2 + \tfrac{1}{2}\sum_{m=-n+1}^{m=n-1}\pi_{n,m-1}\,m^2.$$

In the first sum we set $k = m + 1$, and in the second we set $l = m - 1$. Then

$$\overline{m_{n+1}{}^2} = \frac{(n+1)^2}{2^n} + \tfrac{1}{2}\sum_{k=-n+2}^{k=n}\pi_{n,k}(k-1)^2 + \tfrac{1}{2}\sum_{l=-n}^{k=n-2}\pi_{n,l}(l+1)^2$$

$$= \frac{(n+1)^2}{2^n} + \tfrac{1}{2}\sum_{k=-n}^{k=n}\pi_{n,k}(k-1)^2 - \tfrac{1}{2}\pi_{n,-n}(-n-1)^2$$

$$+ \tfrac{1}{2}\sum_{l=-n}^{l=n}\pi_{n,l}(l+1)^2 - \tfrac{1}{2}\pi_{n,n}(n+1)^2.$$

Now $\pi_{n,n} = \pi_{n,-n} = \dfrac{1}{2^n}$, so only the two sums remain, and they may be combined:

$$\overline{m_{n+1}{}^2} = \tfrac{1}{2}\sum_{k=-n}^{k=n}\pi_{n,k}[(k-1)^2 + (k+1)^2]$$

$$= \tfrac{1}{2}\sum_{k=-n}^{k=n}\pi_{n,k}(2\,k^2 + 2)$$

$$= \sum_{k=-n}^{k=n}\pi_{n,k}\,k^2 + \sum_{k=-n}^{k=n}\pi_{n,k} = n + 1, \quad \text{Q.E.D.} \tag{10.9}$$

from Eq. (10.7) and the fact that the $\pi_{n,k}$ are probabilities whose sum over k is unity.

The distribution of points is spreading with time and we obtain a root mean square displacement

$$\overline{(R^2)}^{1/2} = n^{1/2}\, l \tag{10.10}$$

for equal steps of length l.

When the number of steps n becomes very large, it can be proved that the distribution (10.3) reduces to a Gaussian distribution (see the Appendix).

We shall see later how this result can be applied to Brownian motion. We can also apply it to computing as in the rounding off of errors in a long computation. Then, we might take the maximum case where $|l| = \frac{1}{2}$, in which case the root mean errror $\sqrt{\overline{R_n^2}} \sim \frac{1}{2}\sqrt{n}$. That is, we assume the range of the last digit to be $\pm\frac{1}{2}$. The maximum error, on the other hand, would be proportional to $\frac{1}{2}n$, which corresponds to all the errors adding up, a very improbable situation.

We can extend our discussion to the case where the steps have different lengths. Then we have a random distribution about an average:

$$\overline{R_n^2} = \overline{l^2} \cdot n, \qquad \text{or} \qquad \sqrt{\overline{R_n^2}} = \sqrt{\overline{l^2}} \cdot \sqrt{n}. \tag{10.11}$$

This latter formula may be more suitable for rounding off errors.

3. Shot Effect

We can apply our "random walk" formula to problems of *noise in tubes* (*Shot effect*) and to radioactive transformations. If we consider the radioactive transformation, the substance is emitting particles at an average rate of N particles per second. This is actually a discrete particle emission with no correlation between successive emitted particles.

The actual emission can be written

$$P = Nt + \nu, \tag{10.12}$$

where ν is the correction to the average emission, and corresponds to the noise. This description corresponds closely to emission of electrons from a heated filament, and hence we would have the same type of noise in an electron tube. The emission as a function of time is shown in Fig. 10.4.

We must first show how to reduce this to a "random walk" problem. This can be done in a variety of ways, depending upon the actual conditions of emission. Let us start with a very simple problem corresponding to the following assumption: We assume that we can find a time interval θ sufficiently small so that in this time interval we may have one of two equally probable events occurring (see Fig. 10.5): no emission and emission of one particle. Thus, during this time interval, the change in emission is

$$\Delta t = \theta, \qquad \Delta P = \begin{cases} 0 \\ 1 \end{cases} = \tfrac{1}{2} + \begin{cases} -\tfrac{1}{2} \\ +\tfrac{1}{2} \end{cases}, \tag{10.13}$$

with the result that

$$N = 1/(2\,\theta),$$

and that

$$\Delta \nu = \begin{cases} -\tfrac{1}{2} \\ \tfrac{1}{2} \end{cases}.$$

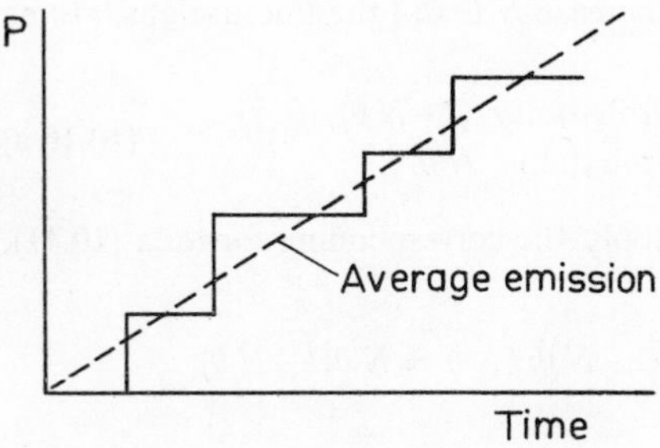

FIG. 10.4. The emission as a function of time is a step function. The average emission is a straight line. The "steps" correspond to the term ν in Eq. (10.12).

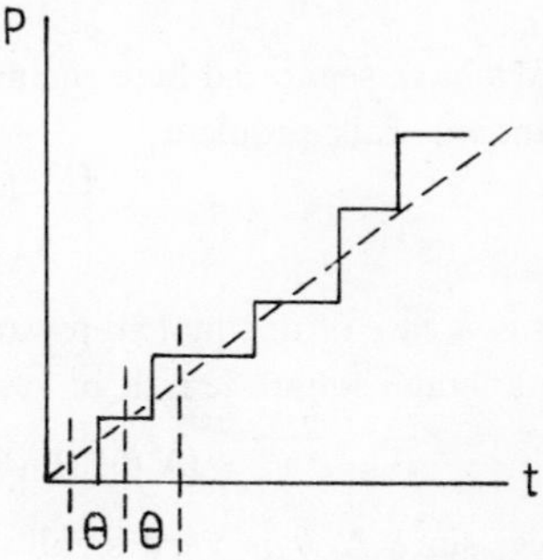

FIG. 10.5. The step function of Fig. 10.4 shown with the time interval θ selected so that during θ the probability of emission is $\frac{1}{2}$.

Thus, if we take $|l| = \frac{1}{2}$, we have reduced the problem to that of a constant drift $N\,t$, with a random walk superimposed. The square average of the random fluctuations is again given by

$$\overline{\nu_n{}^2} = n\,l^2 = (\tfrac{1}{4})\,n, \tag{10.14}$$

where n denotes the total length of time $t = n\,\theta$. During this time interval t, the average emission was

$$\overline{P} = N\,t = n\,\theta\,\frac{1}{2\,\theta} = (\tfrac{1}{2})\,n,$$

hence

$$\overline{\nu_n{}^2} = (\tfrac{1}{2})\,\overline{P}. \tag{10.15}$$

The average square fluctuation, in this special example, is equal to one half of the average number of particles emitted.

A more important physical problem, and a more realistic one, is obtained with different assumptions, corresponding to *completely random emission*. We select a very small time interval θ, and assume that, during this interval, the increase of emission ΔP is

$$\Delta P = \begin{cases} 0 & \text{with probability } 1 - N\theta, \\ 1 & \text{with probability } N\theta \ll 1. \end{cases}$$

The time interval θ is so small that there is no chance for the emission of two, three, or more particles. The average rate of emission is N. The condition can be written in the following way:

$$\Delta P = N\theta + \begin{cases} -N\theta & \text{probability } (1 - N\theta), \\ 1 - N\theta & \text{probability } N\theta. \end{cases} \tag{10.16}$$

We have separated here the average increase $N\theta$ and the fluctuations, giving a random walk problem

$$\Delta \nu = \begin{cases} -N\theta & \text{probability } (1 - N\theta), \\ 1 - N\theta & \text{probability } N\theta. \end{cases} \tag{10.16 a}$$

This is a case of unequal steps, and we apply the corresponding formula (10.11). The average square length of steps is

$$\overline{l^2} = \overline{\Delta \nu^2} = (N\theta)^2 (1 - N\theta) + (1 - N\theta)^2 N\theta = N\theta(1 - N\theta),$$

hence, since $N\theta$ is very small

$$\overline{l^2} = N\theta.$$

We use this result together with Eq. (10.11) and obtain the average square fluctuation about a total time interval t, during which the average emission is $N t$:

$$t = n\theta, \qquad n \text{ large},$$
$$\overline{P} = N t = n N \theta,$$
$$\overline{\nu^2} = n \overline{l^2} = n N \theta = \overline{P}.$$

The average square fluctuation, in a case of completely random emission, is exactly equal to the average number of emitted particles.

4. Brownian Motion

In returning to the discussion of Brownian motion, we shall follow the treatment of H. A. Lorentz[1] and also note a few orders of magnitude:

$$k = 1.38 \times 10^{-16} \text{ ergs/molecule } {}^0\text{K},$$
$$k T = 4.14 \times 10^{-14} \text{ ergs/molecule} \approx 1/40\, e\, v,$$
$$\text{at } T = 300\ {}^0\text{K} \approx 27\ {}^0\text{C}.$$

[1] H. A. Lorentz, "Les théories statistiques en thermodynamique," p. 49, Teubner, Leipzig, 1916; G. L. de Haas - Lorentz, "Die Brownsche Bewegung." Vieweg, Braunschweig, 1913.

Consider a particle immersed in a medium, with coordinates as shown in Fig. 10.6. We shall consider its motion only in the x direction. Since the motion is random, motion in the x direction is independent of motion in the y and z directions. We must introduce a coefficient of viscous damping, w.

Then, the equation of motion of the particle (mass $= m$) is

$$F_x = m \frac{dv}{dt} + w\, v, \qquad (10.17)$$

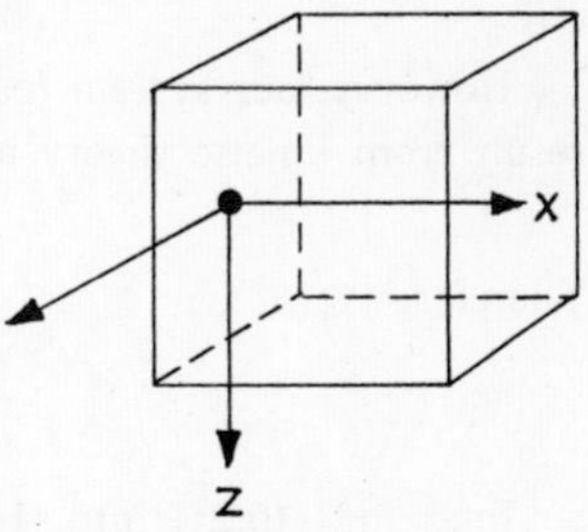

FIG. 10.6. The coordinates x, y, and z of the particle immersed in a viscous medium.

where F_x denotes the random forces which are exerted on the particle. F_x must be random, since in any reasonably small interval of time we will have a very large number of random collisions between the particle and the molecules of the liquid.

Now let us consider an interval of time, τ, sufficiently small so that the change in velocity, Δv, of the particle in the time interval will be small. Then we compute the total impulse of force exerted on the particle in time interval τ:

$$X = \int_0^\tau F_x\, dt. \qquad (10.18)$$

The velocity of the particle will be v_0 at $t = 0$ and v_1 at $t = \tau$, and integrating Eq. (10.17) over the time interval τ gives

$$m(v_1 - v_0) + w\, v_0\, \tau = X. \qquad (10.19)$$

Regrouping terms, we obtain

$$m\, v_1 = v_0(m - w\,\tau) + X. \qquad (10.20)$$

Now, since F_x is completely at random, we can state that

$$\overline{X} = 0, \qquad (10.21)$$

but we must take into account $\overline{X^2}$ which is not zero. We square Eq. (10.20):

$$v_1{}^2 = v_0{}^2\left(1 - \frac{2\,w\,\tau}{m} + \frac{w^2\tau^2}{m^2}\right) + \frac{X^2}{m^2} + \frac{2\,X\,v_0}{m}\left(1 - \frac{w\,\tau}{m}\right), \qquad (10.22)$$

and note that τ is very small, so

$$\frac{w^2\,\tau^2}{m^2} \ll \frac{2\,w\,\tau}{m}.$$

If we now take the average of Eq. (10.22), we find $\overline{X}$ appearing, which we have previously set equal to zero. Therefore, the average of $v_1{}^2$ becomes:

$$\overline{v_1{}^2} = \overline{v_0{}^2}\left(1 - \frac{2\,w\,\tau}{m}\right) + \frac{\overline{X^2}}{m^2}. \tag{10.23}$$

However, our system (particle + liquid) is at some temperature T, and the result from kinetic theory applies, namely

$$\tfrac{1}{2}\,m\,\overline{v^2} = \tfrac{1}{2}\,k\,T.$$

Therefore

$$\overline{v_1{}^2} = \overline{v_0{}^2} = \frac{k\,T}{m}. \tag{10.24}$$

Inserting (10.24) into (10.23) and solving for $\overline{X^2}$:

$$\overline{X^2} = 2\,w\,\tau\,k\,T. \tag{10.25}$$

Thus the average of the square of the impulse of force is not equal to zero. Moreover, in examining Eq. (10.23) by rewriting:

$$\tfrac{1}{2}\,m\,\overline{v_1{}^2} = \tfrac{1}{2}\,m\,\overline{v_0{}^2}\left(1 - \frac{2\,w\,\tau}{m}\right) + \frac{\overline{X^2}}{2\,m},$$

we observe that $(\tfrac{1}{2})\,m\,\overline{v_0{}^2}\,(2\,w\,\tau/m)$ represents the loss of kinetic energy of the particle in passing through the viscous medium, while $\overline{X^2}/2\,m$ represents the compensating energy given to the particle by the random collisions with the molecules. Thus, we observe a two-way mechanism of energy transfer:

$$\begin{cases} \text{Kinetic energy of particle} \rightarrow \text{Molecular agitation,} \\ \text{Molecular agitation} \rightarrow \text{Kinetic energy of the particle.} \end{cases}$$

As a further result, we see that if the viscous damping is large, the compensating transfer is also large. A large viscous term represents a strong coupling between the particle and the surrounding viscous liquid, hence powerful collisions that correspond to large random impulses X. The work done by the random forces comes from the energy of thermal agitation (heat) and returns to heat by the viscous damping.

In order to obtain the mean square displacement of the particle, we shall simplify the discussion somewhat by assuming that at $t = 0$, $v_0 = 0$ and at $t = \tau$, $v = v_1$. We shall also assume that after τ, we no longer have forces acting on the particle; that is, we simply isolate one of the collisions, and treat it and each of the other collisions as an individual event. After τ, then, the motion is damped, and we can write

$$v = v_1\,e^{-\frac{wt}{m}}. \tag{10.26}$$

Solving for x:

$$x = \int_{\tau}^{\infty} v\,dt = v_1 \int_{\tau}^{\infty} e^{-\frac{wt}{m}}\,dt = \frac{v_1 m}{w}\left[e^{-\frac{wt}{m}}\right]_{\tau}^{\infty}.$$

But since τ is small, we can evaluate the exponential between the limits 0 and ∞ instead, and therefore

$$x = \frac{m\,v_1}{w} = \frac{X}{w}, \tag{10.27}$$

from Eq. (10.20) with $v_0 = 0$. This quantity x represents the displacement of the particle resulting from impulse X occurring in time τ. This is a form of random walk, since $\overline{x} = 0$ because $\overline{X} = 0$. But $\overline{X^2} \neq 0$; squaring and averaging Eq. (10.27), we obtain

$$\overline{x^2} = \overline{X^2}/w^2. \tag{10.28}$$

Substitution of Eq. (10.25) into Eq. (10.28) yields

$$\overline{x^2} = \frac{2\,k\,T}{w}\,\tau. \tag{10.29}$$

And for a longer time interval t, containing many small intervals τ, the square motions add independently

$$\overline{x^2} = \frac{2\,k\,T\,t}{w}. \tag{10.30}$$

This has been checked experimentally by observing the position of colloidal particles in suspension as a function of time.

5. Thermal Agitation in an Electric Circuit

We turn, now, to a problem very similar to the Brownian motion: random flow of charge in an electric circuit. Consider the electric circuit shown in Fig. 10.7. The circuit consists of an inductance, a resistance, and an ammeter to read the current, all at some temperature T. The system has one degree of freedom, and therefore

$$\overline{E}_{\text{kin}} = \tfrac{1}{2}\,k\,T = \tfrac{1}{2}\,L\,\overline{i^2}. \tag{10.31}$$

The current fluctuates at random, $\overline{i} = 0$. If we write the equation of motion of the current

$$L\frac{di}{dt} + R\,i = F, \tag{10.32}$$

where F denotes the random emf imposed on the circuit, we see that this equation is identical with the equation of motion of the particle undergoing Brownian motion (10.17). Moreover, the mechanism of energy transfer is similar.

The electron transfers kinetic energy to the molecules of the resistor, and "collisions" of the molecules give kinetic energy to the electron. The compensation is determined now by the mean square of the impulse of the random emf's and we obtain a relation similar to (10.25)

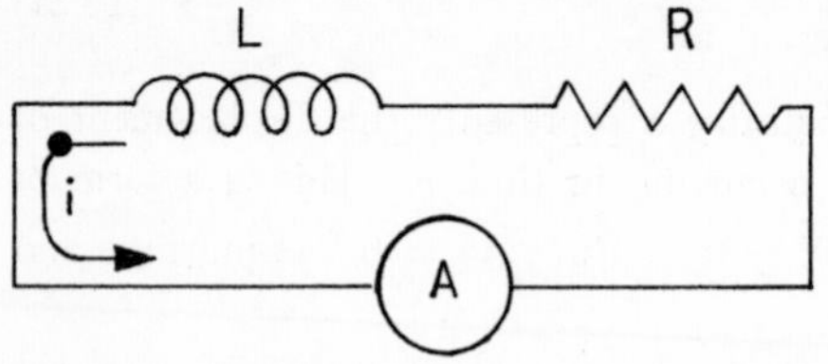

FIG. 10.7. The circuit used in the discussion of noise due to thermal agitation. An inductance, a resistance, and an ammeter are in series, and all are maintained at temperature T.

$$\overline{X^2} = 2\,R\,\tau\,k\,T. \tag{10.33}$$

Charge q takes the place of the displacement x, and follows a condition similar to (10.30):

$$\overline{q^2} = \frac{2\,k\,T}{R}\,t. \tag{10.34}$$

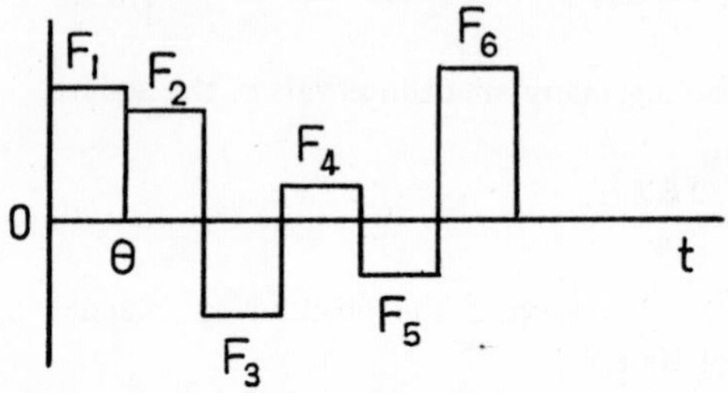

FIG. 10.8. The random force is a step function, constant during each interval from $(n-1)\ \theta$ to $n\,\theta$.

We thus have two sources of noise in an electronic circuit thermal noise, due to the thermal agitation and fluctuations of charge in circuit elements such as resistors, and shot effect in tubes. In a later section we shall analyze the thermal noise in terms of its frequency distribution.

We can construct a somewhat more detailed model to account for the time increase of the mean square impulse of force in Brownian motion (or emf in electric circuit). We assume that the force varies at random with time, as shown in Fig. 10.8, but that the force will be constant in each time interval θ (θ will be very small, and $\tau = n\,\theta$). Since the forces are exerted at random, there will be no correlation, and thus

$$\begin{aligned} \overline{F_i F_k} &= 0, \quad i \neq k, \\ \overline{F_i^2} &= \overline{F^2} \neq 0; \end{aligned} \tag{10.35}$$

we compute

$$X = \int_{t=0}^{t=\tau=n\theta} F\,dt = \theta(F_1 + F_2 + \ldots + F_n),$$

and

$$X^2 = \theta^2(F_1{}^2 + F_2{}^2 + \ldots + F_n{}^2 + 2F_1F_2 + 2F_1F_3 + \ldots). \qquad (10.36)$$

Taking the average, we have

$$\overline{X^2} = \theta^2\overline{(F_1{}^2 + F_2{}^2 + \ldots)}.$$

But from (10.35)

$$\overline{X^2} = n\,\theta^2\,\overline{F^2}, \qquad (10.37)$$

since the average of the cross terms is zero and $\tau = n\,\theta$;

$$\overline{X^2} = \tau\overline{(F^2\,\theta)}, \qquad (10.38)$$

and we have shown that the mean square of impulse of force (or emf) is proportional to time, a result that agrees with our formulas (10.25) and (10.33) and explains the mechanism of this increase.

Appendix

We discussed in Section 2 the problem of random walk and obtained the probability function $\pi_{n,m}$ for reaching a point m in n steps [Eq. (10.3)]

$$\pi_{n,m} = \frac{n!}{2^n \dfrac{n+m}{2}!\,\dfrac{n-m}{2}!}.$$

We now want to investigate what happens when the number n of steps is very large, while m remains finite. We use the Stirling approximation for factorials

$$n! \to \left(\frac{n}{e}\right)^n \sqrt{2\pi n}, \qquad n \gg 1,$$

and obtain, after some cancellations,

$$\pi_{n,m} \to \frac{n^n}{(n+m)^{\frac{n+m}{2}}(n-m)^{\frac{n-m}{2}}} \cdot \frac{\sqrt{2\pi n}}{2\pi\sqrt{\dfrac{n+m}{2}\cdot\dfrac{n-m}{2}}} =$$

$$= \frac{2\sqrt{n}}{\sqrt{2\pi(n^2-m^2)}} \cdot \frac{1}{\left(1+\dfrac{m}{n}\right)^{\frac{n+m}{2}}\left(1-\dfrac{m}{n}\right)^{\frac{n-m}{2}}}.$$

The terms in the denominator are of the type $(1+\varepsilon)^{1/\varepsilon}$ that tends to e for very small ε, but we need a better approximation. Let us expand

$$ln(1+\varepsilon)^{1/\varepsilon} = \frac{1}{\varepsilon}\,ln(1+\varepsilon) = \frac{1}{\varepsilon}\left(\varepsilon - \frac{\varepsilon^2}{2} + \ldots\right) = 1 - \frac{\varepsilon}{2} + \ldots,$$

hence

$$(1+\varepsilon)^{1/\varepsilon} \to e^{1-\varepsilon/2},$$

which gives, with $\varepsilon = m/n$,

$$\left[\left(1+\frac{m}{n}\right)^{\frac{n}{m}}\right]^{\frac{m}{2}+\frac{m^2}{2n}} \to \left[e^{1-\frac{m}{2n}}\right]^{\frac{m}{2}+\frac{m^2}{2n}} = e^{\frac{m}{2}+\frac{m^2}{4n}+\cdots};$$

similarly

$$\left(1-\frac{m}{n}\right)^{\frac{n-m}{2}} \to e^{-\frac{m}{2}+\frac{m^2}{4n}},$$

and finally

$$\pi_{n,m} \to \frac{2\sqrt{n}}{\sqrt{2\pi(n^2-m^2)}}\, e^{-\frac{m^2}{2n}} \to \frac{2}{\sqrt{2\pi\, n}}\, e^{-\frac{m^2}{2n}},$$

a probability distribution of the Gaussian type. We must keep in mind the fact that m always has the same parity as n. For a given n, the distance between successive points is $\Delta\, m = 2$ (see Fig. 10.3). Let us for instance consider the case where n and m are even

$$n = 2\,h, \qquad m = 2\,y, \qquad \Delta\, y = 1, \qquad h \gg y.$$

We can ignore the m^2 term in the denominator of $\pi_{n\,m}$ and write

$$\pi_{h,\,y} = \frac{1}{\sqrt{\pi\, h}}\, e^{-\frac{y^2}{h}}.$$

This is easy to compare with the standard Gaussian formula

$$P = \frac{1}{\sqrt{2\pi}\,\sigma}\, e^{-\frac{y^2}{2\sigma^2}}, \qquad \overline{y^2} = \sigma^2,$$

where σ is the standard deviation. Our formula for $\pi_{h,\,y}$ indicates

$$\sigma^2 = \frac{h}{2}, \qquad \overline{m^2} = 4\,\overline{y^2} = 2\,h = n.$$

which corresponds to our general result of Eq. (10.7).

CHAPTER 11

THERMAL NOISE IN AN ELECTRIC CIRCUIT; NYQUIST'S FORMULA

1. Random Impulses Model

We shall apply some of the results of the last chapter to a discussion of the Nyquist noise formula, which determines the frequency distribution of noise resulting from random thermal emf's.[1]

We recall the following result from Eqs. (10.33) and (10.38): The average of the square of the impulse of emf F, taken over a time interval τ is

$$X = \int_0^\tau F\,dt, \qquad \overline{X^2} = 2\,R\,k\,T\,\tau, \tag{11.1}$$

$$\overline{X^2} = \tau(\theta\,\overline{F^2}), \tag{11.2}$$

where Eq. (11.2) is the result obtained from the model of emf's occurring at random, with each emf, F, constant over the very small time interval θ and

$$\tau = n\,\theta.$$

Thus, combining (11.1) and (11.2)

$$\overline{F^2}\,\theta = 2\,R\,k\,T. \tag{11.3}$$

Although, from our model, we have a random succession of rectangular pulses, the intensity spectrum of this will be the spectrum of a single rectangular pulse since, with the pulses occurring at random (no correlation), the effect of the succession of pulses can be obtained by summing the squares of the amplitudes of the frequency components.

The spectrum of a single pulse of emf of height F and time duration θ, results from Eqs. (8.23) and (8.25):

$$f(t) = \int_{\nu=-\infty}^{+\infty} C(\nu)\cos 2\pi\,\nu\,t\,d\nu = \int_{\nu=0}^{\infty} 2\,C(\nu)\cos 2\pi\,\nu\,t\,d\nu. \tag{11.4}$$

---

[1] J. L. Lawson and G. E. Uhlenbeck, "Threshold Signals," Radiation Laboratory Series **24**. McGraw-Hill, New York, 1950.

We have a superposition of successive cosine terms with amplitude

$$C(\nu) = F\,\theta\left(\frac{\sin \pi\,\nu\,\theta}{\pi\,\nu\,\theta}\right). \tag{11.5}$$

The duration of the pulse is θ and the "nominal" band width $1/\theta$ (Chapter 8, Section 4):

$$\Delta\,\nu = 2\,\nu_M = \frac{1}{\theta}, \qquad -\nu_M \leqslant \nu \leqslant +\nu_M, \qquad \nu_M = \frac{1}{2\,\theta}. \tag{11.6}$$

In a rather crude approximation, the frequency spectrum for a rectangular pulse of height F and duration θ can be considered as extending approximately from $-\nu_M$ to $+\nu_M$, with a constant amplitude

$$C(\nu) = F\,\theta \tag{11.7}$$

for each frequency component.

If we do not want to introduce negative frequencies, we may take

$$0 \leqslant \nu \leqslant \nu_M, \qquad \nu_M = \frac{1}{2\,\theta}, \tag{11.8}$$

and double the amplitude [as in Eq. (11.4)]:

$$C'(\nu) = 2\,C(\nu) = 2\,F\,\theta. \tag{11.9}$$

Let us now consider the succession of pulses of length θ and average $\overline{F^2}$. The average square emf is, according to Eq. (11.3),

$$\overline{E^2} = \overline{F^2} = 2\,R\,k\,T\frac{1}{\theta}, \tag{11.10}$$

and it extends approximately over a frequency spectrum $0 \leqslant \nu \leqslant \nu_M$. Hence we have

$$\overline{E_\nu{}^2} = 4\,R\,k\,T\,\nu_M, \tag{11.11}$$

almost uniformly distributed over the frequency range 0 to ν_M. We can make a proportional reduction for a smaller frequency interval, $\Delta\,\nu$, i. e., between ν and $\nu + \Delta\,\nu$

$$\overline{e^2} = 4\,R\,k\,T\,\Delta\,\nu, \tag{11.12}$$

which is the Nyquist formula.[2]

[2] Some fundamental references are: P. W. Bridgman, Note on the Principle of Detailed Balancing, *Phys. Rev.* **31**, 101 (1928); J. B. Johnson, *ibid.* **29**, 367 (1927); **32**, 97 (1928); H. Nyquist, *ibid.* **32**, 110 (1928); J. Bernamont, Fluctuations de potentiel aux bornes d'un conducteur metallique, *Ann. phys.* [11], **7** (1937); M. Courtines, Les fluctuations dans les appareils de mesures, *Congr. intern. d'electricité*, vol. **2**, Paris (1932).

2. The Nyquist Method

We consider now the Nyquist derivation of the same formula. First we must construct a circuit capable of transmitting a continuous range of frequencies — such as a very long cable (Fig. 11.1). Let the cable have length l, and characteristic impedance Z. We shall terminate the line with resistors R_I and R_{II} and make $R_I = R_{II} = Z$. The entire circuit will be at some temperature T. Each resistor is a source of thermal emf, and thus signals are sent from R_I to be absorbed in R_{II}, and vice versa. These signals cover a wide band of frequencies.

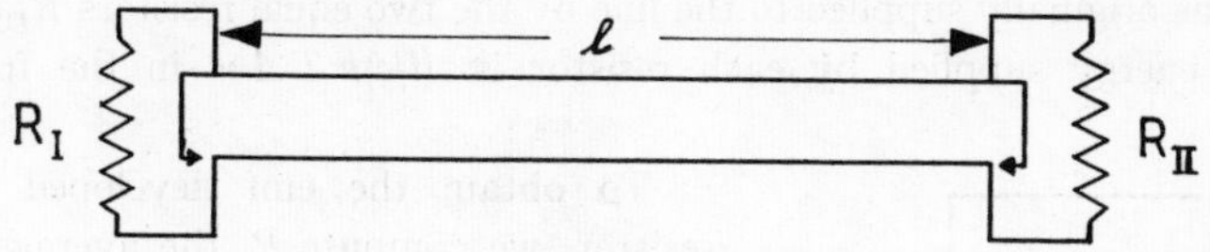

FIG. 11.1. A long cable of length l terminated by resistors R_I and R_{II}, and by switches for shorting out the resistors.

When equilibrium has been reached, we short circuit both ends of the line, and, since we must maintain thermal equilibrium, the signals which are in the line are no longer being absorbed (nor are any emitted), but simply are reflected from both ends of the line. The equilibrium condition of the short circuited line, then, is the one in which the signals which are present set up standing waves, with a node at each short circuited end (Fig. 11.2). These are the "proper" frequencies which can exist on the transmission line and are determined by

$$\frac{n\,\lambda}{2} = l, \qquad (11.13)$$

where each n represents a proper frequency and hence a degree of freedom for the transmission line.

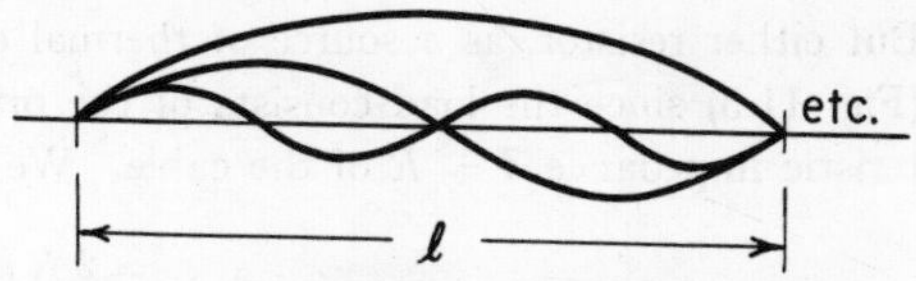

FIG. 11.2. Standing waves in the line with the resistors shorted out.

Since the line may be thought of as a harmonic oscillator for each proper frequency, the average energy for each proper frequency (degree of freedom) must be the sum of the potential energy and kinetic energy, each of which is $(\frac{1}{2})\,k\,T$. Therefore the average energy per degree of freedom is $k\,T$.

To get the energy in the line in a frequency interval $\Delta\,\nu$, we must compute the corresponding number of degrees of freedom, $\Delta\,n$. Thus, from (11.13)

$$n = \frac{2\,l}{\lambda} = 2\,l\,\frac{\nu}{c}, \qquad (11.14)$$

since $\lambda = c/\nu$ where c is the velocity of the wave. Therefore

$$\Delta n = \frac{2l}{c} \Delta \nu \tag{11.15}$$

is the number of degrees of freedom in the frequency interval $\Delta \nu$. The total average energy in $\Delta \nu$, in the short-circuited cable, is

$$\overline{E}_{\text{tot}} = \Delta n \, k \, T = \frac{2l}{c} \Delta \nu \, k \, T, \tag{11.16}$$

and this was originally supplied to the line by the two equal resistors R_I and R_{II}. The total energy supplied by each resistor is $(l/c) k \, T \, \Delta \nu$ in the frequency range $\Delta \nu$.

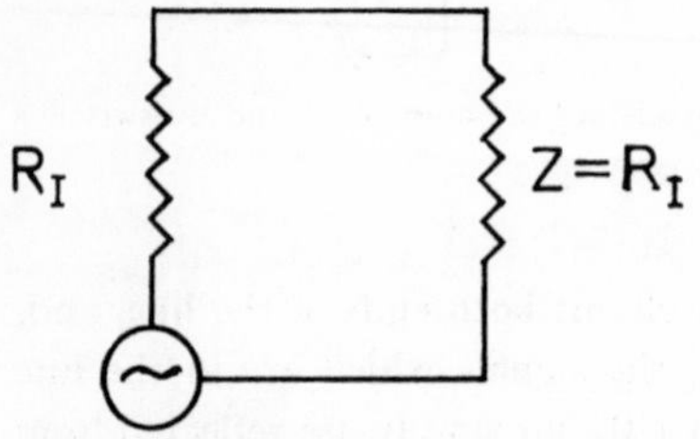

FIG. 11.3. The resistor R_I with the rest of the line replaced by its characteristic impedance $Z = R_I$.

To obtain the emf developed in each resistor, we compute P, the average power, which is the energy per unit time:

$$\overline{P} = \frac{(l/c) \, k \, T \, \Delta \nu}{(l/c)},$$

since l/c is the time required for the signal to travel from R_I to R_{II}. The average power developed in each resistor and sent into the cable is thus

$$\overline{P} = k \, T \, \Delta \nu. \tag{11.17}$$

But either resistor, as a source of thermal emf, drives a load consisting of $2 \, R$ (Fig. 11.3) since the load consists of the original resistance R plus the characteristic impedance $Z = R$ of the cable. We thus have

$$e_\nu = 2 \, R \, i_\nu,$$

and the power developed in Z is

$$\overline{P} = R \, \overline{i_\nu^2} = \frac{\overline{e_\nu^2}}{4 \, R}; \tag{11.18}$$

hence, according to (11.17):

$$\frac{\overline{e_\nu^2}}{4 \, R} = k \, T \, \Delta \nu, \tag{11.19}$$

or

$$\overline{e^2} = 4 \, k \, T \, R \, \Delta \nu, \tag{11.20}$$

which is what we derived previously.

3. Discussion and Applications

As a check on our derivation, we can apply it to a series $L\,R\,C$ circuit, and compute the average of the square of the random current due to thermal emf's. The circuit is shown in Fig. 11.4. The thermal emf is given by Eq. (11.20) or (11.12), and therefore

$$\overline{i_\nu^2} = \frac{\overline{e_\nu^2}}{|Z|^2} = \frac{\overline{e_\nu^2}}{R^2 + \left(L\,\omega - \dfrac{1}{\omega\,C}\right)^2}, \qquad \omega = 2\pi\,\nu. \tag{11.21}$$

If we set

$$\omega_0 = 2\pi\,\nu_0 = 1/\sqrt{L\,C}, \tag{11.22}$$

and use Eq. (11.20), then Eq. (11.21) becomes

$$\overline{i_\nu^2} = \frac{4\,R\,k\,T\,\Delta\,\nu}{R^2 + L^2\left(\omega - \dfrac{\omega_0^2}{\omega}\right)^2}. \tag{11.23}$$

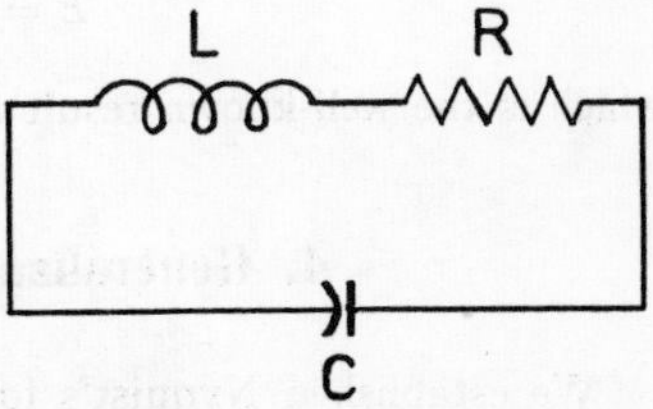

FIG. 11.4. A resistance R, an inductance L, and a capacitance C in series form a harmonic oscillator. Noise is generated in the resistance.

We define a Q_0 factor for the circuit

$$Q_0 = \frac{\omega_0\,L}{R}, \tag{11.24}$$

and obtain

$$\overline{i_\nu^2} = \frac{2}{\pi}\,\frac{k\,T}{L}\,\frac{Q_0}{\omega_0}\,\frac{\Delta\,\omega}{1 + \dfrac{Q_0^2}{\omega_0^2}\left(\omega - \dfrac{\omega_0^2}{\omega}\right)^2}. \tag{11.25}$$

The kinetic energy in the circuit at some frequency ν is

$$\overline{E_{k\nu}} = \tfrac{1}{2}\,L\,\overline{i_\nu^2}, \tag{11.26}$$

and therefore the total kinetic energy must be obtained by summing over all frequencies from $\nu = 0$ to $\nu = \infty$, and the sum may be replaced by an integral:

$$\overline{E}_{\text{kin}} = \sum \overline{E_{k\nu}} = \sum \tfrac{1}{2}\,L\,\overline{i_\nu^2} = \frac{k\,T}{\pi}\,\frac{Q_0}{\omega_0}\int_0^\infty \frac{d\omega}{1 + \dfrac{Q_0^2}{\omega_0^2}\left(\omega - \dfrac{\omega_0^2}{\omega}\right)^2}. \tag{11.27}$$

The integral in equation (11.27) is not too hard to evaluate, and it can be shown[3] that

$$\frac{Q_0}{\omega_0}\int_0^\infty \frac{d\omega}{1+\dfrac{Q_0^2}{\omega_0^2}\left(\omega-\dfrac{\omega_0^2}{\omega}\right)^2}=\frac{\pi}{2}, \tag{11.28}$$

and the total (average) kinetic energy is

$$\overline{E}_{\text{kin}} = \tfrac{1}{2}\, k\, T. \tag{11.29}$$

There is an equal amount $\frac{1}{2}\, k\, T$ for the average potential energy, represented by charges on the condenser, and we finally have, for the total average energy

$$\overline{E} = \overline{E}_{\text{kin}} + \overline{E}_{\text{pot}} = k\, T, \tag{11.30}$$

which is the well-known result for a low-frequency harmonic oscillator.

4. Generalizations of Nyquist's Formula

We established Nyquist's formula for the case of an electric circuit with a resistance R. Noise is generated in the resistance only, where there is a coupling between electric current and thermal agitation in the conductive material. Self inductances and capacities do not introduce any such coupling and give no additional noise terms. In an impedance

$$Z = R + i\, X, \tag{11.31}$$

only the R term contributes to noise.

Instead of an electrical problem, we might discuss a mechanical system with viscous damping. We used the similarity of mechanical and electrical vibrations in Chapter 10, Section 5. It applies just as well for Nyquist's formula. Summarizing the results of Chapter 10 [Eqs. (10.18), (10.25), (10.30), (10.33), and

[3] Putting $\omega = \omega_0\, s$ and splitting the integral in two parts, 0 to 1 and 1 to ∞, we have

$$Q_0\int_0^1 \frac{ds}{1+Q_0^2(s-1/s)^2} + Q_0\int_1^\infty \frac{ds}{1+Q_0^2(s-1/s)^2} = Q_0\int_1^\infty \frac{ds/s^2+ds}{1+Q_0^2(s-1/s)^2}$$

$$= Q_0\int_0^\infty \frac{dx}{1+Q_0^2\, x^2} = \frac{\pi}{2},$$

with $x = s - 1/s$, the limits of which are 0 (for $s = 1$) and ∞ (for $s = \infty$).

(10.34)], and of this chapter, we may state some general results on the noise in any system possessing a damping term R:

$$\overline{X^2} = 2\,R\,k\,T\,t, \tag{11.32}$$

where X is the impulse of the force during a time t;

$$\overline{x^2} = \frac{2\,k\,T}{R}\,t, \tag{11.33}$$

where x is the displacement for a free Brownian motion during a time t;

$$\overline{E}_{\text{kin}} = \tfrac{1}{2}\,k\,T \tag{11.34}$$

is the average kinetic energy per degree of freedom; and

$$\overline{f^2} = 4\,R\,k\,T\,\Delta\,\nu \tag{11.35}$$

is the average square of the forces with frequencies between ν and $\nu + \Delta\,\nu$.

All these results apply in a very general way for low frequencies. Mrs. de Haas-Lorentz discussed a great variety of examples of applications of formulas (11.32), (11.33), and (11.34).[4] The problem of extending Eq. (11.35) to a number of nonelectrical problems was very carefully investigated by Callen,[5] who proved the complete generality of the formula, and discussed the case of problems with different types of constraints. These results represent important applications of thermodynamics applied to irreversible processes.[6]

When frequencies are too high, the situation becomes progressively different. First, one must realize that many new degrees of freedom may begin to play a role. For instance, in an electrical circuit, higher modes based on distributed capacity and self-inductance will appear and be excited by thermal agitation. In a mechanical system, transverse vibrations of different kinds will also be excited. Furthermore, we have the quantum limitations. Our preceeding theory can be used only for low frequencies

$$h\,\nu \ll k\,T, \quad \text{where } h \text{ is Planck's constant.} \tag{11.36}$$

---

[4] H. A. Lorentz, "Les théories statistiques en thermodynamique," Teubner, Leipzig, 1916; G. L. de Haas-Lorentz, "Die Brownsche Bewegung." Vieweg, Braunschweig, 1931.

[5] H. B. Callen, Ph. D. thesis, M. I. T., 1948; R. F. Greene and H. B. Callen, *Phys. Rev.* **83**, 1231 (1951); H. B. Callen and T. A. Welton, *ibid.* **83**, 34 (1951); H. B. Callen and R. F. Greene, *ibid.* **86**, 702 (1952).

[6] L. Onsager, *Phys. Rev.* **37**, 405 (1931); **38**, 2265 (1931); H. B. G. Casimir, *Revs. Modern Phys.* **17**, 343 (1945); S. R. DeGroot, "Thermodynamics of Irreversible Processes." North Holland, Amsterdam, 1951.

For higher frequencies, it is well-known that formula (11.34), for instance, does not apply any more. The average energy of an oscillator ν, is

$$\overline{E}(\nu) = \frac{h\,\nu}{e^{\frac{h\nu}{kT}} - 1}, \tag{11.37}$$

instead of $k\,T$. Similar corrections should be introduced in the other formulas.

The physical background of the situation is clear: a viscous resistance indicates a coupling between a certain motion and thermal agitation. This coupling results in damping out the motion and changing its high-grade energy into low-grade heat. But this transfer of energy cannot go on forever, since it would bring the system completely to rest, and we know that the system must exhibit some sort of Brownian motion at temperature T. Hence the same coupling mechanism which provokes damping must also create random forces acting on the system and maintaining it in thermal agitation. This is the origin of our formulas (11.32) or (11.35). The explanation in the case of the Brownian motion of a particle in water is very simple: collisions of the particle with water molecules result in viscous damping. Random collisions of water molecules with the particle yield the random forces keeping the particle in thermal agitation. The situation is similar in all other examples that can be thought of.

5. Thermal Agitation in a Rectifier[7]

Suppose that a rectifier is in series with a resistance R and a reactance X, as shown in Fig. 11.5. The resistances in the circuit (the resistance R as well as any resistance in the rectifier) will give rise to random emf's due to thermal agitation. The rectifier cannot rectify the random currents induced by these emf's because a rectified current could be used to do work in contradiction to the second law of thermodynamics.

The characteristic curve of the rectifier is shown in Fig. 11.6 and, since it rises more sharply to the right of the origin than to the left, we may conclude that the fluctuations on the left must be greater than on the right. Otherwise the time average of the currents would not be zero, and there would be a rectified current. There may, however, be a rectified voltage, and this is what we wish to compute.

To do this, we write for the random emf (generated in R and r, the resistance of the rectifier) at any instant:

$$\phi = \phi_0 + \sum_{\nu} \phi_\nu, \tag{11.38}$$

[7] L. Brillouin, *Phys. Rev.* 78, 627 (1950).

where the ϕ_ν are the complex exponential terms in the Fourier analysis of the emf. Because the ϕ_ν are complex exponentials, we have the average

$$\overline{\phi_\nu} = 0 \tag{11.39}$$

for all ν, and

$$\overline{\phi} = \phi_0. \tag{11.40}$$

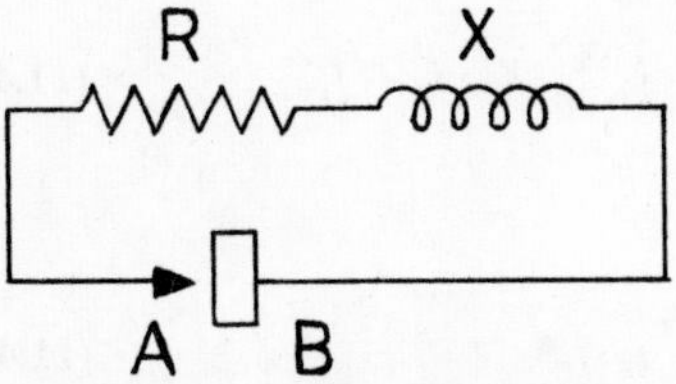

FIG. 11.5. A resistance R, a reactance X, and a rectifier AB in series. Noise is generated in the resistance. There is a rectified emf, but no rectified current.

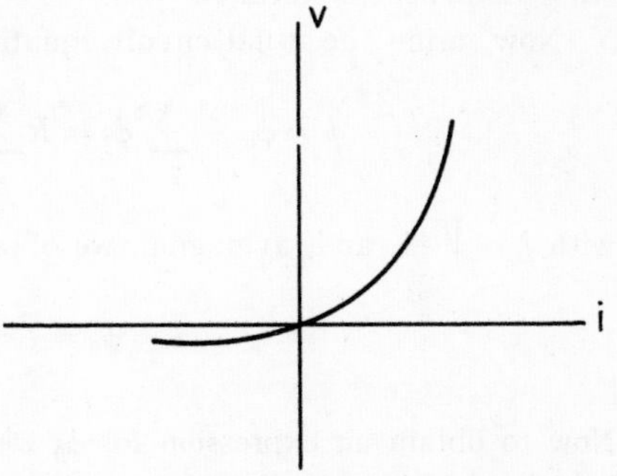

FIG. 11.6. The voltage-current characteristic of a rectifier.

If the rectifier were missing from the circuit, we would have $\phi_0 = 0$. What we wish to compute is ϕ_0, the average constant term due to the rectifier.

The thermal emf's give rise to random currents which we may also expand in a Fourier series:

$$i = \sum_\nu i_\nu. \tag{11.41}$$

There is no i_0 term in this expansion because there can be no rectified current. As before, the i_ν terms are complex exponentials whose averages are zero, so that we have

$$\overline{i_\nu} = 0 \quad \text{for all } \nu, \quad \text{and hence} \quad \overline{i} = 0. \tag{11.42}$$

The potential drop across the rectifier will be given by

$$\begin{aligned} V_A - V_B &= f = r\,i + b \cdot i \cdot i^* \\ &= r \sum_\nu i_\nu + b\left[\sum_\nu i_\nu \cdot i_\nu^* + \sum_\nu \sum_{\mu \neq \nu} i_\nu \cdot i_\mu^*\right], \end{aligned} \tag{11.43}$$

since the random currents are very small so that the rectifier is operated on the portion of its characteristic curve close to the origin, and this portion may be approximated by a parabola. Taking an average, we obtain

$$\overline{f} = b \sum_{\nu} i_\nu \cdot i_\nu^*; \tag{11.44}$$

the cross product terms average to zero, since they, too, are complex exponentials whose exponent is not zero.

Now, using the usual circuit equation, we have

$$\phi = \phi_0 + \sum_{\nu} \phi_\nu = R \sum_{\nu} i_\nu + j \sum_{\nu} X_\nu \cdot i_\nu + f, \tag{11.45}$$

with $j = \sqrt{-1}$, and, averaging, we obtain

$$\overline{\phi} = \phi_0 = \overline{f} = b \sum_{\nu} i_\nu \cdot i_\nu^*. \tag{11.46}$$

Now to obtain an expression for ϕ_0 we use Eq. (11.45) again, and match like exponential terms:

$$\phi_\nu = (R + r + j X_\nu)\, i_\nu. \tag{11.47}$$

The $r\, i_\nu$ term is contributed by f [Eq. (11.43)]. The cross product terms (also contributed by f) $i_\nu \cdot i_\mu^*$ $(\mu \neq \nu)$ are neglected in comparison with the i_ν terms since they are quadratic in the currents, which are small. From Eq. (11.47), we obtain

$$\overline{i_\nu\, i_\nu^*} = \frac{\overline{\phi_\nu \phi_\nu^*}}{(R + r)^2 + X_\nu^2}. \tag{11.48}$$

We can now use Eq. (11.20) to obtain $\overline{\phi_\nu \phi_\nu^*}$ since only the resistances in the circuit give rise to random emf's:

$$\overline{\phi_\nu \phi_\nu^*} = 4(R + r)\, k\, T\, \Delta\, \nu, \tag{11.49}$$

so that, finally, we have

$$\phi_0 = 4\, k\, T(R + r) \sum_{\nu} \frac{\Delta\, \nu}{(R + r)^2 + X_\nu^2} \tag{11.50}$$

for the rectified emf due to the rectifier. If we replace the sum by an integral and assume an inductive reactance, for which $X = 2\pi\, L\, \nu$, we easily obtain

$$\phi_0 = b\, k\, T / L. \tag{11.51}$$

To conclude, we recall that there is no rectified current, and note that the rectified voltage is just equal to the potential drop across the rectifier, so that no work can be done by the circuit. Application of the formula to special examples always shows such a complete compensation of the direct average voltage. The whole procedure is an example of the general method of detailed balancing discussed by Bridgman.[8]

---

[8] P. W. Bridgman, *Phys. Rev.* **31, 101 (1928).**

CHAPTER 12

THE NEGENTROPY PRINCIPLE OF INFORMATION

1. The Relation between Information and Entropy

A quantitative definition of information, based on statistical considerations, was given in Chapter 1. We considered a situation in which there were P_0 different possible cases or events of equal *a priori* probability. Information I_1 is required to reduce the number of possible cases to P_1, and the logarithm of the ratio P_0/P_1 measures I_1 [Eq. (1.6)]:

$$\begin{aligned} &\text{Initially:} \quad I_0 = 0, \qquad P_0 \text{ possibilities,} \\ &\text{Finally:} \quad I_1 > 0, \qquad P_1 \text{ possibilities,} \\ &\qquad\qquad \text{with } I_1 = K \ln(P_0/P_1). \end{aligned} \tag{12.1}$$

In thermodynamical units $K = k =$ Boltzmann's constant.

We now wish to distinguish between two classes of information:

1. Free information I_f, which occurs when the possible cases are regarded as abstract and have no specified physical significance.

2. Bound information I_b, which occurs when the possible cases can be interpreted as complexions of a physical system. Bound information is thus a special case of free information.

The reason for making this distinction is that we are now ready to discuss the relation between information and entropy (and its negative, negentropy), and we prefer to use the term entropy only in the usual thermodynamical sense. Thus only information connected with certain specific physical problems, that is bound information, will be thought of as related to entropy.

To obtain the relation between bound information and entropy, then, we consider the equally probable cases to be the "complexions" used by Planck. Then

	Bound information	Number of complexions	Entropy	
Initially:	$I_{b0} = 0,$	$P_0,$	$S_0 = k \ln P_0;$	(12.2)
Finally:	$I_{b1} \neq 0,$	$P_1 < P_0,$	$S_1 = k \ln P_1.$	

Evidently, in this scheme, the system is not isolated: the entropy is decreased when information is obtained, reducing the number of complexions, and this information must be furnished by some external agent whose entropy will increase. The relation between the decrease in entropy of our system and the required information is obvious, for, by Eq. (12.1)

$$I_{b1} = k(\ln P_0 - \ln P_1) = S_0 - S_1, \tag{12.3}$$

or

$$S_1 = S_0 - I_{b1}. \tag{12.3 a}$$

The bound information appears as a negative term in the total entropy of the physical system, and we conclude

$$\begin{aligned} \text{bound information} &= \text{decrease in entropy } S \\ &= \text{increase in negentropy } N, \end{aligned} \tag{12.4}$$

where we define negentropy as the negative of entropy. This statement represents the "negentropy principle of information." We shall discuss this relation for a variety of examples, and show how information can be changed into negentropy and vice versa.

In the case of free information, we prefer not to think of a connection between information and entropy, since the relation between entropy and the number of cases is defined only if the cases are complexions of a physical system.

2. The Negentropy Principle of Information; Generalization of Carnot's Principle

In the situation described by Eq. (12.2), we have decreased the entropy of the system by means of some external agent. If we now isolate the system, Carnot's principle states that in any further normal evolution of the system

$$\Delta S_1 \geqslant 0, \quad \text{or} \quad \Delta(S_0 - I_{b1}) \geqslant 0. \tag{12.5}$$

The increase in entropy may be either in S_0 or in $-I_{b1}$ or in both. When the system is isolated and abandoned to itself, it naturally evolves towards the average structure of greatest probability, according to its physical condition, which is defined by some fixed values given to some macroscopic parameters (volume, energy, chemical structure, etc.). The system may have been overdetermined even in its "initial" condition, corresponding to an entropy S_0. The additional information I_{b1} required in the formulas (12.2) and (12.3) certainly corresponds to an increased overdetermination. We may have specified many microscopic parameters, the evolution of which cannot be followed in detail. For instance, we may build up the system with certain given quantities of chemical compounds, but later these chemicals may react, and the chemical composition of the system may vary in the course of time, and we are unable to observe this detailed composition. These overspecifications of the structure may be contained either in the S_0 term or in the $-I_{b1}$ term, and the over-all increase in entropy may be difficult to split between these two terms.

An interesting case is obtained when S_0 corresponds to the general structure after free evolution of the isolated system, so that there is no overdetermination in S_0. In such a problem S_0 remains a constant, and Eq. (12.5) reduces to

$$\Delta I_{b1} \leqslant 0, \tag{12.5 a}$$

and

$$N = -S, \qquad \Delta N_1 \leqslant 0, \qquad \Delta(N_0 + I_{b1}) \leqslant 0, \tag{12.6}$$

or $\Delta I_{b1} \leqslant 0$ if there is no overdetermination in the initial state. Using negentropy as a measure of the grade of energy (Chapter 9, Section 2), we obtain Kelvin's principle of the degradation of energy, expressed symbolically in Eq. (12.6). Equality is obtained for reversible transformations, while irreversible transformations yield the inequalities.

The fact that $\Delta I_{b1} \leqslant 0$ [in Eq. (12.5 a)] is in agreement with earlier results on free information that

$$\Delta I_f \leqslant 0, \tag{12.7}$$

obtained when we showed that information (free, since the symbols were abstract, and were not thought of as the complexions of a physical system) was a maximum for equally probable cases.

Section 3 of this chapter will be devoted to a discussion of various examples showing that either class of information can be changed into negentropy, and that information, whether bound or free, can be obtained only at the expense of the negentropy of some physical system. We may thus rewrite Eq. (12.4) as a reversible reaction:

$$I \rightleftarrows N. \tag{12.8}$$

Such a statement implies a generalization of Carnot's principle,[1] if we include both classes of information. For if

$$\Delta I_f \leqslant 0, \qquad \Delta N_1 \leqslant 0,$$

then

$$\Delta N_1 + \Delta I_f \leqslant 0,$$

or

$$\Delta(S_1 - I_f) = \Delta(S_0 - I_{b1} - I_f) = \Delta(S_0 - I) \geqslant 0 \tag{12.9}$$

in a problem which contains free information as well as bound information. In terms of negentropy, we have a degradation principle

$$\Delta(N_0 + I) \leqslant 0. \tag{12.10}$$

[1] L. Brillouin, *J. Appl. Phys.* **24**, 1152 (1953).

The quantity N_0 is now the negentropy of some physical system. The information term contains both bound information, which may produce an increase in N_0 [in the example described by Eq. (12.2), I_{b1} increased N_0 to N_1], as well as free information. The sum of negentropy and information may remain constant in a reversible transformation, and will decrease otherwise. These inequalities apply only to average values. In all applications of Carnot's principle, the possibility of the occurrence of random fluctuations is present.

Let us give an example showing how both bound and free information may enter into a problem. We start with an individual in possession of information, which will be free as long as it remains in his mind and is, thus, not directly connected with any physical system. We follow the losses in this information as it is transmitted to a second individual, and at each step we state whether the loss is of free or of bound information:

A. An individual possesses information which is free.

B. He tells a friend about it in English, say, and the information is now bound: it has been transformed into sound waves, or electric pulses, or some other physical disturbance which may be used for communication. There may be errors in the coding for transmission. This will be a loss of free information, since it occurs before the transformation into a physical disturbance.

C. Due to distortion and thermal noise in the communication system, some of the information may be lost. This is a loss of bound information.

D. The friend is hard of hearing, so that he misses a few words. The loss here is of bound information, but the information received by the friend is now free since it is in his mind.

E. After a while the friend forgets some of the information, and this loss, too, is a loss of free information.

At each step there is a loss of information, the most favorable case being a possibility of no loss. This is the sort of situation which might arise when a stock exchange broker gives, over the telephone, information on stock market quotations.

It should be noted that the losses in steps *B*, *D*, and *E* are borderline cases. Sometimes it is difficult to distinguish between free and bound information, particularly in cases involving a human observer. We must, of course, ignore any element of human value. For example, we exclude the case of a scientist collecting data and then discovering a scientific law as a result of study of the data. Our definitions do not apply to such a problem. It is only by excluding the process of thought that we have been able to develop a satisfactory theory of information. We may, of course, hope that we may later find it possible to extend the theory to include the analysis and discussion of such problems.

Returning to Eqs. (12.6) and (12.10), we may summarize the interrelation between thermodynamics and information theory in the following way:

Negentropy N corresponds to information I.
Temperature T means thermal noise perturbing the transmission of information.
Energy retains its usual meaning.
$\Delta Q = T \Delta S$ gives the heat involved in a certain process.
$\Delta W = T \Delta N = T \Delta I$ corresponds to the mechanical work available.
(12.11)

At high temperature T the noise is higher and the amount of work required for the transmission of certain information is larger, in order to overcome the background noise.

3. Some Typical Physical Examples

We now want to discuss some classical problems of physics, and to show where bound information arises, and the role that it plays. This will be an opportunity for examining some old discussions on the meaning of entropy, and for clarifying a few difficult points.

We consider the case of a ideal monatomic gas in a container of volume V thermally isolated from its surroundings. When steady conditions have been reached, the entropy is:[2]

$$S = k\,n\left[\frac{5}{2} + \ln\left(g\frac{V}{n}\left\{\frac{4\pi\,m\,E}{3\,h^2\,n}\right\}^{3/2}\right)\right], \tag{12.12}$$

where n = number of atoms in the gas, m = mass of an atom, k, h = Boltzmann's and Planck's constants, respectively, E = total energy, and g = number of indistinguishable states on the ground level of the atom.

If the ground state is not degenerate, $g = 1$. This is the case of an atom with no moment of momentum in the ground state ($j = 0$). If there is a moment of momentum j (spin plus orbit), there are $g_j = 2j + 1$ states, which are supposed to be equally probable. The ground state is assumed to be low enough, and the temperature not too high, so that excitation to upper energy levels cannot take place.

The theoretical formula checks very well with experimental data, but many theoretical terms, which are absolutely needed for consistency, are really too

---

[2] See for instance J. E. Mayer and M. G. Mayer, "Statistical Mechanics," p. 115, Eq. (5.19), also pp. 132–140 and 209. Wiley, New York, 1940.

small to be observed in most thermodynamical experiments;[3] let us rewrite Eq. (12.12) in the following ways:

$$\left.\begin{array}{lll} \text{for } g=1: & \text{no degeneracy, } j=0, & S_1, \\ \text{for } g=2: & j=\tfrac{1}{2}, & S_2 = S_1 + k\,n \ln 2, \\ \text{for } g=3: & j=1, & S_3 = S_1 + k\,n \ln 3. \end{array}\right\} \quad (12.13)$$

The case $g = 2$ corresponds to atoms with spin $\frac{1}{2}$ and two orientations $(\pm \frac{1}{2})$. For $g = 3$ we have $j = 1$ and 3 orientations $(-1, 0, +1)$. All orientations are equally probable when the external field is zero; a small external field would split the energy levels and remove the degeneracy.

The differences between S_1, S_2, and S_3 are very small, and furthermore they cannot be directly observed, since we have no way of changing the j value of a given atom. In radioactive transformations, however, we may observe an atom of mass m and spin j disintegrating into another one of mass m' and spin j', in which case these terms would have a physical meaning.

This discussion shows that we should be careful to speak of entropy differences ΔS only if the transformation is physically possible. Otherwise it has no practical meaning. Let us suppose that we have additional information on the state of the gas: for instance, we may happen to know that the gas, at a certain earlier instant of time, occupied a smaller volume V'. This is the case if the gas is in a container V' and we suddenly open the connection with another volume V'':

$$V = V' + V'', \qquad V' < V.$$

The initial entropy S' is smaller than the entropy S after expansion by an amount given by Eq. (12.12):

$$S - S' = k\,n\,(\ln V - \ln V') = I, \tag{12.14}$$

and I measures the information. After we open the volume V'', the gas flows in, density oscillations take place between the two volumes, and the steady state is progressively established with a uniform density throughout the volume V. Increase of entropy and loss of information proceed together. We may say that the gas progressively "forgets" the information.[4]

---

[3] O. Stern, *Revs. Modern Phys.* **21**, 534 (1949); E. Schrödinger, *Proc. Roy. Irish Acad.* **53** A, 189 (1950); K. Darrow, *Bell System Tech. J.* **21**, 51 (1942); **22**, 108 (1943).

[4] J. von Neumann also considers the case of the observer forgetting the information, and states that this process also means an increase of entropy. Here, again, we see the impossibility of always distinguishing clearly between free and bound information. This emphasizes the need for a generalized Carnot principle, as stated in Section 2. For further discussion of this point see J. von Neumann, "Mathematische Grundlagen der Quanten-Mechanik." Springer, Berlin, 1932; also P. Jordan, *Philosophy of Sci.* **16**, 269 (1949).

As another example, let us consider a case of gas *diffusion*. In order to reduce the problem to its essential points, we assume: Two gases, with atoms having the same mass m, and $g = 1$, n_1 atoms of type 1 initially occupy a volume V_1, n_2 atoms of type 2 occupy a volume V_2,

$$n_1 + n_2 = n, \qquad V_1 + V_2 = V, \tag{12.15}$$
$$n_1 = p_1 n, \qquad n_2 = p_2 n, \qquad V_1 = p_1 V, \qquad V_2 = p_2 V, \qquad p_1 + p_2 = 1.$$

The relations (12.15) imply that the initial concentrations of the two constituents and the final concentration are all equal:

$$V_1/n_1 = V_2/n_2 = V/n.$$

Furthermore, we assume equipartition of energy:

$$E_1/n_1 = E_2/n_2 = E/n, \tag{12.16}$$

and all of these conditions together imply that there is no initial pressure or temperature difference between the two gases.

Let us set the bracket in Eq. (12.12) equal to Q:

$$Q = [(4\pi\, m\, E)/(3\, h^2\, n)]^{3/2}.$$

Our assumptions make it clear that Q has the same value for both gases, and retains the same value throughout the process of the mixing of the gases. Hence we have:
Before mixing

$$S_{12} = k(n_1 + n_2)\left[\frac{5}{2} + \ln\frac{V}{n} + \ln Q\right] = S. \tag{12.17}$$

After mixing

$$\begin{aligned} S_{12}' &= k\, n_1\left[\frac{5}{2} + \ln\frac{V}{n_1} + \ln Q\right] + k\, n_2\left[\frac{5}{2} + \ln\frac{V}{n_2} + \ln Q\right] \\ &= S_{12} + k\, n_1(\ln n - \ln n_1) + k\, n_2(\ln n - \ln n_2), \\ S_{12}' &= S_{12} - k\, n(p_1 \ln p_1 + p_2 \ln p_2). \end{aligned} \tag{12.18}$$

The irreversible increase in entropy is

$$\Delta S' = S_{12}' - S_{12} = -k\, n(p_1 \ln p_1 + p_2 \ln p_2) > 0. \tag{12.19}$$

This quantity is positive, since $p_1 < 1$ and $p_2 < 1$ make the logarithms negative. We had, in the initial situation, a certain information I (bound information) about the system

$$I = -k\, n(p_1 \ln p_1 + p_2 \ln p_2), \tag{12.20}$$

and this information was lost in the process of gas diffusion. We may compare Eq. (12.20) with the Shannon formula for information [Eq. (2.1)]. The gas in its state of final mixture corresponds to a situation with *a priori* probabilities p_1 and p_2 for two symbols. Each symbol is represented here by a certain type of atom. Selection of one particular combination of symbols yields information $-k(p_1 \ln p_1 + p_2 \ln p_2)$ per symbol (Shannon). Our initial state of the gas corresponds to selecting the atoms 1 and putting them in V_1, while atoms 2 are put in V_2. This requires information given by Eq. (12.20).

We may now consider a slightly different problem, and assume atoms with spin $\frac{1}{2}$, type 1 corresponding to the orientation $+\frac{1}{2}$, while type 2 means $-\frac{1}{2}$. Collisions will make transitions between the two kinds of atoms, and the final state will correspond to

$$p_1 = \tfrac{1}{2}, \qquad p_2 = \tfrac{1}{2}, \tag{12.21}$$

with entropy

$$S_{12}'' = S_{12} + k\,n \ln 2. \tag{12.22}$$

We again lose information and increase the entropy

$$\Delta S'' = S_{12}'' - S_{12}' = k\,n\,[\ln 2 + p_1 \ln p_1 + p_2 \ln p_2] > 0. \tag{12.23}$$

The final entropy S_{12}'' is equal to the entropy S_2 of Eq. (12.13) for a gas of spin $\frac{1}{2}$ with the two orientations equally probable. Our discussion clearly shows the need for the g term in the entropy formula, and explains its physical significance.

The increase in entropy corresponds to a loss of information, as in our previous examples. Let us compare our formula with the expressions obtained in Fig. 2.4. We found that the selection of one special distribution, out of a set with *a priori* probabilities p_1, p_2 gave an information

$$I_p = -K(p_1 \ln p_1 + p_2 \ln p_2) \tag{12.24}$$

per symbol. The maximum of this quantity is obtained for

$$p_1 = p_2 = \tfrac{1}{2}, \qquad I_{max} = k \ln 2. \tag{12.25}$$

If we now go from the p_1, p_2 case to the $\frac{1}{2}, \frac{1}{2}$ case, there is a net change

$$\Delta I = I_{max} - I_p = k\,[\ln 2 + p_1 \ln p_1 + p_2 \ln p_2] \tag{12.26}$$

per symbol. This is exactly the same formula as in Eq. (12.25).

4. Some General Remarks

From these few problems we may already draw some interesting conclusions.

Acquisition of information about a physical system corresponds to a lower state of entropy for this system. Low entropy implies an unstable situation that will sooner or later follow its normal evolution toward stability and high entropy.

The second principle does not tell us anything about the time required, and hence we do not know how long the system will remember the information. But, if classical thermodynamics fails to answer this very important question, we can obtain the answer from a discussion of the molecular or atomic model, with the help of kinetic theory: the rate of attenuation of all sorts of waves, the rate of diffusion, the speed of chemical reactions, etc., can be computed from suitable models, and may vary from small fractions of a second to years or centuries.

These delays are used in all practical applications: it does not take very long for a system of pulses (representing dots and dashes, for instance) to be attenuated and forgotten, when sent along an electric cable, but this short time interval is long enough for transmission even over a long distance, and makes telecommunications possible.

A system capable of retaining information for some time can be used as a memory device in a computing machine. The examples discussed in the preceding section are not only interesting from a theoretical point of view, but they also show how to attack a practical problem. Let us consider, for instance, the problems of diffusion and spin distribution [Eqs. (12.15)—(12.26)]. They are closely related to magnetic memory devices: spin is always associated with a magnetic moment. Hence a situation like the one described in Eq. (12.15) means that volume V' is magnetized to saturation in a certain direction, while volume V'' has the opposite magnetization. The information stored in this system corresponds to a decrease in entropy. Our discussion shows how this situation is progressively destroyed by diffusion and collisions that increase the entropy and erase the information.

Entropy is usually described as measuring the amount of disorder in a physical system. A more precise statement is that *entropy measures the lack of information* about the actual structure of the system. This lack of information introduces the possibility of a great variety of microscopically distinct structures, which we are, in practice, unable to distinguish from one another. Since any one of these different microstructures can actually be realized at any given time, the lack of information corresponds to actual disorder in the hidden degrees of freedom.

This picture is clearly illustrated in the case of the ideal gas. When we specify the total number n of atoms, their mass m, their degeneracy factor g, and the total energy E [see Eq. (12.12)], we do not state the positions and velocities of each individual atom. This is the lack of information leading to the entropy computed in Eq. (12.12). Since we do not specify the positions and velocities of the atoms, we are unable to distinguish between two different samples of the gas, when the difference consists only in different positions and velocities for the atoms. Hence we can describe the situation as one of disordered atomic motion.

The origin of our modern ideas about entropy and information can be found in an old paper by Szilard,[5] who did the pioneer work but was not well understood at the time. The connection between entropy and information was rediscovered by Shannon,[6] but he defined entropy with a sign just opposite to that of the standard thermodynamical definition. Hence what Shannon calls entropy of information actually represents negentropy. This can be seen clearly in two examples (pages 27 and 61 of Shannon's book) where Shannon proves that in some irreversible processes (an irreversible transducer or a filter) his entropy of information is decreased. To obtain agreement with our conventions, reverse the sign and read negentropy.

The connection between entropy and information has been clearly discussed in some recent papers by Rothstein[7] in complete agreement with the point of view presented in this chapter.

---

[5] L. Szilard, *Z. Physik* **53**, 840 (1929).

[6] C. E. Shannon and W. Weaver, "The Mathematical Theory of Information." U. of Illinois Press, Urbana Ill., 1949.

[7] J. Rothstein, *Science* **114**, 171 (1951); *Phys. Rev.* **85**, 135 (1952).

CHAPTER 13

MAXWELL'S DEMON AND THE NEGENTROPY PRINCIPLE OF INFORMATION

1. Maxwell's Demon: Historical Survey

The problem of Maxwell's demon provides an excellent example for the application of the theory of information, and clearly shows the connection between information and entropy.

The sorting demon was born in 1871 and first appeared in Maxwell's *Theory of Heat* (p. 328), as "a being whose faculties are so sharpened that he can follow every molecule in his course, and would be able to do what is at present impossible to us .... Let us suppose that a vessel is divided into two portions, A and B by a division in which there is a small hole, and that a being who *can see the individual molecules* opens and closes this hole, so as to allow only the swifter molecules to pass from A to B, and only the slower ones to pass from B to A. He will, thus, without expenditure of work raise the temperature of B and lower that of A, in contradiction to the second law of thermodynamics."[1]

The paradox was considered by generations of physicists. M. von Smoluchowski[2] first noticed the possible effect of Brownian agitation of the trap door, which would result in random opening or closing of the door and seriously perturb the operation. This would be of special importance in any automatic device, such as a spring valve, and would completely prevent any long range operation of such a system. Smoluchowski concluded that Brownian motions constitute only an apparent breakdown of the second principle, because of their random unpredictable nature and of the short duration of the motion. A permanent operation of any system is impossible, and the impossibility of a "perpetuum mobile" of the second kind is still certain: a system may move, but only irregularly and not in a systematic way.

The problem of the action of a spring valve is an interesting one: if it were not for its Brownian motion, the spring valve might produce a pressure difference between two connected vessels. The case is similar to the problem of the rectifier,

---

[1] The full passage is quoted by J. H. Jeans, "Dynamical Theory of Gases," 3rd ed., p. 183. Cambridge U. P., New York, 1921.

[2] M. von Smoluchowski, *Physik. Z.* **13**, 1069 (1912).

which we discussed at the end of Chapter 11. An ideal rectifier, acting on individual electrons, would rectify the thermal agitation of electrons, in contradiction with the second principle. But there is no ideal rectifier, and the only result to be expected is an assymetrical thermal agitation, as explained in Chapter 11.

A most important contribution was presented by Szilard[3] in a remarkable paper in which he first explained that the demon is acting on information on the detailed motion of the gas, and is actually changing information into negentropy. We shall discuss later some interesting questions raised by Szilard.

Lewis[4] discussed problems very similar to those investigated in the preceding chapter: gas separation and diffusion. He considered the entropy term connected with the mixture or separation of the gases, and reached conclusions similar to ours.

The question was raised by Slater[5] as to whether the uncertainty principle might play a role in the problem. Maxwell's demon has to measure, simultaneously, the position and velocity of a given atom. The two quantities cannot be measured simultaneously with infinite accuracy, because of the well known limitation:

$$\Delta p \cdot \Delta q \geqslant h, \qquad \text{where} \qquad p = mv. \tag{13.1}$$

This uncertainty may play a role for light atoms (small mass m) and high pressures, when the positions of the atoms should be determined with great accuracy. But the uncertainty limitation would not be of importance for heavy atoms and low pressures, as was shown by Demers.[6]

The essential question is much more fundamental, and was first raised by Demers[6] and Brillouin:[7] *Is it actually possible for the demon to see the individual atoms?* We assume that the whole system is isolated and initially at a given temperature T. The demon is in an enclosure in equilibrium at constant temperature, where the radiation must be black body radiation, and it is impossible to see anything in the interior of a black body. It would not help to raise the temperature. At "red" temperature, the radiation has its maximum in the red, and has exactly the same intensity whether there are no molecules or millions of them in the enclosure. Not only is the intensity the same, but also the fluctuations are the same. The demon would perceive thermal radiation and its fluctuations, but he would never see the molecules.

---

[3] L. Szilard, *Z. Physik* **53**, 840 (1929).

[4] G. N. Lewis, *Science* **71**, 569 (1930).

[5] J. C. Slater, "Introduction to Chemical Physics." McGraw-Hill, New York, 1939.

[6] P. Demers, *Can. J. Research* **22**, 27 (1944); **23**, 47 (1945).

[7] L. Brillouin, *Am. Scientist* **37**, 554, see p. 565 (1949); **38**, 594 (1950); also *J. Appl. Phys.* **22**, 334 (1951).

It is not surprising that Maxwell did not think of including radiation in the system in equilibrium at temperature T. Black body radiation was hardly known in 1871, and it was thirty years before the thermodynamics of radiation was clearly understood, and Planck's theory was developed.

The demon cannot see the molecules, hence he cannot operate the trap door and is unable to violate the second principle. The demon is unable to see the molecules, but he might try to detect them by some other method: he may measure the Van der Waals forces, or the fields due to electric dipoles or magnetic moments. Here the answer is different: all these fields are short distance fields, with intensities decreasing at least in r^{-2}, where r is the distance. The demon would thus detect molecules only when they are very close to the wall and to the trap door. This is too late to be able to operate the trap door without doing any work. The very forces on which the demon would rely, to detect the molecules, would also act on the trap door or on the valve. Work would thus be required to move the door and the problem would become much more involved. It is essential, in Maxwell's assumptions, that a molecule should be detected long before it reaches the wall, at such a distance that all short distance fields can still be safely neglected.

This can be done only with the help of some radiation, and the case of light is the simplest one for discussion.

2. The Demon Exorcised

Let us investigate the possibilities of the demon. We may equip him with an electric torch so that he can see the molecules. The torch is a source of radiation not in equilibrium. It pours negative entropy into the system. From this negative entropy the demon obtains information. Using this information, he operates the trap door, and rebuilds negative entropy, thus completing a cycle:

$$\text{negentropy} \rightarrow \text{information} \rightarrow \text{negentropy}. \qquad (13.2)$$

Demers[6] discussed the over-all procedure, without mentioning the intermediate step, in which the demon obtains the information to be used in the last operation. Demers proved for different examples that the loss in negentropy of the torch was larger than the final gain. In other words the initial increase in entropy is larger than the final decrease, and the over-all balance satisfies Carnot's principle.

Szilard had previously noticed the intermediate step with information. His discussion of the last process (transformation of information into negentropy) was very accurate, but he based the investigation of the first step on a rather artificial model.

Let us start with a crude discussion[7] which will illustrate the most important points. A more accurate investigation, using some results due to Jacobson,[8] will be given later.

In order to discuss an entropy balance, we have to define an isolated system, to which the second principle can safely be applied. Our system is composed of the following elements:

1. A charged battery and an electric bulb, representing the electric torch.
2. A gas at constant temperature T_0, contained in Maxwell's enclosure, with a partition dividing the vessel into two portions, and a hole in the partition.
3. The demon operating a trap door at the hole. The entire system is insulated and closed.[9]

The battery heats the filament to a high temperature T_1:

$$T_1 > T_0. \tag{13.3}$$

This condition is required, in order to obtain visible light

$$h\nu_1 > kT_0, \tag{13.4}$$

that can be distinguished from the background of black body radiation in the enclosure at temperature T_0.[10] During the experiment, the battery yields a total energy E and no entropy. The filament radiates energy E and loses entropy. The change in entropy of the filament is

$$S_f = -E/T_1 = \text{negentropy put into the gas.} \tag{13.5}$$

If the demon does not intervene, the energy E is absorbed in the gas at temperature T_0, and we observe an over-all increase of entropy:

$$S = (E/T_0) + S_f > 0. \tag{13.6}$$

Now let us investigate the work of the demon. He can detect a molecule when at least one quantum of energy $h\nu_1$ is scattered by the molecule and absorbed in his eye (or in a photoelectric cell, if he uses such a device). This represents a final increase of entropy

$$S_d = h\nu_1/T_0 = kb, \qquad \text{where} \qquad h\nu_1/kT_0 = b > 1, \tag{13.7}$$

according to condition (13.4).

[8] H. Jacobson, *Trans. N. Y. Acad. Sci.* **14**, 6 (1951).

[9] We may replace the demon by an automatic device with a "magic eye" which opens the trap door at convenient instants of time. This is a mere problem of designing some ingenious gadget, and it does not modify the general conditions of the problem.

[10] See Eq. (9.45). Condition (13.4) is required to make the average energy $\overline{E}$ of a quantized resonator ν_1 materially smaller than kT_0.

Once the information is obtained it can be used to decrease the entropy of the system. The entropy of the system is

$$S_0 = k \ln P_0, \tag{13.8}$$

according to Boltzmann's formula, where P_0 represents the total number of microscopic configurations (Planck's "complexions") of the system. After the information has been obtained, the system is more completely specified. P_0 is decreased by an amount p and

$$\begin{aligned} P_1 &= P_0 - p, \\ \varDelta S_i &= S - S_0 = k \varDelta (\ln P) = -k(p/P_0). \end{aligned} \tag{13.9}$$

It is obvious that $p \ll P_0$ in all practical cases. The total balance of entropy is

$$\varDelta S_d + \varDelta S_i = k[b - (p/P_0)] > 0, \tag{13.10}$$

since $b > 1$ and $p/P_0 < 1$. The final result is an increase in entropy in the isolated system, as required by the second principle. All the demon can do is to recover a small part of the negentropy and use the information to decrease the degradation of energy.

In the first part of the process [Eq. (13.7)], we have an increase of entropy $\varDelta S_d$, and hence a change $\varDelta N_d$ in the negentropy:

$$\varDelta N_d = -kb < 0, \quad \text{a decrease.} \tag{13.7 a}$$

From this lost negentropy, a certain amount is changed into information and, in the last step of the process [Eq. (13.9)], this information is changed into negentropy again:

$$\varDelta N_i = k(p/P_0) > 0, \text{ an increase.} \tag{13.9 a}$$

This justifies the general scheme (13.2).

3. Discussion

Let us discuss more specifically the original problem of Maxwell. We may assume that, after a certain time, the demon has been able to obtain a difference of temperature $\varDelta T$:

$$\begin{aligned} T_B &> T_A, & T_B &= T + \tfrac{1}{2}\varDelta T, \\ T_B - T_A &= \varDelta T, & T_A &= T - \tfrac{1}{2}\varDelta T. \end{aligned} \tag{13.11}$$

In the next step, the demon selects a fast molecule in A, with a kinetic energy of $3kT(1 + \varepsilon_1)/2$, and directs it into B. Then he selects a slow molecule in B, with kinetic energy $3kT(1 - \varepsilon_2)/2$, and lets it enter A. The demon requires two light quanta in order to observe these two molecules, and hence there is an increase in entropy similar to the one computed in Eq. (13.7):

$$\Delta S_d = 2\,k\,b \qquad \text{with} \qquad b = h\,\nu_1/k\,T > 1. \tag{13.12}$$

The exchange of molecules results in an energy transfer

$$\Delta Q = 3\,k\,T(\varepsilon_1 + \varepsilon_2)/2 \tag{13.13}$$

from A to B, which corresponds to a decrease of the total entropy because of Eq. (13.11):

$$\Delta S_i = \Delta Q\left(\frac{1}{T_B} - \frac{1}{T_A}\right) = -\Delta Q\frac{\Delta T}{T^2} = -\frac{3}{2}\,k\,(\varepsilon_1 + \varepsilon_2)\frac{\Delta T}{T}\cdot \tag{13.14}$$

The quantities ε_1 and ε_2 will usually be small but may exceptionally reach a value of a few units. ΔT is much smaller than T, hence,

$$\Delta S_i = -\frac{3}{2}k\,\eta, \qquad \eta \ll 1,$$

and

$$\Delta S_d + \Delta S_i = k\left(2\,b - \frac{3}{2}\eta\right) > 0. \tag{13.15}$$

Carnot's principle is actually satisfied.

Demers[6] discussed another instance assuming the demon to be in an enclosure at a lower temperature $T_2 \ll T_0$. An experimental set up can be imagined in which the demon could distinguish quanta $h\,\nu$ emitted by the molecules at temperature T_0. We then have a condition

$$h\,\nu > k\,T_2, \qquad T_2 < T_0, \tag{13.16}$$

instead of (13.4) and the discussion proceeds along similar lines.

Whether we use a higher temperature T_1 [Eq. (13.3)] or a lower temperature T_2 [Eq. (13.16)] we always need a temperature difference, otherwise the demon cannot operate. And if we have a temperature difference we do not need the help of a demon. Any thermal engine would do. For instance, if we want to create a temperature difference and if we use a bulb at T_1, the simplest way to do it is to let the radiation heat up one half of the gas, while the other one remains at T_0. This procedure would be much more efficient than the work of the demon!

Our first discussion is crude, because we introduced assumptions corresponding to "usual" conditions, namely: $p \ll P_0$ in Eq. (13.9) or $\Delta T \ll T$ in Eq. (13.11). We shall investigate the problem more carefully in the next section and prove that Carnot's principle is always satisfied, even in very exceptional situations.

We have, nevertheless, discovered a very important physical law in Eq. (13.10): every physical measurement requires a corresponding entropy increase, and there is a lower limit, below which the measurement becomes impossible. This limit corresponds to a change in entropy of the order of k, Boltzmann's constant. A more accurate discussion will prove later that the exact limit is $k \ln 2$, or approximately 0.7 k for one bit of information obtained. As Gabor states it:[11] "We cannot get anything for nothing, not even an observation." This very important law is a direct result of our general principle of the negentropy of information, and will be discussed later. It is very surprising that such a general result escaped attention until very recently.

A general feature of all this discussion is that the quantum conditions were used in the reasoning, but Planck's constant h is eliminated in the final results, which depend only on Boltzmann's constant k. This proves that the results are independent of quanta and of the uncertainty principle, and, in fact, a discussion can be given along classical lines without the introduction of quantum conditions.

4. The Demon's Operation as a Transformation of Information into Negative Entropy

The general problem is of such importance that it requires a closer and more detailed investigation. The discussion was indicated by Jacobson[8] and will be completed in this section. First we want to choose an example that is simpler than the original one invented by Maxwell. Instead of the "temperature demon," we shall consider a "pressure demon." By operating the trap door, this demon lets atoms go from B to C, and prevents atoms in C from escaping back into B. After a while he will obtain a higher pressure in C and a lower pressure in B. The operation is simpler to discuss, and the pressure demon does not require an accurate measurement of velocity, so that we need not consider the uncertainty relation. In order to eliminate unessential parameters, we shall specify the experimental conditions indicated in Fig. 13.1. Between the containers B and C we use a pipe of cross sectional area A equal to the area of the hole and of the trap door. A beam of light from an outside source passes through glass windows, and the scattered light is used to detect the atoms. This detection must be done at some distance x before the trap door, and the velocity of the atoms must be known, at least approximately, in order to determine the time at which to open the door. For example, we might use a system of revolving shutters that would let atoms pass if they have the average velocity, to a reasonable approximation, and would reflect back all atoms with a different speed.

---

[11] D. Gabor, M. I. T. Lectures, 1951.

In such a device we would obtain a good definition of the area A and an approximate definition of the velocities of striking atoms.

We must now define the amount of information needed by the demon for efficient operation. Let us consider a long time interval t that we subdivide into small intervals τ. The demon must know whether to open the door during τ, or to keep it closed. For each interval τ the information required is: Is there one (or more) particle going to hit the trap door of area A from the left? This is a typical "yes" or "no" question. We have an *a priori* probability p_1 for "yes," and p_2 for "no." During a long interval t, we shall have, on the average, N_1 openings of the door, and N_2 intervals with the door closed. We may write

$$t = G\tau, \qquad N_1 = G p_1, \qquad N_2 = G p_2, \qquad p_1 + p_2 = 1. \tag{13.17}$$

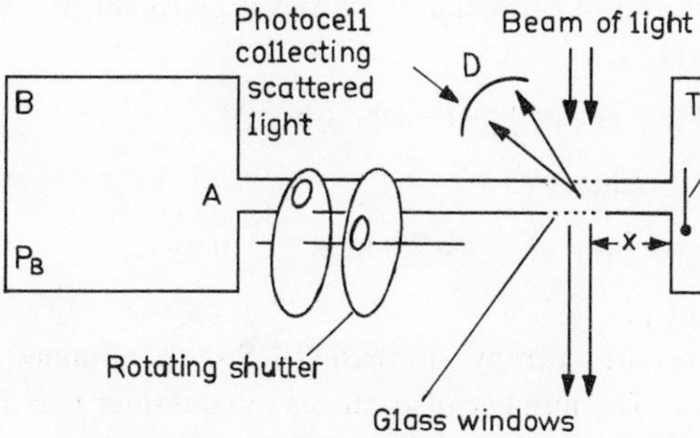

FIG. 13.1. Containers B and C contain particles at pressures of P_B and P_C, respectively. Particles may travel from B to C along a pipe of cross sectional area A. Two rotating shutters with apertures of area A are so adjusted that a particle passing through the left hand shutter will also pass through the right hand shutter if it has, approximately, a certain given velocity. A beam of light passes through glass windows in the pipe for detection of the presence of a particle. The light scattered by a particle is absorbed by the detector D which then opens the trap door so that the particle may pass into C.

Our definitions of information (Chapter 1) apply directly to such a problem, and yield the information per interval τ:

$$I_\tau = -k(p_1 \ln p_1 + p_2 \ln p_2) \text{ in thermodynamical units.} \tag{13.18}$$

Let us now consider the kinetic theory of our problem. The average number of molecules hitting the trap door of area A during a time τ (at a temperature T_0) is proportional to the density of the gas. We have, on the average:

$$\begin{aligned} u &= b A \tau && \text{molecules striking from the left,} \\ v &= r u = c A \tau && \text{molecules striking from the right,} \end{aligned} \tag{13.19}$$

and

$$r = c/b = P_C/P_B, \tag{13.20}$$

where P_B and P_C are the pressures in B and C, respectively. The operation of the shutter selecting molecules from the left with the average velocity will eliminate some molecules coming from the left (by reflection from the second shutter), and therefore Eq. (13.20) should be corrected:

$$r \geqslant P_C/P_B = r_p. \tag{13.21}$$

The relation between p_1 and u is

$$p_1 = 1 - e^{-u}, \qquad p_2 = e^{-u}. \tag{13.22}$$

and when $u \ll 1$, then $p_1 \approx u$ and $p_2 \approx 1 - u$. The derivation of this relation is given in Appendix I at the end of this chapter. From Eq. (13.22), we obtain for the information per interval τ:

$$I_\tau = k[-(1 - e^{-u}) \ln(1 - e^{-u}) + u\, e^{-u}], \tag{13.23}$$

which for small values of u reduces to

$$I_\tau \approx k(-u \ln u + u) = k\, u(1 - \ln u), \qquad u \ll 1, \tag{13.24}$$

neglecting higher powers of u.

We may now compute the entropy decrease ($\Delta S < 0$) obtained by the operation of the trap door. The number of particles in container C is increased in time τ by an amount u (entering from left to right) minus $v\, p_1$ (leaving from right to left) since the door is open only during a fraction p_1 of the total time:

$$\Delta n_\tau = u - r\, u\, p_1 \approx u(1 - r\, u), \qquad u \ll 1, \tag{13.25}$$

and the entropy change is

$$\Delta S_\tau = -k \ln(P_C/P_B) \cdot \Delta n_\tau = -k\, u(1 - r\, u) \ln r_p, \tag{13.26}$$

which is obtained from Eq. (12.12) as follows: we may write Eq. (12.12), which gives the entropy of an ideal monatomic gas, as

$$S = k[\alpha\, n + n \ln(V/n)],$$

where α depends on the mass of the molecules and on their average energy. In our problem the mass is the same for the two containers B and C, and if the average energy is initially the same, it will remain the same throughout the experiment because of the way in which the demon transfers molecules from B to C. The entropy of the system is

$$S = S_B + S_C = k\left\{\alpha(n_B + n_C) + n_B \ln\frac{V_B}{n_B} + n_C \ln\frac{V_C}{n_C}\right\}.$$

Now as molecules are transferred from B to C, the volumes stay constant and

$$\Delta n_C = \Delta n_\tau = -\Delta n_B,$$

so that

$$\Delta S = k\left\{\alpha(\Delta n_B + \Delta n_C) + \Delta n_B \ln \frac{V_B}{n_B} + \Delta n_C \ln \frac{V_C}{n_C}\right.$$

$$\left. + n_B \cdot \frac{n_B}{V_B}\left(-\frac{V_B}{n_B^2}\right)(\Delta n_B) + n_C \cdot \frac{n_C}{V_C}\left(-\frac{V_C}{n_C^2}\right)(\Delta n_C)\right\} = -k\,\Delta n_\tau \ln\left(\frac{V_B}{n_B}\cdot\frac{n_C}{V_C}\right).$$

But from a well-known result of kinetic theory

$$P_B = \frac{n_B \overline{v_B{}^2 m}}{3\,V_B}, \qquad P_C = \frac{n_C \overline{v_C{}^2 m}}{3\,V_C},$$

and since we have already assumed that the average energies are the same, Eq. (13.26) follows immediately.

Formula (13.26) proves that an entropy decrease can be obtained only if $r\,u < 1$, and that the most favorable conditions are

$$r\,u \ll 1, \qquad \text{hence} \qquad u \ll 1, \qquad \text{and} \qquad r_p \approx r. \tag{13.27}$$

This means that the number of molecules escaping backwards remains small.

We are now in a position to compute the efficiency of the demon's operation in the second step of the transformation (13.2):

$$\text{Information} \to \text{Negentropy}.$$

We define the efficiency by the ratio

$$\varepsilon_{II} = -\Delta S_\tau / I_\tau = (1 - r\,u)\cdot(\ln r)/(1 - \ln u), \tag{13.28}$$

according to Eqs. (13.24), (13.26), and (13.27). Let us take

$$r\,u = e^{-\beta} \ll 1, \qquad \text{then} \qquad \beta > 1, \tag{13.29}$$

and

$$u = e^{-\beta}/r, \qquad \text{and} \qquad \ln u = -\beta - \ln r,$$

so that

$$\varepsilon_{II} = \frac{(1 - e^{-\beta})\ln r}{1 + \beta + \ln r}. \tag{13.30}$$

The efficiency is always smaller than one and may reach unity when β is large and r is very large, in which case we certainly have u very small, a circumstance justifying our assumptions (13.24) and (13.27). High efficiency ih the second step of the operation (13.2) is thus obtained for large pressure difference between C and B.

5. The Negentropy Required in the Observation

Next we have to consider the first step, and compute the amount of negentropy required to obtain the information.

In order to know whether a molecule is going to hit the door during a certain interval of time τ, we must use a succession of pulses of radiation, of duration τ. If there is no molecule, the radiation passes through the apparatus (see Fig. 13.1) without being absorbed, and there is no entropy increase. If there is one (or more) molecule, radiation is scattered and absorbed in the photoelectric cell. There will be an entropy increase of E/T_0 if T_0 is the temperature of the system, and E the energy absorbed.

We assumed [Eq. (13.19)] an average number u of molecules hitting the trap door during a certain time τ, and this gave a probability p_1 for one or more hits during τ [Eq. (13.22)]. This means that, on the average, there is an interval t_u between molecules (or groups of molecules):

$$t_u = \tau/p_1. \tag{13.31}$$

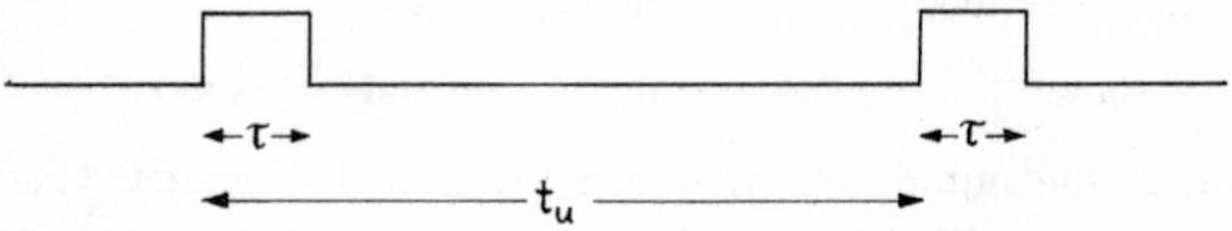

FIG. 13.2. Rectangular pulses of duration τ repeated at intervals t_u.

This is the average interval between successive times when the door is opened. We have to record, in the photoelectric cell, a succession of pulses of duration τ, at intervals t_u, on the average, as indicated in Fig. 13.2. How many quanta do we need, and how large must they be for accurate recording?

A single pulse is represented by a Fourier integral [see Eqs. (8.25)—(8.28)] with a continuous spectrum effectively extending up to

$$\nu_{max} = 1/(2\tau). \tag{13.32}$$

The pulse thus has an infinite number of components, and hence has an infinite energy.

The situation is different for a system of successive pulses repeated (on the average) at intervals t_u. Let us discuss the problem with the simplifying assumption that the repetition rate is exactly t_u, making the whole procedure strictly periodic with period t_u.[12] The system of pulses can be analysed into a Fourier

[12] A more general discussion is given in Appendix II, at the end of this chapter. The replacement of a single pulse (Fourier integral) by a succession of pulses (Fourier series) is just the reverse of the discussion given in Chapter 8, Section 3, for the introduction of the Fourier integrals (Figs. 8.3 and 8.4).

series with a discrete spectrum containing only certain frequencies, as shown in Fig. 13.3. These frequencies are

$$0, \; \nu_u, \; 2\,\nu_u, \; 3\,\nu_u \; \text{ up to } \; n\,\nu_u, \quad \text{with} \quad \nu_u = \frac{1}{t_u} = \frac{p_1}{\tau}. \tag{13.33}$$

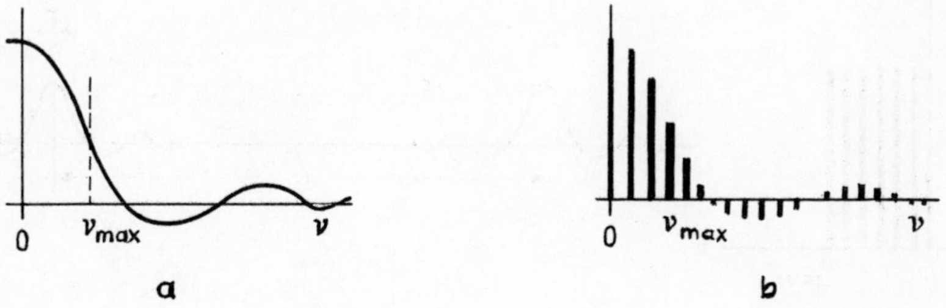

FIG. 13.3. a: Continuous spectrum for a single pulse. b: Discrete spectrum for a succession of pulses. The envelope is the same as the curve for the continuous spectrum.

The maximum frequency must be high enough to enable us to build up short pulses of duration τ, a condition which again results in a limitation similar to (13.32) or, approximately

$$\nu_{max} = n\,\nu_u \approx \frac{1}{2\tau}. \tag{13.34}$$

Here we should notice that our simplified periodic model can be used only as long as t_u is larger than $2\,\tau$, so that the zero pulse $(t_u - \tau)$ does not become shorter than the active pulse τ. Altogether we obtain $n + 1$ components (including the zero frequency)

$$n \approx \frac{1}{2\,\tau\,\nu_u} = \frac{1}{2\,p_1} = \nu_{max}\,t_u. \tag{13.34 a}$$

Let us take an example and assume an amplitude $A/2$ for the zero frequency, and a constant amplitude A for all other frequencies. Let us further assume that each proper frequency contains only a cosine term and no sine term. The resulting signal system is

$$f(t) = A(\tfrac{1}{2} + \cos\Phi + \cos 2\,\Phi \ldots + \cos n\,\Phi) = A\,\frac{\operatorname{Sin}(n + \frac{1}{2})\Phi}{2\sin\frac{1}{2}\Phi}, \tag{13.35}$$

according to Lagrange's identity, which we have already used [Eq. (8.61)], with

$$\Phi = 2\pi\,\nu_u \cdot t = 2\pi\,t/t_u.$$

We thus obtain a succession of rounded pulses (no longer rectangular pulses), as shown in Fig. 13.4. Their shape is given by Eq. (13.35) with a maximum amplitude $(n + \frac{1}{2})\,A$, at time zero, and the first zeros on the two sides at

$$\pm\,(n + \tfrac{1}{2})\,\Phi_1 = \pi, \qquad \pm\, t_1 = t_u/(2\,n + 1).$$

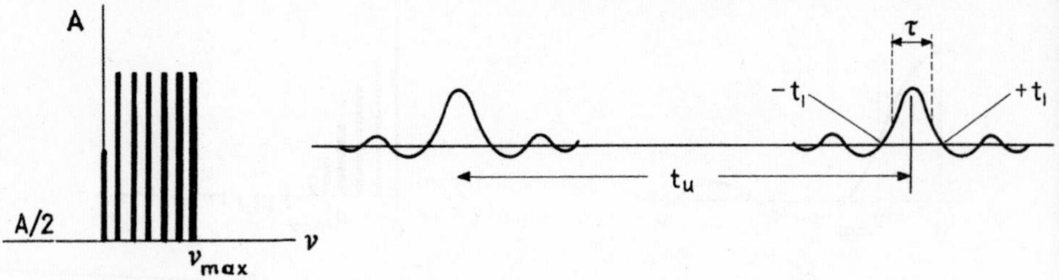

FIG. 13.4. The system of rounded pulses of effective duration τ, repeated at intervals t_u, of Eq. (13.35), and their Fourier spectrum.

The total interval of time from one zero to the next is $2\,t_1$, but the effective or "nominal" duration (discussed in Chapter 8, Sections 4 and 5) of the pulse corresponds approximately to one half of this interval, during which the amplitude is actually high. We thus define

$$\tau = t_1 = t_u/(2\,n + 1) \qquad \text{or} \qquad n + \tfrac{1}{2} = t_u/2\,\tau, \tag{13.36}$$

a relation that replaces our approximate condition (13.34 a). The repetition rate of the pulses is t_u.

We compute the average energy in the pulse system with the help of Parseval's equation [Eq. (8.12)]:

$$\overline{f^2} = \frac{1}{t_u}\int_0^{t_u} f^2\,dt = \tfrac{1}{4}\,A^2 + \sum_1^n \tfrac{1}{2}\,A^2 = \tfrac{1}{2}\,A^2(n + \tfrac{1}{2}).$$

The zero frequency term in (13.35) contributes by its square, while terms in $A^2 \cos^2 m\,\Phi$ give $(\frac{1}{2})A^2$ each. The average power (energy per second) in the pulse system is represented by $b\,\overline{f^2}$, with a numerical factor b, whose value depends on the units:

$$\overline{P} = b\,\overline{f^2} = (n + \tfrac{1}{2})\,\tfrac{1}{2}\,b\,A^2. \tag{13.37}$$

Almost all of the energy is concentrated in the short pulses τ. This can easily be verified: The maximum amplitude $(n + \frac{1}{2})\,A$ at time zero corresponds to a peak power

$$P_M = b(n + \tfrac{1}{2})^2 A^2 = 2(n + \tfrac{1}{2})\,\overline{P},$$

according to Eq. (13.37), and Eq. (13.36) gives

$$P_M \tau = \overline{P}\, t_u, \tag{13.37 a}$$

which proves that the energy in the pulse is equal to the total energy during t_u. We must now investigate the thermal excitation of the different degrees of freedom, and we first assume all the frequencies to be comparatively low

$$h\nu < k\,T$$

where T is the temperature of the system. We have obtained, in Eq. (13.34), $n + 1$ degrees of freedom per time interval t_u, a result which agrees with the discussion in Chapter 8 [Eq. (8.57)]. The term with zero frequency has an average energy $(\frac{1}{2})\, k\,T$ and the n vibrational terms have average energy of $k\,T$ each. Altogether, the average thermal energy for a time interval t_u is

$$\overline{E_T} = (n + \tfrac{1}{2})\, k\,T = k\,T\, t_u/2\,\tau, \tag{13.38}$$

according to Eq. (13.36). This energy is evenly distributed over t_u.

The probability for light absorption in the photocell is proportional to the energy available during each time interval: During the pulse τ, it amounts to

$$E_1 = P_M \tau + \overline{E_T}\cdot \tau/t_u = \overline{P}\, t_u + \tfrac{1}{2}\, k\,T,$$

according to Eqs. (13.37 a) and (13.38).

During the rest period $t_u - \tau$ we obtain

$$E_2 = \overline{E_T}(t_u - \tau)/t_u = \tfrac{1}{2}\, k\,T\big((t_u/\tau) - 1\big).$$

This term E_2 will give spurious absorptions resulting in detrimental irregular openings of the trap door. We want to reduce these errors of operation and we take

$$E_1 = \alpha\, E_2, \qquad \alpha \gg 1; \tag{13.39}$$

hence

$$\overline{P}\, t_u + \tfrac{1}{2}\, k\,T = \tfrac{1}{2}\,\alpha\, k\,T\big((t_u/\tau) - 1\big).$$

Since α is large, and τ/t_u is small, this condition reduces to

$$\overline{P} \approx \alpha\, k\,T/2\,\tau, \tag{13.40}$$

and $\overline{P}\, t_u$ represents the energy of the radiation absorbed, during t_u, in the photocell. The average energy absorbed during an interval τ is $\overline{P}\,\tau$, and the corresponding average entropy increase, per interval τ, amounts to

$$\Delta S_\tau = \overline{P}\,\tau/T = \tfrac{1}{2}\,\alpha\, k. \tag{13.41}$$

All of our approximations are based on the assumption

$$t_u \gg \tau, \qquad u \ll 1.$$

We can now discuss the efficiency in the first step of the demon's operation, when negentropy is changed into information. Using Eqs. (13.18) and (13.24) for the information per interval τ, we obtain an efficiency

$$\varepsilon_I = I_\tau / \Delta S_\tau \leqslant 2(-p_1 \ln p_1 - p_2 \ln p_2)/\alpha \approx 2\,u(1 - \ln u)/\alpha. \qquad (13.42)$$

The last expression is valid for very small values of u. Values of u too close to unity are difficult to discuss. The efficiency ε_I might be higher in that region. For smaller values of u it becomes smaller and smaller.

Summarizing the results, we see that

ε_I = efficiency in the first step, is maximum when $u \approx 1$,

ε_{II} = efficiency in the second step, is maximum for very small u.

Let us compute the over-all efficiency:

$$\varepsilon_0 = \varepsilon_I \cdot \varepsilon_{II} = \frac{2\,u(1 - r\,u)\ln r}{\alpha}, \qquad (13.43)$$

using Eqs. (13.28) and (13.42). As in Eq. (13.29), we take

$$r\,u = e^{-\beta} = \eta < 1,$$

and obtain

$$\varepsilon_0 = \frac{2\,\eta(1-\eta)\ln r}{\alpha}\,\frac{\ln r}{r} \leqslant \frac{\ln r}{2\,r\,\alpha}, \qquad (13.44)$$

since the optimum value of η is $\frac{1}{2}$. The last expression is maximum for $r = e$, giving $u = \eta/r = e/2$, a small value for which all of our approximations ahould hold:

$$\varepsilon_{0max} = 1/(2\,e\,\alpha) \approx 1/(5.44\,\alpha), \qquad \alpha \gg 1.$$

The over-all efficiency drops to zero for $r = 1$ (equal pressures in B and C) and also when r is very large (high pressure in C). We thus prove that the over-all efficiency is always smaller than one, and that both ε_I and ε_{II} also remain below unity, even under very abnormal circumstances, when the pressure ratio r is large.

6. Szilard's Problem: The Well-Informed Heat Engine

Szilard published in 1929[3] a very remarkable paper on the problem of Maxwell's demon, and discovered for the first time the connection between information and entropy. This was really pioneer work, and the importance of this paper was overlooked until recent developments of the theory brought it back into the foreground. We want now to investigate some interesting questions raised by Szilard, and to discuss recent work by Gabor[11] on these problems.

Szilard considers the following case: a closed cylinder, of volume V, can be split into two parts V_1 and V_2 by sliding in a partition at a certain position. The cylinder contains just one molecule. At the time when the observer introduces the partition, he has some way of knowing whether the molecule happens to be in V_1 or in V_2. Let us suppose that the molecule is in V_1. The partition is then moved, as a piston, along the cylinder, and the volume V_1 is slowly expanded to the original value V, while the whole system is maintained at a constant temperature T by a thermostat. The molecule will collide with the piston many times during such a slow operation, and these collisions result in an average pressure similar to the one of an ideal gas. A certain amount of work is done. The partition is then removed sidewise, put again into its original position, and the operation can be repeated anew. This system yields mechanical work. It uses only one temperature, but it requires information on the position of the molecule, and we have to discuss how this information is connected with entropy changes. Our precise definition of information, and the results obtained in the previous examples will enable us to simplify the discussion and to make it more accurate.

In Szilard's scheme the successive steps are taken in the following order:

A. Slide the partition in, at a certain position.

B. Discover whether the molecule is in V_1 or in V_2.

C. Accordingly, move the piston up or down.

The first step A requires no discussion. As for B, we must think of an experimental device for locating the molecule. We may use a beam of light B_1 passing through V_1 and another beam B_2 passing through V_2. Two photoelectric cells C_1 and C_2 may receive the light scattered from V_1 and V_2, respectively. We first use the beam B_1. If we have light scattered in C_1, this proves that the molecule is in V_1. If C_1 does not detect any light, nothing is proved:

the molecule may not be in V_1,
the molecule may fail to scatter light,
or the light quantum scattered may have missed C_1.

We then repeat the scattering experiment with the second beam B_2 in V_2. Finally a quantum $h\nu$ is scattered, either from V_1 or from V_2, and we locate the molecule. The absorption of $h\nu$ in one of the photocells corresponds to an entropy increase

$$\Delta S = h\nu/T \geqslant k, \tag{13.45}$$

according to our previous discussion [Eq. (13.7)]. A more detailed investigation [see Eq. (14.17)] slightly lowers the limit and gives

$$\Delta S \geqslant k \ln 2 = 0.7\, k. \tag{13.45 a}$$

We now compute the information obtained. The probability p_1 for finding the molecule in V_1 is obviously V_1/V, and the probability that the molecule is in V_2 is V_2/V:

$$p_1 = V_1/V, \qquad p_2 = V_2/V, \qquad p_1 + p_2 = 1.$$

Let us first consider the two cases separately. We can use our formulas (1.5) and (1.6) and compute:

$$\begin{aligned} &\text{molecule in } V_1\text{:} \quad \text{information } i_1 = k \ln (V/V_1) = -k \ln p_1, \\ &\text{molecule in } V_2\text{:} \quad \text{information } i_2 = k \ln (V/V_2) = -k \ln p_2. \end{aligned} \tag{13.46}$$

And the average information per operation is

$$\bar{I} = p_1 i_1 + p_2 i_2 = -k(p_1 \ln p_1 + p_2 \ln p_2) > 0, \tag{13.46 a}$$

which corresponds to Shannon's formula [Eq. (2.1)]. Each individual operation may yield information smaller than or larger than the entropy increase ΔS required to obtain it, but the *average information* (13.46 a) is smaller than the *average entropy increase* per operation:

$$\overline{\Delta S} \geqslant \bar{I}. \tag{13.47}$$

The equal sign is obtained when the two volumes V_1 and V_2 are equal:

$$V_1 = V_2 = \tfrac{1}{2} V, \qquad p_1 = p_2 = \tfrac{1}{2}, \qquad \bar{I} = k \ln 2,$$

which corresponds to the maximum average information. We may have fluctuations in the information obtained in individual operations. In the long run, however, the average information is smaller than the cost paid for it in negentropy, ΔN. The generalized Carnot principle of Chapter 13 is satisfied on the average, with positive and negative fluctuations:

$$\Delta N = -\Delta S, \qquad \Delta(N + I) \leqslant 0. \tag{13.47 a}$$

Let us now discuss the entropy changes in the gas, and the final operation C of the engine. The entropy of an ideal gas [Eq. (12.12)] is

$$S = S_0 + k \ln V.$$

At the instant the partition slides into position, we obtain a certain decrease of entropy:

$$\begin{aligned} &\text{either} \quad \Delta\sigma_1 = k \ln(V_1/V) = k \ln p_1 < 0, \text{ if the molecule is in } V_1, \\ &\text{or} \quad \Delta\sigma_2 = k \ln p_2 < 0 \text{ if the molecule is in } V_2. \end{aligned} \tag{13.48}$$

The probabilities of the two alternatives are p_1 and p_2 respectively. We note that the entropy decrease ($-\Delta\sigma_1$ or $-\Delta\sigma_2$) is always exactly equal to the individual information (i_1 or i_2), since Eqs. (13.46) and (13.48) are identical, except for sign. Furthermore, the average entropy decrease in the gas, per operation, is

$$\overline{\Delta \sigma} = p_1 \Delta \sigma_1 + p_2 \Delta \sigma_2 = -I. \tag{13.49}$$

When we move the piston and increase the volume to its original value V we restore the original entropy value. The work done, W, is equal to the heat Q taken from the heat reservoir (assuming a slow reversible operation):

$$W = Q = \int_{V_1}^{V} p\, dV = k\,T \int_{V_1}^{V} \frac{dV}{V} = k\,T \ln (V/V_1), \qquad p\,V = k\,T,$$

using Boyle's law for one molecule and considering case 1 (the molecule in V_1). The entropy increase during this period of expansion is

$$Q/T = k \ln(V/V_1) = -\Delta \sigma_1 > 0,$$

and similarly if the molecule is in V_2. This last operation simply justifies the validity of Eqs. (13.48) and shows how the initial entropy decrease is obtained. Altogether, there is a net entropy increase $\Delta S - I$ [Eq. (13.47)] in the complete cycle of operation.

We have thus proved, for this example, that information corresponds to negative entropy [Eqs. (13.47) and (13.49)], but we had to be careful about fluctuations, because we assumed that we first operated the partition without previous knowledge on the position of the molecule.

7. Gabor's Discussion

Gabor[11] investigated a similar problem, but with a different procedure in the operation of the engine. He reverses the order of the first two operations *A* and *B*, and proceeds in the following manner:

A. Make sure that the molecule is in V_1 (Szilard's step *B*),
B. Slide in the partition (Szilard's step *A*),
C. Move the piston.

Gabor assumes that a light beam illuminating the volume V_1 is used to provide the information. His complete machine is sketched in Fig. 13.5. A single molecule is moving in a cylinder V, maintained at the temperature T. The lower part of the cylinder (volume V_1) has transparent walls and is flooded by a light beam from a heated filament, emitting a certain frequency ν. A system of mirrors and lenses keeps the light circulating without absorption, unless some light is scattered by the molecule, and absorbed in the photosensitive elements. When this happens, a relay sets the mechanism in motion: a frictionless piston slides into the cylinder, and two mirrors slide down and cut off the light beam. The molecule progressively raises the piston and does mechanical work.

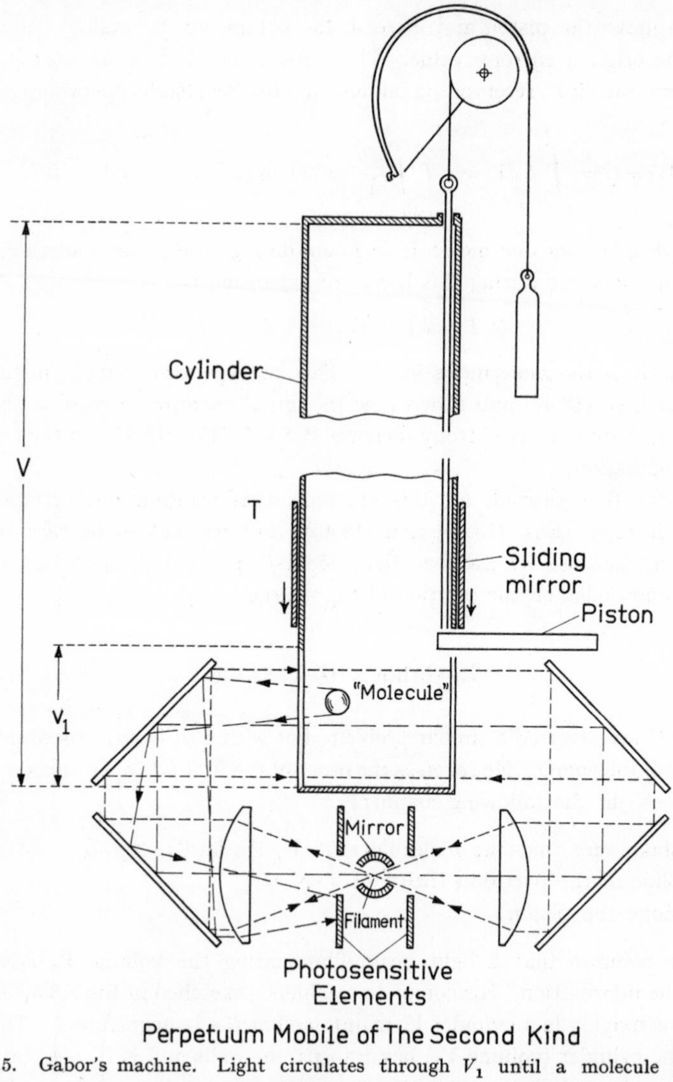

FIG. 13.5. Gabor's machine. Light circulates through V_1 until a molecule is present and scatters a photon to one of the photosensitive elements. When this happens a relay slides the piston into the cylinder, sliding mirrors cut off the illuminating beam, and the molecule raises the piston.

The entropy change when we introduce the piston is a decrease:

$$\Delta S_1 = k \ln(V_1/V) = k \ln p_1 < 0, \tag{13.50}$$

and the expansion period corresponds to an increase restoring the original entropy value. When the expansion is completed, the piston slides aside and is brought back to its initial position (this part of the mechanism is not shown in Fig. 13.5). The entropy decrease (13.50) can be made as large as we wish by increasing the volume V. The difficult point is now to prove that the amount of light required for the observation also increases with V in such a way that the initial increase of entropy should always be larger than $|\Delta S_1|$.

Let us consider the first part of the operation, when we are waiting for the molecule to enter volume V_1 and scatter light. The average waiting time t_u is proportional to V, and the flash of scattered light has a duration τ proportional to V_1. Altogether, our observation must give two pieces of information:

A. The molecule is in V_1, instead of in V.

B. This happens during an interval τ of the total time t_u.

The situation here is different from that in the experiment of Fig. 13.1, where the position was defined by the geometry of the apparatus, and the only observation required was on time. We can compute the total amount of information required by using Eq. (12.1):

$$I = k \ln(P_0/P_1),$$

where P_0 = the number of equally probable possibilities in the general case, and P_1 = the number of equally probable possibilities when the information I is given. Here we obviously have

$$P_0/P_1 = (t_u/\tau)\,(V/V_1) = (V/V_1)^2, \qquad \text{since} \qquad t_u/\tau = V/V_1. \tag{13.51}$$

Hence the measure of information in this type of experiment is

$$I = k \ln(V/V_1)^2 = 2\,k \ln(V/V_1) = -2\,k \ln p_1. \tag{13.52}$$

The information I is twice as large as the entropy decrease ΔS_1 of Eq. (13.50) which measures the negentropy obtained with the help of the information I. The transformation of information into negentropy has an efficiency $\frac{1}{2}$.

Next we want to compute the initial increase of entropy which was needed to obtain this information. In the whole volume, of total length L (proportional to V), we must build up a beam of light covering only a length L_1 (proportional to V_1). This can be done by properly superimposing a certain number of proper vibrations of the length L. These proper modes of vibrations have wavelengths

$$2\,L,\ L,\ 2L/3,\ \ldots,\ 2\,L/M,$$

and the shortest wavelength must be of the order of $2\,L_1$ in order to give a good definition of the length L_1. Hence we have

$$M = L/L_1 = V/V_1 \tag{13.53}$$

for the number of proper vibrations in the volume V. For each of these modes, we have a flash time τ repeated at intervals t_u. This situation is similar to the one discussed in Section 5, Eqs. (13.39) and (13.41), and requires an entropy increase

$$(\alpha\, k\, t_u)/(2\,\tau), \qquad \text{with} \qquad t_u \gg \tau \qquad \text{and} \qquad \alpha \gg 1,$$

per mode. Altogether we find

$$\Delta S = (M\,\alpha\, k\, t_u)/(2\,\tau) = (\alpha\, k/2)\,(V/V_1)^2 \tag{13.54}$$

for the total entropy cost of the observation. Let us compare this result with the formula (13.52) for the information:

$$\left.\begin{aligned} &\Delta S - I = k[(\alpha F/2) - \ln F] > 0, \qquad \alpha \gg 1 \\ &\text{with} \\ &F = (V/V_1)^2 = (1/p_1)^2. \end{aligned}\right\} \tag{13.55}$$

This expression is always positive. When p_1 decreases indefinitely, F increases to infinity, and so does the bracket in Eq. (13.55). This is the explanation of Szilard's problem. Further details will be found in Chapter 15.

Appendix I

We want to prove the formula (13.22) and use a reasoning due to H. Jacobson. We take an extremely short time interval θ, so small that there cannot be more than one molecule hitting the area A during θ:

$$\text{Probability of one hit:} \quad \alpha\,\theta <<< 1,$$

$$\text{Probability of no hit:} \quad 1 - \alpha\,\theta.$$

Now we consider the interval $\tau = m\,\theta$ and we have

$$\pi_0 = (1 - \alpha\,\theta)^m: \quad \text{probability of no hit during } \tau,$$

$$\pi_1 = m\,\alpha\,\theta(1 - \alpha\,\theta)^{m-1}: \quad \text{probability of one hit during any one of the } m \text{ intervals } \theta,$$

$$\pi_2 = \frac{m(m-1)}{2}\,(\alpha\,\theta)^2\,(1 - \alpha\,\theta)^{m-2}: \quad \text{probability of two hits during } \tau,$$

$$\pi_n = \frac{m!}{n!(m-n)!}\,(\alpha\,\theta)^n\,(1 - \alpha\,\theta)^{m-n}: \quad \text{probability of } n \text{ hits during } \tau.$$

Obviously

$$\pi_0 + \pi_1 + \ldots + \pi_n + \ldots + \pi_m = [\alpha\,\theta + (1 - \alpha\,\theta)]^m = 1,$$

Furthermore, when θ becomes very small and m very large

$$\pi_0 = (1 - \alpha\,\theta)^m = (1 - \alpha\,\theta)^{\frac{\alpha\tau}{\alpha\theta}} \to e^{-\alpha\tau}.$$

But π_0 is just our earlier p_2 of Eq. (13.22) and $\alpha\,\tau = u$ which justifies the formula (13.22). Furthermore

$$p_1 = \pi_1 + \pi_2 + \ldots \pi_m = 1 - e^{-\alpha\tau} = 1 - e^{-u}$$

is the probability for one or more hits.

Appendix II

We may generalize the reasoning used in relation to Eq. (13.33). Instead of assuming equidistant pulses, let us assume that m pulses are distributed at random over a certain very long time t:

$$t = m\,\tau/p_1,$$

where

$$m \gg 1, \quad \text{and} \quad p_1 = \text{probability of occurrence of an active interval } \tau.$$

We also assume that this succession of pulses is repeated in the following intervals of length t, giving a periodicity with a long period t. This periodic distribution has a spectrum with the frequencies $0, \nu_0, 2\,\nu_0, \ldots, n\,\nu_0$ [see Eqs. (13.34)—(13.36)], with

$$\nu_0 = 1/t = p_1/(m\,\tau), \qquad n\,\nu_0 = \nu_{max} \approx 1/(2\,\tau).$$

The maximum value n is now

$$n = 1/(2\,\tau\,\nu_0) = m/(2\,p_1).$$

The discussion given in Eqs. (13.37)—(13.41) applies directly to this case, and gives an average increase in entropy, per interval τ:

$$\Delta S_\tau = \alpha\,k/2,$$

as in Eq. (13.41).

CHAPTER 14

THE NEGENTROPY PRINCIPLE OF INFORMATION IN GENERAL PHYSICS

1. The Problem of Measurements in Physics

We have been able to reach, thus far, a few definite conclusions, which may be summarized as follows:

A. Information can be changed into negentropy, and vice versa. If the transformation is reversible, there is no loss, but an irreversible transformation always corresponds to a loss.

B. Any experiment by which information is obtained about a physical system produces, on the average, an increase of entropy in the system or in its surroundings. This average increase is always larger than (or equal to) the amount of information obtained. In other words, information must always be paid for in negentropy, the price paid being larger than (or equal to) the amount of information received. An observation is always accompanied by an increase in entropy, and thus involves an irreversible process.

C. The smallest possible amount of negentropy required in an observation is of the order of k. A more detailed discussion will give the value

$$\begin{aligned} \text{minimum of negentropy} &= k \ln 2 = 0.7\, k \\ &\approx 10^{-16} \text{ in c g s degrees Kelvin} \end{aligned} \qquad (14.1)$$

as the exact limit, a result which agrees with an earlier discussion of Szilard. In binary digits this minimum represents just one bit.

D. These remarks lead to an explanation of the problem of Maxwell's demon, which simply represents a device changing negentropy into information, and back into negentropy.

We want to investigate more carefully the conclusions B and C. This will lead to a discussion of the problem of reliability and accuracy in a physical experiment. The reader may have noticed the fact that we had to introduce, in the discussion of Chapter 13, an arbitrary factor α [Eqs. (13.39) and (13.54)], which was assumed to be large enough, in order to reduce errors of observation and detrimental operations of the system. This factor α insures *reliability* in the experimental device. This is a point of great importance which we will discuss in detail. We shall also investigate the question of the minimum negentropy required for an observation, and justify the rule (14.1).

It was in the discussion of Maxwell's demon that we first discovered the general results B and C. The observer, whether physicist or demon, requires sources of negentropy since every observation is always made at the expense of the negentropy of the surroundings. Thus he needs batteries, power supply, compressed gases, etc., all of which represent sources of negentropy. He also needs light in his laboratory in order to be able to read ammeters or other instruments.

What is the smallest possible amount of negentropy required for an observation? Let us suppose that we want to read an indication on an ammeter maintained at temperature T. The needle and its spring represent an oscillating system with a very low proper frequency. The needle exhibits a Brownian motion of oscillation, with an average kinetic energy $k\,T/2$, and an average total energy

$$\overline{E_t} = k\,T. \tag{14.2}$$

Ising[1] considers that an energy

$$E_I \geqslant 4\,\overline{E}_t = 4\,k\,T \tag{14.3}$$

is required to obtain a correct reading. This energy will be dissipated in friction, Joule effect, viscous damping of the ammeter, etc., after the reading is made. This means an increase of entropy for the entire system of

$$\Delta S = E_I/T \geqslant 4\,k. \tag{14.4}$$

Thus $4\,k$ is needed for a reliable observation on the basis of Ising's criterion. We now want to show that $k \ln 2 = 0.7\,k$ is the limit, for which we just obtain a 50% chance that the observation is correct, with a 50% chance that the deflection observed might simply be due to thermal agitation.

2. Observations Made on an Oscillator

Let us consider a harmonic oscillator of frequency ν with quantized energy levels $E_n = n\,h\,\nu$. The problem of the ammeter, above, will correspond to the limit of very low frequency. We obtained in Eqs. (9.31) — (9.44), some general results on the statistical properties of such a resonator when it is maintained at a temperature T. The energy level $n\,h\,\nu$ has a probability

$$\begin{gathered} p_n = B\,e^{-nx} = e^{-nx} - e^{-(n+1)x} \qquad \text{with} \qquad x = \frac{h\,\nu}{k\,T}, \\ \sum_{n=0}^{\infty} p_n = \sum_{n=0}^{\infty} B\,e^{-nx} = 1, \quad B = 1 - e^{-x}. \end{gathered} \tag{14.5}$$

[1] G. Ising, *Phil. Mag.* [6] **51**, 827 (1926); M. Courtines, Les fluctuations dans les appareils de mesures," Congr. intern. d'électricité, vol. 2, Paris, (1932).

Hence

$$\left.\begin{aligned} P_{n \geqslant q} &= p_q + p_{q+1} + \ldots = e^{-qx}, \\ P_{0<n<q} &= p_0 + p_1 + \ldots p_{q-1} = 1 - e^{-qx}, \end{aligned}\right\} \tag{14.5 a}$$

for the probabilities of states above $(q-1)$ and below q, respectively. We may define a median quantum number m by the condition

$$P_{n<m} = P_{n \geqslant m},$$

which yields

$$e^{-mx} = \tfrac{1}{2} \qquad \text{or} \qquad m\,x = \ln 2 \approx 0.7,$$

so that

$$E_m = m\,h\,\nu = k\,T \ln 2. \tag{14.6}$$

This median value can be compared with the average value

$$\bar{n} = \sum_{n=0}^{n=\infty} n\,p_n = 1/(e^x - 1). \tag{14.7}$$

For low frequencies

$$h\nu \ll k\,T \qquad \text{and} \qquad x \ll 1,$$

so that Eq. (14.7) gives

$$\bar{n}\,x = 1 \qquad \text{or} \qquad \bar{E} = \bar{n}\,h\,\nu = k\,T, \tag{14.8}$$

and we notice that the median value is smaller than the average value. The situation is different for high frequencies, which are discussed in the next section.

Next we compute the average quantum value for states $n \geqslant q$:

$$\bar{n}_q = \frac{\sum_{n=q}^{\infty} n\,p_n}{P_{n \geqslant q}} = \frac{B\,e^{-qx} \sum_{r=0}^{\infty} (q+r)\,e^{-rx}}{e^{-qx}}, \qquad n = q + r,$$

and using conditions (14.5) and (14.7), we obtain

$$\bar{n}_q = q + \bar{n}, \qquad \text{since} \qquad \bar{r} = \bar{n}. \tag{14.9}$$

The average quantum value $\overline{n'_q}$ for the group of states $n < q$ is obtained directly from the relation

$$P_{n<q}\,\overline{n'_q} + P_{n \geqslant q}\,\bar{n}_q = \bar{n},$$

which yields

$$\overline{n_q'} = \bar{n} - \frac{q}{e^{+qx} - 1} \qquad \text{for} \qquad n < q. \tag{14.10}$$

Let us apply these results to the median value

$$q = m: \qquad \begin{aligned} \overline{n_m} &= m + \bar{n}, \qquad & n \geqslant m; \\ \overline{n_m'} &= \bar{n} - m, \qquad & n < m. \end{aligned} \tag{14.11}$$

For low frequencies

$$\begin{aligned} \overline{n_m} &= \bar{n}(1 + \ln 2) \approx 1.7\,\bar{n}, \\ \overline{n_m'} &= \bar{n}(1 - \ln 2) \approx 0.3\,\bar{n}. \end{aligned} \tag{14.12}$$

We may now consider the problem of making an observation and discussing its reliability. Suppose that we observe, at a certain instant of time t, an energy corresponding to $n \geqslant q$ quanta. The chance that this high quantum number may be due to thermal fluctuations is $P_{n \geqslant q}$. The chance that the resonator would have obtained normally $n < q$, and then absorbed some additional quanta (from an outside source) to reach a level above q is $P_{n<q}$. If we accept equal chances for these two cases, we must choose for q the median value

$$q = m = (\ln 2)/x.$$

If, on the other hand, we take the Ising value for a "reliable" observation [Eq. (14.3)], we have

$$q_I = (1/x) \cdot 4$$

and

$$(P_{n \geqslant q})/(P_{n<q}) = e^{-4}/(1 - e^{-4}) = 1/(e^4 - 1) \approx 1/54, \tag{14.13}$$

which gives a chance of about 2% for errors due to thermal agitation.

At time t, we observe more than q quanta on the resonator. In case this is due to thermal fluctuations, the average excess energy has been obtained from the surrounding thermostat T, and according to Eq. (14.9), the average energy, in this case, will be

$$\overline{E_q} = \overline{n_q}\, h\nu = q\, h\nu + \bar{n}\, h\nu. \tag{14.14}$$

If q quanta actually are absorbed from an outside source, the excess energy $q\,h\nu$ comes from this source, and is added to the normal $\bar{n}\,h\nu$ average, giving again (14.14). At any rate, the excess energy $q\,h\nu$ is dissipated later on, by friction, viscosity, or ohmic losses, and is absorbed by the surrounding thermostat at temperature T. If Eq. (14.14) was the result of fluctuations, this means simply that the thermostat gets back some of the energy it had previously lost. If

Eq. (14.14) results from actual absorption from an outside source, we have q quanta finally absorbed by the thermostat, and hence an entropy increase occurs:

$$\Delta S = q h \nu / T = q k x = \begin{cases} k \ln 2 & \text{if} \quad q = m, \\ 4 k, & \text{Ising.} \end{cases} \tag{14.15}$$

This entropy increase of the surrounding thermostat is the cost paid for the observation. Its lowest value $k \ln 2$, or approximately $0.7\,k$, is obtained when we accept a 50% chance of error.

It is very curious that by selecting a limit $m < \bar{n}$ [Eqs. (14.6) and (14.8)], we nevertheless have a certain amount of energy absorbed to bring the resonator back to normal. This is because the limit m may be lower than the average $\bar{n}$ but [Eq. (14.12)] the average $\overline{n_m}$ of quanta above m is larger than $\bar{n}$.

The result is general and applies to low or high frequencies, although the numerical example in this section was selected for low frequencies.

3. High-Frequency Resonator and the Cost of an Observation

Let us now consider a resonator with high frequency, when $h\nu$ can be of the order of kT or larger than kT. The quantity x is no longer a small quantity, and condition (14.6) for the median value will usually not yield an integer. We thus have to choose the next larger integer:

$$q \geqslant m \qquad \text{integer.} \tag{14.16}$$

The reliability of the observation is then better than 50%, and the ΔS is higher than $k \ln 2$ [Eq. (14.15)], if all the excess energy is dissipated and transferred to the thermostat at temperature T.

Let us now select a different case, that corresponds to the problem of Maxwell's demon. We have molecules in an enclosure at temperature T, and we use an additional source of light, emitting quanta $h\nu$, in order to see the molecules. A molecule is observed when it scatters at least one quantum $h\nu$, which is later on absorbed by a photoelectric cell or in the eye of the observer. This quantum $h\nu$ must be above the limit of the black body radiation, in order to be distinguishable from that general background.

We previously assumed [Eqs. (13.4) and (13.38)] that these requirements lead to a condition

$$h\nu \geqslant kT.$$

We now want to show that we may lower the limit to

$$h\nu \geqslant kT \ln 2. \tag{14.17}$$

In order to do this, we note first that the smallest amount of energy that can be absorbed is one quantum. Further, if we wish an observation of one (or more) quantum on the resonator to have a 50% reliability, we must take $m = 1$. This, together with Eqs. (14.6) and (14.7), requires:

$$m = \overline{n} = 1 \qquad \text{and} \qquad x = h\nu/kT = \ln 2. \tag{14.18}$$

The average value and the median value coincide, and correspond to an absorption of just one quantum.

The ground state with zero quanta has a probability $\frac{1}{2}$, equal to the total probability of all states with 1, 2, 3, or more quanta. If we observe one quantum (or more) on the resonator, the chance that it might be due to actual absorption is 50% and the chance that it may be due to fluctuations is 50%. When this quantum is dissipated and reabsorbed by the surrounding medium at temperature T, we obtain an entropy increase, for the medium, of

$$\Delta S = k \ln 2. \tag{14.19}$$

Hence the limit k used in Chapter 13, Section 3, should be corrected to $k \ln 2$, thus improving slightly the efficiency of the demon's operation.

If, in an enclosure at T, we consider a resonator with higher frequency

$$h\nu > kT \ln 2 \qquad \text{or} \qquad x > \ln 2,$$

we obtain $m < 1$, and we have to take $q = 1$, according to Eq. (14.16). This will give a reliability better than 50%, and a ΔS larger than $k \ln 2$. In all of these examples, the observation gives us exactly one bit of information, a "yes" or "no" answer to a certain question:

Has energy been absorbed by a certain resonator?

Is there a gas molecule at a certain location?

One binary digit of information represents $k \ln 2$, and must be paid for by more than $k \ln 2$ in negentropy.

We must note that the information is valid for a short period of time only: the resonator's damping soon dissipates the excess energy, or the molecule moves away from the observed position. This law of decay corresponds to a typical characteristic of the second principle.

The preceding discussion clearly shows that the second principle holds only on the average, as was specified in item B of Section 1. The second principle is always limited by the possibility of unpredictable fluctuations. It may happen that one particular observation could be made at exceptionally low cost, but we have no way to foresee when and how this may happen. Only averages can safely be predicted.

An amount of information corresponding to a sizable number of bits results in an extremely small contribution to the entropy of the system, on account of the factor of 10^{-16} in Eq. (14.1). The problems we discuss are of no great importance for thermodynamics, but the connection between entropy and information is fundamental for the theory of information, which cannot be built consistently without it. Furthermore we shall consider special conditions where the entropy cost of an observation may become very much higher than the limit (14.1).

4. Experiments Requiring Many Simultaneous Observations at Low Frequencies

We discussed in Sections 2 and 3 a very simple example, in which an experiment was based on the observation of one single oscillator, and we found a limit

$$\Delta S = k \ln 2$$

for the entropy increase corresponding to a fifty-fifty chance that the observation might be correct. This limit was obtained for low frequencies. If we include the case where high frequencies may be required (Section 3), we can summarize the results in the following manner:

$$\Delta S \geqslant A_1 k \qquad \text{where} \qquad A_1 = \begin{cases} \ln 2\text{: low frequencies } h\nu \leqslant kT \\ h\nu/kT\text{: high frequencies } h\nu > kT \end{cases} \tag{14.20}$$

is the entropy increase for a single observation. In practice, high frequencies are not excited in the black body radiation, and one quantum $h\nu$ of energy is enough to give a reliable observation.

It should be noted that, in the discussion of the preceding sections, it is assumed that an observation is given by a reading of an energy above E_l on the resonator. A negative reading, i. e. an observation of low energy on the resonator, is not thought of as yielding any information for the reasons given in Chapter 13, Section 6 in connection with the discussion of Szilard's heat engine. The essential reason for the restriction that information is obtained only from positive results (an observation of high energy on the detector) is that it is not clear how the reliability of a negative reading can be defined.

We want now to consider the more complex problem in which observations on n oscillators are required in an experiment. In some cases the observations must be made simultaneously on the n receivers, but in other instances we may observe them successively. The observation may require that only one of these resonators exhibits, at a certain instant of time, an energy larger than a certain limit E_l, but in other experimental devices the observation may be based on high energy observed on a certain number m of the resonators:

$$1 \leqslant m \leqslant n.$$

All the resonators are assumed to be maintained in a thermostat at a constant temperature T, and we first consider the case of low frequencies $(h\nu \ll kT)$. The problem is to determine the limit E_l which yields an over-all chance of $\frac{1}{2}$ for a correct observation, and a chance of $\frac{1}{2}$ for a spurious observation due to fluctuations.

Let us consider an arbitrary limit E_l and discuss the case of one of the n oscillators. We have the following probabilities from Eq. (14.5 a):

$$P_1 = e^{-E_l/kT} \tag{14.21 a}$$

is the probability that the thermal fluctuations give to this resonator an energy larger than E_l, while

$$P_2 = 1 - e^{-E_l/kT} \tag{14.21 b}$$

is the probability that the fluctuations give to the resonator an energy below E_l. When we observe n resonators, we easily compute the following table of probabilities, in which only thermal fluctuations enter:

TABLE 14.1

$P_{n,n} = P_1^n$	probability that all n resonators have energy $\geqslant E_l$;
$P_{n,n-1} = n P_1^{n-1} P_2$	probability that any one of the resonators has energy $< E_l$, while the remaining $(n-1)$ resonators have energy $\geqslant E_l$;
$P_{n,n-2} = \frac{n(n-1)}{2} P_1^{n-2} P_2^2$	probability that any two resonators are below E_l, while $(n-2)$ of the resonators are above E_l;
$P_{n,n-m} = \frac{n!}{m!(n-m)!} P_1^{n-m} P_2^m$	probability that any m of the resonators have energy below E_l while the other $(n-m)$ resonators have energy $\geqslant E_l$;
$P_{n,0} = P_2^n$	probability that all resonators have energy below E_l.

The sum of the probabilities for these different cases is obviously unity since

$$\sum_{m=0}^{n} P_{n,n-m} = P_1^n + \dots + \frac{n!}{m!(n-m)!} P_1^{n-m} P_2^m + \dots + P_2^n$$

$$= (P_1 + P_2)^n = 1^n = 1.$$

Let us now specify experimental conditions for an observation. We first assume that an observation gives a positive result when any one of the n oscillators exhibits an energy larger than E_l. We have a probability $P_2{}^n$ that this may not be due to fluctuations, and a probability $1 - P_2{}^n$ that one or more oscillators may have been raised above E_l by thermal fluctuations. Thus the probability of a correct observation is $P_2{}^n$, since the observed energy larger than E_l must, in this case, be the result of absorption of energy from an outside source. The probability of a spurious observation resulting from fluctuations is $1 - P_2{}^n$. We now require that a correct observation have a probability of $\frac{1}{2}$, and we thus obtain the condition

$$P_2{}^n = (1 - e^{-A_n})^n = \tfrac{1}{2}, \qquad \text{with} \qquad E_l = A_n k T, \tag{14.22}$$

or

$$e^{-A_n} = 1 - (\tfrac{1}{2})^{1/n}. \tag{14.22 a}$$

For $n = 1$, we recognize our earlier result (14.15)

$$E_{l1} = k T \ln 2, \qquad A_1 = \ln 2.$$

When n is larger, E_l must increase, since the right hand side of Eq. (14.22 a) becomes smaller and smaller, with increasing n. Hence e^{-A_n} also decreases. We may take the logarithm of each side of Eq. (14.22), and obtain an asymptotic expression for A_n:

$$n \ln(1 - e^{-A_n}) \approx - n\, e^{-A_n} \approx - \ln 2,$$

or

$$A_n \approx \ln n - \ln(\ln 2) \approx \ln n + 0.3667. \tag{14.23}$$

The following table gives some values of the coefficient A_n:

$n =$	1	2	4	100	10.000
$A_n \approx$	0.69	1.23	1.84	4.95	9.58

(14.24)

To return to the experiment, the excited resonator has received its excess energy from an outside source, when the observation is correct, or, if the observation is spurious, it has received this energy from the thermostat. In either case this excess energy will be absorbed in the thermostat later on, and result in a net entropy increase, for the case of a correct observation, of

$$\Delta S = E_l/T = A_n k.$$

The discussion here is exactly similar to the earlier one given in Eqs. (14.14) and (14.15).

We must emphasize, in this new problem, that the computed ΔS represents a lower limit only. The actual increase may be larger than $k A_n$. We observe an absorption of energy from the outside source only when enough is absorbed to raise one resonator above E_l. But many other resonators may absorb some energy from the outside source in smaller amounts that will not raise them above E_l, and hence will escape our attention. This absorbed energy also goes to the thermostat later on and contributes an additional unknown increase of entropy. We thus arrive, finally, at the condition

$$\Delta S \geqslant A_n k. \tag{14.25}$$

Since A_n is an increasing function of n, the lower limit of the entropy increase becomes larger as the number of resonators necessary for the experiment increases.

Equations (14.22), (14.22 a), (14.23), and (14.24) for A_n were obtained on the assumption that only one of the resonators gave a positive reading. These equations are, however, valid for the case in which we obtain $m (1 \leqslant m \leqslant n)$ positive readings, if we require that the probability that all of them are genuine is $\frac{1}{2}$. This means, as before, that we must equate to $\frac{1}{2}$ the probability that, so far as fluctuations are concerned, all n of the oscillators have energy below E_l. Thus all the earlier equations for A_n still hold. We must, however, modify Eq. (14.25) for the entropy increase, because we now have energy $m E_l$ to be absorbed by the thermostat. Thus

$$\Delta S = m E_l / k T = m A_n k,$$

or, if we take into account the uncertainty in the negative readings

$$\Delta S \geqslant m A_n k. \tag{14.26}$$

We have used only a small part of Table **14.1** in this discussion. Other problems, such as one in which only a certain fraction of the positive readings are to be regarded as genuine, would make use of the other probabilities given.

The case of high frequencies is different. One single quantum $h\nu$ per resonator is enough for a reliable observation, and obviously represents the minimum energy required. These frequencies do not appear, in practice, in the black body radiation. Hence we take

$$E_l = h\nu = A k T, \qquad A = h\nu / k T.$$

Summarizing these results, we see that an experiment requiring n simultaneous observations on n resonators contained in a thermostat corresponds to an entropy increase of

$$\Delta S = A k \tag{14.27}$$

for each resonator whose energy exceeds E_l, with

$$A = \begin{cases} A_n \text{ given by Eqs. (14.23) and (14.24) for low frequencies } h\nu \ll kT, \\ h\nu/kT \text{ for high frequenzies } h\nu \gg kT. \end{cases} \tag{14.28}$$

The intermediate case of $h\nu \approx kT$ should be discussed separately for each special problem.

5. Problems Requiring High Reliability

Our preceding discussions were based on the assumption that we might be satisfied with a 50% probability for errors in our experiments. This very low limit was chosen in order to yield the lowest value of entropy increase compatible with any measurement. It is interesting to extend the investigation to problems requiring higher reliability, and to see how the entropy cost will be increased.

Let us emphasize here the distinction introduced between reliability and accuracy. Accuracy will be specifically discussed in Chapter 15, and can be defined in the following manner: We measure a quantity x over a total field of observation l, with a possible error Δx. We consider the quantity

$$\mathcal{A} = l/\Delta x \tag{14.29 a}$$

as defining the accuracy of the experiment. If, for instance, we use a meter subdivided into millimeters, $\mathcal{A} = 1000$. With a yard stick having subdivisions of $\frac{1}{4}$ of an inch, we define $\mathcal{A} = 144$.

Reliability corresponds to a different problem: Given an experimental procedure, with certain accuracy requirements, there always remains the possibility that thermal fluctuations may give spurious readings and result in incorrect indications. This will occur with a certain probability. Instead of considering the limit where this probability is $\frac{1}{2}$, we now want to discuss problems where the probability of error would be reduced to

$$P = 1/r, \quad r > 2, \quad \text{probability of errors due to thermal agitation.} \tag{14.29 b}$$

The Ising condition [Eqs. (14.3), (14.4), (14.13), and (14.15)] corresponds to $r = 54$.

Let us start with the case of an experiment using a single reading on a low-frequency oscillator. The discussion of Section 2 applies immediately. We must select a limit q giving

$$P_{n \geqslant q} = e^{-qx} = 1/r$$

according to Eq. (14.5 a), and we obtain

$$\ln r = qx = qh\nu/kT. \tag{14.30}$$

The energy limit on the resonator is $q\,h\,\nu$. After the observation has been made, this additional energy is dissipated in the damping of the resonator [Eq. (14.14)] and this results in an entropy increase [Eq. (14.15)] in the thermostat T

$$\Delta S = q\,h\,\nu/T = k \ln r. \tag{14.31}$$

The entropy cost increases logarithmically with the reliability r.

Let us now consider an experiment involving many observations, in order to extend the results of Section 4. Our earlier Eq. (14.22) is now replaced by

$$P = (1 - e^{-A_n})^n = 1 - 1/r \qquad \text{with} \qquad E_l = A_n\,k\,T, \tag{14.32}$$

where P is the probability that positive readings on m of the n resonators are all genuine, and E_l is the energy limit on each of the n resonators. The preceding result, Eq. (14.31) corresponds to $n = 1$, and

$$A_1 = \ln r. \tag{14.33}$$

For high values of both r and n we can obtain an asymptotic expression, because A_n becomes very small. Taking the logarithms of boths sides in (14.32), we have

$$n \ln(1 - e^{-A_n}) \approx -n\,e^{-A_n}, \qquad \ln(1 - 1/r) \approx -1/r,$$

and hence

$$n\,e^{-A_n} \approx 1/r$$

or

$$A_n \approx \ln(r\,n), \qquad r\,n \gg 1. \tag{14.34}$$

The coefficient A_n, for low frequencies, may vary, in practice, from 0.7 to a few hundreds. This formula should be a good approximation even for small values of n, since it gives the correct value for $n = 1$. The energy finally dissipated on the m resonators is $m\,A_n\,k\,T$ and the total entropy cost is

$$\Delta S \geqslant k\,m\,A_n = k\,m \ln(r\,n). \tag{14.35}$$

The case of high frequencies is, again, different. One single quantum $h\,\nu$ per resonator is enough for an observation since these frequencies do not, in practice, appear in the black body radiation:

$$\begin{aligned} &E_l = h\,\nu = A\,k\,T, \qquad A = h\,\nu/k\,T, \qquad h\,\nu \gg k\,T \\ &\qquad\qquad \Delta S \geqslant m\,k\,A. \end{aligned} \tag{14.36}$$

We thus arrive at a coefficient

$$A = \begin{cases} A_n \text{ given by Eq. (14.34) for low frequencies } h\,\nu \ll k\,T, \\ h\,\nu/k\,T \text{ for high frequencies } h\,\nu \gg k\,T. \end{cases} \tag{14.37}$$

The transition from low to high frequencies would be more difficult to discuss, and would depend upon the particular problem under consideration.

In all the examples discussed thus far in this chapter, we assumed that the observation was performed with a certain number n of oscillators maintained at a temperature T by a thermostat. At a certain instant of time, we observed the energies on these oscillators, and later on the equilibrium of temperature between the oscillators and the thermostat was progressively reestablished. A certain amount of energy was redistributed and the entropy of the thermostat was increased. These conditions are the simplest ones for discussion, but the case of high frequencies requires a more accurate discussion.

6. A More Accurate Discussion of Experiments Using High Frequencies

The conditions assumed in the preceding sections give a satisfactory theory for the case of low frequencies, but some experiments actually require the use of high frequencies and one may wonder whether, in these cases, the entire energy needed for the experiment must always be finally dissipated. Equation (14.36) certainly defines the total amount of energy required for an observation, but instead of using, as a receiver, an oscillator maintained at a temperature T, we may think of another device, such as a photoelectric cell at temperature T. The radiation used in the experiment may fall on a piece of metal from which it ejects an electron with a kinetic energy

$$E_{k_0} = h\nu - W_0, \tag{14.38}$$

where W_0 represents the work done in extracting the electron from the cathode. The electron may then be decelerated through an electric field, thus losing energy W_1, which corresponds to electric work done. The electron finally reaches a fluorescent screen at temperature T and is absorbed. At the instant when this absorption takes place, the electron has a low kinetic energy

$$E_{k_1} = h\nu - W_0 - W_1, \tag{14.39}$$

and this energy is changed into heat, giving an entropy increase

$$\Delta S = (h\nu - W_0 - W_1)/T \tag{14.40}$$

in the screen. If the decelerating field is weak, this ΔS will be just a little smaller than $h\nu/T$. If the field is too strong, the electron cannot reach the screen and observation is made impossible. The experiment can only give a positive result when the electron reaches the screen with an energy larger than the thermal fluctuations in the screen, and this brings us back to the problem discussed in the preceding section.

We wish to emphasize the distinction between the following two quantities:

$$\Delta E = n h \nu, \tag{14.41}$$

representing the smallest total energy required in the experiment, using n receiving cells, and

$$\Delta S = k n A_n, \tag{14.42}$$

which is the smallest entropy increase for an observation of reliability r on n receivers. A_n is the coefficient previously defined in Eqs. (14.23), (14.24), and (14.34). For high frequencies we have

$$\Delta Q = T \Delta S < \Delta E. \tag{14.43}$$

Only part of the total energy ΔE is changed into heat ΔQ, while the difference can be recovered as electrical or mechanical work ΔW:

$$\Delta W = \Delta E - \Delta Q. \tag{14.44}$$

In most experimental devices, however, we do not care whether the energy ΔE is actually changed into heat or is recovered, although the preceding discussion is important for the validity of the theory.[2]

Thus, the use of high frequencies to obtain a given quantity of information proves more expensive, in terms of negentropy, than the use of low frequencies, unless some special device is introduced to convert part of the energy associated with the high frequency into work. It is still, however, necessary to retain enough of the energy to activate a low-frequency detector, so that the earlier results on low-frequency resonators yield the minimum cost of the observation. The introduction of a special device to minimize the loss of energy, in the high-frequency case, may simply be thought of as a device to convert what is initially a situation requiring the use of high frequencies to a situation for which low frequencies are satisfactory.

At this point it is interesting to mention also the photographic method. When a quantum $h\nu$ strikes a photographic plate, an atom is ionized, and an electron is emitted with a kinetic energy E_{k_0} given by Eq. (14.38), where W_0 now represents the threshold of ionization. The electron travels a certain distance and is finally stopped in the emulsion losing its energy E_{k_0} partly in work done, and partly in heat produced during many collision processes. Here W_0 is much larger than kT (since ionization is not produced by thermal fluctuations), and

[2] The author is very much indebted to Professor N. Bohr and Dr. J. R. Oppenheimer for their criticisms and discussions at a meeting held in December, 1954, at the Institute for Advanced Studies in Princeton.

the heat produced in the emulsion will be greater than kT (otherwise the electron would not travel far enough and could be brought back by thermal agitation). Conditions are not very different from those just discussed and lead to similar conclusions. The process of developing the plate need not be considered. It is simply an amplification (and a costly one in terms of entropy) changing a microscopic effect into a macroscopic one, which can be observed directly.

7. An Example Showing the Minimum Negentropy Required in an Observation

We shall now discuss a simplified example for which it is actually possible to show the existence of a minimum negentropy required in an observation. We consider again the problem, discussed in Chapter 13, Section 4, of how to locate a particle with a beam of light. Let us take a succession of light pulses, as represented in Fig. 14.1, with the light on during τ_1, and off during τ_2. The whole period is

$$\text{period } \tau = \tau_1 + \tau_2: \quad \text{function } f(t) = \begin{cases} 1, & |t| < \dfrac{\tau_1}{2}, \\ 0, & \dfrac{\tau_1}{2} < |t| < \dfrac{\tau}{2}, \end{cases} \tag{14.45}$$

Such a pulse system requires a bandwidth, which is essentially defined by the length of the short pulse. If we assume $\tau_1 < \tau_2$ we obtain

$$0 < \nu < \nu_M, \quad \nu_M \approx \frac{1}{2\tau_1}, \tag{14.46}$$

according to our Eq. (13.32).

Instead of the pulse system $f(t)$ we now consider the reverse pulses $F(t)$, as shown on Fig. 14.2:

$$F(t) = \begin{cases} 0, & |t| < \dfrac{\tau_1}{2}, \\ 1, & \dfrac{\tau_1}{2} < |t| < \dfrac{\tau}{2}, \end{cases} \quad \text{period } \tau, \tag{14.47}$$

$$F(t) = 1 - f(t). \tag{14.48}$$

The two functions f and F obviously have the same Fourier spectrum, although one of them has short pulses with long intervals, and the other one has long pulses with short intervals. The maximum frequency ν_M is, in both cases, associated with the shorter interval τ_1 or τ_2. This maximum frequency is minimum when f and F are similar with

$$\tau_1 = \tau_2 = \tau/2, \qquad \nu_M = 1/\tau. \tag{14.49}$$

This will obviously correspond to the smallest amount of energy required for an observation, and hence to the smallest increase in entropy. Let us examine this situation more carefully.

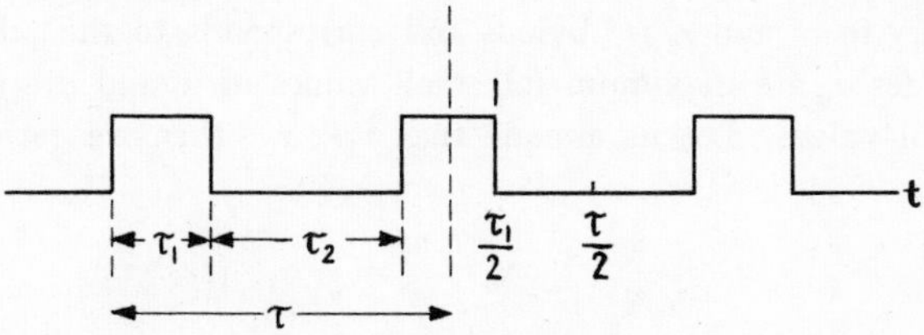

FIG. 14.1. Light pulses of duration τ_1 repeated at intervals τ. The light is off during $\tau_2 = \tau - \tau_1$.

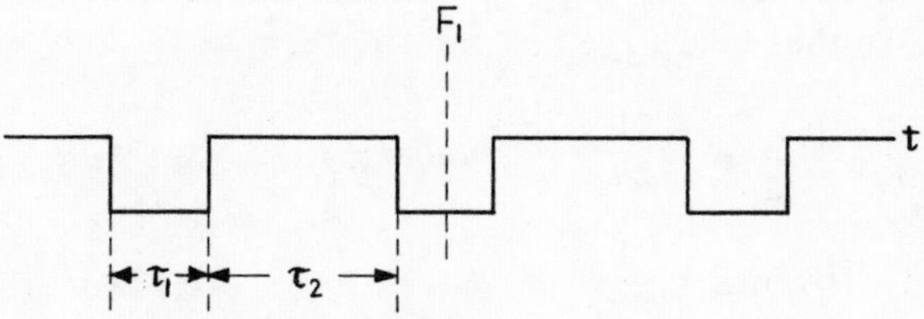

FIG. 14.2. Light pulses of duration τ_2 repeated at intervals τ. This curve is just the reverse of that in Fig. 14.1.

First, we may easily compute the information. We use a succession of pulses $f(t)$ (Fig. 14.1) and we observe light scattered by the molecule. This means that a molecule happens to be in the beam of light during one of the τ_1 pulses. The total *a priori* number P_0 of possibilities is proportional to τ and, after we get this information, the number of possibilities P_1 is proportional to $\tau_1 < \tau$. We use formula (1.6) and obtain the information

$$I = k \ln(P_0/P_1) = k \ln(\tau/\tau_1). \tag{14.50}$$

The shorter the pulse time τ_1 is, the higher is the accuracy and the larger will be the information.

In order to compute the entropy used in an observation, we first analyze the Fourier Spectrum of our function (14.45)

$$f(t) = \frac{\tau_1}{\tau} + \sum_{n=1}^{\infty} a_n \cos n\phi,$$

$$\phi = \frac{2\pi t}{\tau}, \qquad a_n = \frac{2}{\pi n} \sin \frac{\pi n \tau_1}{\tau} = \frac{2}{\pi n} (-1)^{n+1} \sin \frac{\pi_n \tau_2}{\tau}. \tag{14.51}$$

The symmetry in τ_1 and τ_2 is obvious and corresponds to the relation (14.48). The amplitudes a_n are maximum for small values of n, and drop progressively to very small values. Let us assume that $\tau_1 < \tau_2$; then we get the first zero amplitude for

$$n_0 = \frac{\tau}{\tau_1}, \qquad \nu_0 = \frac{n_0}{\tau} = \frac{1}{\tau_1} \qquad (\tau_1 < \tau_2).$$

We must now remember the existence of *noise*. Very small amplitudes in our spectrum (14.51) will be completely blurred by the signal distortion by noise. Let us assume that we can just as well erase these high frequencies and keep only a finite Fourier Spectrum up to $(\frac{1}{2})\,\nu_0$ (one half the frequency of the first zero amplitude). We thus take

$$\begin{aligned} A:\ \nu_{max} &= \frac{1}{2\tau_1}, \qquad n_{max} = \frac{\tau}{2\tau_1}, \qquad (\tau_1 < \tau_2), \\ B:\ \nu_{max} &= \frac{1}{2\tau_2}, \qquad n_{max} = \frac{\tau}{2\tau_2}, \qquad (\tau_2 < \tau_1). \end{aligned} \tag{14.52}$$

The case $\tau_1 = \tau_2$ requires special attention. Our condition (14.52) gives $n_{max} = 1$ in that case, which means that we are using the approximation

$$f = \frac{1}{2} + \frac{2}{\pi} \cos \frac{2\pi t}{\tau} \qquad \tau_1 = \tau_2 = \frac{1}{2}\tau$$

with just one term, as shown on Fig. 14.3, instead of the rectangular curve.

In order to overcome thermal noise, each of the components we keep must have an energy of the order of $k\,T$. Altogether, the total energy in the finite spectrum is

$$E = n_{max}\,\alpha\,k\,T + \beta \frac{k\,T}{2}, \tag{14.53}$$

with numerical coefficients α, β of the order of unity. The last term corresponds to the energy needed in the constant term in order to exceed $(\frac{1}{2})\,k\,T$. This energy is scattered and absorbed (in a photocell for instance) during an observation, and results in an increase of entropy

$$\Delta S = k\{\alpha\, n_{max} + \tfrac{1}{2}\beta\} \tag{14.54}$$

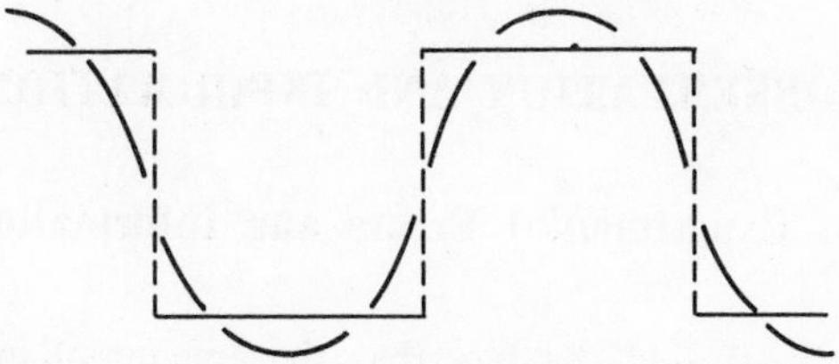

FIG. 14.3. Approximation of the system of pulses with $\tau_1 = \tau_2 = \tau/2$ by the first two terms of the Fourier series:
$f = \frac{1}{2} + (2/\pi)\cos(2\pi\, t/\tau)$.

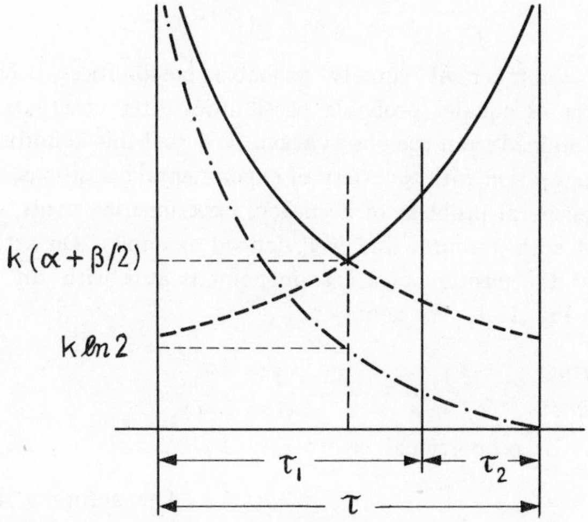

FIG. 14.4. Information and the associated increase in entropy plotted as a function of $\tau_1 = \tau - \tau_2$ for $0 < \tau_1 < \tau$.
I: — · — · — · S: solid curve
unused portion of $(\alpha\, n_{max} + \beta/2)$: - - - -

which varies according to our relations (14.52). The curve is minimum for $\tau_1 = \tau_2 = \frac{1}{2}\tau$ and its general shape is plotted on Fig. 14.4, where the curve of I [Eq. (14.50)] has also been drawn. This example proves again two things: The entropy increase is always larger than the information obtained. The amount of entropy required in an observation cannot go beyond a lower limit which, in our problem is $k(\alpha + \frac{1}{2}\beta)$.

CHAPTER 15

OBSERVATION AND INFORMATION

1. Experimental Errors and Information

We have already stressed the fact that the amount of information to be obtained from an experiment is closely related to the accuracy of the experimental set-up. We started (Chapter 12) with the definition of information:

$$I_1 = k \ln(P_0/P_1), \tag{15.1}$$

where P_0 = number of equally probable possibilities before observation, P_1 = number of equally probable possibilities after observation, and I_1 = information obtained from the observation. We used this definition in Chapters 13 and 14 in connection with a variety of experimental conditions. We now want to discuss the general problem of accuracy, experimental errors, and information. Let us start with a simple and well defined example. On a total length L we observe that the position of a certain point is at x with an error of Δx, as indicated in Fig. 15.1. We define

$$\begin{aligned} &\text{Absolute error:} && \varepsilon_a = \Delta x, \\ &\text{Relative error:} && \varepsilon_r = \Delta x/x, \\ &\text{Comparative or proportional error:} && \varepsilon_c = \Delta x/L . \end{aligned} \tag{15.2}$$

The accuracy $\mathcal{A}$ of the experiment was defined in Eq. (14.29), as the reciprocal of ε_c:

$$\mathcal{A} = 1/\varepsilon_c = L/\Delta x. \tag{15.2 a}$$

This definition fulfills the requirement that increasing accuracy should correspond to smaller and smaller comparative errors.

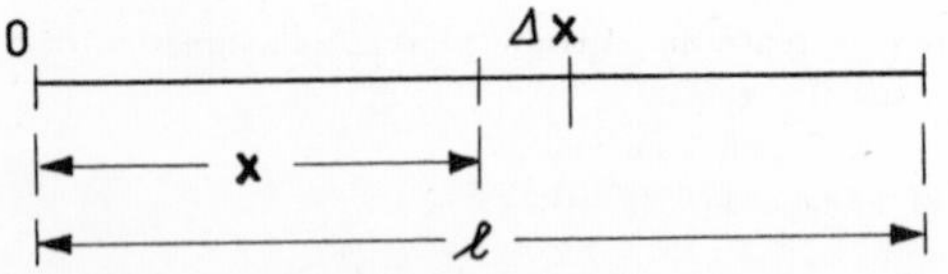

FIG. 15.1. A particle is located, with error Δx, at position x out of a possible range of positions L.

The absolute and relative errors are familiar to the physicist. The comparative error ε_c does not seem to have been mentioned very often. Nevertheless, it is the quantity that is of importance in connection with information theory. The amount of information obtained from the observation is, by Eq. (15.1):

$$\Delta I = k \ln(L/\Delta x) = -k \ln \varepsilon_c = k \ln \mathcal{A}. \tag{15.3}$$

It contains the ratio of the uncertainty Δx (that remains after the observation is made) to the original uncertainty L, corresponding to the whole field of observation. In an optical instrument, this would lead to the consideration of the ratio of the resolving power to the total field of aperture of the instrument.

We have already had to use similar definitions in connection with time measurements (Chapter 14, Section 7). We discussed the case of a short pulse of duration τ, repeated at intervals t, and we found that the important quantity to consider was the ratio τ/t, since it appears both in the expression for information and in the formula for the entropy cost of the operation. We shall discuss now similar problems in space and time, and investigate how to measure the position x, y, z of a particle at a time t, with errors $\Delta x, \Delta y, \Delta z$, and Δt. The definition requires the introduction of the quantities a, b, c, and θ covering the range of admissible values of x, y, z, and t. If this field of observation is not specified, then the information obtained in the measurement cannot be defined and the entropy cost appears as infinite.

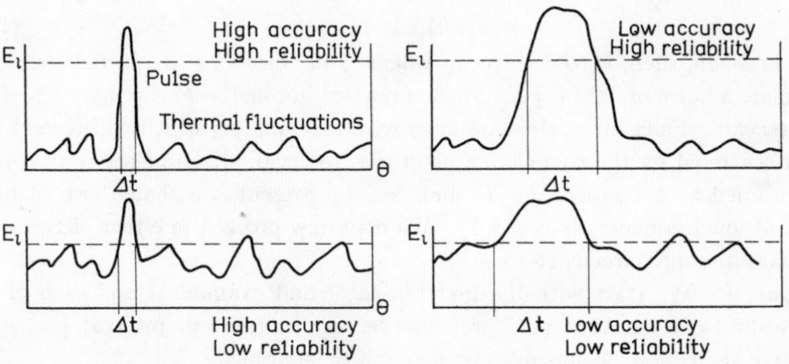

FIG. 15.2. Examples of pulses with thermal noise yielding the four combinations of high and low accuracy with high and low reliability.

Let us remind the reader of the distinction made between "accuracy" and "reliability." In Chapter 14, we defined reliability by considering the possibility of incorrect readings due to thermal fluctuations in the measuring device. A simple drawing shows the difference between these two expressions. In Fig. 15.2, we assume that we are using pulses propagating along a line, and that these pulses are observed in a convenient receiving system. The total duration of the pulse system is θ, and the shortest pulses our receiving system can measure correspond to Δt. The accuracy is $\theta/\Delta t$.

In setting up the receiver, we have chosen a certain limit E_l to the intensity which it records. Pulses of intensity lower that E_l are not recorded, while those of intensity greater than E_l are recorded. If E_l is very much higher than the average thermal fluctuations, the reliability is high, since there is little chance for fluctuations to reach the limit. A low E_l, too close to the intensity of the thermal fluctuations, yields a low reliability. The general situation is illustrated in Fig. 15.2.

2. Length Measurements with Low Accuracy

We start with a very simple problem: the measurement of length with, say, a meter stick. The stick is subdivided into small sections Δx (1 mm, for instance), and we lay the meter stick beside the object to be measured, with the two origins in coincidence. Light is necessary for us to see the stick and the object, and we must look at each subdivision along the stick until we find the one containing the other end of the object to be measured. For the precise discussion, we abstract the procedure as follows: we consider a particle located somewhere along the interval 0 to L on the x-axis, and we wish to measure its position with an accuracy Δx. To do this we divide the segment L into n intervals, each of length Δx:

$$n = L/\Delta x = 1/\varepsilon_c = \mathcal{A}. \tag{15.4}$$

The problem, then, is to discover in which of the intervals the particle lies. We circulate a beam of light (by a system of mirrors, for instance) through each of the n intervals. Each interval is equipped with a resonator, which will receive any light scattered by the particle if it is in that interval. Each of the resonators is maintained at a temperature T, and, for the present, we shall think of using light of low frequency ($h\nu \ll kT$). We may now proceed in either of two ways to make the measurement:

Case I: We start with the first resonator and examine it and each of the succeeding ones in turn until we observe, say in the i-th interval ($i \leqslant n$), a positive deflection, which may be genuine or spurious.

Case II: We examine all n of the resonators, and observe, say, j positive deflections ($1 \leqslant j \leqslant n$), one deflection corresponding to the particle and the other ones being spurious.

We wish to compute the information obtained and the associated entropy increase to show that

$$\Delta(S-I) \geqslant 0$$

in each of these two cases. To do this, we make use of the results of Chapter **14** on observations requiring the use of many resonators. As in Chapter **14**, we assign no significance to a negative reading. Only positive readings (observation of high energy on the resonator) are regarded as yielding information. And, again as in Chapter 14, the entropy increase computed will be a lower bound.

Case I: In case I we observe the particle in interval number i, with $i \leqslant n$. Thus the particle has been located in one position out of an *a priori* possible i positions, and hence the information obtained is

$$\Delta I = k \ln i. \tag{15.5}$$

Observations on i resonators have been made, and, of these, one resonator has absorbed energy which will later be dissipated in the thermostat, so that the accompanying entropy increase is

$$\Delta S \geqslant k A_i \tag{15.5 a}$$

according to Eq. (14.26). If i is large, we have, using Eqs. (15.5), (15.5 a), and Eq. (14.23) for A_i:

$$\Delta(S - I) \geqslant k[\ln i - \ln(\ln 2)] - k \ln i = -k \ln(\ln 2) > 0. \tag{15.6}$$

Of course, i may not be large: we may observe the particle in the first or second interval. In this case, we cannot use the asymptotic expression (14.23) for A_i, although the inequality (15.6) still holds. We give, in Table 15.1, the results for some low values of i:

TABLE 15.1

	i			
	1	2	3	4
A_i	0.69	1.23	1.58	1.84
$\Delta I/k$	0.00	0.69	1.10	1.39
$\Delta(S-I)/k$	0.69	0.54	0.48	0.45

Case II: In this case we have j positive readings so that the number of possible positions for the particle has been reduced from the original n to j. The information obtained is thus

$$\Delta I = k \ln(n/j). \tag{15.7}$$

In this case j resonators have absorbed energy which must later be dissipated with an accompanying increase in entropy of

$$\Delta S \geqslant k j A_n, \tag{15.7 a}$$

since observations have been made on all n of the resonators. We have again made use of Eq. (14.26). Under the assumption that n is large enough to permit use of the asymptotic expression for A_n [Eq. (14.23)], we obtain, using Eqs. (15.7) and (15.7 a):

$$\Delta(S-I) \geqslant k\{j[\ln n - \ln(\ln 2)] - \ln(n/j)\} = k[\ln j + (j-1)\ln n - j\ln(\ln 2)] > 0. \tag{15.8}$$

Equation (15.8) is the same as Eq. (15.6) if $j = 1$, that is, if only one resonator gives a positive reading. For $j > 1$, case *II* yields less information and a larger increase in entropy.

In the following sections we shall make use of the results for case *II*, with $j = 1$. This case yields the smallest difference (among the examples discussed) between entropy increase and information, and, at the same time, enables us to assume that n is large so that the asymptotic expression for A_n may be used.

It should be noted that other possible arrangements of the apparatus will yield still larger entropy increases for the same amount of information. For example, one might arrange the resonators to receive the light directly with a positive reading indicating that the particle is not present. In this case one looks for a negative reading indicating that the particle blocks the passage of light through the interval. It is readily verified that this experiment results in a much larger entropy increase, since most of the resonators absorb energy.

3. Length Measurements with High Accuracy

The preceding discussion is based upon the assumption of low accuracy, when the error Δx in length measurement is not too small, so that low frequencies can be used in the beam of light. When this error Δx is very small, it becomes necessary to use a short wavelength λ and a high frequency in the illuminating radiation, so that the beam illuminates just one interval at a time. Concentration of light on a single interval Δx cannot be practically obtained unless the wavelength λ is shorter than $2\Delta x$:

$$\lambda \leqslant 2\Delta x. \tag{15.9}$$

Three different devices for illumination have been sketched in Fig. 15.3. The first one (*A*) uses a wave guide of thickness d equal to Δx. This wave guide has a low-frequency cut-off corresponding to $\lambda/2 = d$, and can only transmit frequencies above this limit. This is exactly condition (15.9). The beam diverges on emerging from the wave guide with an angle φ which becomes smaller and smaller as the frequency becomes higher and higher. Illumination can be sharply concentrated upon a single interval Δx. In Fig. 15.3 B we use a lens of aperture θ.

The focus obtained has a width

$$\Delta x = \lambda/(2 \sin \theta)$$

according to the well known formula for resolving power. This again yields condition (15.9). In Fig. 15.3 C we try to use a long wavelength λ with a flat screen having a hole of width Δx, but the diffraction below this diaphragm scatters light upon the neighboring intervals, and the concentration of light upon just a single interval Δx cannot be achieved.

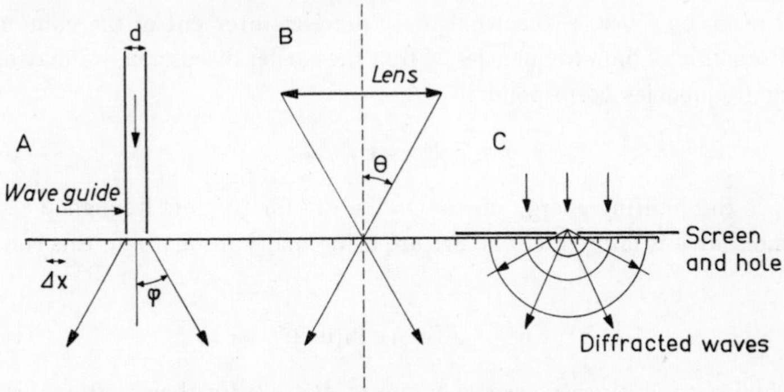

FIG. 15.3. Three devices for concentrating light on an interval Δx: A: A wave guide of thickness $d = \Delta x$. B: A lens of aperture θ. C: A screen with an aperture of width Δx.

It thus appears that the frequency used in the observation must, if we are to have sharp concentration, satisfy the condition

$$\nu = c/\lambda \geqslant c/(2 \Delta x). \tag{15.10}$$

We now define a characteristic length associated with the temperature T, at which the resonators used in the observation are maintained:

$$h \nu / k T = h c/(2 k T \Delta x) = \Delta x_T/(2 \Delta x) \tag{15.11}$$

with

$$\Delta x_T = h c/k T \approx 1.44/T, \tag{15.12}$$

where we have used the minimum value of ν consistent with the condition (15.10).

We may recall that the conditions of Section 2 require low frequency, so that

$$h \nu / k T \ll 1,$$

and this implies that

$$\Delta x \gg \Delta x_T/2, \tag{15.13}$$

which means that the accuracy may be low since a lower limit is placed on the length of the interval Δx.

To obtain high accuracy, on the other hand, we require

$$\Delta x \ll \Delta x_T/2, \tag{15.13 a}$$

which implies [from Eq. (15.11)] that

$$h\nu/kT \gg 1. \tag{15.14}$$

We shall need, however, a somewhat more precise statement of the value for $h\nu$ for the discussion of high frequencies. From the earlier discussion, we may assume that high frequencies correspond to

$$h\nu > E_l = kTA_n, \tag{15.14 a}$$

where E_l is the limiting energy on the oscillators for the low frequency case. If we assume that n is large (i. e. that we are using many resonators), this condition becomes

$$h\nu > kT[\ln n - \ln(\ln 2)]. \tag{15.14 a}$$

For this high-frequency case, we can compute $\Delta(S-I)$ for the situation described at the end of Section 2 (observations taken on n resonators, only one reading positive). Since absorption of a single quantum is sufficient for the single positive reading, we have:

$$\begin{aligned} \Delta S &= h\nu/T > k[\ln n - \ln(\ln 2)], \\ \Delta I &= k \ln n, \\ \Delta(S-I) &> k\ln(\ln 2) > 0. \end{aligned} \tag{15.15}$$

as for the low-frequency case. Actually the entropy increase here may be much larger since ν may be very large. We must not, however, forget the discussion of Chapter 14, Section 6, where the possibility of reducing the fraction of the energy $h\nu$ dissipated was introduced. We cannot, however, improve on the low-frequency case, since sooner or later an observation must be made, on a low-frequency device, if not on a high-frequency one. The generalized Carnot principle is thus satisfied, and we shall discuss later the role played by the large energy required in the experiment. Similar situations will be found in other examples.

The remaining case, $h\nu \approx kT$ will require special discussion for each individual case. If, for example, A_n is small so that Eq. (15.14 a) holds, but Eq. (15.14) does not, we have a situation requiring detailed discussion based on the exact expressions for the various averages necessary for deriving the value of A_n.

4. Efficiency of an Observation

The efficiency $\mathcal{E}$ of an experimental method of observation can be defined as the ratio of the information obtained ΔI to the cost in negentropy $|\Delta N|$, which is the entropy increase ΔS accompanying the observation:

$$\mathcal{E} = \Delta I / |\Delta N| = \Delta I / \Delta S, \qquad \Delta N = -\Delta S. \tag{15.16}$$

When the accuracy is low, we obtain the conditions of Section 2, and for case *II*, with only one positive reading, we have

$$\mathcal{E} = \Delta I / \Delta S = (\ln n)/A_n \approx \frac{1}{1 - \dfrac{\ln(\ln 2)}{\ln n}} \approx 1 + \frac{\ln(\ln 2)}{\ln n} \tag{15.17}$$

for large n and reliability 2. The higher is the accuracy ($\mathcal{A} = n$, large), the higher will be the efficiency $\mathcal{E}$ of the observation, and the efficiency approaches unity for very large n.

Formula (15.17) applies for the case of low reliability, with a probability of $\frac{1}{2}$ that the observation is due to thermal fluctuations. We may use the formulas of Chapter 14, Section 5 for problems requiring high reliability. We found [Eq. (14.34)] that if reliability r and n are both large

$$A_n = \ln(r\,n), \qquad r \gg 1, \qquad n \gg 1,$$

which yields an entropy increase of

$$\Delta S = k \ln(r\,n), \tag{15.18}$$

and an efficiency

$$\mathcal{E}_r = \Delta I / \Delta S \approx (\ln n)/(\ln r\,n) = 1/[1 + (\ln r)/(\ln n)]. \tag{15.19}$$

The efficiency will depend on the relative values of n and r.

We have noted that high accuracy requires the use of high frequency. If, however, suitable devices are introduced to reduce dissipation of energy, the above relations which hold for the low-frequency case, will also be valid for the high-frequency case. Without such devices, Eq. (15.19) is modified, and we have

$$\mathcal{E}_r = \Delta I / \Delta S \approx (\ln n)/(h\,\nu), \tag{15.19 a}$$

with $h\,\nu > E_l \approx \ln r\,n$, so that the efficiency is reduced.

5. Measurement of Distance with an Interferometer

The method of measurement of length, or position, discussed in the preceding sections, yields a relatively small associated increase of entropy; that is to say that the efficiency of the measurement, at least for low reliability, is close to unity, and the efficiency increases with the accuracy. This method also yields a fairly high efficiency for higher reliability with the exact value of the efficiency depending, according to Eq. (15.19), on both reliability and accuracy.

Interferometric measurements, on the other hand, will appear as very costly in terms of entropy increase, and the efficiency will be seen to be low even for low reliability. The essential reason for this, as we shall see, is the necessity of recording many positive readings.

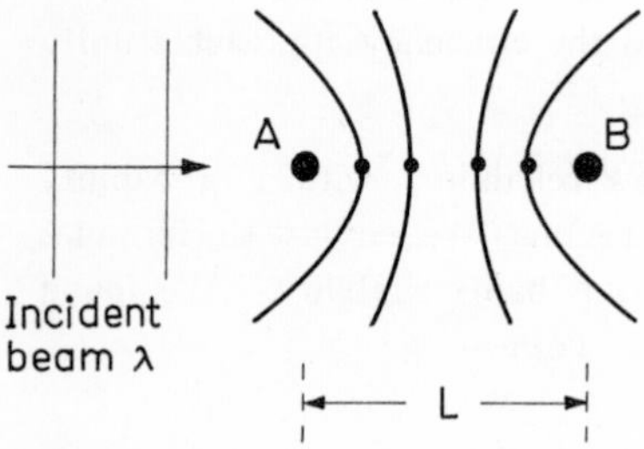

FIG. 15.4. Interference fringes produced by light scattered by two particles A and B a distance L apart.

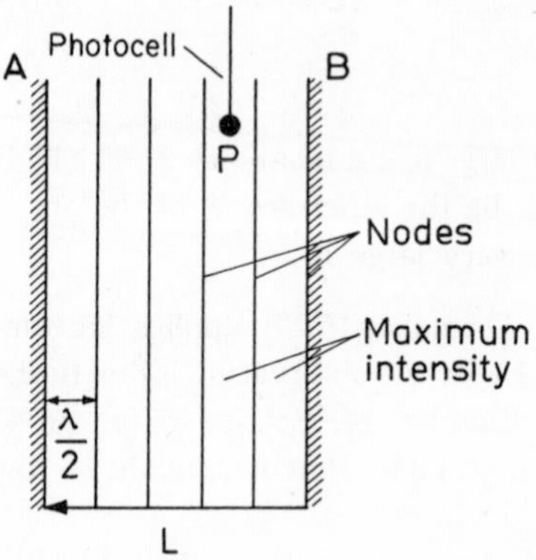

FIG. 15.5 Standing waves between two parallel reflecting plates A and B a distance L apart. The photocell P is used to determine the planes of maximum intensity.

To measure the distance L between two points A and B, we think of locating material particles at A and B, shining light on them, and then observing the interference pattern in the light scattered by the particles. The number n of fringes between A and B gives the number of half wavelengths along the distance L between them (see Fig. 15.4):

$$n\,\lambda/2 = L. \tag{15.20}$$

If we want to be more specific, we must consider an actual interferometer, for instance a Fabry-Perot apparatus used for measuring the length of a standard meter. Reducing the method to its essential features, we may think of two parallel reflecting plates A and B, and a system of standing waves between them, as shown in Fig. 15.5. To find the distance between them, we count the number of planes of maximum intensity between A and B. This could be done by using a photocell P and moving it progressively from A to B. The relation (15.20) gives the frequency of the light

$$\nu = n\, c/2\, L. \tag{15.21}$$

If we need q quanta $h\,\nu$ absorbed in the photocell P in order to observe properly the position of one plane of maximum intensity, then we shall need altogether an amount of radiation energy

$$\Delta E = n\, q\, h\, \nu = n^2\, q\, h\, c/2\, L. \tag{15.22}$$

For low frequencies the number q will be high, but for high frequencies one single quantum per fringe ($q = 1$) may be sufficient. We shall discuss this point carefully.

If all the energy ΔE is absorbed and changed into heat in the thermostat, the corresponding entropy increase during the observation will be

$$\Delta S = \Delta E/T = n^2\, q\, h\, c/2\, L\, T = k\, n^2\, q\, \Delta x_T/2\, L. \tag{15.23}$$

Here we introduce again the characteristic distance Δx_T for a temperature T, defined in Eq. (15.12). Let us assume that we use the smallest acceptable number q of quanta for the existing experimental conditions. We shall discuss this point later. We thus measure the length L with an error that may not exceed $\lambda/2$:

$$\Delta L \approx \lambda/2 = L/n. \tag{15.24}$$

Hence, if conditions (15.23) are realized, we obtain

$$\Delta S = k\, n\, q\, \Delta x_T/(2\, \Delta L). \tag{15.25}$$

Let us now discuss the question of the number q of quanta required to observe the position of a fringe.

A. *Large Distance, Low Accuracy*

These conditions correspond to small quanta and low frequencies, observed on resonators in a thermostat at temperature T:

$$\begin{gathered} h\,\nu \ll k\, T, \\ h\,\nu/k\, T = n\, h\, c/2\, L\, k\, T = \Delta x_T/(2\, \Delta L) \ll 1. \end{gathered} \tag{15.26}$$

We are now working under the conditions specified in Chapter 14, Section 4, where we discussed in a general way an experimental device using a large number n of simultaneous observations. We obtained the following result, for the case of reliability 2 (probability of $\frac{1}{2}$ for error due to fluctuations):

$$E_l = q\, h\, \nu = A_n\, k\, T \qquad \text{with} \qquad A_n > 0.7.$$

This gives

$$q = A_n k T/h\nu = 2 A_n \Delta L/(\Delta x_T) \gg 1.$$

The coefficient A_n was found to amount to a few units. Higher reliability leads to a larger coefficient A_n. From Eq. (15.25) we may compute the entropy increase for case A, since there is no doubt in this case that all the energy ΔE is dissipated in this observation:

$$\Delta S = k n A_n. \tag{15.27}$$

We may think of this observation as measuring the position of B relative to A, say, so that, as in the earlier discussion, the information obtained is

$$\Delta I = k \ln(L/\Delta L) = k \ln n, \tag{15.28}$$

and the efficiency of the observation is, for large n,

$$\mathcal{E} = \Delta I/\Delta S = (\ln n)/(n A_n) \approx \frac{\ln n}{n[\ln n - \ln(\ln 2)]} \approx \frac{1}{n}\{1 + [\ln(\ln 2)]/(\ln n)\} \leqslant 1, \tag{15.29}$$

which is much smaller than in the earlier cases, where only one positive observation is required. If we had required higher reliability, with a lower probability for spurious observations due to thermal fluctuations, we would have used the expression for A_n from Chapter 14, Section 5. The entropy increase ΔS would be n times that for the corresponding case of Section 3, and the efficiency would, accordingly, be lower by a factor of $1/n$.

Whatever the reliability, A_n is always larger than $\ln n$, and the negentropy principle of information yields our generalized Carnot principle

$$\Delta(S - I) = k(n A_n - \ln n) \geqslant 0. \tag{15.30}$$

B. Short Distances or High Accuracy and Low Temperature

These circumstances require high frequencies

$$h\nu \gg kT, \qquad h\nu/kT = (\Delta x_T)/(2\Delta L) \gg 1. \tag{15.31}$$

Here we are operating well beyond the limit of the spectrum of black body radiation at temperature T. We may use a low intensity of one quantum only for each fringe, and so the total amount of energy needed for the measurement is

$$q = 1, \qquad \Delta E = n h\nu = n h c/(2\Delta L), \qquad \Delta L = L/n. \tag{15.32}$$

We are now in the situation discussed in Chapter 14, Section 6, and we must distinguish between the total energy required, and the fraction of it which must finally be dissipated into heat ΔQ. As explained there, we may use a photoelectric cell with a decelerating field, at least theoretically (in practice it would be a very inefficient device!). This will allow us to decrease the energy dissipation to the same value as for the low frequencies used in case A, and formulas (15.27) — (15.30) still apply.

The fact remains, however, that a large energy ΔE is required for the experiment, as shown by Eq. (15.32), which we can rewrite in the following way

$$\Delta E \cdot \Delta L = n h c/2, \qquad n = L/(\Delta L) = \mathcal{A} = \text{accuracy}. \tag{15.33}$$

We shall discuss later on the physical meaning of this relation, which shows that the energy ΔE required may increase without limit as ΔL becomes smaller and smaller.

6. Another Scheme for Measuring Distance

The preceding discussion emphasizes the great difficulty of measuring extremely small distances by interferometric means, and the very high cost of such experiments. In view of the importance of this result, it is useful to show that other and different methods would be at least as costly. One might think, for instance, that the difficulties encountered in the preceding section might be due to the fact that we used wavelengths much shorter than the distances to be measured. This led to extremely short wavelengths in a problem involving very small distances. We may use a different procedure and rely on low frequencies and wavelengths much longer than the distance L to be measured. We thus consider the following conditions:

$$h\nu \ll kT, \qquad \text{hence} \qquad \lambda \gg \Delta x_T, \tag{15.34}$$

according to Eq. (15.24) and the definition of Δx_T in Eq. (15.12). Also we have

$$\lambda \gg L. \tag{15.35}$$

This situation is sketched in Fig. 15.6. We shall observe, in this case, the intensity of light scattered by the particles A and B in both the forward direction and the backward direction. Waves scattered forward by A and B are in phase. Let α be the amplitude scattered by each particle. The total intensity of the waves scattered forward is

$$I_f = 4\alpha^2, \tag{15.36}$$

while waves scattered backward have a phase difference φ and exhibit a resulting intensity

$$I_b = 4\alpha^2 \cos^2(\varphi/2) \approx 4\alpha^2(1 - \varphi^2/4), \tag{15.37}$$

with

$$\varphi = 4\pi L/\lambda, \tag{15.38}$$

which is small because of Eq. (15.35), so that the expansion of $\cos^2(\varphi/2)$ in Eq. (15.37) is valid. The difference i of I_f and I_b yields a measure of L:

$$i = I_f - I_b = I_f\phi^2/4 = I_f 4\pi^2(L/\lambda)^2. \tag{15.39}$$

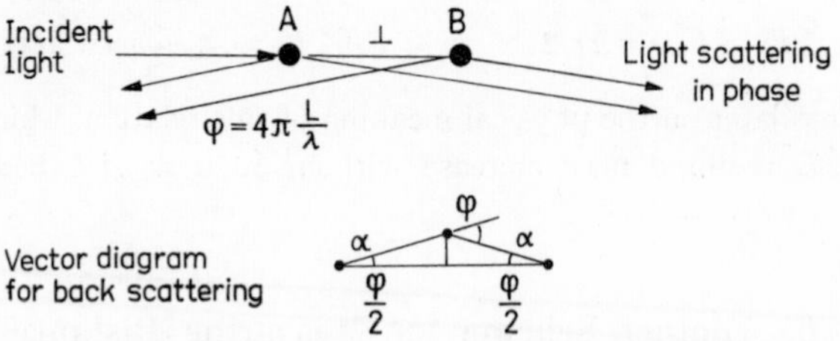

FIG. 15.6. Light of low frequency scattered forward by particles A and B is in phase. That scattered backward is out of phase by $\varphi = 4\pi L/\lambda$. The vector diagram for the backward scattering is also shown. The amplitude is α.

In order to measure I_f and I_b, we must absorb the scattered light in some photoelectric cells or in tuned receivers. We thus dissipate a total energy $I_f + I_b$, and this sum is approximately equal to $2 I_f$. The corresponding entropy increase is

$$\Delta S = 2 I_f/T = i(\lambda/L)^2/2\pi^2 T, \tag{15.40}$$

according to Eq. (15.39). The thermal agitation in the receivers is of the order of $k T$ [according to Eq. (15.34)], and hence we have an error $k T$ in both I_f and I_b so that

$$\Delta i = 2 k T \tag{15.41}$$

is the error in the difference i. We must use large intensities in order to obtain a reasonable accuracy. If we assume that

$$i = \beta k T, \qquad \beta \gg 1, \tag{15.41 a}$$

and

$$I_f = f k T,$$

then, from Eqs. (15.39) and (15.41 a),

$$i = \beta k T = f k T \cdot 4\pi^2 \cdot (L/\lambda)^2,$$

which yields, by Eq. (15.38),

$$\beta/f = 4\pi^2 \cdot (L/\lambda)^2 \ll 1 \qquad \text{or} \qquad f \gg \beta \gg 1.$$

Now from Eqs. (15.41) and (15.41 a), we obtain

$$(\Delta i)/i = 2/\beta, \tag{15.42}$$

while from Eq. (15.39), we have

$$\Delta i = \Delta I_f \cdot 4\pi^2(L/\lambda)^2 + I_f \cdot 4\pi^2(L/\lambda^2) \cdot 2 \Delta L$$

or

$$(\Delta i)/i = (\Delta I_f)/I_f + 2(\Delta L)/L = (1/f) + 2(\Delta L)/L = 2/\beta$$

from Eq. (15.42). This, together with the condition $f \gg \beta$, yields

$$(\Delta L)/L \approx 1/\beta. \tag{15.42 a}$$

The coefficient β thus appears as the accuracy $\mathcal{A}$ in the measurement of L, so that the expression (15.40) for the entropy increase ΔS_l becomes, on using Eq. (15.41 a),

$$\Delta S_l = k(\mathcal{A}/2\pi^2)\,(\lambda/L)^2, \tag{15.43}$$

where we are using long wavelengths $\lambda \gg L$. We must compare this result with the formulas obtained in Section 5. Again, we consider the two cases A and B.

A. Short Wavelengths, Large Distances, Eqs. (15.26) and (15.27)

The condition here is

$$L \gg \Delta x_T. \tag{15.44}$$

The entropy cost for short wavelengths was

$$\Delta S_{S,A} = k\,n\,A_n, \quad \text{with} \quad n = \mathcal{A} \quad \text{and} \quad A_n \approx \ln(r\,n), \tag{15.45}$$

for reliability r in our experiment. Finally, the short-wave method yields

$$\Delta S_{S,A} = k\,\mathcal{A}\ln(r\,\mathcal{A}), \tag{15.46}$$

which means $k\,\mathcal{A}$ multiplied by a numerical factor of a few units or a few tens at most.

With the use of long wavelengths, we have a ΔS_l defined in Eq. (15.43). We must satisfy condition (15.35), and we take

$$\lambda = \gamma L, \qquad \gamma \gg 1.$$

A γ value of a few tens will suffice, and condition (15.34) is automatically satisfied, on account of Eq. (15.44). Finally

$$\Delta S_l = k\,\mathcal{A}\gamma^2/2\pi^2, \tag{15.47}$$

with a numerical coefficient $\gamma^2/2\pi^2$, which amounts to a few tens. Hence in this first case *A* the two methods lead to similar orders of magnitude for the negentropy cost of the measurement.

B. Short Wavelengths, Small Distances, Eqs. (15.31), (15.32), and (15.34)

Let us now assume that

$$L \ll \Delta x_T. \tag{15.48}$$

The energy needed, with short wavelengths, was, according to Eq. (15.32)

$$\Delta E = n^2 h c/2 L = k T n^2 \cdot \Delta x_T/2 L$$

of which only a fraction is necessarily dissipated. Taking, however, the most unfavorable case (all the energy dissipated), we obtain an increase of entropy:

$$\Delta S_{S,B} \geqslant k n^2 \Delta x_T/2 L = k \mathcal{A}^2 \Delta x_T/2 L. \tag{15.49}$$

In using formula (15.43) for the case of long wavelengths, we turn again to the conditions (15.34) and (15.35). The more stringent condition is now (15.34), and we assume

$$\gamma' h \nu = k T \qquad \text{with} \qquad \gamma' \gg 1,$$

which yields

$$\lambda = \gamma' \Delta x_T \qquad \text{and} \qquad \lambda/L = \gamma'(\Delta x_T/L).$$

Here a coefficient γ' of a few units is large enough to make the thermal energy practically $k T$, as required in Eq. (15.41). We thus have

$$\Delta S_l = k \mathcal{A}(\gamma'^2/2\pi^2)(\Delta x_T/L)^2. \tag{15.50}$$

The factor $(\gamma'/\pi)^2$ is of the order of a few units. For small distances L, the entropy cost increases in L^{-2} in Eq. (15.50) for long wavelengths, as compared with only L^{-1} in Eq. (15.49) for short wavelengths. For sufficiently small distances, the method using short wavelengths thus yields a smaller entropy cost than the method with long wavelengths, and, in fact, for extremely small distances the long wavelengths are very costly for this case. The procedure of Section 5 is more favorable than the method investigated here.

This discussion is not quite complete. The entropy increase depends on the accuracy $\mathcal{A}$: it increases in $\mathcal{A}^2$ for short wavelengths, and in $\mathcal{A}$ for long wavelengths. For a given accuracy, however, the general conclusions reached above are valid, at least for sufficiently small distances. The case of moderately small distances would require closer examination, but it does not appear that anything of real importance would arise from this case.

7. The Measurement of Time Intervals

Having discussed the measurement of length in some detail, we now turn to another fundamental problem: the measurement of time. In most clocks, some mechanism is used to move hands in front of a dial. This simply reduces the observation of a time interval to the measurement of an angle, or of a length. The observation, in such a case, proceeds as in the preceding sections.

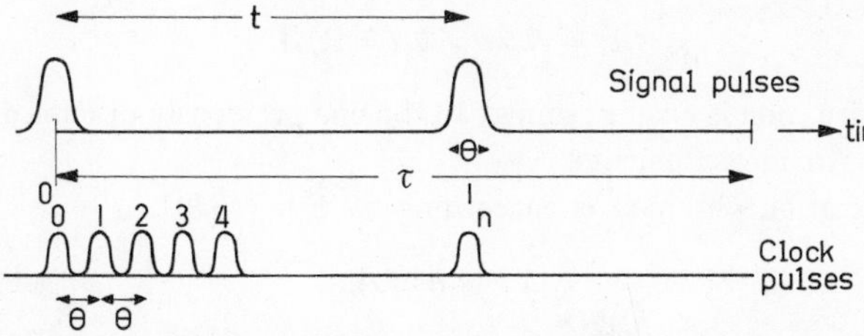

FIG. 15.7. Two signals of duration θ are sent at a time interval t apart, out of a possible range of time τ. An electronic clock emits short pulses at intervals θ, which activate receivers for the signals whose time spacing we wish to measure.

This procedure is, however, not very accurate, and we shall consider another type of time measurement which corresponds essentially to the method used in electronic timing devices, where very high accuracy can be achieved. A time interval t is defined as the distance in time between two pulses, which may be electric pulses sent along a line to a receiver. The situation is sketched in Fig. 15.7. The first pulse coincides with a pulse coming from an electronic timing device. This electronic clock sends a succession of short pulses at intervals θ and θ is also the length of the signal pulse at time t. Each pulse from the clock is used to switch on a certain receiver. Receivers numbered 1, 2, 3, . . . , n are successively connected to the line, from which the signal pulse is supposed to come. If there is no signal during the interval when the receiver is switched on, nothing happens. If there is a signal, the receiver is activated. We thus note, for instance, that receiver number 0 and receiver number n have been activated, and we conclude that the length of the time interval t is

$$t = n\,\theta. \tag{15.51}$$

The switching mechanism does not require, in principle, any energy. It can be operated by changing the voltage on a crystal diode, with no current flowing unless a signal pulse comes in. The operation can also be reduced to changing the voltage on a gating grid in an electron tube. When the signal pulse arrives, it must be recorded, and this means energy dissipation. We may think of using a tuned receiver, but usually an amplifier is needed. This is just an auxiliary device to increase the power, and we are not going to consider the energy required in the amplifying system itself.

In such a problem, we have to specify the total duration τ of the experiment in order to be able to define the amount of information and the entropy cost. We use definitions similar to those introduced in Section 1. We consider the comparative error ε_c and the accuracy $\mathcal{A}$:

$$\varepsilon_c = \Delta t/\tau = \theta/\tau = 1/\mathcal{A}. \tag{15.52}$$

The over-all situation is exactly similar to the one previously discussed in connection with length measurements.

The information obtained is [according to Eq. (15.3)]:

$$\Delta I = k \ln \mathcal{A}, \tag{15.53}$$

while the entropy cost is

$$\Delta S \geqslant 2\, k\, A_{n+1}, \tag{15.54}$$

since we have observed $(n + 1)$ resonators, with positive readings on two of them. We may use the value of A_{n+1} given by Eq. (14.23) for the case of reliability 2 (50% chance of error), or

$$A_{n+1} = \ln[r(n+1)]$$

for a problem requiring high reliability (Chapter 14, Section 5). The generalized Carnot principle holds

$$\Delta(S - I) \geqslant 0. \tag{15.55}$$

In the problem of time measurements, we always remain under the conditions corresponding to case A of Section 5, by virtue of the uncertainty relation. Pulses of duration θ require a band width

$$\Delta \nu = 2\, \nu_M = 1/\theta.$$

We want to prove that this condition yields low frequencies:

$$h\, \nu_M < k\, T, \qquad \text{hence} \qquad \theta = 1/(2\, \nu_M) > h/2\, k\, T, \tag{15.56}$$

a condition which can be written

$$\theta > \Delta\, x_T/2\, c = (1.44 \cdot 10^{-10})/6\, T \text{ seconds}, \tag{15.57}$$

where T is the Kelvin temperature, and $\Delta\, x_T$ is the characteristic length of temperature T defined in Eq. (15.12). Condition (15.56) is practically always fulfilled. This condition can be examined from the point of view of the uncertainty relation. It is well known that the time t and the energy E represent a pair of conjugate variables. Hence when we measure t with an accuracy Δt, we certainly introduce an unknown perturbation ΔE in the energy E:

$$\Delta E \cdot \Delta t \approx h. \tag{15.58}$$

This uncertainty ΔE must be compared with the normal energy fluctuations ε resulting from the thermal agitation at the temperature T:

$$\overline{\Delta_1 E} \approx \sqrt{\overline{\varepsilon^2}} = \sqrt{n}\, k\, T, \tag{15.59}$$

where n represents the number of "active" degrees of freedom of the system, namely the number of vibrations of low frequency $(h\nu \leqslant k T)$. High-frequency vibrations are not excited, in practice, and contribute very little to energy fluctuations. We thus have to compare ΔE and $\Delta_1 E$:

Case A.

$$\text{If} \quad \Delta E \ll \Delta_1 E \quad \text{then} \quad \Delta t \gg h/(\sqrt{n}\, k\, T). \tag{15.60}$$

This is the case considered in this section. The perturbation due to the time measurement is negligible and can be ignored. Conditions (15.57) and (15.60) differ only in the factor $\sqrt{n}$.

Case B.

$$\text{If} \quad \Delta E \geqslant \Delta_1 E, \quad \text{then} \quad \Delta t \leqslant h/(\sqrt{n}\, k\, T). \tag{15.61}$$

These conditions would result in a large perturbation of the system. Too large an accuracy in the definition of time might even destroy the system under observation, since it would require high frequencies, yielding large quanta $h\nu$, of the order of $\Delta_1 E$ or more.

8. Observation under a Microscope

The problems of distance and time measurements have been discussed in the preceding sections, and their applications cover almost entirely the field of physical experiments. Measurement of an electric current, for instance, results from a reading on an ammeter, which is a measurement of position of the needle on the dial, and this can be reduced to a length measurement. Measurement of length, of time intervals, and counting are the principal experimental methods of observation, and our discussion shows how the negentropy principle of information applies to these problems.

The question is, however, of such importance, that we shall investigate some additional examples. Let us first discuss how we can define the position of a particle with the help of a microscope, concentrating light on a focus F as shown in Fig. 15.8. This requires a certain frequency range and a very large number of photons falling on the lens, in order to give good definition of the focus. The problem is completely specified only when we limit the field of the apparatus as indicated in Fig. 15.8. The light passes through a wave guide, which we may choose of rectangular cross section, with sides a and b in the directions x and y, respectively. The wave guide defines a discrete set of proper waves,[1] the superposition of which can result in a focus at a certain level $z = 0$, the focal plane.

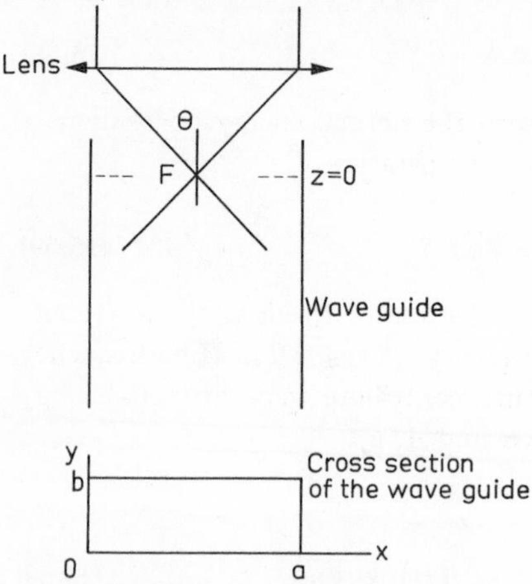

FIG. 15.8. The wave guide limits the range of observation by the microscope lens of aperture θ. The focus F of the lens is at the level $z = 0$ of the rectangular wave guide.

Let us select the H (transverse electric) waves with a vertical magnetic field whose magnitude must have a zero normal derivative on the boundary:

$$H_z = \sum_{l,\,m} A_{lm} \cos \frac{\pi l x}{a} \cos \frac{\pi m y}{b} \cos \omega \left(t - \frac{z}{V_{lm}} \right), \tag{15.62}$$

where l and m represent the number of nodes in the x and y directions respectively, while V_{lm} is the phase velocity of this particular wave in the z direction. The integers l and m can run from 0 to ∞ but the combination 0,0 is excluded. The wave propagation equation

$$\nabla^2 H_z - \frac{1}{c^2} \frac{\partial^2 H_z}{\partial t^2} = 0 \tag{15.63}$$

yields

$$\omega^2 \left(\frac{1}{c^2} - \frac{1}{V_{lm}{}^2} \right) = \left(\frac{\pi l}{a} \right)^2 + \left(\frac{\pi m}{b} \right)^2. \tag{15.64}$$

---

[1] See, for instance, C. G. Montgomery, R. H. Dicke, and E. M. Purcell, "Principles of Microwave Circuits," M. I. T. Radiation Lab. Series, Vol. 8, pp. 34, 37, 55. McGraw-Hill, New York, 1948.

The phase velocity V_{lm} is larger than c, while the group velocity U_{lm} is smaller than c. Both velocities approach the limit c for high frequencies. As V_{lm} becomes infinite (and U_{lm} approaches zero), we obtain a low-frequency cut-off:

$$\frac{1}{c^2}\,\omega_{l,m}{}^2 = \left(\frac{\pi l}{a}\right)^2 + \left(\frac{\pi m}{b}\right)^2, \tag{15.65}$$

and since

$$\omega_{lm}/c = 2\pi/\lambda_{lm}$$

the corresponding wavelength is given by

$$4/\lambda_{lm}{}^2 = (l/a)^2 + (m/b)^2.$$

A given l, m wave can be generated by a plane wave entering the wave guide at an oblique angle and being reflected back and forth from the walls. Let us designate by ϕ_x, ϕ_y, and θ the angles made by the incident ray with the x, y, and z axes, respectively. We will have

$$\left.\begin{aligned} &\cos\phi_x = \pm\, l\,\lambda/2\,a, \qquad \cos\phi_y = \pm\, m\,\lambda/2\,b, \\ &\text{and hence} \\ &V_{l,m} = \frac{c}{\cos\theta} > c, \\ &\frac{\omega^2}{c^2}\sin^2\theta = \left(\frac{\pi l}{a}\right)^2 + \left(\frac{\pi m}{b}\right)^2, \end{aligned}\right\} \tag{15.66}$$

or

$$\frac{4}{\lambda^2}\sin^2\theta = (l/a)^2 + (m/b)^2.$$

Cut-off conditions correspond to $\theta = \pi/2$. In the case of Fig. 15.9, we obviously excite the higher l, m components through the oblique rays in the convergent beam. A convenient superposition of terms [Eq. (15.62)] may be used to construct a focus F. When the frequency of the beam ω is given, Eq. (15.65) provides an absolute limitation to the l, m values, since they must always yield $\omega_{lm} < \omega$. When the angle θ_0 of angular aperture is given, Eq. (15.66) gives a stronger limitation to the l, m values. High accuracy in the definition of a focus will require high l, m terms in the sum, and this, in turn, requires high frequency ω and a large aperture θ_0.

Our problem, however, is different. We shall be satisfied with a limited accuracy in the definition of the focus, and we want to relate this accuracy to the information obtained in the observation. We take a finite number of terms of the sum (15.62):

$$0 \leqslant l \leqslant l_M, \qquad 0 < m \leqslant m_M, \tag{15.67}$$

and we use a frequency above the limits given by Eq. (15.66). Conditions (15.67) yield a focal spot of finite dimensions:

$$\Delta x \geqslant a/l_M, \qquad \Delta y \geqslant b/m_M. \tag{15.68}$$

We cannot separate the variables z and t since our waves are propagating freely in the z direction, and we assume that the wave guide is either infinite, or else so terminated as to avoid reflections. What we can do is to use short pulses of duration τ as we did in Chapter 13, and, in order to obtain a finite number of degrees of freedom, we must use pulses repeated periodically on an interval t. This gives us, for each wave, a number of degrees of freedom [Eq. (13.36)]:

$$n \geqslant t/2\tau. \tag{15.69}$$

Altogether our beam has $l_M \cdot m_M \cdot n$ degrees of freedom of frequency ω. Let us assume a low frequency at a temperature T: $h\nu < kT$. Each degree of freedom will have an energy kT, and therefore the total thermal energy will be

$$E_T = l_M \cdot m_M \cdot n\,k\,T. \tag{15.70}$$

If we want to observe a focus that can be distinguished from the thermal background, we must use an energy E at least equal to $A\,E_T$, where A is the coefficient defined in Chapter 14, Sections 4 and 5. When an observation is made, the radiation energy is scattered by the particle under consideration, and the energy is absorbed in some photoelectric cells. This results in an entropy increase:

$$\Delta S = E/T \geqslant l_M \cdot m_M \cdot n\,k\,A, \tag{15.71}$$

or, by use of Eqs. (15.68) and (15.69)

$$\Delta S \geqslant A\,k\,F/2 \quad \text{with} \quad A > 1 \quad \text{and} \quad F = \frac{a}{\Delta x} \cdot \frac{b}{\Delta y} \cdot \frac{t}{\tau} \cdot \tag{15.72}$$

The information obtained is, according to Eqs. (15.1) and (15.3),

$$\Delta I = k \ln F, \tag{15.73}$$

a quantity which is always smaller than ΔS. Our negentropy principle of information is satisfied, since

$$\Delta(S - I) \geqslant k[(A\,F/2) - \ln F] > 0, \tag{15.74}$$

an inequality very similar to the one obtained in Gabor's discussion of Szilard's problem [Eq. (13.55)]. The expression (15.74) is always positive. It has a minimum value for $F = 2/A$, and this minimum value is $k[1 - \ln(2/A)] > 0$, since A is larger than unity.

When the field of observation is very large and the accuracy is high, the quantity F becomes very large and the entropy cost ΔS of an observation is very much larger than the information ΔI obtained. This remark may have some important implications in many physical problems. Observation of a focus without time and field limitations would make the entropy cost infinite, but this does not correspond to any physical problem.[2]

9. Discussion of the Focus in a Wave Guide

We now return to conditions (15.67) and investigate more carefully the conditions near a focus in a wave guide. We must keep in mind the fact that the pipe's boundaries act as perfect mirrors, reflecting the pipe's cross section indefinitely up and down, and right and left, as indicated in Fig. 15.9. A focus $F_{0,0}$ within the pipe has its images at $F_{-1,0}$, $F_{0,-1}$, $F_{-1,-1}$, in the next rectangles,

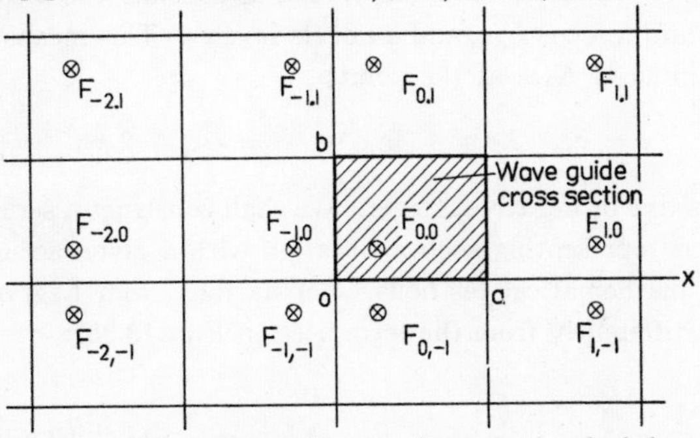

FIG. 15.9. The wave guide's cross section is shown in the shaded area with the focus of the lens at $F_{0,0}$. Because the walls of the guide are perfect reflectors, images of the focus will be produced as shown.

and so on indefinitely. How can we represent such a situation with a system of waves of the type of Eq. (15.62)? We first note that the focal plane $z = 0$ is characterized by the fact that all components are in phase in the expansion (15.62). For a different z value, these same components are no longer in phase because of their different V_{lm} velocities, and the beam spreads out. Considering only the focal plane $z = 0$, we have

$$H_{z=0} = \sum_{l,m} A_{lm} \cos l\theta \cos m\psi \cos \omega t, \tag{15.75}$$

[2] This problem has been discussed by G. Toraldo di Francia, *J. Opt. Soc. Amer.* **45**, 497 – 501 (1955).

with

$$\phi = \pi\, x/a, \qquad \psi = \pi\, y/b.$$

We may split the double Fourier series into two separate series, one in x and the other in y, thus obtaining

$$\left.\begin{aligned} H_{z=0} &= X(x)\,Y(y)\cos\omega t, \\ X(x) &= \sum_l X_l \cos l\phi, \qquad 1 \leqslant l \leqslant l_M, \\ Y(y) &= \sum_m Y_m \cos m\psi, \qquad 1 \leqslant m \leqslant m_M, \\ A_{lm} &= X_l\, Y_m. \end{aligned}\right\} \tag{15.76}$$

We exclude $l = 0$ and $m = 0$, in order to eliminate the forbidden term 0,0.

The problem is symmetric in x and y. Let us consider the x coordinate only. We want to obtain a focus $F_{0,\,0}$ and all of its images. This means that we must have sharp maxima of $X(x)$ at the points

$$x = x_0 + 2\,p\,a \qquad \text{and} \qquad x = -\,x_0 + 2\,p\,a, \tag{15.77}$$

where p is a positive or negative integer. We shall construct a series with a finite number of terms representing such a situation with a given accuracy, but first we need a few mathematical relations. Let us start from Lagrange's identity, written a little differently from the form used in Eq. (13.35):

$$\cos\phi + \cos 2\phi + \ldots + \cos l_M\phi = \sum_1^{l_M} \cos l\phi = \tfrac{1}{2}\left(\frac{\sin(l_M + \frac{1}{2})\,\phi}{\sin\frac{1}{2}\phi} - 1\right)$$

$$= \frac{\sin\dfrac{l_M}{2}\,\phi\,\cos\dfrac{l_M+1}{2}\,\phi}{\sin\dfrac{\phi}{2}}. \tag{15.78}$$

The result is obtained by simple trigonometric transformations based on the relations

$$(l_M + \tfrac{1}{2})\,\phi = \frac{l_M}{2}\,\phi + \frac{l_M+1}{2}\,\phi,$$

$$\tfrac{1}{2}\phi = -\,\frac{l_M}{2}\,\phi + \frac{l_M+1}{2}\,\phi.$$

We now take

$$1 \leqslant l \leqslant l_M, \qquad X_l = \cos l\,\phi_0, \qquad \phi_0 = \pi\, x_0/a, \tag{15.79}$$

which yields

$$X(x) = \sum_0^{l_M} \cos l\phi \cos l\phi_0 = \tfrac{1}{2} \sum_1^{l_M} [\cos l(\phi - \phi_0) + \cos l(\phi + \phi_0)],$$

or, if we use Eq. (15.78)

$$X(x) = \frac{\sin \frac{l_M}{2}(\phi - \phi_0) \cos \frac{l_M + 1}{2}(\phi - \phi_0)}{2 \sin \frac{\phi - \phi_0}{2}} + \frac{\sin \frac{l_M}{2}(\phi + \phi_0) \cos \frac{l_M + 1}{2}(\phi + \phi_0)}{2 \sin \frac{\phi + \phi_0}{2}}. \tag{15.80}$$

The first term yields sharp maxima at

$$\phi = \phi_0 + 2\,p\pi$$

when its denominator is zero. The second term gives maxima at

$$\phi = -\phi_0 + 2\,p\pi$$

and this gives the complete system of the focus and its images defined by Eq. (15.77). The system degenerates when ϕ_0 is zero, that is, when the focus is at one corner of the wave guide.

The series of coefficients (15.79) gives exactly the conditions required. Let us consider the original focus itself and its neighborhood

$$x = x_0 + \delta x, \qquad \phi = \phi_0 + \delta\phi, \qquad \delta x = a\,\delta\phi/\pi. \tag{15.81}$$

The second term in Eq. (15.80) is negligible. The first term has a maximum value of $l_M/2$ at the focus ($\delta\phi = 0$), and has its first zeros at

$$\delta\phi = \pm\pi/(l_M + 1)$$

when the cosine term in the numerator of the first term is zero. The width of the maximum can be practically defined as $\frac{1}{2}$ of the distance between the first zeros to the right and to the left:

$$\begin{aligned} \Delta\phi &= (2\,\delta\phi)/2 = \pi/(l_M + 1), \\ \Delta\, x &= a/(l_M + 1) \approx a/l_M. \end{aligned} \tag{15.82}$$

When l_M is large, this condition reduces to our earlier relation (15.67).

Similar considerations apply to the y coordinate. It is easy to verify that these conditions correspond exactly to the usual definition of resolving power. Let us consider a square aperture, and take equal limits along x and y:

$$a = b = r, \qquad \Delta x = \Delta y, \qquad l_M = m_M = M.$$

The radius of the focus is

$$\Delta r = \sqrt{(\Delta x)^2 + (\Delta y)^2} = r \sqrt{\frac{1}{{l_M}^2} + \frac{1}{{m_M}^2}} = \sqrt{2}\, r/M.$$

The limiting angle θ_0 is obtained from Eq. (15.66):

$$\frac{4\,\nu^2}{c^2} \sin^2 \theta_0 = \left(\frac{l_M}{a}\right)^2 + \left(\frac{m_M}{b}\right)^2 = 2\left(\frac{M}{r}\right)^2, \tag{15.83}$$

so that

$$\Delta r = c/(\nu \sin \theta_0) = \lambda/(\sin \theta_0), \tag{15.84}$$

which is the usual formula for the resolving power as a function of wavelength λ and angular aperture θ_0.

10. Examples and Discussion

The reader may wonder why we obtained similar relations in Eqs. (15.67) and (15.69), except for a factor $\frac{1}{2}$ in Eq. (15.69). The reason is that we need a system of standing waves along x and y. Standing waves are built out of two similar waves propagating in opposite directions. These two opposite waves result from reflections in the sides of the wave guide. In the z direction we have only one propagating wave, and no reflected wave. This accounts for the factor $\frac{1}{2}$ in the number n of degrees of freedom in Eq. (15.69). We have already explained, at the beginning of Section 9, that all the component waves are exactly in phase on the focal plane $z = 0$, and get rapidly out of phase for different z values, because of their different velocities V_{lm}. We could equally well consider the focus as resulting from a convergent beam, with a maximum angle θ_0 defined by Eq. (15.83). The beam diverges beyond the focus, and θ_0 gives the angle of divergence.

Instead of a sharp focus, we may need a long needle-like beam. This can be obtained by using a high frequency and small angles θ. Formulas (15.66) or (15.83) show the possibility of adjusting these parameters in such a way that the integers l and m remain large and the beam has a small cross section.

We also have the possibility of producing, at least approximately, a plane beam of given thickness. This can be done by taking a cylindrical lens and small angles θ, with long slits limiting the beam in the x direction, but not in the y direction, as indicated in Fig. 15.10. The wave expansion (15.76) would be, in the focal plane,

$$H_{z=0} = X(x) \cos \omega t$$

with no dependence on y. The resulting beam is

$$H = \sum_{l=1}^{l_M} X_l \cos l\phi \cos \omega(t - (z/V_l)), \tag{15.85}$$

with $m = 0$. A high frequency ω, much above the cut-off frequency

$$\omega \gg \omega_{l_M} = \pi c\, l_M / a \tag{15.86}$$

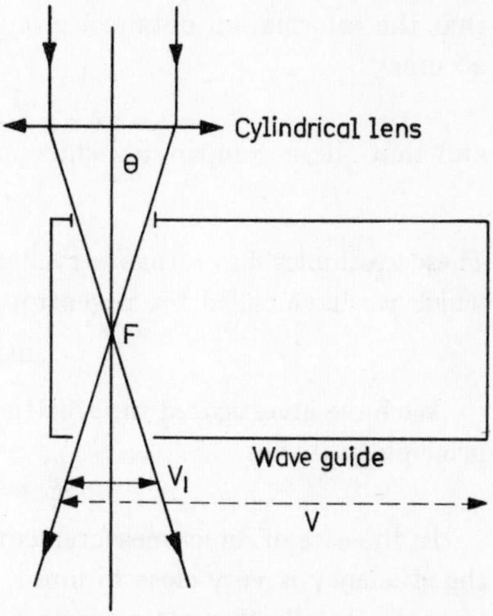

FIG. 15.10. A beam of small divergence produced by a cylindrical lens, and suitable for use in Szilard's machine.

will give a beam with a very small divergence. These conditions correspond to the problem of Szilard's machine discussed in Chapter 13, Section 6. Figure 15.10, rotated through 90 degrees, corresponds to the situation in Fig. 13.5. In this case we have $\Delta y = b$, and the expression for F in Eq. (15.72) reduces to

$$F = \frac{a}{\Delta x} \cdot \frac{t}{\tau} = (V/V_1)^2. \tag{15.87}$$

This is exactly the value of F used in Eq. (13.55), and the combination of Eqs. (15.74) and (15.87) is identical with the earlier result of Chapter 13, obtained by a different method.

Our Eqs. (15.72) and (15.74) contain the numerical coefficient A, whose values were discussed in Chapter 14, Section 5. For low frequencies, this coefficient has the value A_n which may reach a few units, but some experimental conditions may require high frequencies which lead to a much larger value for A:

$$A = \begin{cases} A_n & \text{when} \quad h\nu \ll kT \\ h\nu/kT & \text{when} \quad h\nu \gg kT. \end{cases} \tag{15.88}$$

The first case holds for "classical" observations. The second case certainly corresponds to an observation perturbing the observed system and requiring quantum conditions.

11. Summary

In all of the examples discussed in this and earlier chapters, we have found that the information obtained in an experiment depends logarithmically on the accuracy:

$$\Delta I = k \ln \mathcal{A}, \tag{15.89}$$

and that the accompanying entropy increase satisfies the inequality

$$\Delta S \geqslant \Delta I. \tag{15.90}$$

These examples have thus served to verify the generalized Carnot principle, which we have called the negentropy principle of information:

$$\Delta(S - I) \geqslant 0. \tag{15.91}$$

We have investigated the efficiency of observations, which, by the negentropy principle, satisfies

$$\mathcal{E} = \Delta I / \Delta S \leqslant 1. \tag{15.92}$$

In the case of direct measurement of length (Sections 2 and 3 of this chapter), the efficiency is very close to unity, and the negentropy cost of the observation is small. In all other cases considered, however, the efficiency is much less than unity and the entropy increase depends at least linearly on the accuracy:

$$\Delta S = a\mathcal{A} + b. \tag{15.93}$$

The constant b is usually small. The coefficient a is a constant in some cases, and in others is a logarithmic function of $\mathcal{A}$. The interferometric method of distance measurement and the measurement of position by a microscope both lead to entropy increases of the form given by Eq. (15.93). Evidently in these cases the efficiency decreases rapidly with increasing accuracy.

We have seen that, generally speaking, efficiency is higher for low frequencies. The exception occurs in cases where quantum conditions enter because of very high accuracy requirements. Under such circumstances, the use of high frequencies is more favorable, even though the efficiency is still very low. In this case, however, we can increase the efficiency by introduction of suitable devices to reduce the dissipation of energy. In effect this procedure converts a high-frequency problem into a low-frequency one, and the corresponding results for low frequencies can thus be made to apply in all cases.

It should, perhaps, be remarked that the direct method of measurement of distance, which gave a very high efficiency, is not one which can easily be used in the laboratory for the measurement of small distances because of the difficulties in the design of suitable apparatus. Very small distances are always measured by interferometric means, and thus, in practice, the low efficiencies found in most of the examples are the ones we must consider.

CHAPTER 16

INFORMATION THEORY, THE UNCERTAINTY PRINCIPLE, AND PHYSICAL LIMITS OF OBSERVATION

1. General Remarks

We have discussed a variety of experiments, and we have obtained a general result: the negentropy principle of information, which says that any information resulting from a physical observation must be paid for by an increase in entropy in the laboratory. On the average, this entropy increase is larger than the information obtained when both quantities are measured in the same system of units. These conditions represent a new limitation on the possibilities of observation, and we want to compare it with the well known uncertainty relations.

There has been a great deal of discussion, during the last half century, on the relations between classical physics and quantum physics. The original point of view of N. Bohr, expressed in his principle of "complementarity" and his interpretation of the uncertainty relations, seems to remain the sound and logical approach to the problem. Recent discussions[1] have clearly emphasized the importance of the questions involved. Physics starts, historically and actually, on the classical level, with experiments made at the human scale, and fundamental definitions (length, time, mass, general laws) based on these experiments. From this solid ground, the physicist proceeds to the investigation of atomic problems and discovers the quantum conditions, with all the limitations involved in the uncertainty principle, and wave mechanics. Consistency requires that these new laws should, in the limit of very large quantum numbers, reduce to classical laws. Bohr emphasized repeatedly the fact that a measuring apparatus is always described in classical terms, but he also introduced the "correspondence principle," according to which quantum laws must lead to classical laws in the limit, when Planck's constant h can be considered as negligibly small.

Bohm states that "quantum theory presupposes the classical concepts in describing this level." How can we define classical physics? Elsasser characterizes

[1] W. Elsasser, *Phys. Rev.* **52**, 987 (1937); *Phil. Sci.* **18**, 300 (1951); *in* "Louis de Broglie Physicien et Penseur," p. 87. Albin Michel, Paris, 1953; N. Bohr and L. Rosenfeld, *Phys. Rev.* **78**, 794 (1950); L. Rosenfeld, *in* "Louis de Broglie Physicien et Penseur," p. 43. Albin Michel, Paris, 1953; D. Bohm, "Quantum Theory." Prentice-Hall, New York, 1951.

this stage by the possibility of nonperturbing experiments, in which a clear distinction can be drawn between the observer and the system under observation. A typical example is an optical observation of a mechanical system, a falling body, for instance. The experiment does not appreciably perturb the system, and can be repeated many times with consistent results. It has the fundamental property of reproducibility. It is not easy to state precise conditions for such nonperturbing observations. A few points may, however, be stressed: The system under experimentation must contain many particles and a large number of quanta. The accuracy of the experiment must not be too high. An obvious condition is that one must operate far from the limits of the uncertainty relations:

$$\Delta p \cdot \Delta q >>> h \quad \text{and} \quad \Delta E \cdot \Delta t >>> h. \tag{16.1}$$

The errors Δp, Δq, ΔE, and Δt must not be too small, in order to assure the possibility of simultaneous determination of p, q, E, and t.

We can also introduce another condition, which now results from the discussion presented in this book. The entropy cost ΔS of the observation should be negligible, when compared with the total entropy S_0 of the system under observation:

$$\Delta S \ll S_0,$$

and hence

$$\Delta I \leqslant \Delta S \ll S_0, \tag{16.2}$$

since the information ΔI obtained is always smaller than the entropy cost ΔS. These conditions are certainly necessary but they may not be sufficient. The general scheme is the following: At first the system and the measuring device are not coupled. During the observation a coupling is established, with a certain amount of interaction. After the observation, the system and the measuring device are uncoupled. During the observation there are changes in the p, q, E, and S of the system, and these unknown changes occur during the time interval Δt of the experiment. The observation can be considered as "nonperturbing" if these unknown changes are extremely small when compared with the accuracy of the experiment. Conditions (16.1) and (16.2) are thus necessary. Let us, for instance, consider the case of Eq. (16.2). The experiment results in an increase ΔS in the total entropy of the observed system and of the measuring device. When the systems are uncoupled after the experiment, part of this ΔS will be associated with the observed system, and the rest with the observing apparatus, but it is, in general, impossible to distinguish clearly between these two parts. Hence we must require that the total increase ΔS should always be very small when compared with the entropy S_0 of the observed system.

Elsasser considers, as an example, the problem of the molecules in a gas. It is possible, in principle, to measure very accurately the positions of all the molecules, but such an observation would require a beam of light of very high frequency. Interaction of this light with the molecules would transfer to them very high impulses and greatly alter the entire system. This is clearly not a nonperturbing observation, and is forbidden by conditions (16.1) and (16.2). On the other hand, measurements of volume, pressure, and density can be made under conditions (16.1) and (16.2), provided the accuracy is not too high.

2. An Observation is an Irreversible Process

In order to avoid misunderstanding and to clarify the situation, we must specify that the entropy increase ΔS required for the observation has no relation whatsoever with entropy changes occurring in the system itself, as long as no measurement is performed.

Let us, for instance, consider a system undergoing an adiabatic transformation.[2] There is no entropy change within the system, but the adiabatic transformation goes on unnoticed and unobserved, when the system is not coupled with a device permitting observation. We assume that this adiabatic transformation involves variations in the physical variables (p, v, T, etc.), but, as long as we do not measure these variables, we have no way of knowing what is

---

[2] An adiabatic transformation is described as a succession of states of equilibrium. If the system is contained in a cylinder of length L with a moving piston, the motion δx of the piston must be very small during a time δt large enough to allow for the perturbation to travel back and forth many times over the distance L. This requires $\delta x/\delta t = v <<< c$, where c is the velocity of the perturbation. For radiation, c is the velocity of light; for a gas, c is the thermal velocity of the molecules; for a solid or a liquid, c is the velocity of sound.

Adiabatic transformations of quantized systems have been discussed by many authors. Bohm (*loc. cit.*, Chapter 20, in ref. 1) states the condition

$$\frac{h}{(\Delta E)^2}\frac{\partial E}{\partial t} \ll 1,$$

where E is the energy, and ΔE is the energy difference to the next quantum state. Let us consider standing waves over a distance L, with N nodes, so that $L = N\lambda/2 = N c/(2\nu)$, and hence $E = n h \nu = h c n N/(2L)$ and $\Delta E = h\nu = h c N/(2L)$, if there are n quanta $h\nu$ of oscillation on our standing wave. Then

$$\frac{\partial E}{\partial t} = -h c n N v/(2L^2), \qquad \text{with} \qquad v = \frac{\partial L}{\partial t},$$

and Bohm's condition for an adiabatic transformation reads

$$2 n v/(N c) \ll 1,$$

a relation similar to our earlier $v <<< c$.

going on. In order to observe p, v, T, etc., we must couple the system with some physical instruments, and we thus introduce a slight perturbation. The observation itself is an irreversible process involving an increase ΔS in the entropy of the laboratory. We always have to read the position of a pointer in front of a scale (distance measurements) and to note time intervals. These fundamental observations were discussed in Chapter 15, and every physical observation can be reduced to these elements.

In this example, we clearly see the distinction between the entropy changes occurring in an isolated (and hence unobserved) system and the entropy increase ΔS required for an observation and due to the coupling between the observed system and the measuring instruments.

An observation is essentially an irreversible process. From a purely thermodynamical point of view, we have proved that no observation can be made without an accompanying increase of entropy in the physical system itself or in the equipment used for the experiment, and coupled with the system during the observation:

$$\Delta S > 0. \tag{16.3}$$

If we take the more general point of view described in the preceding chapters, we include the information I in the entropy, and the condition is

$$\begin{aligned} &\Delta(S - I) \geqslant 0, \\ &\Delta S \geqslant \Delta I > 0. \end{aligned} \tag{16.4}$$

In both cases, an increase of entropy is inevitable whenever an observation is performed, and hence, since an increase of entropy implies irreversibility, irreversibility appears as characteristic of an observation.

Similar remarks have previously been made by many authors, and especially by J. von Neumann, in the discussion of some paradoxical problems of quantum mechanics. One should never speak of a system being in a certain state unless he makes a measurement of some quantity involved. This process of measurement is irreversible, and determines, at least partially, the future behavior of the system.

3. General Limitations in the Accuracy of Physical Measurements

We have discovered difficulties in the measurement of distance with very high accuracy, especially when extremely small distances are involved. The characteristic length Δx_T, corresponding to a given temperature T, and defined by Eq. (15.12)

$$\Delta x_T = hc/kT \approx 1.44/T \text{ cm.}, \tag{16.5}$$

where T is measured in degrees Kelvin, is, in effect, the boundary between small and large distances. The increasing difficulty of measuring smaller and smaller distances indicates that the fundamental assumptions of Euclidean space (and time) must be considered only as an idealization, which cannot and should not be regarded as valid in the limit of extremely small distances. The mathematical definition of "infinitely small" distances corresponds to impossible physical conditions. We shall return to this problem in Section 4.

A connection between quantum mechanics and information theory can be clearly recognized in various problems which we have discussed. Quantum limitations are needed in the discussion, because we live in a quantized world. When, however, the experiment performed is on the classical level, we note that Planck's constant h does not appear in the final results, which contain only Boltzmann's constant k. We thus recognize that the negentropy principle of information is actually a new principle, and cannot be reduced to quantum and uncertainty relations. Planck's constant h cannot be eliminated from the final results when the experiment performed reaches the quantum level, and the two theories are linked at this level in a more complicated way.

This can be shown in the problems discussed in Chapter 15, Sections 3 and 5. Large distances (case A) correspond to a classical problem. The measurement of very short distances reaches the quantum level. Extremely short distances and very low temperatures involve the limitations of both quantum conditions and information theory in their measurement.

In all of our general discussion, so far, we have attempted to reduce the problems to their fundamental elements, and we have systematically ignored the energy degraded in all sorts of amplifying processes. Amplifiers are always needed in the experimental devices. They perform, essentially, the following duty: to convert a quantum effect, by increasing its amplitude, into an effect that can be recorded on an apparatus operating on the classical level. The role of an amplifier has been very clearly defined by Elsasser. A few examples will illustrate the general situation: A photographic plate can react to one single quantum, and the developing process is the amplifier which yields a visible black spot (classical effect). A photoelectric cell may record a single quantum, when connected to an electronic amplifier. A Geiger counter can detect a single charged particle, and the amplification results here from the ionic discharge. A cloud chamber is a similar example. As long as the amplifier does not include a feed-back loop, it can be ignored and does not modify the observation, although, of course, it will contribute to the entropy increase associated with the observation. Amplifiers with feed-back constitute a very important problem, and their role has been emphasized by Wiener in his theory of cybernetics.

As noted above, classical conditions obtain for a case A (Chapter 15, Section 3 and 5) measurement, when ΔL is larger than Δx_T. Exceptional situations arose for case B

$$\Delta L < \Delta x_T, \tag{16.6}$$

which correspond to high accuracy, very low temperature, and extremely small distances. Under such conditions we have to distinguish between the energy ΔE required for the observation and the fraction of it which must be degraded into heat, and results in an entropy increase. In many practical cases the entire energy ΔE is actually dissipated into heat, but we have shown in Chapters 14 and 15 that most of this dissipation could be avoided, and that the entropy increase ΔS might (at least theoretically) be reduced to the value obtained in classical observations, and be just slightly larger than ΔI, the amount of information obtained.

In Chapter 15, we investigated the problem of length measurement, and we found that the most economical method was the one discussed in Sections 2 and 3. The efficiency was given in Eq. (15.17):

$$\mathcal{E} = \Delta I/\Delta S = 1 + [\ln(\ln 2)]/\ln n. \tag{16.7}$$

For an accuracy, say, of 100

$$L/\Delta L = \mathcal{A} = n = 100, \tag{16.8}$$

Equation (16.7) yields

$$\mathcal{E} = 1 + [\ln(\ln 2)]/\ln 100 = 1 - \frac{0.3667}{\ln 100} \approx 1 - 0.08 = 0.92. \tag{16.9}$$

Interferometric measurements, discussed in Sections 5 and 6, and microscopic observations, discussed in Section 8, gave a much lower efficiency.

Classical conditions (case A) correspond to the case where the energy required for the observation is entirely changed into heat, and the energy needed is thus given directly by the relation

$$\Delta E = T\Delta S. \tag{16.10}$$

This is the situation when the error ΔL in the length measurement is not too small, and remains larger than Δx_T.

In case B, however, we want to reduce the error ΔL and reach conditions (16.6), and the situation is completely changed. The theoretical minimum increase of entropy ΔS can be maintained at a low value, but the energy ΔE required in the experiment becomes larger and larger:

$$\Delta E > T\Delta S. \tag{16.11}$$

This point deserves closer consideration, and will be discussed now.

4. The Limits of Euclidean Geometry

Let us summarize the fundamental difficulties related to the measurement of extremely small distances, and investigate the general limitations that they impose on physical definitions.

In order to measure a length L with an error ΔL, we must use radiation of wavelength

$$\lambda \leqslant 2 \Delta L. \tag{16.12}$$

We discussed this condition very carefully in Chapter 15, and we compared different methods of measurement; we found that long wavelengths might occasionally be used, but that their cost in energy or negentropy was very much higher than for short wavelengths. A short wavelength λ [Eq. (16.12)] corresponds to a large momentum

$$p = h/\lambda \geqslant h/(2 \Delta L), \tag{16.13}$$

and this radiation will interact with the system under observation and transmit to the system a change of momentum ΔP, which may vary from $-p$ to $+p$, and hence

$$\Delta P = 2p \geqslant h/\Delta L, \tag{16.14}$$

which is the usual uncertainty relation. The new point, which we want to emphasize, is that a large momentum p always involves a large energy, and, accordingly, the measurement of a length with a very small error ΔL always requires a large expense in energy.

Let us first assume that we are using electromagnetic radiation. The case of other radiations will be discussed in the next section. If we use light, a wavelength λ corresponds to a quantum $h\nu$:

$$h\nu = hc/\lambda \geqslant hc/(2 \Delta L). \tag{16.15}$$

The smallest amount of energy ΔE with which we can perform an experiment is $h\nu$, and therefore

$$\Delta E = h\nu, \qquad \Delta E \cdot \Delta L \geqslant hc/2. \tag{16.16}$$

There is no precise limitation to the small distances or lengths that can be measured, but the amount of energy required for the experiment increases as $(\Delta L)^{-1}$, and will soon become a formidable obstacle to the measurements. Experiments performed under the conditions of case B will certainly greatly perturb the observed system. Very high frequencies must be used, and these would produce large recoil impulses, pair creations, etc.

These remarks indicate clearly that the actual cost in equipment and machinery required in nuclear experimentation corresponds to the increased cost in energy. After all, the cost of operating a big cyclotron or synchrocyclotron is in proportion to the high energy needed for each observation and dissipated in the target.[3]

Mathematicians can define infinitely small distances, but this is an abstraction corresponding to impossible physical conditions. For instance, let us consider a given laboratory, with a certain limited amount of energy. If all of this energy is required to measure a certain distance, then this distance is the smallest one which is observable in this laboratory.

It has often been suggested that many of the difficulties of quantum theory could be eliminated by the introduction of some sort of minimal length. A fixed minimum length could hardly be justified on the basis of the preceding remarks. We hesitate to extend the example of the laboratory, with a limited amount of energy available, to include the entire universe, because of the difficulty of making precise definitions of its extent and content. Nevertheless, we can say that measurements of shorter and shorter distances present ever increasing difficulties, and the increasing cost of the observation of such distances might be the new factor needed in the theory.

Our Eq. (16.16) is very similar to Eq. (15.33):

$$\Delta E \cdot \Delta L \approx n h c/2, \tag{16.17}$$

and bears a close similarity to the uncertainty relation (16.14). The conditions (16.16) have, however, a meaning entirely different from that of the uncertainty relation. In the uncertainty relation ΔE represents the error in the energy E. In Eq. (16.16), on the other hand, ΔE is the amount of energy required for the experiment, and at least partially changed into heat during the process of measuring L with an approximation ΔL. The two relations thus have only formal similarity; their physical meanings are very different.

5. Possible Use of Heavy Particles Instead of Photons

We have discussed a variety of experimental structures under the assumption that a light beam was used for the illumination. One must consider the possibility of using other types of waves, such as waves associated with material particles of mass m, instead of photons with zero mass. We start, again, from Eqs. (16.12)

---

[3] L. Brillouin, *J. Appl. Phys.* **24**, 1152 (1953); **25**, 887 (1954).

and (16.13) which apply to any kind of radiation, and we now consider use of a particle of rest mass m_0. We must compute the kinetic energy of this particle. The particle has a momentum p and a kinetic energy E_{kin}, given by

$$p = h/\lambda = m_0 v/\sqrt{1-\beta^2}, \qquad \text{with} \qquad \beta = v/c; \tag{16.18}$$

$$E_{\text{kin}} = m_0 c^2 \left[\frac{1}{\sqrt{1-\beta^2}} - 1\right] = c\sqrt{m_0{}^2 c^2 + p^2} - m_0 c^2. \tag{16.19}$$

Approximations can be computed for extreme cases: For photons or particles of small rest mass, we have

$$m_0 c \ll p = h/\lambda, \qquad E_{\text{kin}} \approx p c - m_0 c^2; \tag{16.20}$$

while for heavy particles, one obtains

$$m_0 c \gg p = h/\lambda, \qquad E_{\text{kin}} \approx p^2/2 m_0. \tag{16.21}$$

For a given p and variable rest mass m_0, the curve representing E_{kin} as a function of m_0 is shown in Fig. 16.1.

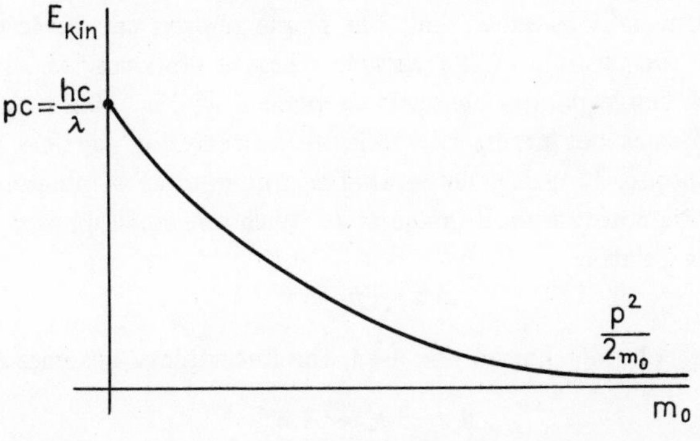

FIG. 16.1. The kinetic energy plotted as a function of m_0 with a given fixed momentum p. The curve approaches $p^2/2\,m_0$ asymptotically for $m_0 c \gg p$.

At first sight it might seem interesting to use heavy particles, thus reducing the amount of energy E_{kin} required for the experiment. This is, however, not possible when very small distances d are being measured. Suppose, for instance

$$\Delta L = d = 10^{-13}, \qquad p \approx 3 \cdot 10^{-14}.$$

according to Eq. (16.14). We must compare p with $m_0 c$, in order to determine whether Eq. (16.20) or Eq. (16.21) applies:

Electron:	$m_0 \approx 10^{-27}$	$m_0 c \approx 3 \cdot 10^{-17}$	Case (16.20)
Proton:	$m_0 \approx 2 \cdot 10^{-24}$	$m_0 c \approx 6 \cdot 10^{-14}$	Intermediate
Heavy nucleus:	$m_0 \approx \frac{5}{3} \cdot 10^{-22}$	$m_0 c \approx 5 \cdot 10^{-12}$	Case (16.21).

A reduction in the energy required could be obtained by using very heavy nuclei, but these nuclei have larger cross sections, and would be unfit for measuring lengths smaller than their diameters.

Altogether photons, mesons, electrons, and nucleons are the only particles that can be used, in practice, for the illuminating beam, and they all yield similar results when the distance d is extremely small. The difficulties discussed in Sections 3 and 4 are really fundamental and cannot be eliminated.

6. Uncertainty Relations in the Microscope Experiment

The methods of information theory were used in Chapter 15, Sections 8 and 9 for the discussion of observations under a microscope. This is a typical problem frequently introduced in connection with the uncertainty relations. In this discussion it is usually assumed that one single photon can be used to obtain information on the position of the particle. This is obviously an oversimplified assumption. A single photon observed at point I of Fig. 16.2 may come from anywhere, and does not necessarily indicate a scattering particle at M. The discussion of Chapter 15 clearly shows that a large number of photons is required to define unambiguously a focal image at I. With one single photon one obtains the uncertainty relation:

$$\Delta x \cdot \Delta p_x \approx h, \tag{16.22}$$

but, when many photons have to be used, the uncertainty becomes much larger

$$\Delta x \cdot \Delta p_x \approx A\, h, \tag{16.23}$$

with a numerical factor A which may become very large. This is typical of an experimental device in which the position x is measured by some optical system, without the use of material screens, diaphragms, or shutters. Let us discuss this point carefully.

The conditions of observation are sketched in Fig. 16.2. We want to measure x over an interval a, with an error Δx, but we are no longer interested in y or b or Δy. In the proper waves, given by Eq. (15.62), we are concerned with the factor $\cos(\pi l x/a)$ and the values of l, while we ignore the factor $\cos(\pi m y/b)$

and the values of m whenever this is feasible. We may, for instance, choose $b > a$, thus making the ground wave $l = 0$ and $m = 1$, since these values yield the lower cut-off frequency in Eq. (15.65). This wave will represent the incident beam, arriving through the wave guide, and incident on the particle M:

$$\textit{Incident beam:} \qquad l = 0, \qquad m = 1. \tag{16.24}$$

This incident beam represents the superposition of two plane waves with

$$\cos\phi_y = \pm\,\lambda/2\,b,$$

according to Eq. (15.66). We may also allow m to assume both positive and negative values, so that $m = \pm\,1$. The angles, ϕ_x and ϕ_y, were defined in Chapter 15, Section 8, and, in general, we have

$$\cos\phi_x = l\,\lambda/2\,a, \qquad \cos\phi_y = m\,\lambda/2\,b,$$

and we shall consider l and m as positive or negative integers.

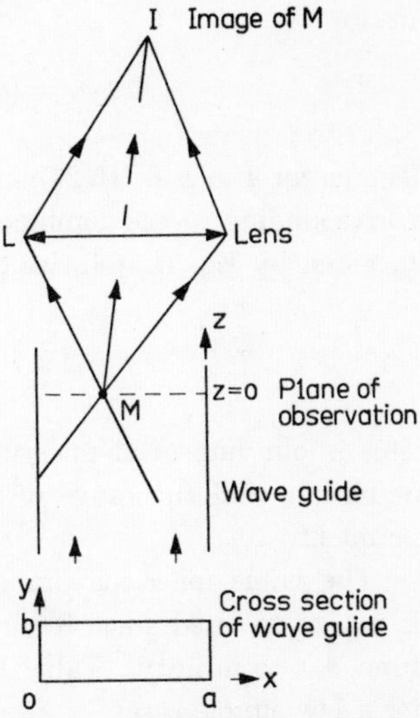

FIG. 16.2. Conditions of observation when a wave guide and lens are used to detect a particle at the focus M.

Light scattered from particle M may contain proper waves with all possible values of l and m. We can eliminate most of the terms by using a cylindrical lens of length b at L. This device cancels out all terms except for $m = 0$. We may thus describe the scattering process as a transition

$$\begin{array}{ll} \text{in } l: & \text{from } 0 \text{ to } l, \\ \text{in } m: & \text{from } 1 \text{ to } 0. \end{array} \tag{16.25}$$

In order, however, to account for the positive and negative signs in $\cos\phi_x$ and $\cos\phi_y$, we must consider transitions

$$\begin{array}{ll} \text{in } l: & \text{from } 0 \text{ to } \pm\,l, \\ \text{in } m: & \text{from } \pm\,1 \text{ to } 0. \end{array} \tag{16.25 a}$$

A change δl during the scattering of a photon results in an impulse δp_x to the particle M:

$$\delta p_x = (h/\lambda)\,\delta(\cos\phi_x) = h\,l/2\,a. \tag{16.26}$$

The $\pm$ sign is now contained in l, and the value l may run from $-\,l_M$ to $-\,1$, or from $+\,1$ to $+\,l_M$. The value $l = 0$ is excluded because l and m cannot both be zero. Condition (15.69) requires that we must use n terms in each wave in order to define t with an error $\tau = \Delta t$. Since impulses δp_x can be positive or negative, we compute the sum of squares, and denote it by $(\Delta p_x)^2$:

$$(\Delta p_x)^2 = \sum_n \sum_l (\delta p_x)^2 = n(h/2a)^2 \cdot 4[1 + 4 + 9 + \ldots + l_M^2], \qquad (16.27)$$

or

$$\Delta p_x = (h/a) \left[\frac{n}{3} l_M(l_M + 1)(l_M + \tfrac{1}{2})\right]^{1/2}.$$

The factor 4 in Eq. (16.27) arises because there are four cases from Eq. (16.25 a) corresponding to the combinations of $\pm l$ and ± 1. Now, using the value for l_M given by Eq. (15.68), we obtain

$$\Delta p_x \cdot \Delta x = h \left[\frac{\tau}{6 \Delta t}\left(1 + \frac{\Delta x}{a}\right)\left(\frac{a}{\Delta x} + \tfrac{1}{2}\right)\right]^{1/2}. \qquad (16.28)$$

This is our improved uncertainty relation, which takes into account the time definition, and the range of variation of the variable x in the microscope experiment.

The value for τ may range from $2\Delta t$ up to infinity. The value $\tau = \Delta t$ is not to be used since it yields no information. The parameter a may range from Δx to infinity. Table 16.1 contains the results of numerical computation for a few simple cases.

TABLE 16.1

$\frac{\tau}{\Delta t}$	$\frac{a}{\Delta x}$	$\left[\frac{\tau}{6\Delta t}\left(1 + \frac{\Delta x}{a}\right)\left(\frac{a}{\Delta x} + \frac{1}{2}\right)\right]^{1/2}$
2	1	1
2	2	$\sqrt{5/2} = 1.12$
2	3	$\sqrt{14/3} = 1.25$
3	1	$\sqrt{1.5} = 1.22$
3	2	$\sqrt{7.5/2} = 1.37$
large values		$[a\tau/(6 \cdot \Delta t \cdot \Delta x)]^{1/2}$

When the accuracy is very low, and most of the definition is due to screens and obstacles ($a = \Delta x$), the usual uncertainty occurs. We may, however, be interested in cases where the time definition and the measurement of distance are obtained primarily through the optical system, and this leads to much higher uncertainty. Let us take, for example,

$$\tau/\Delta t = 6000, \qquad a/\Delta x = 1000: \quad \Delta x \cdot \Delta p_x = h \cdot 10^3. \tag{16.29}$$

We thus arrive at the conclusion that the uncertainty may become very large in the measurement of the position of a "free" particle: a particle free to move over a large distance during a long time, without disturbance from material screens, shutters, or other mechanical devices. Such mechanical devices obviously can on longer be used anyway when small distances, shorter than 1 Ångstrom unit, are under consideration, and our discussion is of greatest value in this range.

7. Measurement of Momentum

We assumed, in the microscope experiment, that we knew the initial velocity of the particle, and we tried to measure the position. The results were not very favorable. Let us try the reverse procedure. We start by measuring the position x at time t with great accuracy. This gives a large unknown impulse to the particle [Eq. (16.28)], but this does not matter, since we did not know the original velocity anyhow. Then we can measure the velocity v_x and also p_x by Doppler effect.[4] The usual argument gives

$$\Delta x \cdot \Delta p_x \approx h. \tag{16.30}$$

The standard discussion is based on the assumption that one single photon $h\nu'$ may suffice for a good measurement of the frequency ν' in the Doppler effect, provided a long wave packet of total duration θ can be used:

$$\Delta \nu' \cdot \theta \approx 1. \tag{16.31}$$

We now want to investigate this problem more carefully and to take advantage of the remarks based on the theory of information. We intend to show that one single photon is not enough, and we shall discuss how the number of photons required in the experiment is related with exact specifications on the experimental procedure. This will lead us to a modified uncertainty relation:

$$\Delta x \cdot \Delta p_x \approx n h, \qquad n \geqslant 1, \tag{16.32}$$

where n depends upon the conditions of observation. This practical limit may be lowered to the earlier limit (16.30) when conditions are selected in such a way as to make n nearly unity.

[4] See, for instance, D. Bohm, *loc. cit.*, p. 105, in ref. 1.

The discussion on information showed us that we must always define the range of variation and the error in the quantities to be measured. In our present problem, we take

$$\begin{aligned} &\text{time } t \text{ of observation:} && \text{error } \Delta t = \theta, && \text{range } \tau; \\ &\text{velocity } v_x \text{ of the particle:} && \text{error } \Delta v_x, && \text{range } u. \end{aligned} \tag{16.33}$$

As in earlier examples, we introduce the range τ in time by assuming that flashes of duration θ are repeated at intervals τ. These light signals can be obtained by superimposing n different frequencies

$$n = \tau/2\Delta t = \tau/2\theta. \tag{16.34}$$

These frequencies extend over a frequency range $\delta\nu = 1/\theta$. We also specify in Eq. (16.33) the range u of velocities over which we want to operate. We shall design a system capable of measuring velocities between v_0 and $v_0 + u$ with an error Δv. This means that we must use m resonators tuned on m different Doppler frequencies ν', each resonator being able to receive a frequency band $\Delta \nu'$ corresponding to Δv:

$$m = u/(\Delta v), \qquad \Delta \nu' = \nu \cdot \Delta v/c, \tag{16.35}$$

where ν is the average initial frequency. The measurement is possible, provided that the original frequency range $\delta \nu$ of Eq. (16.34) is smaller than the $\Delta \nu'$ introduced in (16.35). The problem of an experiment requiring m simultaneous observations was discussed in Chapter 14, and it was shown that one should select for each resonator an energy limit E_l, given by

$$E_l = A_m k T. \tag{16.36}$$

If one observes an energy E on a resonator, such that $E < E_l$, the resonator is regarded as unexcited; while $E > E_l$ means that the resonator is excited. If we assume a high reliability r for the experiment, we have, from Chapter 14,

$$A_m \approx \ln(r\,m) \qquad \text{for} \qquad r \gg 1 \qquad \text{and} \qquad m \gg 1. \tag{16.37}$$

These conditions can be satisfied by using a single quantum $h\nu'$ if

$$h\nu' > A_m k T.$$

The energy E_l will correspond to a single quantum on each frequency ν' if we take

$$h\nu' = E_l \approx A_m k T, \tag{16.38}$$

and we have n different frequencies ν' covering a band $\delta\nu$ [Eq. (16.34)] in order to define the instant of time measurement. Finally the energy dissipated is $n h \nu'$, and the entropy increase is

$$\Delta S = n h \nu'/T \approx n A_m k = k n \ln(r\,m). \tag{16.39}$$

The information obtained is

$$\Delta I = k \ln[(\Delta t/\tau) \cdot (\Delta v/u)] = k \ln(n\, m/2), \tag{16.40}$$

and the generalized second principle is satisfied:

$$\Delta(S - I) = k[(n-1) \ln m + n \ln r - \ln(n/2)] > 0. \tag{16.41}$$

The numerical factor n may be small, but is always larger than 2. We have assumed high reliability and high accuracy $(r \gg 1,\ m \gg 1)$ and therefore ΔS is much larger than ΔI.

Since we are using n quanta, we obtain a recoil n times greater than in the usual discussion, and the uncertainty relation is given by Eq. (16.32).

As an example, let us take

$$r = e^{10}, \qquad m = e^{10}, \qquad A_m = 20,$$

where the value of A_m is computed from Eq. (16.37). These values give, from Eq. (16.38),

$$h\nu' \approx 20\, k\, T.$$

If the experiment is made at room temperature, this condition indicates frequencies near the visible range. Information theory and quantum conditions do not appear in contradiction; on the contrary, they are complementary to one another.

For applications to field theory, we shall use Eq. (16.30), which represents the lower limit of Eq. (16.32).

8. Uncertainty in Field Measurements

Uncertainty relations for a field theory have been discussed by Bohr and Rosenfeld[5] for the case of electromagnetic fields. A probe of volume V and charge ε is used during a time τ. The momentum p_x is measured at t, and takes on another value p_x' at time $t + \tau$. The average field $\overline{E_x}$ over V during τ is

$$\overline{E_x} = (p_x' - p_x)/\varepsilon\, \tau. \tag{16.42}$$

The position x of the probe is measured with an error Δx, and results in an error Δp_x in p_x' and p_x. We contend that we can use, in this case, the relation (16.30).

[5] N. Bohr and L. Rosenfeld, *Kgl. Danske Videnskal. Selskab. Mat.-fys. Medd.* **12**, paper 8 (1953); W. Heitler, "The Quantum Theory of Radiation," Chapter 2, p. 76. Oxford U. P., New York, 1944.

We first measure x, then p_x at time t (see Section 6). Then we measure p_x' at time $t + \tau$ and finally x'. The last determination imparts to the particle a large unknown momentum, but this is no longer of significance. The error in p_x gives an error in the field

$$\Delta \overline{E_x} \approx h/(\varepsilon \tau \cdot \Delta x) \approx h/(e \tau Z \cdot \Delta x), \tag{16.43}$$

where $\varepsilon = Z e$, and e is the electronic charge. Observations under a microscope enable us to measure the field from its action on a free particle, with no physical obstacles perturbing this field. In this formula, we may take for Δx the diameter of the particle, and $Z \Delta x$ is a characteristic of the particle used as a probe. It may range from 10^{-13} for an electron up to 10^{-10} for a heavy nucleus ($Z = 96$, $\Delta x \approx 10^{-12}$). In order to define a time interval τ we need a beam of light with frequencies ranging from 0 to ν_M:

$$\nu_M = \tfrac{1}{2} \tau, \tag{16.44}$$

and hence

$$\varepsilon \cdot \Delta \overline{E_x} \cdot \Delta x \approx 2 h \nu_M. \tag{16.45}$$

This formula has a simple interpretation, since $\varepsilon \overline{E_x} \Delta x$ is the work done by the field $\overline{E_x}$ over a distance Δx. This work cannot be measured with great accuracy because we may have emission or absorption of quanta $h \nu_M$ coming from the beam of light used to define the time interval τ.

Altogether our discussion does not modify the fundamental formula (16.43) of Bohr and Rosenfeld, but it emphasizes some difficulties in regard to the uncertainty relations. The usual uncertainty relations correspond to an absolute theoretical limit, but this limit cannot be reached in many experimental devices, where, in general, a much higher uncertainty is obtained. This is especially true when the position of a nearly free particle is to be measured.

CHAPTER 17

THE NEGENTROPY PRINCIPLE OF INFORMATION IN TELECOMMUNICATIONS

1. The Analysis of Signals with Finite Band Width

In Chapter 8, we discussed the general problem of signal analysis, and we were able to prove (Section 6) that a system of signals representing a message of total duration τ and finite band width

$$0 \leqslant |\nu| \leqslant \nu_M \tag{17.1}$$

contained only a finite number of degrees of freedom:

$$N = 2\,\nu_M \tau + 1. \tag{17.2}$$

When the total duration τ is large, we may approximate Eq. (17.2) as

$$N \approx 2\,\nu_M \tau. \tag{17.3}$$

This very important result was obtained by two methods: the Fourier analysis of a periodically repeated system of messages in Chapter 8, Section 6, and the sampling method for a single message in Section 7. In the Fourier method, the degrees of freedom correspond to the amplitudes of the first N harmonics in the Fourier series. With Shannon's sampling method, the function $f(t)$ representing the message is measured at N equidistant points, with a constant interval

$$\theta = \tau/N \approx 1/(2\,\nu_M) \tag{17.4}$$

between them, and it was shown how to reconstruct the original function from these sampled values [Eq. (8.70)]:

$$f_m = f(m\,\theta), \tag{17.5}$$

$$f(t) = \sum_m f_m \frac{\sin \pi(2\,\nu_M t - m)}{\pi(2\,\nu_M t - m)}.$$

We also discussed (in Section 8) another representation, based upon Gabor's "information cells":

$$\Delta\nu \cdot \Delta t = 1, \tag{17.6}$$

each of which contains two components, one symmetrical, and one anti-symmetrical. There are

$$n = \nu_M \tau \tag{17.7}$$

such cells, giving

$$N = 2n = 2\nu_M \tau$$

distinct components to be specified for the definition of a message.

2. Signals and Thermal Noise: Representation in Hyperspace

The analysis of Chapter 8 applies to any kind of signals and messages. How can we use it for thermal noise of finite band width ν_M observed during a time τ? In each cell we can define the average intensity, but the phase is random. We thus have n components, each of them representing a harmonic oscillator which has an average energy kT. We assume low frequencies, and ignore quantum conditions. We arrive at the same conclusion if we consider the Fourier analysis of the entire system, with its N components, and take an average kinetic energy of $kT/2$ for each sine term and for each cosine term. Or, we may start from Shannon's N sampled values and assign an average kinetic energy of $kT/2$ to each of them. Altogether, the noise energy is, on the average,

$$\overline{E_n} = NkT/2 = \nu_M \tau k T, \tag{17.8}$$

and the noise power is

$$P_n = \overline{E_n}/\tau = \nu_M k T. \tag{17.8 a}$$

This corresponds to signals propagating along a line in one direction: for instance, the signal is generated at the left input and propagates to the right. The result is identical with Eq. (11.17) where we discussed the same problem from Nyquist's point of view.

Thermal noise is defined by its average power and its fluctuations (see Chapters 9, 10, and 11). If the noise power were exactly constant it could be easily eliminated and compensated, but the perturbation really comes from the unpredictable fluctuations, which are always of the same order of magnitude as the average power.

Let us now consider a signal (or message) given by a certain arbitrary function of maximum frequency ν_M, and duration τ. The function has N degrees of freedom $X_1, X_2, \ldots, X_m, \ldots, X_N$ as defined in the preceding section. It can be represented by a point with coordinates $X_1, X_2, \ldots, X_m, \ldots, X_N$ in an N-dimensional space S_N.[1] Each set of "cells" will correspond to a coordinate system in S_N, and a change in coordinates in the hyperspace means a change in the cell system. We use orthogonal functions to represent the given function, and the total energy will be proportional to the sum of the squares of the coordinates. By a proper choice of units, we may write

$$E = \sum_{m=1}^{m=N} X_m^2 = R_N^2, \tag{17.9}$$

with no special numerical coefficient. When the energy is given, the point must lie on a hypersphere of radius R_N. The volume of such a sphere is known to be

$$V_N = C_N \cdot R_N^N \qquad \text{with} \qquad C_N \approx (2\pi e/N)^{N/2} \tag{17.10}$$

for large N. The constant C_N depends upon the number N of dimensions. A very interesting feature of a space S_N, with a large number N of dimensions, is that the volume V_N is mostly concentrated near the surface. We may prove this by showing that a small increase ΔR_N in the radius may cause a very large increase in volume:

$$(\Delta V_N)/V_N = N(\Delta R_N)/R_N. \tag{17.10 a}$$

When N exceeds $R_N/(\Delta R_N)$ this expression may become larger than unity! Thus, we should remember that practically the whole volume of such a hypersphere is concentrated within a thin layer near the surface.

3. The Capacity of a Channel with Noise

A given unperturbed signal is represented by a certain point M in the hyperspace S_N. If noise is present, the point will be displaced a certain distance, within a sphere centered at M. The radius of this sphere is given by $\overline{E_n}^{1/2}$, where $\overline{E_n}$ is the average noise energy. We do not know where the new point M' will be, within this sphere, on account of the uncertainty in the noise. Hence, we should not use another signal represented by a point too close to point M. The problem is to compute exactly how many points can safely be distinguished from one another, or, in other words, how many different messages can be distinguished in the presence of noise.

Let us start with a simple discussion, which we shall examine more carefully later on: The total energy is the sum of the energy E for the signal and the

[1] This method is very completely discussed by C. E. Shannon, *Proc. I. R. E.* **37**, 10 (1949).

average energy $\overline{E_n}$ for the noise. According to Eq. (17.9), this sum defines a hypersphere of radius

$$R' = (E + \overline{E_n})^{1/2}. \tag{17.11}$$

for the signal plus the noise. A signal is the center of a small sphere of radius

$$r = \overline{E_n}^{1/2}, \tag{17.12}$$

and we must assume that noise, added to a given signal, blacks out a sphere of radius r about the point M representing the signal proper. The question is: how many of these small spheres of radius r can be contained in the large sphere of radius R'? Certainly the ratio of the volumes gives an upper limit to this number:

$$G = R'^N / r^N = [(E + \overline{E_n})/\overline{E_n}]^{N/2} = [1 + (P/P_n)]^{N/2}, \tag{17.13}$$

where P and P_N are the average powers in the signal and in the noise, respectively. We defined in Eq. (4.3) the capacity of a channel as the limit

$$C = K \lim_{\tau \to \infty} \left(\frac{\ln G(\tau)}{\tau} \right), \tag{17.14}$$

where $G(\tau)$ is the total number of distinct messages of length τ that can be sent over the channel. Comparing Eqs. (17.13) and (17.14), we obtain

$$C = K \lim_{\tau \to \infty} (N/2\tau) \cdot \ln[1 + (P/P_n)];$$

but N is given by Eq. (17.3), and hence

$$C = K \nu_M \ln[1 + (P/P_n)], \tag{17.15}$$

where K = a constant depending on the units used, ν_M = the upper limit of the frequency band, P = the average signal power, and P_n = the average noise power. Equation (17.15) is known as the Hartley-Tuller-Shannon formula.[2]

4. Discussion of the Tuller-Shannon Formula

A result of such importance requires a more detailed discussion in order to justify the approximations introduced and to prove that the limit (17.13) can actually be reached. First of all, we must be sure to include the effect of fluctuations and unpredictable variations in noise. All of this is contained in the general statistical formula Eq. (9.32):

$$p(E, T) = B e^{-\beta E}, \qquad \beta = 1/kT, \tag{17.16}$$

[2] An excellent discussion by M. Leifer and W. F. Schreiber may be found in *Advances in Electronics* **3**, 306 (1951).

where $p(t)$ is the probability of a "complexion" (or quantum state) of energy E at temperature T, and B is a coefficient determined by the condition that the sum of the p's must be unity. This can be applied directly to noise. Let $x_1, x_2, \ldots, x_m, \ldots, x_n$ be the variables representing noise alone. Then Eq. (17.9) yields

$$E_n = \sum_m x_m{}^2 = r^2 \tag{17.17}$$

for the total noise energy. On the other hand, we have a volume dV [Eq. (17.10)] between r and $r + dr$, and the number of quantized complexions is proportional to that volume. We thus obtain the probability that a point lies between r and $r + dr$:

$$p(r, T)\, dr = B'\, e^{-\beta r^2}\, r^{N-1}\, dr, \tag{17.18}$$

since

$$dV = N\, C_N\, r^{N-1}\, dr.$$

B' is a new normalization constant. The new probability $p(r, T)$ exhibits a very sharp maximum at a certain r value, when

$$\begin{aligned} \frac{\partial}{\partial r}(r^{N-1}\, e^{-\beta r^2}) &= (N-1-2\,\beta\, r^2)\, r^{N-2}\, e^{-\beta r^2} = 0, \\ r_{mp}{}^2 &= (N-1)/2\,\beta = (N-1)\, k\, T/2. \end{aligned} \tag{17.19}$$

It is easy to prove that for very large values of N this maximum becomes sharper and sharper. Equation (17.19) gives the most probable value of r^2, and hence the most probable value of the noise energy:

$$E_{mp} = r_{mp}{}^2 = (N-1)\, k\, T/2 \approx N\, k\, T/2 = \overline{E_n}, \qquad N \gg 1. \tag{17.20}$$

This is a typical example of the coincidence between the most probable value E_{mp} and the average value $\overline{E_n}$ when the number of variables, N, becomes exceedingly large. We have already obtained an example of this phenomenon in Chapter 4 (see Sections 7 and 8).

In our problem, the message is represented by a point with coordinates X_m in the hyperspace with N dimensions, and the signal plus noise gives a point with coordinates

$$X_m' = X_m + x_m \qquad \text{with } x_m \text{ random.}$$

The preceding discussion proves that this new point with coordinates X_m' must practically lie on the surface of a sphere of radius r_{mp} centered on the original point M. These are exactly the conditions assumed in Eqs. (17.12) and (17.13) for the derivation of the Tuller-Shannon formula.

These conditions apply only for low frequencies, when $h\nu$ is much smaller than kT, and the quantum states can be considered as infinitely close together. Under these circumstances, the noise can be defined as Gaussian noise. The distribution, along a certain variable x_m, is independent of the other variables, and follows a law in $e^{-\beta x_m^2}$ according to Eqs. (17.16) and (17.17). Gaussian noise does not apply to a quantized system unless the quanta $h\nu$ can be considered as infinitely small. Figure 17.1 is a sketch showing the geometry of the situation,

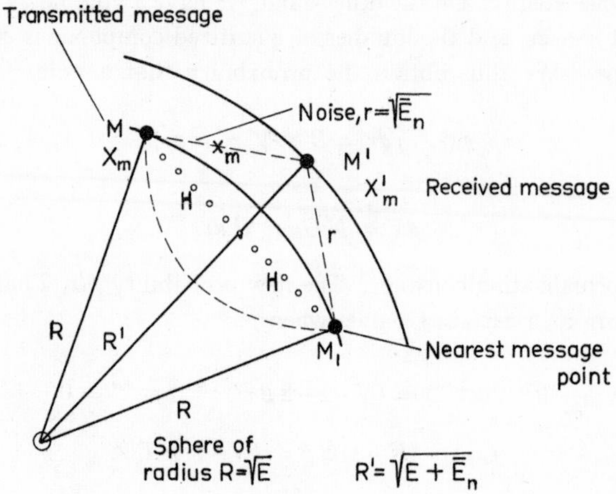

FIG. 17.1. Plane section of the hypersphere in N dimensions showing two "nearest" message points and the effect of noise.

and taking into account the results of Eq. (17.10) that the points within a sphere must practically lie on the surface of the sphere. Point M, representing the original message of energy E, is on a sphere of radius $E^{1/2}$. The message plus noise is represented by point M' on the sphere of radius $(E+\overline{E_n})^{1/2}$, and the distance MM' is $r=\overline{E_n}^{1/2}$ [Eqs. (17.12) and (17.19)]. M_1 represents a possible position for another message point that could just be confused with M since it is at the same distance r' from M'. The distance MM_1 thus represents the smallest possible distance between distinguishable message points. Figure 17.1 is a plane section of the hyperspace, defined by the three points M, M', and M_1. The distance $MM_1=2H$ has its limit when MM' is perpendicular to OM and $M'M_1$ is perpendicular to OM_1. This means that the area A of the triangle OMM' is

$$A_{OMM'}=H(\overline{OM'})/2=(\overline{MM'})\,(\overline{OM})/2; \tag{17.21}$$

hence

$$H R' = R r, \qquad \text{and} \qquad H = \sqrt{\frac{E \cdot \overline{E}_n}{E + \overline{E}_n}} < r = \sqrt{\overline{E}_n}. \tag{17.22}$$

The distance $2H$ between points M and M_1 is actually smaller than the distance $2r$, where r is the radius of the noise sphere around M.

We now have to investigate how to distribute our message points M in the sphere R of volume

$$V = C_N R^N = C_N E^{N/2}, \tag{17.23}$$

in order to insure a transmission with a probability of error as small as we like. Let

$$\eta = e^{-\alpha} \ll 1 \tag{17.24}$$

be the probability of error that we can tolerate. We distribute our message points with a constant average density throughout the volume V. One possible way to obtain this constant density may be to use just a random distribution in the volume, as suggested by Shannon. Let G_1 be the total number of such message points. Any message point falling within a sphere of radius H around our point M may be confused with M and result in an error. This represents a volume

$$u = C_N H^N. \tag{17.25}$$

Message points falling in the remaining volume $V - u$ do not produce any possibility for error. The probability of an error is obviously proportional to G_1 and to u/V, and we want

$$\mathcal{E} = G_1 u/V \leqslant \eta. \tag{17.26}$$

This means that we can use a number of points

$$G_1 \leqslant \eta V/u = \eta (R/H)^N = \eta [(E + \overline{E}_n)/\overline{E}_n]^{N/2} \tag{17.27}$$

according to Eqs. (17.12), (17.13), and (17.15). This can be rewritten

$$G_1 \leqslant \eta G, \tag{17.28}$$

when G is the quantity defined in Eq. (17.13). The maximum number G_1 corresponds to the equality in Eq. (17.28), and yields a channel capacity C_1:

$$C_1 = K \lim_{\tau \to \infty} [(\ln G_1)/\tau] = K \lim_{\tau \to \infty} \left[\frac{\ln G}{\tau} + \frac{\ln \eta}{\tau} \right],$$

or, according to Eq. (17.24),

$$C_1 = C - \lim_{\tau \to \infty} (\alpha/\tau). \tag{17.29}$$

The capacity of the channel can be brought arbitrarily close to the theoretical limit C previously defined in Eq. (17.15). All we need is a distribution of message points with constant average density in the sphere of radius R.

5. A Practical Example

We based our preceding discussion on the consideration of the complete long messages of total duration τ. Let us now investigate how such a message could be constructed from some standard signals. We start with the cell system of Section 1. Any cell system will do: for example, the cell system corresponding to the Fourier series, or that corresponding to Shannon's sampling method. We have [Eqs. (17.7) and (17.8)]:

$$n = \nu_M \tau \tag{17.30}$$

cells, each of them with a noise energy

$$\overline{e_n} = k\,T. \tag{17.31}$$

The total noise energy is, on the average,

$$\overline{E_n} = n\,\overline{e_n} = n\,k\,T.$$

Let us select an energy level E for a given signal in a certain cell. This signal is perturbed by noise, which adds an average energy $\overline{e_n}$ to the signal E, with fluctuations of the same order of magnitude, thus practically convering an energy band $2\,\overline{e_n}$. According to this rather crude discussion, we may try to select in each cell a set of energy levels $2\,\overline{e_n}$ apart, and to use them as elementary signals. The signals themselves will have energies up to a certain maximum value:

$$e_s = 0, \qquad 2\overline{e_n},\ 4\overline{e_n},\ \ldots,\ 2(m-1)\overline{e_n}, \tag{17.32}$$

and the total energies, for the signal plus noise, will be

$$e_t = e_s + \overline{e_n} = \overline{e_n},\ 3\overline{e_n},\ 5\overline{e_n},\ \ldots,\ (2\,m-1)\overline{e_n}.$$

We thus have m distinct signals per cell. A complete message of duration τ is obtained by specifying the signal energies in the n cells. The total energy of the message, on the average, is

$$\begin{aligned} \overline{E_s} &= n\,\overline{e_s} = n(m-1)\,\overline{e_n}, \\ \overline{E_s} + \overline{E_n} &= n\,m\,\overline{e_n}. \end{aligned} \tag{17.33}$$

These definitions correspond to our previous ones. If the message time τ is long, E_s will differ very little from its average, and all the messages will, in practice, have the energies given in Eq. (17.33). This is, again, a case of coincidence of the most probable value with the average value.

The number of distinct messages obtained in this manner is

$$G' = m^n ,$$

and the capacity of the channel is

$$C' = K \lim_{\tau \to \infty} [(\ln G')/\tau] = K \nu_M \ln m. \tag{17.34}$$

But, according to Eq. (17.33)

$$m = 1 + (\overline{e_s}/\overline{e_n}) = 1 + (\overline{E_s}/\overline{E_n}) = 1 + (\overline{P_s}/P_n), \tag{17.35}$$

with $\overline{P_s} = P_M/2$, where P_M is the maximum signal power. Hence the capacity C' is equal to the limit capacity given by the Tuller-Shannon formula (17.15). This model will be used for comparison in our further discussion.

This discussion justifies the choice of the spacing $2\,\overline{e_n}$ introduced in Eq. (17.32), since it yields Shannon's formula. A closer spacing would give obvious overlapping between energy bands corresponding to two successive signal levels. A broader spacing might give a greater safety in transmission, but it would not use the channel to its full capacity.

Some additional remarks may be useful to show the connection with the analysis presented in the preceding section. We first want to prove that equidistant energy levels [Eq. (17.32)] correspond to a uniform density of signal points in the hyperspace with $N = 2\,n$ dimensions. Let us consider a certain cell, say the i-th, which will contain two degrees of freedom, one a sine type and the other a cosine type. Let us call them X_i and Y_i. The $2\,n$ coordinates X_i, Y_i represent the hyperspace with N dimensions. Let us assume a uniform density $\rho(X_i, Y_i)$ for the signal points in the plane $X_i\, Y_i$. This gives, on the average, in a small region $dX_i\, dY_i$, a number of points

$$dG = \rho(X_i, Y_i)\, dX_i\, dY_i.$$

We now select an annular region between r_i and $r_i + dr_i$ with

$$r_i^2 = X_i^2 + Y_i^2 = E_i, \tag{17.36}$$

with E_i the corresponding energy value. The average number of signal points in this region is

$$dG = \rho(X_i, Y_i)\, 2\pi\, r_i\, dr_i = \pi\, \rho(X_i, Y_i)\, dE_i,$$

and we obtain a uniform density

$$\rho'(E_i) = \pi\, \rho(X_i, Y_i) \tag{17.37}$$

along the energy scale for the i-th cell. This corresponds to the assumption made in Eq. (17.32).

In Eq. (17.32) we used equidistant energy levels, all equally probable, up to a certain maximum. We may introduce another assumption and consider energy levels with an *a priori* probability of

$$\pi_i = B\, e^{-\gamma E_i} \tag{17.38}$$

for the energy E_i in the i-th cell. This gives a probability of

$$\pi_i = B\, e^{-\gamma r_i^2} = B\, e^{-\gamma (X_i^2 + Y_i^2)} \tag{17.39}$$

in the N-dimensional hyperspace. The problem is very similar to the one already discussed in Eqs. (17.16) and (17.20). The new constant γ simply replaces our former β, and we discuss signal energy instead of noise energy. All signal points practically lie on a sphere

$$R^2 = (N-1)/(2\gamma) = \overline{E}, \tag{17.40}$$

and $\overline{E}$ is the average energy value for the signals.

6. The Negentropy Principle Applied to the Channel with Noise

We have emphasized, in the earlier chapters, the principle that any information obtained about a physical system is paid for by a corresponding amount of negative entropy taken from the system, and, conversely, that any information stored or transmitted by a physical system corresponds to an increase of negentropy in the system.

The principle can be verified in the examples we have under discussion. We shall discuss a paper by Raymond[3] on this subject, and show how it must be corrected for an erroneous numerical factor $\frac{1}{4}$.

The cable, along which we want to transmit a message, is initially at a temperature T. It has, under normal conditions, an entropy S_0, and exhibits a noise level corresponding to an average power P_n, for the band width ν_M and a certain direction of propagation [Eqs. (11.17) and (17.8 a)]:

$$P_n = k\, T\, \nu_M. \tag{17.41}$$

This is where Raymond used an incorrect factor 4 in his Eq. (4), and this led to a troublesome factor $\frac{1}{4}$ in his Eq. (5).

---

[3] R. C. Raymond, *Am. Scientist* **38**, 275 (1950); see also C. A. Desoer, *Mass. Inst. Technol. Research Lab. Electronics, Quart. Progr. Rept*; **46** (1951). J. H. Felker, *Proc. I. R. E.* **40**, 728 (1952); D. A. Bell, *Am. Scientist* **40**, 682 (1952); L. Brillouin, *J. Appl. Phys.* **25**, 595 (1954).

When we transmit a message we use an average power P during a certain time τ, and no heat. The entropy of the cable is not modified at first, but if we do not receive the message, and leave it on the cable, it will propagate back and forth, and be progressively attenuated by Joule effect in the resistances, until all the energy $P\tau$ has been changed into heat. This final stage corresponds to an entropy S larger than the original S_0. The negentropy ΔN initially introduced on the cable by the process of signal transmission is, accordingly, represented by the difference

$$\Delta N = S - S_0. \tag{17.42}$$

This is the quantity which we must compute.

We may first assume a rather strong coupling between the signals and the physical system (the cable). This is Raymond's assumption "that the heat capacity of the closed system is so large that the change in temperature with operation of the communication device is negligible." This leads to a final entropy

$$S = S_0 + P\tau/T, \tag{17.43}$$

and hence, with the help of Eq. (17.41):

$$\Delta N = P\tau/T = k\nu_M P\tau/P_n. \tag{17.44}$$

The negentropy ΔN represents information flowing at the rate of $\Delta N/\tau$ per second, and hence the channel capacity (per second) is

$$C_1 = \Delta N/\tau = k\nu_M P/P_n. \tag{17.45}$$

If we compare this result with Shannon's formula (17.15)

$$C_{sh} = k\nu_M \ln[1 + (P/P_n)], \tag{17.46}$$

we see that the two formulas agree only for very small values of the ratio P/P_n, when the logarithm can be expanded, and the expansion reduced to its first term only.

Shannon's formula was obtained under special assumptions, which actually do not correspond to the model just discussed. Shannon assumed a lossless cable, with no ohmic resistance. This means that there is no coupling between the electric currents flowing on the cable and the physical cable itself. The source of noise is supposed to be outside the cable, and to act independently. There is no direct mechanism here to produce the final increase of entropy that was found in our previous example. If we retain the idea of no coupling between the signals and the cable, we must assume a dissipation mechanism of a different nature. The increase in entropy might be due to signal distortion, or to irregular changes in the spacing of current pulses and in the intensity of the pulses.

The initial state is an organized system of pulses carrying the desired information, and the final state is a disorganized and disordered succession of pulses distributed at random, and carrying no intelligible information. Our system has n oscillating degrees of freedom (the cells of Section 1), and a random distribution of energy E_r corresponds to a temperature T [Eq. (17.8)]:

$$E_r = n\,k\,T. \tag{17.47}$$

If we now assume the energy E_r to be progressively increased by steps dE_r, the entropy increase is

$$S - S_0 = \int_{E_1}^{E_2} (dE_r)/T = n\,k \int_{E_1}^{E_2} (dE_r)/E_r = n\,k \ln(E_2/E_1). \tag{17.48}$$

The initial state E_1 corresponds to noise power P_n only, with a duration τ. The final energy level E_2 is obtained after all the additional energy $P\,\tau$ has been distributed at random among the n oscillators, and added to the noise power:

$$E_1 = P_n \tau, \qquad E_2 = (P_n + P)\,\tau. \tag{17.49}$$

Hence, we have for the negentropy

$$\Delta N = S - S_0 = n\,k \ln[(P_n + P)/P_n].$$

This yields a channel capacity (per unit time) of

$$C_2 = \Delta N/\tau = k(n/\tau) \ln[1 + (P/P_n)] = k\,\nu_M \ln[1 + (P/P_n)], \tag{17.50}$$

which is identical with Shannon's formula (17.46). The difference between our earlier result (17.45) and the new one (17.50) arises because the original model was maintained at a constant temperature T, while the new model exhibits a rise in temperature proportional to the rise in random energy E_r, with Eq. (17.47) valid at all times. This rise in temperature decreases the entropy difference (17.48) and results in a lower capacity for the channel.

The logarithm appears here in a similar fashion to the well known $\ln V$ term in the entropy of an ideal gas [Eq. (12.12)]. The situation in this problem is very similar to the one already discovered in Chapter 13, Section 7 [Eq. (13.55)] when we found information I increasing as the logarithm of a certain quantity F, while the entropy change ΔS was a linear function of F. In the problem of telecommunication we have similar formulas: information I [or channel capacity C, Eqs. (17.46) and (17.50)] is the logarithm of

$$F = 1 + (P/P_n),$$

while entropy change [Eq. (17.44)] is proportional to $F - 1$ in Raymond's model, which represents the real physical problem of dissipation.

In conclusion, we must emphasize the physical meaning of this discussion: Shannon's formula really represents a limit that corresponds to optimum conditions with maximum efficiency in the transformation of negentropy into information. This results from the fact that the computations based on information (Section 3) or on negentropy [Eq. (17.50)] give identical results, provided all quantities are measured in the same system of units. If information is measured in bits and entropy in thermodynamical units, then one finds that each bit corresponds to $k \ln 2 \approx 10^{-16}$ in thermodynamical units, since this is the ratio of units. This proves again (see Chapter 14) that one bit of information can never be obtained for less than $k \ln 2$ in negentropy cost.

7. Gabor's Modified Formula and the Role of Beats

Gabor,[4] after discussing the "cell" system which we explained in Chapter 8, investigated very thoroughly the energy levels which can be used, in each cell, to represent distinguishable signals. This original discussion is based on quantum theory, but for all practical applications the quanta $h\nu$ are so small that a classical theory can be used. When this is done, one realizes that the new terms in Gabor's formula correspond to beats between signal and noise. These beats result in increased energy fluctuations. If we superimpose a signal of amplitude A_1 and a noise of amplitude A_2 with variable phase ψ, we obtain

$$I = A_1 \cos \omega t + A_2 \cos(\omega t + \psi), \tag{17.51}$$

$$I^2 = A_1^2 \cos^2 \omega t + A_2^2 \cos^2(\omega t + \psi) + 2 A_1 A_2 \cos \omega t \cos(\omega t + \psi).$$

Let us now average over a few periods of oscillation, assuming a slow variation of A_2 and ψ:

$$\overline{I^2} = A_1^2/2 + A_2^2/2 + A_1 A_2 \cos \psi. \tag{17.52}$$

The power over such a relatively short interval of time is

$$\overline{P} = P_1 + \overline{P_2} + 2(P_1 \overline{P_2})^{1/2} \cos \psi. \tag{17.53}$$

The average over a long interval of time will contain only the first two terms, since $\cos \psi$ will be zero, on the average:

$$\overline{\overline{P}} = P_1 + \overline{P_2}. \tag{17.54}$$

[4] D. Gabor, *Phil. Mag.* [7] **41**, 1161 (1950).

The last term of Eq. (17.53) represents beats between signal and noise. It plays an important role in the power fluctuations Δp:

$$\overline{P} = \overline{\overline{P}} + \Delta p, \tag{17.55}$$

$$\overline{\Delta p^2} = \overline{P_2{}^2} + 4\, P_1\, \overline{P_2 \cos^2 \psi} = (\overline{P_2})^2 + 2\, P_1\, \overline{P_2},$$

since for thermal noise we have

$$(\overline{P_2})^2 = \overline{P_2{}^2} \qquad \text{and} \qquad \overline{\cos^2 \psi} = \tfrac{1}{2}.$$

From. Eq. (17.55), we see that fluctuations increase with the signal power P_1.

These results can be used for the computation of the number m of distinguishable power levels. Let us choose steps $2(\overline{\Delta p^2})^{1/2}$ to be consistent with Shannon's formula [see Eq. (17.32)]. This is twice the size of the steps originally proposed by Gabor. Let us say that P_M is the maximum power used in signal transmission. The number of steps (including one for $P = 0$) is

$$m_G = 1 + \int_0^{P_M} dP/(2\sqrt{\overline{\Delta p^2}}) = 1 + (\tfrac{1}{2}) \int_0^{P_M} dP/\sqrt{\overline{P_2{}^2} + 2\, P\overline{P_2}}$$

$$= (\tfrac{1}{2}) \sqrt{1 + 2\frac{P_M}{\overline{P_2}}} + \tfrac{1}{2}. \tag{17.56}$$

For small values of the ratio P_M/P_2, the number m_G reduces to $1 + \frac{1}{2}(P_M/P_2)$, which is identical to formula (17.35). For large signal-to-noise ratio, the m_G value increases more slowly with P_M than expression (17.35), which corresponds to Shannon's formula.

According to experimental conditions of observation, it will be necessary to investigate whether the additional fluctuations due to beats may be of importance or not. This discussion will determine whether to use Shannon's or Gabor's formula. Gabor's formula (17.56) results in the following expression for the capacity of the channel

$$C_G = K\, \nu_M \ln m_G = K\, \nu_M \ln \left\{ [1 + \sqrt{1 + 2\, P_M/\overline{P_2}}]/2 \right\}, \tag{17.57}$$

where P_M is the maximum power of the signals. This is obtained by using Eq. (17.34) with Gabor's m_G value. When a long time τ is selected, the $\overline{\cos \psi}$ average becomes zero and beats can be ignored, a situation which justifies the use of Shannon's formula in the limit.

CHAPTER 18

WRITING, PRINTING, AND READING[1]

1. The Transmission of Information; Live Information

We have discussed in the preceding chapter the problem of telecommunications, and we followed the conventional line of attack, as developed by Shannon, Wiener, and the group at the Bell Telephone Laboratories. The problem is restricted to the simplest case of a communication from one person to another, either by telegraph or by some telephonic device. This is a well defined and very important problem, the results of which can be extended to a variety of similar situations; one person talking directly to another, for instance.

The theory is, however, not necessarily restricted to this special case, and it can be extended to much more general problems, provided that special attention is given to the conditions of operation. We intend to discuss these general problems in the present chapter, and to show that our negentropy principle of information enables us to investigate all possible circumstances of communication, and to draw some important conclusions on their fundamental laws.

The first interesting problem is broadcasting. Here we have one person communicating with many other people:

A. One speaker talking before a microphone connected to N different cables with N different receivers.

B. One given telegram sent to N different stations.

C. A speaker in front of an audience in an auditorium.

D. Radio broadcasts.

In cases A and B, we evidently have examples of our earlier "person to person" communication, with N channels operated in parallel. The transmitter must provide the power required for all the channels. If the channels are identical, we simply have to provide power N times greater than that required for one channel. The cases C and D are less favorable, because of the large amount of power which is not utilized: sound waves absorbed in walls, furniture, and other sound absorbing materials, in case C; radio waves lost and dissipated in space, in case D.

---

[1] These problems were discussed by the author at a Harvard seminar (Oct. 1951), a lecture at Brown University (Feb. 1952), and an invited paper at the American Physical Society, Washington meeting (May, 1952). See also L. Brillouin, *J. Appl. Phys.* **25**, 595 (1954).

Except for these very large additional losses, these last cases are similar to the first ones, A and B. Altogether, we may reduce these problems to examples of single channels operated in parallel.

These problems have some common characteristics:

1. Power and negentropy are propagated together with information.

2. The receiver absorbs the energy and negentropy in the same operation by which information is received. We characterize this situation by the expression "live information." The information is transmitted with the energy required for its detection.

3. In the process of transmission, some energy is degraded, some negentropy is lost, and information is lost by the same mechanism.

4. In all of the examples, the generalized Carnot principle, stating that information must be paid for by an amount of negentropy greater than or equal to the information obtained, applies.

2. The Problem of Reading and Writing

We find a completely different situation when we examine another type of transmission of information: writing and reading. There is obviously a certain expenditure of energy in the process of writing, but we find no trace of this energy on the written page. There is no visible negentropy left either; yet the information is there, completely dissociated from these other elements. This is not an isolated example, since a similar situation is found in all cases of recorded information: printed matter, phonograph records, magnetic tape, punched tape and punched cards, blueprints, etc. In all these examples, we have information stored and unconnected with either energy or negentropy. Furthermore, we may recover the information without destroying it. This seems to offer the possibility of unlimited multiplication of the information.

As an example, suppose that an author writes a book and the book is published. We do not consider the problem of thinking and the work of the author. This is the human element, which we have been very careful never to include in our discussions (see Chapters 1 and 20). It does not make any difference whether we consider a book written by an author, or a mere collection of numerical data, such as stock exchange quotations, weather observations, etc. If the manuscript is N letters long, it contains a certain amount of information. Our definitions do not go beyond this point. Now we suppose that 1000 copies of the book are printed, and that each copy is read by 100 persons. The total amount of information has been multiplied by a factor of 10^5, while it appears that the corresponding increase in entropy is not comparable. Of course, the increase in information will be diminished by causes such as misprints, errors of transmission, lack of understanding, etc., but the multiplicative factor can still be, in practice, very large. The problem requires a closer examination in order to show how the negentropy principle applies to these situations.

3. Dead Information and how to Bring it Back to Life

We characterize the preceding situations as cases of stored dead information, with no energy or negentropy connected with it. In order to read out the information, we must reenergize it. An additional source of energy is absolutely necessary for the reading, and this source of energy provides the negentropy which is changed into new information.

We need a source of light to read a book. The phonograph does not work without a motor to turn the record. A blind person reading a book printed in the Braille alphabet has to move his finger along the paper, and exert sufficient pressure to distinguish the print from other irregularities on the page, and this motion and pressure require work. We need light and photoelectric cells to read punched tape, or we may use a battery and brushes passing current through the holes of a punched card. In all of these examples, the amount of negentropy taken from the external source can be demonstrated to be larger than the information obtained. The case of reading a punched tape is a typical example, for which we can compute both entropy and information, and verify the relation between them.

Information in binary digits	0	1	0	0	1	1	1	0	1	0	0	1
Punched tape	0		0	0				0		0	0	

FIG. 18.1. Diagram showing tape with holes punched for the zeros in a message coded in binary digits.

Let us assume that we have information recorded on punched metallic tape in binary digits. As indicated in Fig. 18.1, the zeros are represented by holes, and the ones by unperforated tape sections. Each section of tape contains one bit of information, or

$$\Delta I = k \ln 2 \quad \text{per section} \tag{18.1}$$

in thermodynamical units, when k is Boltzmann's constant. Our reading device is shown in Fig. 18.2. It uses a source of light, with a beam of light striking on the metallic tape. If there is a hole, the beam falls into the photoelectric cell P_1. If there is no hole the beam is reflected into the photoelectric cell P_2. We might think of eliminating the second cell P_2 and concluding that we have a one whenever P_1 is not actuated. We must, however, recall that we have always required that a "negative" reading is to have no significance. Thus each section of the tape will require at least one quantum $h\nu$, and this energy will be absorbed either in P_1 or in P_2. In order to be distinguished from the background of thermal radiation, the quantum $h\nu$ must be high enough so that

$$h\nu \geqslant kT \ln 2, \tag{18.2}$$

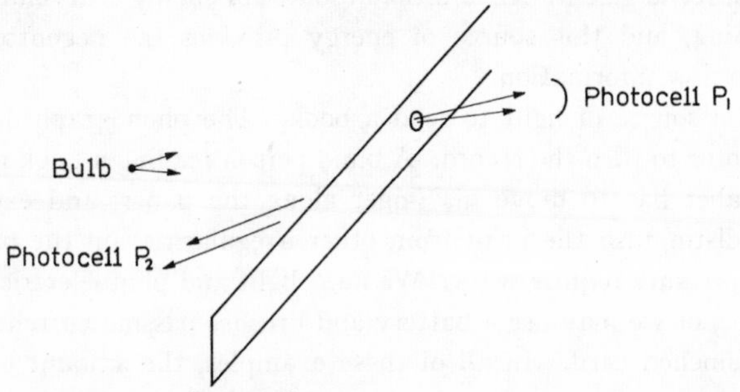

FIG. 18.2. The reading device for the tape of Fig. 18.1. The photocell to the right receives light through the punched holes, while the photocell to the left receives light reflected from the unpunched positions.

as was proved in Chapter 14, Section 3 [Eq. (14.17)]. When the quantum is absorbed, there is a loss in negentropy (an increase ΔS in entropy):

$$\Delta S = h\nu/T \geqslant k \ln 2, \tag{18.3}$$

and we have the relation

$$\Delta(S - I) \geqslant 0, \tag{18.4}$$

which shows that our generalized Carnot principle of Chapter 12 is satisfied. In this simple case we prove that the information comes from the negentropy of the light beam, and we can theoretically reach the limit corresponding to an efficiency unity. The problem escaped notice because of the very small quantity of negentropy required:

$$k \ln 2 \approx 10^{-16} \quad \text{in cgs Centigrade degrees.} \tag{18.5}$$

The preceding type of punching is not very reliable, since the "ones" are not really recorded. A plain piece of tape, with no holes would be read as a succession of ones, which is wrong. A safer method would be to use two different levels for the holes as indicated in Fig. 18.3, and two photoelectric cells receiving the light that may pass through either hole. This arrangement still, however, requires the absorption of one quantum per digit, so that the relations (18.1) — (18.4) would still be valid.

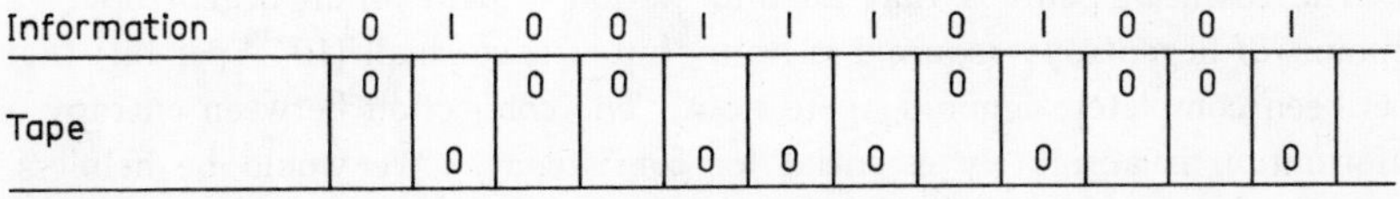

FIG. 18.3. A superior method of punching tape using holes on two levels, one level for the zeros, and the other level for the ones.

Instead of using light, we might use a system of brushes and a battery passing a current through the holes. The current is read on an ammeter or recorded in a relay. According to the discussion of Chapter 14, Section 2, the limit in this case is again $k \ln 2$ per reading. In a mechanical device, such as a phonograph record, small positive or negative pulses can be detected only if the mechanical system yields an energy larger than $k\,T \ln 2$ per pulse, which corresponds to an entropy increase of $k \ln 2$. Similar remarks apply to pulses recorded on magnetic tape. In every case, the negentropy lost in the reading operation is larger than, or at best equal to, the information obtained, and the generalized Carnot principle [Eq. (18.4)] is always satisfied.

Similar remarks apply to the problem of information recorded in blue prints. Each time we need the information, we must read the blueprints. This reading operation absorbs negentropy, from a light source, and part of this negentropy is converted into the information needed, say, for the construction of a device according to the blueprint. We shall return to these problems later.

4. Writing and Printing

We can now consider another problem: how much negentropy is spent in the process of writing? This negentropy is lost, but we obtain a new copy of the information, so that the printing mechanism is another example of the transformation of negentropy into information.

Photographic printing is the simplest example to discuss: we place the punched tape on photographic paper, and shine light through each hole. Each time, at least one quantum $h\nu$ of light is used, in order to print the position of the hole. The situation is similar to the case of Section 3, and leads to similar conclusions: printing a new copy costs exactly as much as reading it. The new copy of the information is paid for in negentropy.

In all of these discussions, we have ignored typical irreversible processes: developing the photographic paper, amplifying the electric impulses, etc. All of these refinements of the technique cost a great deal of negentropy, and the total cost of a reading or a printing operation will be very much higher than the limit which we have computed.

The essential point is that all information is paid for in negentropy. The amount of negentropy required is finite, but it is so small (10^{-16} per bit) that it has been completely ignored up to now. The connection between entropy and information is absolutely essential for consistency. We would be helpless to discuss the problems in this chapter without this connection. The very small value of 10^{-16} of negentropy required per bit of information plays, however, a very important role in modern life, and makes it possible to communicate information at a negligible cost.

We must now mention a law of decay: any system on which information has been recorded will deteriorate in the course of time. Furthermore the information itself may progressively lose its validity. For both reasons, recorded information follows a general law of decay, which is consistent with the generalized Carnot principle. The decay will, however, be much slower for dead (recorded) information than for live information.

5. Discussion of a Special Example

Writing and reading are currently used to such a large extent in everyday life that we do not realize how often we need them. Let us consider, for instance, the procedure followed when sending a telegram. The following steps occur:

A. The sender writes the telegram at the telegraph office.

B. The operator reads the telegram and translates it into impulses of current on the transmitter.

C. The current impulses are received at the receiver and a mechanism prints the message.

D. The local operator reads the address and sends the copy of the telegram to this address.

E. The telegram is read by the addressee.

We have omitted two other steps because they involve thought, and our present theory is unable to treat this process:

A_0. The sender composes his telegram so as to convey some information to the addressee.

F. The addressee comprehends the meaning of the telegram.

Restricting the procedure to the steps A, B, C, D, and E, we note that these steps involve the processes:

A. Writing;
B. Reading, coding, transmitting;
C. Decoding, printing;
D, E. Reading.

Each operation of writing, reading, or printing involves a cost in negentropy, according to the discussion of Sections 3 and 4. The operations of coding and decoding usually require the use of memory devices from which the code numbers have to be read. This process, also, has a certain cost in terms of negentropy. The operation of transmission and reception, discussed by Shannon, has been analysed in Chapter 17. Copies of the telegram will be in the hands of the various people involved, and these copies correspond to dead information which can be read over and over again, provided they are properly reenergized.

The memory devices, mentioned above, will be treated more fully in Chapter 19 on computing machines, where reading and writing operations are mechanized, and use up a certain amount of negentropy each time they occur.

6. New Information and Redundancy

We have shown in Section 3 that the reading operation requires an entropy increase ΔS which is larger than, or at best equal to, the amount of information ΔI obtained by the reader. We now ask the following question: Is this information to be considered new information, or should it be considered only as redundancy, carrying no new information, since it is only a repetition of information contained in the written document? This question is on the border of philosophy, but we may try to give a practical answer to it. When a certain person reads a book for the first time, he certainly obtains information, and this should be counted as new information for the reader. If he reads it again a second and a third time, he obtains only redundancy, and no new information.

From an absolute point of view, we might imagine an ideal scholar, knowing everything that is known to human beings. For this ideal philosopher, every new book contains information. Other readers, however, only obtain redundant information, since it is already known to the ideal scholar. This is a rather unrealistic point of view.

In order to distinguish among the various possible points of view on information and redundancy involved in reading and printing of copies, we introduce the following definitions:[2]

Absolute Information: any piece of information available to any human being on earth, this information being counted only once, whatever the number of

[2] L. Brillouin, *Am. Scientist* **38**, 594 (1950).

people knowing it might be. An ultrasecret document would thus carry as much information as an issue of the New York Times containing the same number of letters.

Distributed Information: the product of the amount of absolute information and the number of people who share that information. This second definition seems more realistic than the more philosophical "absolute information," and this is the point of view we have taken in this chapter. There are, however, problems where the definition of absolute information may be the better one to choose, and the distinction between the two should be kept in mind.

CHAPTER 19

THE PROBLEM OF COMPUTING

1. Computing Machines

We must now consider the question of computing machines, and discuss their action on information. It has been often hinted that a computing machine actually manufactures new information. This is not really the case. Machines are able to process information; they take the raw material and they give out a finished product, but the total amount of information has not been increased. In the best ideal circumstances, information may be kept constant during the computing, but under normal conditions there will be some loss and the final information will be smaller than the input.

Let us consider the problem more carefully. There are two distinct phases in it: programming and actual computing. The programming is done by the scientists who intend to use the machine. They discuss the problem, select the mathematical laws to be used, prepare a program of arithmetic operations to be performed in a certain sequence. All these operations are written down on a medium that the machine can read: punched tape, magnetic tape, etc. This part of the work requires thinking and knowledge from the scientists. It might be called information in a general sense, but this is typically a case where our definitions of information do not apply. We repeatedly emphasized the point that our statistical definition of information did not include any human consideration, and that we could not, at least for the moment, discuss the problem of thinking.

Once a punched tape has been prepared for the program of operation, we might count the number of bits in it and compute how much information there is in this final program. It does not seem that this statement would have much importance.

The next step is to consider the machine with its specified program, and to examine how it actually works. We feed in certain numerical data at the input. The machine operates on these data, according to the given program, and computes the final data which represent the output. If the machine makes no error in computing, it operates exactly like a coding machine. It uses the information contained in the input data and translates it into the output data, which can at best contain all the information of the input, but no more.

The machine may be compared with a transmission channel, including coding and decoding. Under ideal conditions, the message is correctly transmitted, and the information content is kept constant. Errors and approximations in the computing result in a loss of information. The work done by the machine can best be compared to the work of a translator: a translator is given a dictionary and the rules of grammar that enable him to translate into English a paper originally written in Japanese. The dictionary and the grammar correspond to the program of operation. The Japanese paper is the input, and the English translation represents the output. The total information was present in the input, and can (at best) be found in the output.

In a similar way, a machine computing firing tables, for instance, is given a program that takes into account the laws of motion of a projectile and atmospheric conditions. The input is represented by the initial position and velocity. The output is the point of impact and final velocity. The input data logically contain the solution, but we are unable to read it directly. It is a coded message which requires decoding, and this is just another way of saying "translating." If the machine works perfectly it must be reversible: given the impact it may compute backward and obtain the initial conditions. In a similar way, a translator may translate back into Japanese, and should recover the original paper or its equivalent. Ideal operating conditions correspond to reversibility, hence to conservation of information.

The over-all reversibility is obtained by a succession of steps which may include irreversible processes, such as writing data into a memory device and reading them out at a later time.

Each of these operations implies a certain cost in negentropy (see Chapter 18, Sections 3 and 4). The operation of the machine, on a certain program, will actually cost a certain amount of negentropy (energy degraded). This is of importance from a technical point of view, but it does not modify our conclusion, and one may imagine that this cost of operation will be reduced in future and better machines.

Let us quote here a very interesting discussion, written more than a century ago, by Edgar A. Poe. This author considers a variety of automatons and more particularly the calculating machine devised by Babbage. The following quotation defines very exactly our present point of view:

"But if these machines were ingenious, what shall we think of the calculating machine of Mr. Babbage? What shall we think of an engine of wood and metal which can not only compute astronomical and navigation tables to any given extent, but render the exactitute of its operations mathematically certain through its power of correcting its possible errors? What shall we think of the machine which can not only accomplish all this, but actually print off its elaborate results, when obtained, without the slightest intervention of the intellect of man? It will, perhaps, be said in reply, that a machine such as we have described is altogether above comparison with the Chess-Player of Maelzel. By no means — it is altogether beneath it — that is to say, provided we assume (what should never for a moment be assumed) that the Chess-Player is a *pure machine*, and performs its operations without any immediate human agency. Arithmetical or algebraical calculations are, from their very nature, fixed and determinate. Certain *data* being given, certain results necessarily and inevitably follow. These results have dependence upon nothing, and are influenced by nothing but the *data* originally given. And the question to be solved proceeds, or should proceed, to its final determination, by a succession of unerring steps liable to no change, and subject to no modification. This being the case, we can without difficulty conceive the *possibility* of so arranging a piece of mechanism, that upon starting it in accordance with the *data* of the question to be solved, it should continue its movements, regularly, progressively and undeviatingly toward the required solution, since these movements, however complex, are never imagined to be otherwise than finite and determinate."[1]

2. The Computer as a Mathematical Element

The role of a computing machine is interesting to analyze, when the machine is working on input data resulting from an experimental procedure. These data come from observations on a certain physical system, and the series of observations usually gives a continuous function $f(t)$. Since any physical system has a finite band width, this is also the case for $f(t)$.

A digital computer operates on sampled signals. The sampling operation corresponds exactly to the problem discussed in Chapter 8, Sections 6 and 7. If we want to use the complete information contained in the continuous function, we must sample at intervals θ.

$$\theta = \frac{1}{2\,\nu_M} \qquad f_m = f(m\,\theta). \tag{19.1}$$

Our original function f is practically defined only over a finite time interval τ, but in order to obtain a precise mathematical problem, we must specify the behavior of the function from $-\infty$ to $+\infty$, as we did in Chapter 8, Section 6. Let us again assume a periodic function with period τ satisfying conditions (8.52).

[1] Edgar A. Poe, "Maelzel's Chess Player," 1836.

The input of the computer is represented by the N sampled values f_m and if τ is large we have

$$N = 2\,\nu_M\,\tau \tag{19.2}$$

[Eq. (8.51)]. From these sampled values we can compute the Fourier components and vice versa [Eqs. (8.63) and (8.63 a)]:

$$A_n = \frac{1}{N}\sum_{m=1}^{N} f_m\, e^{-i n m \omega_0 \theta}, \qquad \omega_0 = \frac{2\pi}{\tau}, \tag{19.3}$$

$$f_m = \sum_{n=-n_M}^{+n_M} A_n\, e^{i n m \omega_0 \theta}. \tag{19.4}$$

The computer operates on the sampled values f_m and gives output values ψ_μ:

$$\psi_\mu = F_\mu(f_1 \ldots f_m \ldots f_N). \tag{19.5}$$

In general, the functions F_μ representing the computer's program may be very complicated. If, however, we limit our discussion to a *linear mathematical problem*, the operation will be represented by a matrix $(M_{\mu m})$

$$\psi_\mu = \sum_{m=1}^{N} M_{\mu m}\, f_m, \tag{19.6}$$

and the matrix represents the program of computation. We have N different m values in the input, but we may have a different number N_1 of μ values in the output. There may also be a certain amount of redundancy both in input and output data. If we do not want to change the band width of the over-all system, our N_1 output data will require a different time τ_1 for the duration of the output continuous function

$$\Psi(t) = \sum_{\mu=1}^{N_1} \psi_\mu\, g(t-\mu\,\theta), \qquad \tau_1 = N_1\,\theta, \tag{19.7}$$

which is rebuilt according to the rules of Chapter 8 [Eq. (8.60)] and can again be analyzed in a Fourier series [as in Eq. (8.58)].

$$\Psi(t) = \sum_{\beta=-\beta_M}^{+\beta_M} \alpha_\beta\, e^{i\beta\omega_1 t}, \qquad \text{with} \qquad \beta_M\,\nu_1 = \nu_M, \qquad \nu_1 = \frac{1}{\tau_1}, \qquad \omega_1 = \frac{2\pi}{\tau_1}. \tag{19.8}$$

The relation between the Fourier coefficients α_β and the sampled output data ψ_μ is exactly similar to Eq. (19.3)

$$\alpha_\beta = \frac{1}{N_1} \sum_{\mu=1}^{N_1} \psi_\mu \, e^{-i\beta\mu\omega_1\theta}. \tag{19.9}$$

From Eqs. (19.4) — (19.9), we can obtain directly the relation between the input spectrum A_n and the output spectrum α_β, assuming a linear computation represented by the matrix $M_{\mu m}$

$$\alpha_\beta = \frac{1}{N_1} \sum_{\mu=1}^{N_1} \sum_{m=1}^{N} \sum_{n=-n_M}^{n_M} M_{\mu m} \, A_n \, e^{i(nm\omega_0 - \beta\mu\omega_1)\theta}. \tag{19.10}$$

If we assume that the number N_1 of output data is equal to the number N of input data, the formula simplifies. The M matrix is a square matrix and

$$N_1 = N, \qquad \tau_1 = \tau, \qquad \omega_1 = \omega_0, \qquad n_M = \beta_M,$$

$$\alpha_\beta = \frac{1}{N} \sum_{\mu=1}^{N} \sum_{m=1}^{N} \sum_{n=-n_M}^{n_M} M_{\mu m} \, A_n \, e^{i(nm - \beta\mu)\omega_0\theta}, \tag{19.11}$$

with $-n_M \leqslant \beta \leqslant n_M$. The quantity $(n\,m - \beta\,\mu)$ is a positive or negative integer, and the α_β coefficients of the output spectrum are rational functions in

$$z = e^{-i\omega_0\theta} = e^{-i\pi/\tau\nu_M}. \tag{19.12}$$

These formulas entirely support the point of view developed in the preceding section: the machine is processing the information, but not manufacturing any new information. The operation can be reversed when the matrix is non-singular and can be inverted. This means that an inverse matrix J can be found

$$(M) \cdot (J) = (J) \cdot (M) = 1. \tag{19.13}$$

Let us call $J_{m'\mu'}$ the elements of this inverse matrix that represents the reverse program of operation of the machine. Conditions (19.13) mean

$$\sum_{m=1}^{N} M_{\mu m} \, J_{m\mu'} = \delta_{\mu\mu'} = \begin{cases} 1 & \mu = \mu' \\ 0 & \mu \neq \mu' \end{cases},$$
$$\sum_{\mu=1}^{N} J_{m'\mu} \, M_{\mu m} = \delta_{mm'}, \tag{19.14}$$

and the reverse operation of the machine is represented by a relation similar to (19.11):

$$A_{n'} = \frac{1}{N} \sum_{m'=1}^{N} \sum_{\mu'=1}^{N} \sum_{\beta'=-n_M}^{n_M} J_{m'\mu'} \alpha_{\beta'} e^{i(\beta'\mu' - n'm')\omega_0 \theta}. \tag{19.15}$$

The proof is easy, and uses Eqs. (19.14) together with Eq. (8.63 b):

$$\frac{1}{N} \sum_{m=1}^{N} e^{ipm\omega_0\theta} = \delta_{p0} = \begin{cases} 1 & p = 0 \\ 0 & p \neq 0 \quad \text{integer.} \end{cases} \tag{19.16}$$

We use Eq. (19.11) in Eq. (19.15) and obtain (with $\beta' = \beta$)

$$A_{n'} = \frac{1}{N^2} \sum_{m'\mu'\beta'\mu m n} J_{m'\mu'} M_{\mu m} A_n e^{i(nm - n'm')\omega_0\theta} e^{i\beta'(\mu'-\mu)\omega_0\theta}. \tag{19.17}$$

Summing on β' in the last exponential and using Eq. (19.16) gives $\delta_{\mu'-\mu,0}$; hence $\mu' = \mu$. We then sum $\Sigma_\mu J_{m'\mu} M_{\mu m}$ and obtain $m' = m$ according to Eq. (19.14). The last step is to sum $e^{i(n-n')m\omega_0\theta}$ on m and this gives $n = n'$ according Eq. (19.16), so that, finally, we obtain

$$A_n = A_n. \qquad \text{Q.E.D.}$$

We have obtained a complete representation of a machine operating on a linear reversible program, where no information is lost but no new information is created either. There will certainly be a small loss of information due to rounding-off errors in computation.

Computation on a linear program represented by a rectangular matrix M will

lose information if $N_1 < N$

produce redundancy if $N_1 > N$.

Nonlinear programs [Eq. (19.5)] would be harder to analyze.

We shall discuss a slightly different problem in the next section which corresponds to another possible use of the computer.

3. The Computer as a Circuit Element, Sampling and Desampling (Linvill and Salzer)

A computing machine can be incorporated in a control system, and many important applications result from this procedure. The problem has been very carefully investigated by Linvill[2] and Salzer.[3] Here the data come from observation on a certain mechanism, and the results of the computation are used to control the operation of this mechanism. The computer is just a part of the control system and should be analyzed as a circuit element. The whole control system operates on continuous signals with a finite band width, and the computer uses sampled values. The difference from the problem discussed in the preceding section is the following: We assumed in Section 2 that we had available for computation the whole set of data corresponding to a complete experiment of total duration τ, and that we were discussing these results at leisure, after the experiment had been completed. In a control device we must compute right away, using all the data obtained up to a certain time t, in order to be able to control the operation of the mechanism as soon as possible. In such a problem, the total duration of the experiment is not defined in advance. The method of the preceding section must be replaced by the Shannon sampling method (see Chapter 8, Section 7). In order to use all the information contained in the passing band, without introducing unnecessary redundancy, we sample again at intervals θ, as in Eq. (19.1). The original function can be reconstructed by Shannon's procedure [Eq. (8.69)] with the impulse functions

$$g_s(t) = \frac{\sin 2\pi \nu_M t}{2\pi \nu_M t} = \frac{1}{2\nu_M} \int_{\nu=-\nu_M}^{\nu_M} e^{i2\pi\nu t}\, d\nu, \tag{19.18}$$

and

$$f(t) = \sum_m f_m\, g_s(t - m\theta) = \int_{\nu=-\nu_M}^{\nu_M} A(\nu)\, e^{i2\pi\nu t} d\nu. \tag{19.19}$$

The Shannon impulse functions g_s extend to a certain distance both forward and backward. This means that the function $f(t)$ at time t cannot be obtained if we have only the past values $(m < 0)$ available.

---

[2] W. K. Linvill, Doctor thesis, Mass. Inst. Technol., Cambridge, Mass., 1950: *Proc. I. R. E.* **40**, 230 (1952).

[3] J. M. Salzer, Doctor thesis, Mass. Inst. Technol., Cambridge, Mass., 1951: *Proc. I. R. E.* **40**, 231 (1952); **41**, 901 (1953); **42**, 457 (1954); and I. R. E. Electronics Group, University of California, Los Angeles, May 15, 1952; also Hughes Aircraft Co. Memo No. 338, 1954.

Linvill uses a different impulse function $g_L(t)$ representing a very sharp impulse, as shown in Fig. 19.1. We may define such a sharp impulse with a formula similar to (19.18):

$$g_L(t) = \frac{\sin 2\pi \nu_1 t}{2\pi \nu_1 t} = \frac{1}{2\nu_1} \int_{-\nu_1}^{\nu_1} e^{i 2\pi \nu' t} d\nu', \tag{19.20}$$

where $\nu_1 \gg \nu_M$. The function so obtained is called $\tilde{f}(t)$:

$$\tilde{f}(t) = \sum_m f_m g_L(t - m\theta) = \int_{-\nu_1}^{\nu_1} \tilde{A}(\nu') e^{i 2\pi \nu' t} d\nu'. \tag{19.21}$$

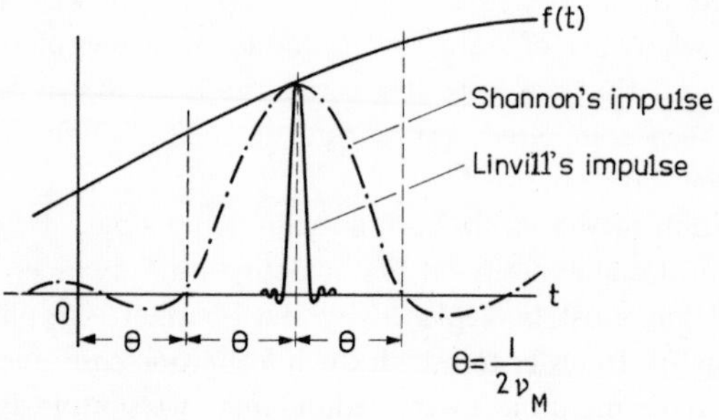

FIG. 19.1. Shannon's and Linvill's impulse functions for reconstructing the function $f(t)$.

From Eqs. (19.18) and (19.19), we compute

$$A(\nu) = \frac{1}{2\nu_M} \sum_m f_m e^{-i 2\pi \nu m \theta}, \qquad -\nu_M \leqslant \nu \leqslant \nu_M, \tag{19.22}$$

while Eqs. (19.20) and (19.21) yield

$$\tilde{A}(\nu') = \frac{1}{2\nu_1} \sum_m f_m e^{-i 2\pi \nu' m \theta}, \qquad -\nu_1 \leqslant \nu' \leqslant \nu_1. \tag{19.23}$$

If we compare Eqs. (19.22) and (19.23), we note that the spectrum $\tilde{A}(\nu')$ is identical with $A(\nu)$ for low frequencies, and reproduces this spectrum periodically in the higher frequency bands:

$$-\nu_M \leqslant \nu' \leqslant \nu_M: \qquad \tilde{A}(\nu') = \frac{\nu_M}{\nu_1} A(\nu); \tag{19.24}$$

and, if, for instance, we take $\nu_M \leqslant \nu \leqslant 3\nu_M$ and set $\nu' = \nu + 2\nu_M$

$$\tilde{A}(\nu') = \frac{1}{2\nu_1} \sum_m f_m e^{-i 2\pi \nu m \theta - i 2\pi m} = \frac{\nu_M}{\nu_1} A(\nu), \tag{19.25}$$

since $2\,\nu_M\,\theta = 1$. In general, if

$$(2\,k - 1)\,\nu_M \leqslant \nu \leqslant (2\,k + 1)\,\nu_M,$$

we take

$$\nu' = \nu + 2\,k\,\nu_M,$$

and we obtain

$$\tilde{A}(\nu') = \frac{\nu_M}{\nu_1} A(\nu). \tag{19.26}$$

Summarizing these results, we have

$$\frac{\nu_1}{\nu_M} \tilde{A}(\nu') = \sum_{k=-\infty}^{\infty} A(\nu' - 2\,k\,\nu_M). \tag{19.27}$$

The sampling method of Linvill gives a function $\tilde{f}(t)$ that can readily be computed from past values since its impulses are sharply located. It differs from the original function through its additional spectra of higher order. The process of desampling is simply a filtering process which retains only the $|\nu| \leqslant \nu_M$ band. This operation gives the original $f(t)$ back again, except for a constant coefficient ν_M/ν_1.

4. Computing on Sampled Data at Time t

The computation proceeds on data known at time t. The input data are

$$f_m = f(m\,\theta), \qquad m \leqslant m_t, \qquad m_t\,\theta = t. \tag{19.28}$$

The output data available at this time are

$$\psi_\mu = \psi\,(\mu\,\theta) \qquad \mu \leqslant m_t - 1. \tag{19.29}$$

If the computation proceeds according to *a linear program*, we may write a relation (Salzer)

$$\psi_{m_t} + \sum_{k=1}^{k_1} b_k\,(m_t)\,\psi_{m_t - k} = \sum_{h=0}^{h_1} a_h(m_t)\,f_{m_t - h}, \tag{19.30}$$

where we use k_1 previously computed output values and the $h_1 + 1$ last input data. The coefficients b_k, a_h may still contain the time (through m_t). An important case occurs for a *linear, time invariant* program of computation with constant b_k and a_h coefficients. Replacing the ψ_{m_t-k} output values by their linear expressions in terms of input values, we may write

$$\psi_{m_t} = \sum_{h=0}^{h_2} c_h f_{m_t-h}. \tag{19.31}$$

The number h_2 of terms included in the sum is larger, and may even become infinite, yielding an infinite series. This formula makes a comparison with our results of Section 2 possible. We take

$$m_t = \mu, \qquad m_t - h = m, \qquad h = \mu - m, \tag{19.32}$$

$$\psi_\mu = \sum_{m=\mu}^{\mu-h_2} c_{\mu-m} f_m. \tag{19.33}$$

Comparing with Eq. (19.6), we obtain the matrix of the transformation:

$$M_{\mu m} = \begin{cases} 0 & m > \mu \\ c_{\mu-m} & \mu - h_2 \leqslant m \leqslant \mu \\ 0 & m < \mu - h_2 \end{cases} \tag{19.34}$$

Such a matrix is represented in the following table, for the case $h_2 = 3$,

$m \downarrow$ / $\mu \rightarrow$	0	1	2	3	4	5	6	7
0	c_0	c_1	c_2	c_3	0	0	0	0
1	0	c_0	c_1	c_2	c_3	0	0	0
2	0	0	c_0	c_1	c_2	c_3	0	0
3	0	0	0	c_0	c_1	c_2	c_3	0
4	0	0	0	0	c_0	c_1	c_2	c_3

(19.35)

All matrix elements below the diagonal are zero. All rows have similar constant coefficients, simply displaced by μ positions to the right. This very special matrix yields simpler results than the more general matrix of Section 2.

5. The Transfer Function for the Computer

Let us now investigate the relation between input and output spectra. We expand the f and ψ functions in Fourier integrals, similar to Eq. (19.19), and obtain

$$f_m = \int_{-\nu_M}^{\nu_M} A(\nu)\, e^{i2\pi\nu t}\, d\nu, \qquad t = m\,\theta, \tag{19.36}$$

$$\psi_m = \int_{-\nu_M}^{\nu_M} \alpha(\nu)\, e^{i2\pi\nu t}\, d\nu. \tag{19.37}$$

We now substitute these expressions in Eq. (19.30), and obtain integrals in $e^{2\pi i\nu t}\, d\nu$ on both sides. The left side has a coefficient

$$\alpha(\nu) + \sum_{k=1}^{k_1} b_k\, \alpha(\nu)\, e^{-i2\pi\nu k\theta}, \tag{19.38}$$

while on the right hand side, we have

$$\sum_{h=0}^{h_1} a_h\, A(\nu)\, e^{-i2\pi\nu h\theta}. \tag{19.38 a}$$

The two functions in Eq. (19.30) being equal, their Fourier transforms are also equal:

$$\alpha(\nu) + \sum_k b_k\, \alpha(\nu)\, e^{-i2\pi\nu k\theta} = \sum_h a_h\, A(\nu)\, e^{-i2\pi\nu h\theta}. \tag{19.39}$$

From this relation we obtain the transfer function:

$$W(\nu) = \frac{\alpha(\nu)}{A(\nu)} = \frac{\sum_{h=0}^{h_1} a_h\, e^{-i2\pi\nu h\theta}}{1 + \sum_{k=1}^{k_1} b_k\, e^{-i2\pi\nu k\theta}} = \frac{a_0 + a_1 z + a_2 z^2 + \ldots + a_{h_1} z^{h_1}}{1 + b_1 z + b_2 z^2 + \ldots + b_{k_1} z^{k_1}}, \tag{19.40}$$

which gives the ratio of output spectrum to input spectrum for the computing system under consideration. It comes out as a rational function of

$$z = e^{-i2\pi\nu\theta}, \qquad \text{with } \theta = \text{the sampling interval.} \tag{19.41}$$

It is a very remarkable fact that the type of computation represented by Eq. (19.30) can be analyzed in this way, and yields at each frequency an output spectrum $\alpha(\nu)$ depending only upon the input spectrum $A(\nu)$ at the same frequency. The transfer function (19.40) was obtained by Salzer, and enabled him to discuss a variety of problems in which computers and ordinary circuits were interconnected in a complex control device.

We might just as well have started from Eq. (19.31), where we assumed that a resolution of the preceding system had been obtained, in order to eliminate the ψ_{m-k}. This relation gives, as before,

$$W(\nu) = \frac{\alpha(\nu)}{A(\nu)} = \sum_{h=0}^{h_2} c_h e^{-i 2\pi \nu h \theta}, \tag{19.42}$$

a polynomial or an infinite series in z.

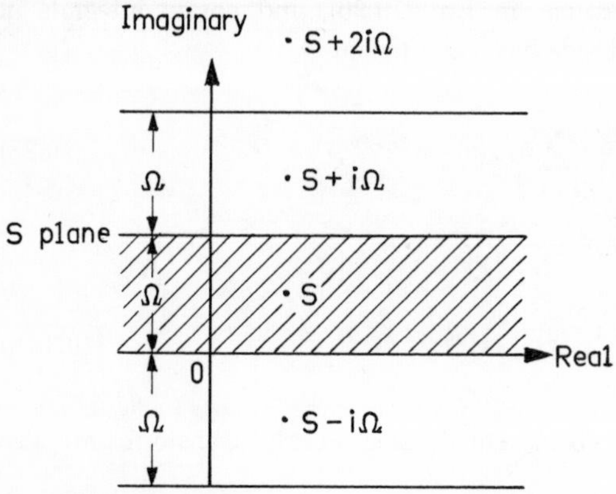

FIG. 19.2. Horizontal strips of the complex s plane in which the values of $\tilde{A}(s)$ are repeated.

All this discussion agrees completely with the point of view developed in the preceding sections about the role of the computer: it represents an automatic device for processing information, just as a machine tool processes metal pieces. There is no new information created, and the output of the computer contains just the same amount of information as the input (in the ideal case of no losses) simply coded in a different manner.

We have based our discussion on the Fourier method, while Linvill and Salzer used the Laplace transform. The two procedures are equivalent, and Salzer's formulas may be obtained by simply changing $i\,\omega$ into s:

$$s = i\,\omega, \qquad \omega = -i\,s, \qquad z = e^{-i\omega\theta} = e^{-s\theta}. \tag{19.43}$$

For the generality of the discussion, it is recommended that s be considered as a complex quantity, but θ (the sampling interval) is always a real quantity. We found that the sampled data $\tilde{f}(t)$ have a periodic spectrum $\tilde{A}(\nu)$ (see Section **3**):

$$\tilde{A}(\omega + n\,\Omega) = \tilde{A}(\omega), \quad \text{with } n \text{ an integer,} \qquad \text{and} \quad \Omega = 4\pi\,\nu_M = 2\pi/\theta \quad \text{real.} \tag{19.44}$$

This property is easily translated for the variable s, and means

$$\tilde{A}(s - i\,n\,\Omega) = \tilde{A}(s - 2\pi\,i\,n/\theta) = \tilde{A}(s). \tag{19.45}$$

In the s complex plane, the $\tilde{A}$ function assumes the same values in successive strips, as shown in Fig. 19.2. When the function is known over one of these strips (the cross-hatched strip, for instance), it is known over the entire plane, since it repeats periodically over the other strips.

6. Circuits Containing a Computer, The Problem of Stability

The preceding analysis proved that a computer working on a given program can be considered as a circuit element with a certain transfer function $W(\nu)$ depending on the frequency ν. When the computer is in series with a conventional circuit, the rest of the circuit is characterized by another transfer function $W_1(\nu)$ and the whole system then has a transfer function

$$W_{\text{total}}(\nu) = W(\nu) \cdot W_1(\nu). \tag{19.46}$$

This remark enables one to discuss the problem of the circuit with computer along the lines of well known methods of circuit analysis. The characteristic point is that the transfer function $W(\nu)$ for the computer is a rational function of the variable z in (19.41) while a conventional circuit yields a transfer function which is rational in ω.

One of the important points for discussion is the problem of *stability*. A computer may take a function $f(t)$ and multiply it by a factor C, thus acting as an amplifier. Furthermore, the general type of program discussed by Salzer [Section 4, Eq. (19.30)] uses a certain number of earlier output values in the computation of the output at time t. This means that the program involves a system of feedback. Having a machine which can operate as an *amplifier with feedback*, we certainly have a problem of stability to discuss, since an amplifier with feedback is able to sustain continuous oscillations when the feedback is strong enough.

This point being of fundamental importance, let us elaborate on it and consider a conventional amplifier α with a feedback β, as shown in Fig. 19.3. A voltage E_1 on the amplifier yields an output $G(t)$:

$$G = \alpha E_1, \qquad \alpha \text{ complex.} \tag{19.47}$$

A fraction β of this output is fed back into the amplifier, and added to the original input $I(t)$, so that

$$E_2 = \beta G = \alpha \beta E_1, \quad \beta \text{ complex},$$

$$E_1 = I + E_2 = I + \alpha \beta E_1, \tag{19.48}$$

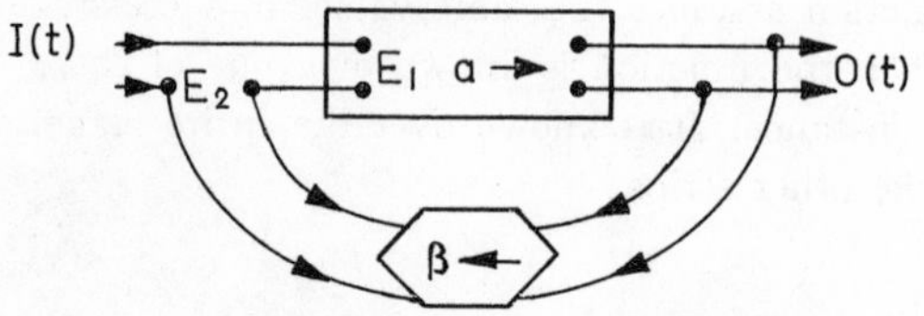

FIG. 19.3. Amplifier α with feed-back β.

from which we obtain

$$E_1 = I/(1 - \alpha \beta),$$

$$G = I \alpha/(1 - \alpha \beta). \tag{19.49}$$

This gives a transfer function

$$W_a = G/I = \alpha/(1 - \alpha \beta), \tag{19.50}$$

for the amplifier with feedback. This expression is very similar to the transfer function of Eq. (19.40) obtained for the computer, if we assume

$$\alpha(\nu) = \sum a_h z^h, \qquad z = e^{-2\pi i \nu \theta}, \qquad -\alpha \beta = \sum b_k z^k. \tag{19.51}$$

A function of type (19.50) possesses a certain number of poles when

$$\alpha \beta = 1, \tag{19.52}$$

a condition which may be fulfilled for specified frequencies. At these frequencies we may obtain a finite output G for a zero input I, since W is infinite: the system is self-oscillating. The position of the poles in the complex plane $s = \sigma + i \omega$ is of fundamental importance, and will be discussed in the next section.

Summarizing the situation, we may say:

A. The computer is similar to an *active network*.

B. The stability of a program of computation can be discussed along similar lines to the problem of stability of active networks.

C. One may study the amplitude and phase characteristics of a given program, and also the locus, impulse response, Nyquist diagram, etc.

D. The band width of the computer is directly defined in terms of the sampling interval θ [Eq. (19.1)]:

$$\text{Maximum frequency:} \quad \nu_M = 1/2\theta. \tag{19.53}$$

Salzer has shown, by numerous examples, the efficiency of this method of discussion. He has also explained how to match a circuit with a computer or vice versa. The matching problems encountered here are similar to those of circuit theory.

7. Discussion of the Stability of a Program

A computer working on a given program is characterized by a transfer function $W(s)$ and the output $\alpha(s)$ is proportional to the input $A(s)$ multiplied by W as shown in Eq. (19.40):

$$\alpha(s) = A(s)\, W(s). \tag{19.54}$$

As long as $|W|$ remains finite, the output is finite and $|W|$ represents the amplification obtained. If $|W|$ becomes infinite, we may obtain an output while using no input. This occurs at the poles of the function $W(s)$. Let

$$s = \sigma + i\,\omega \tag{19.55}$$

be such a pole. The output is

$$\alpha(s)\, e^{st} = \alpha(s)\, e^{\sigma t + i\omega t}. \tag{19.56}$$

If σ is positive or zero, the oscillations increase with time or are sustained. When σ is negative, the resulting oscillations are damped. They might be excited in a transient, but would eventually disappear.

Instability thus corresponds to poles of the transfer function with a positive real part. These poles are on the right side of the imaginary axis of the variable s. Because of periodicity, a given pole P_1 occurs in each strip of height Ω. A pole P_2 on the left side of the imaginary axis gives no instability. Figure 19.4 illustrates the general situation; poles with negative σ (no instability) are indicated by dots, while those with σ non-negative (corresponding to instability) are indicated by crosses. The recurrences of a pole P_1 in successive strips of height Ω are shown as P_1', P_1'', ...

Instead of the s plane, we may consider the z complex plane, shown in Fig. 19.5. The formula

$$z = x + i\,y = e^{-s\theta}, \tag{19.57}$$

represents a conformal mapping of the s plane on to the z plane. The origin 0 in the z plane means $z = 0$, and corresponds to $s = +\infty$. The circle of radius 1 in the z plane corresponds to the imaginary axis in the s plane

$$s = i\,\omega \qquad z = e^{-i\omega\theta}$$

and the interior of this z unit circle represents the right hand side of the s plane. A pole P_1 (and its images P_1', P_1'', ...) on the right hand side of the s plane corresponds to a pole p_1 within the unit circle in the z plane. A pole P_2 on the left in the s plane is represented by a point p_2 outside the unit circle in the z plane.

The problem of discussing the location of the poles of the transfer function may now be stated more accurately. Our transfer function W of Eq. (19.40) can be written in the following way:

$$W = \frac{P(s)}{Q(s)} = \frac{\Sigma a_h z^h}{1 + \Sigma b_k z^k}. \tag{19.58}$$

Once the common roots of P and Q have been eliminated, the poles of W correspond to the remaining roots of Q:

$$Q = 1 + \Sigma b_k z^k = 0. \tag{19.59}$$

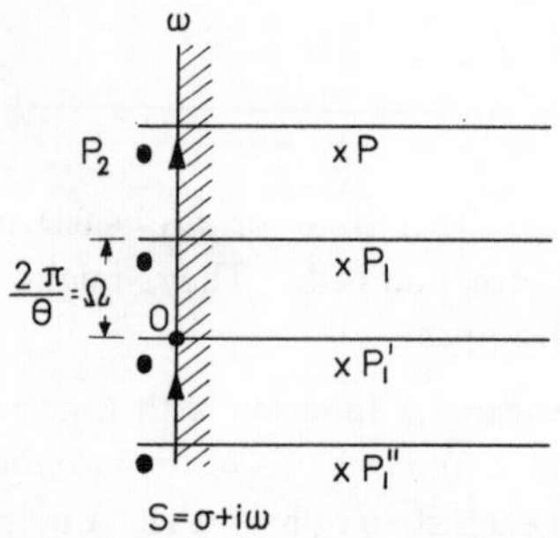

FIG. 19.4. In the complex s plane, a pole P_1 on the right of the imaginary axis corresponds to instability, while a pole P_2 on the left does not yield instability. The repetition in successive strips is shown with stable poles indicated by dots and unstable poles by crosses.

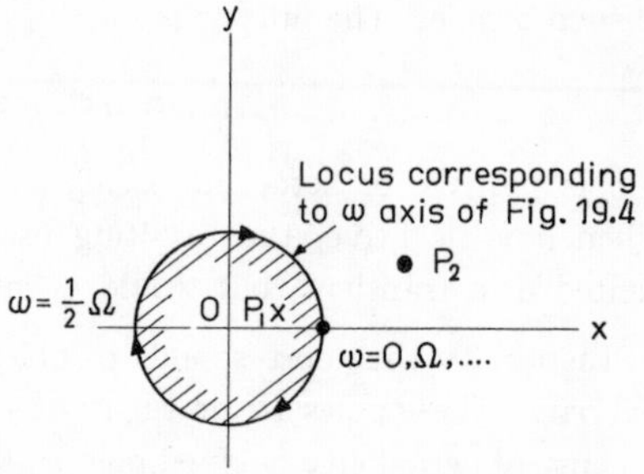

FIG. 19.5. The conformal mapping $z = e^{-s\theta}$ of the complex s plane on to the complex z plane. The imaginary axis ω of the s plane is mapped into the unit circle of the z plane. Poles corresponding to P_1 (unstable) of Fig. 19.4 map inside the unit circle, while poles corresponding to P_2 (stable) map outside.

We may now consider another conformal mapping, from the z complex plane into the Q complex plane, as shown in Fig. 19.6. The origin $Q = 0$ of the Q plane corresponds to all the roots of the function Q [Eq. (19.59)]; hence it represents all the poles of the transfer function W. The point $Q = 1$ in the Q plane is obtained for $z = 0$, the origin on the z plane. The unit circle of the z plane is mapped into a curve L (the locus) in the Q plane, and the interior of the unit circle maps into the interior of the locus L. If a pole P_1 is located inside the unit circle of the z plane, then the origin of the Q plane lies in the area bounded by the locus L, as shown in Fig. 19.6b. This situation corresponds to instability. Figure 19.6a shows a locus L with the origin on the outside, and corresponds to stability.

Salzer has discussed a variety of examples and proved the great practical value of the method. Very often, a rough sketch of the locus L is all that is required to determine stability. The amount by which the locus avoids the origin is an indication of relative stability. The frequency of closest approach to the origin is very often the resonant frequency of the program of computation.

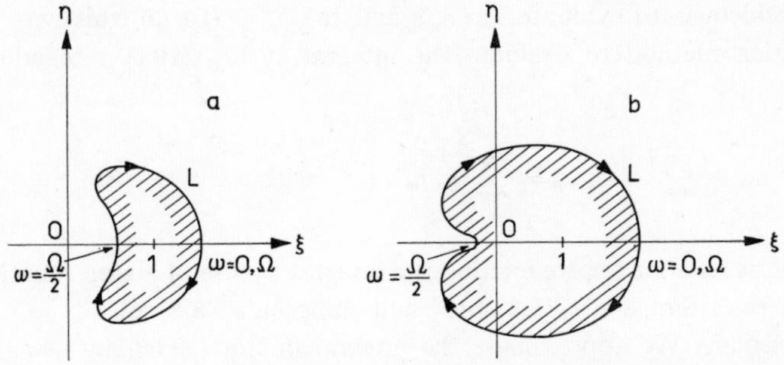

FIG. 19.6. The complex Q plane is the conformal mapping
$$Q = \xi + i\eta = 1 + \sum_k b_k z^k.$$

a: An example in which the origin of the complex Q plane lies outside the locus L. This case corresponds to stability.

b: An example in which the origin of the complex Q plane lies inside of the locus L. This case corresponds to instability.

The transfer function W of a program of computation is always given by a function of the type (19.40) or (19.58). When the transfer function of an operation is known, the realizability of the operation by a computer is proven if the transfer function can be written as a fraction (19.40) or (19.58). This is the main result of Salzer's discussion, and a very important one indeed.

8. A Few Examples

We give now a few examples of transfer functions corresponding to some typical problems of computation.

A. The Computer Operating as an Integrator

In this case the output ψ is to be the definite integral of the input $f(t)$, so that we may set

$$\psi_m = \psi_{m-1} + \int_{(m-1)\theta}^{m\theta} f(t)\, dt = \psi_{m-n} + \int_{(m-n)\theta}^{m\theta} f(t)\, dt = \int_0^{m\theta} f(t)\, dt. \qquad (19.60)$$

The last expressions follow by iteration of the equality between the first two expressions. The transfer function is given by Eq. (19.40) or by Eq. (19.58):

$$W = \frac{\Sigma\, a_n z^n}{1 + \Sigma\, b_n z^n}, \tag{19.61}$$

and the problem is to evaluate the a_n's and the b_n's. To do this we use an approximation method to evaluate the integral of Eq. (19.60), together with Eq. (19.30):

$$\psi_m + \sum_n b_n \psi_{m-n} = \sum_n a_n f_{m-n} \qquad \text{with} \qquad f_k = f(k\,\theta). \tag{19.62}$$

We give the results for approximating the integral by use of a step function, the trapezoidal rule, Simpson's "1/3 rule" and Simpson's "3/8 rule."

Step function. We approximate the integral in Eq. (19.60) by using a step function for $f(t)$, and computing the areas of the resulting rectangles of width θ and heights $f_1, f_2, \ldots, f_m$:

$$\psi_m - \psi_{m-1} = \int_{(m-1)\theta}^{m\theta} f(t)\, dt = f_m \cdot \theta.$$

Comparison with Eq. (19.62) yields

$$b_1 = -1, \qquad a_0 = \theta, \qquad b_j = a_k = 0 \qquad \text{for} \qquad j > 1, \qquad k > 0,$$

and hence from Eq. (19.61), the transfer function is

$$W_0 = \theta/(1 - z). \tag{19.63}$$

Trapezoidal rule. Use of the trapezoidal rule with $n = 1$ in Eq. (19.60) yields

$$\psi_m - \psi_{m-1} = \int_{(m-1)\theta}^{m\theta} f(t)\, dt = (\theta/2)\,(f_m + f_{m-1}),$$

which gives, from Eq. (19.62),

$$b_1 = -1, \qquad a_0 = a_1 = \theta/2, \qquad b_j = a_k = 0 \qquad \text{for} \qquad j > 1, \qquad k > 1.$$

This transfer function, thus, is

$$W_1 = (\theta/2)\;[(1 + z)/(1 - z)]. \tag{19.64}$$

Simpson's 1/3 rule. For Simpson's 1/3 rule we must take $n = 2$ in Eq. (19.60):

$$\psi_m - \psi_{m-2} = \int_{(m-2)\theta}^{m\theta} f(t)\, dt = (\theta/3)\,(f_{m-2} + 4\, f_{m-1} + f_m),$$

from which we obtain

$$b_2 = -1, \quad a_0 = a_2 = \theta/3, \quad a_1 = 4\,\theta/3, \quad b_j = a_k = 0 \quad \text{for} \quad j \neq 2, \quad k > 2,$$

and the transfer function is

$$W_2 = (\theta/3)\,[(1 + 4\,z + z^2)/(1 - z^2)]. \tag{19.65}$$

Simpson's 3/8 rule. In a similar way we use $n = 3$ for Simpson's 3/8 rule, and obtain

$$W_3 = (3\,\theta/8)\,[(1 + 3\,z + 3\,z^2 + z^3)/(1 - z^3)]. \tag{19.66}$$

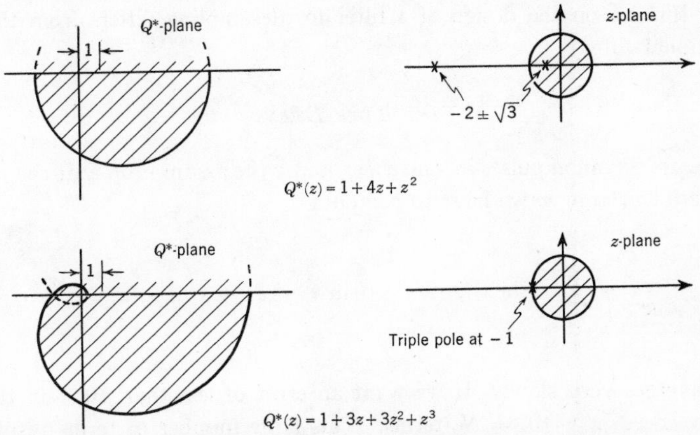

FIG. 19.7. Curves showing the instability of the differentiation programs corresponding to W_2^{-1} and W_3^{-1} in both the Q^* and z planes. Q^* represents the denominator of the transfer function (numerator of the corresponding W). Note that both loci enclose the origin of the Q^* plane. [Reproduced by courtesy of J. M. Salzer, *Proc. I. R. E.* **42**, 547 (1954).]

B. *The Computer Operating as a Differentiator*

Now the output ψ is to be the derivative of the input f. Since differentiation is the operation inverse to integration, the transfer function of an ideal differentiator should be the reciprocal of that for the ideal integrator. This means that W_0^{-1}, W_1^{-1}, W_2^{-1}, and W_3^{-1} ought to represent suitable differentiation programs.

It turns out, however, that only W_0^{-1} and W_1^{-1} are stable, while W_2^{-1} and W_3^{-1} are unstable. The situation is indicated in Fig. 19.7, taken from Salzer's paper, where the poles in the z plane and the shape of the locus in the Q plane have been sketched.

C. *Desampling*

The desampling procedure may be accomplished by replacing the Linvill pulses by Shannon pulses again, or by filtering out all frequencies $\nu > \nu_M$ very accurately. The first procedure results in no phase shift and no change in intensity for $\nu < \nu_M$ and thus gives a transfer function of 1. The second procedure requires zero intensity for $\nu > \nu_M$ and thus yields $W = 0$ for this range of frequencies. This is hardly realizable.

Most filters maintain high intensity transmission in the passing band, but exhibit a phase shift. This is of no importance for telephony because the ear is fairly insensitive to phase. In rebuilding our function, however, phase is essential, and for this reason the design of a filter for desampling differs from that of a conventional filter.

D. *Time Delays*

If we use Shannon pulses in $(\sin x)/x$, under the assumption that the function is constant for large x, we have to compute

$$\sum_{\substack{\text{over large} \\ \text{values of } x}} (\sin x)/x \approx \int_{x \text{ large}}^{\infty} [(\sin x)/x]\, dx \approx (\cos x)/x.$$

This converges very slowly. If we want an error of less than 10^{-n} in the final result, we need $x > 10^n = N$ terms. This large number of terms results in a delay, since the function at t will not be known correctly until N terms later, which means a delay of $N\,\theta$.

CHAPTER 20

INFORMATION, ORGANIZATION, AND OTHER PROBLEMS

1. Information and Organization

We have been able to analyze the information content of a written sentence, of a set of numbers, and of many other situations to which our statistical definition of information could be directly applied. We may, in a similar way, compute the information contained in a blue print, provided this blue print can be represented by a finite number of symbols. Let us consider, for instance, the wiring diagram of some electrical device. We may number from 0 to N all the terminals appearing on the diagram, and represent the diagram by giving the numbers of the terminals connected together: the bracket (1023–0216) would mean that we must connect terminal 1023 to terminal 0216. For a finite number of terminals, there is a finite number P of possible connections, out of which the wiring diagram selects one special system. It, therefore, contains information

$$I = K \ln P, \tag{20.1}$$

according to the definitions of Chapter 1. Let us again emphasize the exact meaning of such a definition: it does not distinguish between a wiring diagram corresponding to a working model and another diagram that would yield a worthless structure, with short circuits or other defects. The information we compute is just the information given to the man who is to do the wiring, and says nothing about what the device is going to do.

The questions as to why this diagram has been selected and how it works are not considered. This was the problem of the scientist or the engineer who designed the device. It required thinking and scientific discussion, and perhaps other human processes, all of which are beyond the scope of our present methods of investigation.

Let us take a specific example: the electric device contains n circuit elements, each of them with m terminals, and q terminals for external connections (including ground or open connection). Altogether we have

$$N = n\,m + q \tag{20.2}$$

terminals, each of which can be connected to any other one, giving

$$P = N^N$$

different possibilities. The information contained in one wiring diagram is

$$I = K \ln P = K N \ln N. \tag{20.3}$$

Taking $K = \log_2 e \approx 1.4$, we obtain the information in bits:

$$I = N \log_2 N.$$

We take, as reasonable orders of magnitude,

$$n = 999, \qquad m = 10, \qquad q = 10,$$

which yields

$$N = 10000 \approx 2^{13.3}, \qquad I = 133000 \text{ bits.}$$

This is a large figure in bits, but if we compute it in entropy units, we must multiply it by 10^{-16}, which is approximately the ratio of units, and we obtain a negentropy of

$$-S = 1.33 \cdot 10^{-11},$$

which is completely negligible.

The machine built according to our specifications contains such a structural negentropy, which represents the information or organization of the machine. This negative term is, however, completely negligible, when compared with the total entropy of the machine. This example exhibits some characteristic features of the whole theory:

The negentropy principle of information requires that every piece of information be associated with a corresponding negative term in the physical entropy of a system. This association is essential for consistency and was proved by the discussions of Chapters 8 to 18.

In practice, these negative terms can be ignored in most problems because of the small coefficient (10^{-16}) introduced by the change from binary digits (bits) to thermodynamical units. Specific organizations may contain a very large amount of information in bit units. Let us consider, for instance, a telephone network of a size comparable to the American system. The order of magnitude of subscribers may be of a few tens of millions, but let us be generous and assume one hundred million subscribers:

$$N = 10^8.$$

A direct application of an equation of the type (20.3) shows that at any given instant of time, the amount of information contained in the entire system is of the order of magnitude of

$$I = N \log_2 N \approx 40 \cdot 10^8 = 4 \cdot 10^9 \text{ bits,}$$

and this is still a very small quantity ($4 \cdot 10^{-7}$) in entropy units.

It is difficult to imagine any piece of machinery containing an amount of information much higher than in the preceding example, but if we think of living organisms we find a completely different order of magnitude. The number of cells may be of the order of 10^{12} and it is difficult to estimate the number of chemical molecules interconnected in a living organism. Here the information contained in the living organism may reach values of significance in the entropy scale. But, as yet, this is an unexplored domain of research.

2. Information Contained in a Physical Law

We have tested, on a variety of examples, the usefulness of our statistical definition of "quantity of information." We may now attempt to extend this definition to more general problems, and to suggest some possible new fields of application.

In Chapters 14 to 16, we investigated the information obtained in a physical experiment, and we found that the amount of information could not be defined unless the field of observation and the accuracy of the experiment were explicitly stated. We shall find a similar situation when we inquire about the information contained in a physical law. In order to be able to give a precise answer to such a question, we must, first of all, state the question precisely and specify exactly the conditions under which the law was obtained and how it is going to be used.

Consider, for example, the law of ideal gases:

$$f(p, v, T) = p\,v/T = R = \text{constant.} \tag{20.4}$$

We must state explicitly the field of application, specify to which gas we want to apply it, over what range of variation of the variables p, v, and T, and how large is the accuracy that we expect to obtain.

A physical law is only a summary of experimental results, and the validity of the law cannot be discussed unless experimental conditions are specified. Keeping the example above in mind, we may discuss the problem in general terms. We assume that we have been observing a certain physical system and measuring certain variables $x_1, x_2, \ldots, x_n$. For each variable x_i we specify the range of variation X_i, and the smallest interval of observation α_i:

$$\text{variable } x_i, \qquad \text{range } X_i, \qquad \text{error of observation } \delta x_i = \alpha_i, \tag{20.5}$$

$$(\text{total number of experimental points on } X_i) = X_i/\alpha_i.$$

After discussing the results, we conclude that a certain expression

$$f(x_1, x_2, \ldots, x_n) = C = \text{constant} \tag{20.6}$$

correctly represents the experimental facts, with an error δf never exceeding some number ϕ. But this is not yet a complete statement of the problem. We must add another quantity, namely the total range of variation F for the function f. This total *a priori* range of variation depends upon the previous knowledge we had, before starting our experiments. If we know nothing about the system, F must be defined in terms of the limits of our measuring devices. The function f is, thus, finally defined over a total interval F with steps ϕ, and hence with a number of possible values F/ϕ, which were all equally probable before we started our observations. We thus have

$$N = (X_1 X_2 \ldots X_n)/(\alpha_1 \alpha_2 \ldots \alpha_n) \tag{20.7}$$

distinct points of observation in the $x_1 \ldots x_n$ hyperspace, and for each point we may expect any one of the F/ϕ values of f. The number of possibilities is thus

$$\begin{aligned} P_0 &= (F/\phi)^N && \text{before the experiments,} \\ P_1 &= 1^N = 1 && \text{after the experiments,} \end{aligned} \tag{20.8}$$

and the information is defined by Eqs. (1.5) and (1.6):

$$I = K \ln(P_0/P_1) = K N \ln(F/\phi) = K N (\ln F - \ln \phi). \tag{20.9}$$

The domain of variation of the variables was assumed in Eq. (20.5) to be a parallelopiped. This is an unnecessary restriction. We may have a volume U of any shape in the hyperspace $x_1 \ldots x_n$ and we denote by α the small volume corresponding to errors in one observation. This gives

$$N = U/\alpha \tag{20.10}$$

instead of Eq. (20.7), and

$$I = (K U/\alpha)(\ln F - \ln \phi) \tag{20.11}$$

is the information contained in the physical law. This formula satisfies the following general requirements: The more precise is the data (i. e., the smaller α and ϕ are), or the broader is the field of observation U, the larger will be the information. The use of the logarithm, as noted in Chapter 1, is required to insure the additivity of independent observations.

We may now discuss the meaning of the quantity F, by comparing the information obtained in successive steps of increasing accuracy. Suppose that a first series of observations gives a function f_1 with an error ϕ_1, while a second and more accurate series of experiments yields a function f_2 with a lower error ϕ_2. This is the case, for instance, when Boyle's law (20.4) is replaced by a van der Waals' formula. Our Eq. (20.11) yields the corresponding increase of information:

$$\Delta I = I_2 - I_1 = (K\,U/\alpha) \cdot (\ln \phi_1 - \ln \phi_2). \tag{20.12}$$

The formula is identical with (20.11) except for the replacement of F and ϕ by ϕ_1 and ϕ_2. The quantity $\ln F$ has been eliminated. It actually plays the role of an additive constant, similar to the unknown additive constant in many entropy formulas.

This example shows that our statistical definition of information can be applied to a great variety of examples and leads to interesting results.

MacKay[1] has discussed the problems of scientific information in two recent papers, in which he tried to prove that different definitions should apply in different fields of application. He calls "selective information" the quantity that we have defined as "information," and he has introduced the terms of "structural information" and "metrical information." These last terms are used in connection with problems of accuracy in experimental devices. Our inquiry and discussion tends to prove that all of these problems can and should be discussed with the same definitions and the same formulas. If this were not the case, we would certainly find inconsistencies, because the fields of application of the different formulas overlap, and we would have three different and unrelated theories of information, instead of one. We definitely feel that only a single theory is needed, and that it can cover the entire field very adequately.

3. Information Contained in a Numerical Table

We find an interesting example in the problem of the information contained in a numerical table. The question has often been raised, and a comparison suggested between

A. A table of random numbers,

B. A table representing a given function.

The general answer is simple: our table contains N positions, corresponding to N values of the variable x. For each value of x, the table gives the value of

[1] D. M. MacKay, *Phil. Mag.* [7] **41**, 289 (1950); Symposium on Information Theory London, *Trans. I. R. E.* (*P. G. I. T.*) p. 60. (1953).

another variable $y(x)$, represented by a number of n decimal digits, or b binary digits. The numbers n and b are related, on the average, by

$$b \approx 3.3\, n. \tag{20.13}$$

Altogether, the table contains

$$I = N\, b \tag{20.14}$$

bits of information, whatever the law relating y to x may be. In case A, for a table of random numbers, the set of numbers y must satisfy certain average relations, exhibit no average correlation, etc., but, once the table is given, there is nothing random about it. It just represents a table like any other one, and it can be said to represent a certain function $y(x)$, which will have, in general, no continuity and no derivative, but still is a function of the discrete variable x.

If the table represents a certain function $y(x)$, we may distinguish different cases:

B_1: Assuming that we know nothing in advance of the function, the numerical table still contains information $N\, b$, as in Eq. (20.14).

B_2: We may have some advance knowledge of the function. We might, for instance, have proofs that the function possesses first, second, ..., n-th derivatives, except at certain points of the interval (certain values of x). This advance information should then be subtracted from the information given by Eq. (20.14), and the information contained in the table is

$$I = N\, b - I_0, \qquad I_0 = \text{advance information}. \tag{20.15}$$

For instance, let $\Delta\, x$ be the difference between two successive values of x in the table, and let us assume that we know that the increase $|\Delta\, y|$ corresponding to an increase $\Delta\, x$ cannot exceed b' in binary digits. Then we have

$$-2^{b'} \leqslant \Delta\, y \leqslant +2^{b'}. \tag{20.16}$$

For the first value of the function, at $x = 0$, there are 2^b possible values for y. For the next value the range is reduced to

$$2 \cdot 2^{b'} = 2^{b'+1}.$$

Altogether, the number of possibilities is

$$P = 2^b \cdot (2^{b'+1})^{N-1},$$

and the information in bits is

$$I = \log_2 P = b + (N-1)\,(b' + 1), \tag{20.17}$$

a quantity which is smaller than $N\, b$, since $b' + 1$ is smaller than b.

B_3: We may even assume that we know, in advance, exactly what the tabulated function is, in which case the table does not give us any new information at all.

The usual case is case B_2, where we have only a partial knowledge of the tabulated function, and we need a table for more detailed information. Our definitions show that the information is maximum for a table of random numbers, of which we know nothing in advance.

4. General Remarks

The theory of information originated in telecommunications and most of its present applications are still in this field. We have tried to prove that the theory can also be very useful in pure science and especially in physics. The similarity between information and entropy was stressed by Shannon, and, as a matter of fact, it goes back to an old paper by Szilard, who did the pioneering work at a time when the practical value of the theory was not yet recognized.

Information and physical entropy are of the same nature. Entropy is a measure of the lack of detailed information about a physical system. The greater is the information, the smaller will be the entropy. Information represents a negative term in the entropy of a system, and we have stated a negentropy principle of information.

Whenever we make an observation on a physical system, we must have all sorts of sources of negentropy. We use this negentropy, and we increase the total entropy of the laboratory containing the system under observation and the measuring instruments. As a result, we obtain a certain amount of information about the system. The increase in entropy is, however, always larger than the information gained. This result represents an extension of Carnot's principle, and we have tested its validity on a great variety of examples. We thus proved that the theory of information cannot be built as a separate entity. The connection with thermodynamics is so close that consistency requires a physical theory of information. This proof is the aim of the present book.

In practice, the theory yields, in most problems, extremely small contributions to the entropy of a physical system. Information is usually measured in bits (binary digits), and entropy in thermodynamical units. The ratio of these units is approximately 10^{-16}, and this means that a very large number of bits (say 10^6) still represents a negligible contribution (10^{-10}) to entropy. The connection is, however, indispensable for consistency. Many of the problems discussed in Chapters 16 and 17 have been stumbling blocks on the road. They could not have been solved without the help of our "physical theory," and their interpretation requires this new form of the theory.

The very small value of the negentropy corresponding to rather large amounts of information is the fundamental reason why transmission of information is usually so inexpensive. Writing, printing, and electrical communication cost very little in entropy units. Their cost in dollars is correspondingly low. Modern life is based on these facts, and would be completely different in a world where the negentropy of information had a larger value.

The fact that our discussions have dealt with such minute quantities should not be regarded as discouraging. Relativity theory seemed, at the beginning, to yield only very small corrections to classical mechanics. New applications to nuclear energy now prove the fundamental importance of the mass-energy relation. We may also hope that the entropy-information connection will, sooner or later, come into the foreground, and that we will discover where to use it to its full value. The problem of measuring extremely small distances, treated in Chapter 16, is a first example, and others may soon follow.

5. Examples of Problems beyond the Present Theory

The present theory of information completely ignores the value of the information handled, transmitted, or processed. This point has been very carefully emphasized throughout this book. Many other writers seem not to have realized the importance of this restriction, and many misunderstandings about the possibilities of the present theory resulted from this situation. It is only by ignoring the human value of the information that we have been able to construct a scientific theory of information based on statistics, and this theory has already proved very useful. There are, however, many problems that cannot be discussed along these lines. The aim of this section is to state briefly some of these questions, and to show how they all converge towards the same general problem: how to introduce into the theory the element of value.

This new element is needed every time one considers information as a basis for prediction and for practical use. Let us first briefly summarize the present situation: We assume, for instance, a telegram to be sent in a binary code (0 or 1), and to contain n binary digits. If there is no redundancy in the coding, this telegram contains a total of n bits of information. Whether the telegram is of importance to the user, or not, is not considered.

At the scientific meetings in Milan, in April 1954, Dr. Couffignal (Paris) raised the following question: After the telegram has been sent, the author adds one binary digit with the following meaning:

0: All wrong; pay no attention to the telegram.

1: Telegram is all right; you can use it.

Informationwise, this means just the addition of one bit of information, making the total $(n + 1)$, instead of n. Practically, the situation is different:

0 (No) destroys all the value of the information in the telegram;

1 (Yes) simply adds redundancy.

Thus, we may say that "no" (0) carries a negative information equal, in absolute value, to the total information in the telegram. The present theory considers information as always positive and never negative. What appears here is clearly a distinction between a statistical measure of information (present theory) and the practical value of this information to the user.

The self-checking and self-correcting codes, discussed in Chapter 6, correspond to practical problems very similar to the preceding one. After a telegram containing n bits, we add a 0 or a 1, whichever makes the total number of 1's even. The receiver checks the total number of 1's:

If it is odd, there may be 1, 3, 5, ... mistakes,

If it is even, we may have no mistakes, or 2, 4, 6, ... mistakes.

The first case obviously corresponds to the "no" signal in Couffignal's problem.

The additional signals for checking or correction do not add any information. According to the present theory, these signals simply add redundancy. The practical *value* of the information is, however, here in question.

Instead of classifying a statement as true or false ("yes" or "no," above), we may decide to give the probability p that the statement is true. Suppose that we choose a scale of 8 ($= 2^3$), and decide that a number m $(0 \leqslant m \leqslant 8)$ corresponds to $p = m/8$, neaning that the statement is true, on the average, in m cases out of 8, and false in $(8 - m)$ cases out of 8. Informationwise, this means just adding three bits of information to the telegram, totaling $(n + 3)$ bits instead of n. As far as the value for the user is concerned, it might be a reasonable guess to say that the value is just $p\,n$. In many cases, however, the user may not be interested at all when the chance of error is above some stated minimum, say 50%, in which case the practical value would be zero for probabilities 0, 1/8, 2/8, 3/8, and take some increasing value when the probabilities are 4/8, 5/8, 6/8, 7/8, 1.

The problem of reliability of a scientific observation was discussed in Chapter 14. Any physical measurement contains a possibility for errors. The reliability r of the experimental method was defined by stating that there was a probability $1/r$ for error due to thermal fluctuations, and a probability of $(1 - 1/r)$ for a correct observation. This is a problem very similar to the preceding one, and it was completed by the assumption that the smallest value of r to be considered was $r = 2$, giving a 50% chance for correctness.

Computing machines were discussed in Chapter 19, and it was shown that computing is very similar to translating, coding, and decoding. In the most favorable case, the computation will retain the full information contained in the input (initial data), but usually some information may be lost on account of approximations introduced in the procedure. Informationwise, computing does not add any new information, but only repeats it in a different language, and possibly with some losses. But computing, like decoding and translating, certainly adds to the practical value of the information, and makes it more meaningful for the user. The problem of information contained in the computing program is another aspect of the question, which has, so far, not been carefully explored, although it was raised at the Milan meetings.

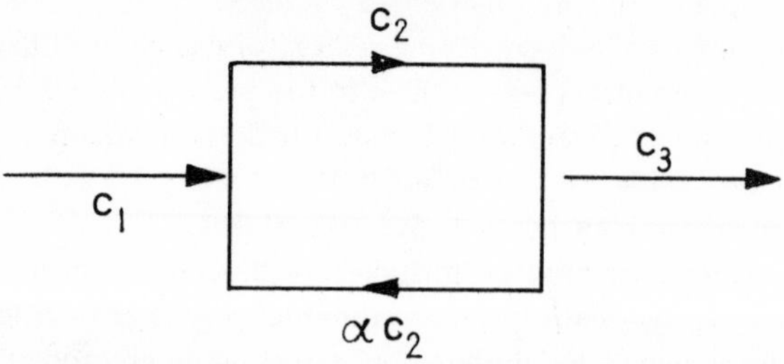

FIG. 20.1. Schematic diagram of the channel capacities in a feedback circuit.

In other discussions, the problem of circulation of information along certain channels, with or without feedback, appeared to be a very important question for practical users. Feedback has very different properties when it is positive than when it is negative. Our definition requires information to be a positive quantity, which can never become negative. Hence, what is involved in feedback channels is not information itself, but, again, the value of the information. How to define the value in such problems is an open question. So far it seems that the only conclusion we can reach is the following one (and it is of no great practical value): Consider Fig. 20.1 in which an input channel C_1 yields, on the average, C_1 bits per second (capacity of C_1). This information travels along C_2 and a fraction α $(0 < \alpha < 1)$ comes back through the feedback loop. Channel C_2 must be able to transmit

$$C_1(1 + \alpha + \alpha^2 + \ldots) = C_1/(1-\alpha) \text{ bits/sec.}$$

so that its capacity is

$$C_2 = C_1/(1-\alpha),$$

and the output has capacity C_3 given by

$$C_3 = C_2 - \alpha C_2 = C_1.$$

This, however, does not even touch the well-known problems of feedback circuits. This type of problem might, however, be discussed by the methods of Linvill and Salzer, developed in Chapter 19.

A variety of problems suggest the importance of discussing the practical value of information for the user. Whereas the measure of information, as presently defined, is an absolute quantity, the value certainly is *relative* to a certain user. It is suggested that these problems might be discussed from an empirical point of view, by trying, for each case, to discover a reasonable definition of the value, and then by comparison of the different problems, to attempt to discover some common properties of the various definitions, and to find out whether a theory could be developed that could be applied to the different special cases. Such a discussion would probably make the theory of information much more valuable for practical applications, and might open up new lines of research of great importance.

At any rate, one point is immediately obvious: any criterion for "value" will result in an evaluation of the information received. This is equivalent to selecting the information according to a certain figure of merit. Some pieces of information will be found important and retained with their full value, while other pieces of information will be found of no value and will be discarded. This problem is very similar to the process of filtering. A filter is a well-known element in the general theory, and it is characterized by two important properties: it is irreversible, and it decreases the total amount of information. In a similar way we can state the following result:

The relative value for a certain user $\leqslant$ absolute information. This is already a point of departure of general validity, and the problem is to define in general terms the different filtering methods used for the evaluation of relative value.

6. Problems of Semantic Information

The theory developed in this book is based exclusively on statistical data. According to our definitions, sentences which are very rare carry a large amount of information. The problem of value, which we discussed briefly in the preceding section, is not considered in our theory. We have also completely ignored another problem: that of meaning. Whether or not the message made sense to either the sender or the receiver was regarded as completely irrelevant. Some work on this semantic problem has recently been done by Ville[2] in France, and by Carnap and Bar-Hillel[3] in the United States.

---

[2] J. Ville, 18th Intern. Congr. of Philosophy of Sci., Paris (1949), published in *Actualités Sci. et Ind.* **1145**, 101-114 Hermann Paris (1951).

[3] R. Carnap and Y. Bar-Hillel, An outline of a theory of semantic information, *Mass. Inst. Technol. Research Lab. Electronics, Tech. Rept.* No. **247** (1952); *Brit. J. Phil. Sci.* **4**, 147-157 (1953).

The work of Carnap and Bar-Hillel is based on the methods and symbolism of symbolic logic. We shall give here a brief outline of their development, which is restricted (partly for the sake of simplicity, and partly because of the limitations of the methods of inductive logic, on which much of the discussion is based) to sentences in a very simple language. They examine a number of possible definitions for the measure of the information contained in a given sentence, and analyze the advantages and disadvantages of each. Their analysis excludes considerations of value, and also of interpretation, from consideration: whether the receiver interprets a message in accordance with the intent of the sender is ignored.

In all of the definitions given, a sentence such as $17 \times 19 = 323$ carries no information. The reason for this is that the receiver of a message is visualized as in possession of all the possible logical deductions from the structure of the given language system, so that such a sentence is redundant. Only sentences, at least part of whose content is not implied by the structure of the language, are thought of as containing information.

Carnap and Bar-Hillel use the following very simple language as a basis for discussion: the language consists of a finite number n of nouns (called "individuals" in their paper) and π of adjectives (called "predicates" in their paper), and the single verb "has" or "is." Thus, if a is a noun (or individual) and P is an adjective (or predicate), "$P\,a$" is read as "a has the property P" or, more simply, "a is P." Also the language has the following connectives, which may be used to build up longer sentences:

$\sim$ not:	negation; $(\sim P\,a)$ means "a is not P;"
$\vee$ or:	disjunction; $(P\,a \vee Q\,b)$ means "a is P or b is Q;"
and:	conjunction; $(P\,a . Q\,b)$ means "a is P and b is Q;"
$\supset$ if ... then:	implication;
$\equiv$ if and only if:	equivalence.

The choice of the π adjectives in the language is somewhat restricted. They are not to overlap in meaning in any way, nor may any adjective imply anything about the use or nonuse of any other adjective. The vocabulary of the language is then completed by introducing for each of the π adjectives P its opposite or negation, which may be denoted by $\sim P$ or by a new symbol, and frequently both.

The sentences in this language are classified as logically false (self-contradictory, such as $P\,a \cdot \sim P\,a$), factual (logically indeterminate, such as $P\,a$), and logically true (tautological, such as $P\,a \vee \sim P\,a$).

One very obvious way to define the information content of a sentence in such a language is as follows: There is a finite number of sentences which can be constructed, and there are certain logical relations among these sentences. The information of a particular sentence i could be defined as a suitably chosen function of the number of sentences implied by i. There are at least two ways of developing this definition,[4] and the reader is referred to Carnap's book for details, since the connection of these definitions with our point of view is rather remote.

The M. I. T. paper[3] contains definitions more closely related to those that we have used. These definitions are based on a particular type of factual sentence, the "state description" denoted by Z. A state description is a sentence consisting of the conjunction of πn simple ("atomic") sentences, and containing each of the n nouns associated with each of the adjectives, or its negation, but not both. There are πn possible associations of nouns and adjectives, and, since each association can occur in two ways (either with the adjective or with its negation), there are, altogether, $2^{\pi n}$ possible state descriptions. A state description completely describes a possible state of the universe of discourse in question, and the definitions of information will involve the *a priori* probabilities of the state descriptions. There is no *a priori* basis in the structure of the language for assigning any particular set of probabilities to the state descriptions, although certain properties of an acceptable set of probabilities limits the choice to some extent. In problems such as we have discussed in this book, the properties of the physical system we want to describe would indicate the choice of probabilities. We might, for instance, discuss temperatures, and designate those above 40 °F. by "high," and those below 40 °F. by "low." It is obvious that the probabilities of "high" and "low" at the North Pole will differ from those at the equator.

For a sentence i (which is, in general, not a state description), the range of i, denoted by $R(i)$, is the set of those state descriptions in which i holds. Thus the sentence i implies that the universe is in one of the states Z of $R(i)$. Definitions of information based on point set theory can be introduced at this stage. We are, however, more interested in quantitative definitions, that is definitions yielding a numerical measure of information. To this end we introduce a measure function, which satisfies the following conditions:

A. For each state description Z, there is a measure $m(Z)$ such that

$$0 \leqslant m(Z) \leqslant 1.$$

This quantity may be interpreted as the *a priori* probability for the state description Z.

B. The sum of the $m(Z)$, taken over all Z, is unity.

C. For any false sentence f, $m(f) = 0$.

---

[4] Carnap, "Logical Foundations of Probability." U. of Chicago Press, Chicago, Ill., 1950.

D. For any nonfalse sentence i, we define $m(i)$ as the sum of $m(Z)$ over all the Z contained in the range $R(i)$.

E. All nouns are treated on a par, that is $m(i)$ is invariant under permutation of the nouns occurring in the sentence i.

F. All adjectives are treated on a par, that is $m(i)$ is invariant under permutation of the adjectives occurring in i.

G. Any adjective may be replaced by its negation without changing the value of $m(i)$.

H. If two sentences i and j have no adjectives in common, they are said to be inductively independent, and

$$m(i.j) = m(i) \times m(j).$$

I. The number of nouns not mentioned in the sentence i does not influence the value of $m(i)$.

Such a measure function is called a "proper m-function," and Carnap considers that it may be properly regarded as a probability: what he calls "absolute logical probability." Conditions E, F, and G introduce relations among the probabilities of the different state descriptions, but do not uniquely determine them. The properties of $m(i)$ can be used to deduce many theorems and relations, necessary for the detailed development of the theory. Among these relations, we shall have use for the following one:

$$m(i) + m(\sim i) = 1.$$

Since $R(i)$ and $R(\sim i)$ contain no state descriptions in common (a state description cannot imply both i and its negation) and every state description is either in $R(i)$ or in $R(\sim i)$ (every state description implies either i or its negation), therefore

$$m(i) + m(\sim i) = \sum_{\text{all } Z} m(Z) = 1.$$

The simplest definition of information given in terms of the measure function is called the "content measure" (or "cont") by Carnap and Bar-Hillel, and it is given by

$$\text{cont}(i) = m(\sim i) = 1 - m(i).$$

The content measure has many interesting properties, and is in qualitative agreement with the definitions used in this book in the following sense. If $m(i)$ is small, then cont(i) is relatively large. But $m(i)$ small means that relatively improbable state descriptions are allowed, so that cont(i) is a measure of rarity.

A second definition, the "measure of information" (inf) is more closely related to our definition. It is given by

$$\inf(i) = -\log_2 m(i) = \log_2[1/\{1 - \text{cont}(i)\}].$$

The same qualitative agreement of this definition with ours holds as for cont(i). Further, condition (H) on the function $m(i)$ can be shown to yield additivity of the measure of information for the conjunction of inductively independent sentences. Consideration of the following special case, will, however, show much more clearly the close connection of the two definitions. We select for the measure function:

$$m(z) = 1/N \qquad \text{for all } Z,$$

where N is the total number of state descriptions. We are thus assuming that the state descriptions are equally probable. This assumption is consistent with the conditions imposed on our measure function. If we let N_r be the number of state descriptions in the range $R(i)$, then the definition for inf(i) yields

$$\inf(i) = -\log_2(N_r/N) = \log_2(N/N_r).$$

This equation is identical with the one we have used throughout the book, if we identify the state descriptions with the equally probable cases in some given situation. Initially there are N possible cases (the N state descriptions). Knowledge of the sentence i reduces the possible number to N_r, so that the information given by the sentence i, according to our earlier definitions, is

$$I = \log_2(N/N_r) \text{ bits}.$$

For a state description Z, $R(Z)$ contains only Z, and

$$I = \log_2 N \text{ bits}.$$

Carnap and Bar-Hillel give further detailed development of these semantic definitions, and discuss applications to various problems of inference and deduction. In this brief outline, we have tried only to show the connection between their problems and those to which this book is devoted.

Author Index

B

Babbage, C., 268
Balser, M., 67, 70
Bar-Hillel, Y., 297, 298, 300, 301
Bell, D. A., 254
Bell, D. E., 3
Bernamont, J., 142
Bohm, D., 229, 231, 241
Bohr, H., 78
Bohr, N., 197, 229, 243, 244
Boltzmann, L., 44, 119, 123
Bridgman, P. W., 142, 151
Brillouin, L., 79, 110, 111, 114, 119, 148, 154, 163, 236, 254, 259, 265

C

Callen, H. B., 147
Carnap, R., 297, 298, 300, 301
Casimir, H. B. G., 147
Cheatham, T. P., 102
Churchill, R. V., 80
Clausius, R., 116
Couffignal, L., 294
Courtines, M., 142, 185

D

Darrow, K. K., 114, 157
de Groot, S. R., 147
de Haas-Lorentz, G. L., 134, 147
Demers, P., 163, 164, 167
Desoer, C. A., 254
Devé, H., 103
Dewey, G., 22
Dicke, R. H., 220
Dickson, L. E., 50
di Francia, G. T., 223

E

Einstein, A., 127, 128
Elias, P., 60, 67
Elsasser, W., 229, 231, 233
Emde, F., 81

F

Felker, J. H., 254
Fine, H. B., 50
Fine, P. C., 114

G

Gabor, D., 90, 99, 168, 176, 179, 257, 258
Gibbs, J. W., 44, 119, 123
Gilbert, E. N., 66, 70
Golay, M. J. E., 67
Greene, R. F., 147

H

Hamming, R. W., 63, 65, 70
Harker, D., 112
Harrison, C. W., 60
Heitler, W., 243

I

Ising, G., 185, 187
Iskenderian, H. P., 119

J

Jacobson, H., 165, 168, 182
Jahnke, E., 81
James, R. W., 111, 112
Jeans, J. H., 162
Johnson, J. B., 142
Jordan, P., 157

K

Kelvin, Lord, 114, 116
Khintchine, A., 102
Kretzmer, E. R., 60

L

Labrouste, H., 103
Labrouste, Y., 103
Lawson, J. L., 141
LeCorbeiller, P., 88
Lee, Y. W., 102
Leifer, M., 248

Levy, M., 103
Lewis, G. N., 163
Linvill, W. K., 273, 274, 275, 278, 296
Lorentz, H. A., 44, 134, 147
Luhn, P., 58

M

MacDonald, D. K. C., 71
MacKay, D. M., 291
Mandelbrot, B., 32, 44, 46, 47
Maxwell, J. C., 44, 119, 162, 164, 168
Mayer, J. C., 114, 156
Mayer, M. G., 114, 156
Milne-Thomson, L. M., 49
Montgomery, C. G., 220

N

Nyquist, H., 128, 142

O

Oliver, B. M., 59, 60
Onsager, L., 147
Oppenheimer, J. R., 197
Osgood, W. F., 20

P

Patterson, A. L., 112
Pepinsky, R., 112
Perrin, J., 128
Planck, M., 44, 119, 127, 152
Poe, E. A., 268, 269
Pratt, F., 22
Purcell, E. M., 220

R

Raymond, R. C., 254, 255, 256
Reed, I. S., 67
Rosenfeld, L., 229, 243, 244
Rothstein, J., 161

S

Salzer, J. M., 273, 275, 278, 279, 280, 283, 285, 286, 296
Schreiber, W. F., 248
Schrödinger, E., 116, 157
Shannon, C. E., 4, 11, 19, 22, 24, 25, 26, 27, 29, 32, 38, 44, 47, 55, 57, 58, 69, 94, 99, 161, 247, 251, 255, 259, 265, 293
Silverman, R. A., 67, 70
Slater, J. C., 163
Smoluchowski, M., 162
Sokolnikoff, E. S., 36, 80, 82
Sokolnikoff, I. S., 36, 80, 82
Stern, O., 157
Szilard, L., 161, 163, 164, 176, 293

T

Tait, P. G., 116
Tolman, R. C., 114

U

Uhlenbeck, G. E., 141

V

Ville, J., 297
von Neumann, J., 157, 232

W

Wagner, C. A., 70
Walker, R. M., 75
Weaver, W., 4, 22, 27, 29, 69, 161
Welton, T. A., 147
Wheeler, H. A., 88
Whittaker, E. T., 99
Wiener, N., 102, 233, 259
Wiesner, J. B., 102

Z

Zemansky, M. W., 114
Zipf, G. K., 22, 46, 47

Subject Index

A

Accuracy, definition of, 194, 202
efficiency of observation as a function of, 209, 210
high, condition for, 208, 209
effect of, 219, 230
and high frequencies, 206–208, 209
illumination devices for, 206, 207
and low temperature, 212, 213, 234
measurement of length with, 206–208, 212, 213, 234
negentropy cost of, 223
total energy required for, 196–198, 208, 212, 213
information as a function of, 199, 203, 218, 228, 289, 290
low and low frequencies, 204–206
measurement of length with, 204–206, 211, 212
and uncertainty, 240, 241
of measurements, 184, 202–219
limitations of, 232–236
ultimate, 128
relation to comparative error, 218
and reliability, distinction between, 194, 203, 204
ultimate of measurements, 128
unlimited, impossibility of, 125
Adjective or predicate, 298
Agitation, disordered, 129
thermal, 123–129
and Brownian motion, 125, 128, 134–137
coupled with ordered motion, 148
in a crystal, 124
and disordered motion, 125
in an electric circuit, 137–139, 141–151
at high frequencies, 147
energy of, 123
and work done by random forces, 136
Agitation, thermal
errors due to, probability of, 187, 194
noise due to, 125, 138
in a rectifier, 148–151, 163
and reliability, 187, 194, 204, 209, 295
Amplification and transfer function, 281
Amplifier with feedback, 279
transfer function of, 280
Amplifying processes, energy degraded in, 233
Autocorrelation, 101, 104
function, 101, 102, 112
Wiener's, 112
Avogadro's number, 119, 128

B

Band-pass system, 87
Band width, finite, 87–89, 245, 246, 269, 270, 273
and length of signals, 29, 87, 88
nominal, 87, 142
and sampling interval, 280
Beats between signal and noise, 257, 258
Binary code, 51–53, 54–58
example of, 52
Binary coding, by letters, 51, 52
by words, 55
Binary channel, capacity of with noise, 69
Binary digit of information, negentropy equivalent of, 189, 257, 288
Binary digit(s), 2, 261, see also "Bits"
Binary signals, 62
Bit of information, negentropy equivalent of, 189, 257, 288
"Bits," 2, 30, 288, 292, 293
average number per letter, 5, 8, 25
Black body radiation, and high frequencies, 190, 193, 195
and Maxwell's demon, 162–168, 188
and Planck's formula, 125
Blueprints, information contained in, 287

Boltzmann constant, 3, 30, 233
and negentropy cost of information, 168
Boltzmann-Planck formula, 120, 122, 166
Bragg's condition, 111
Broadcasting, negentropy principle applied to, 259
Brownian motion, 134–137, 138, 147, 148, 185
displacement in, 147
and perpetuum mobile of second kind, 162
and thermal agitation, 125, 128, 134–137

C

Cable, transmission, 254–257
Capacity, of a binary channel with noise, 69, 70
of a channel, 28–43
in bits per second, 30
definition of, 28, 29
with feedback, 296
with noise, 247–258
Raymond's model, 254–257
Shannon's model, 247–248
and rate of flow of information, 30, 40
for sequential coding, 38
for symbols with equal length, 39
with unequal length, 43
Carnot's principle, 114, 164, 167
generalization of, 153–156
and negentropy principle of information, 153–156, 293
verification of, 178, 208, 218, 228, 243, 262, 263, 264
and random fluctuations, 155
Cell, fundamental of lattice, 106, 110, 112
miscellaneous, use of for filing, 71, 72, 73, 75
number of signals per, for maximum efficiency, 75–77
of reciprocal lattice, 106
Cells, Gabor's information, 99–101, 245
number of in a living organism, 289
optimum size of, in filing, 71, 73, 74, 75
in quantum mechanics, 101
Channel, binary, capacity of with noise, 69, 70
capacity of, 28–43
Channel, capacity of, definition of, 28, 29
in bits per second, 30
with feedback, 296
with noise, 247–258
Raymond's model, 254–257
Shannon's model, 247–248
and rate of flow of information, 30, 40
for sequential coding, 38
for symbols with equal length, 39
with unequal length, 43
matching a code with, 38
language with, 30
noiseless, theorem for, 38
Characteristic curve of a rectifier, 148, 149, 150
Characteristic equation of a difference equation, 32, 33, 35, 37
Characteristic impedance, 143, 144
matching, 44
Characteristic length, 207, 232, 234
Checking, mechanism, 62
by parity, 62, 66
positions, 63, 65
signal, 62
sums, 66
Chess player of Maelzel, 269
Circuit, electric, noise in and thermal agitation, 125, 137–139, 141–151
element, computer as, 273–275
Circuits containing a computer, 279, 280
transfer function for, 279
Code, binary, 51–53, 54–58
example of, 52
figure of merit of, 68
matching with a channel, 38
ternary, 53
Codes, error correcting and detecting, 62–70
self-correcting, efficiency of, 67
and self-checking, and value, 295
Coding, 26, 27
based on letter groups and correlation, 58
best, 38, 40, 41, 43
and cost, 44
and distribution of symbols, 38, 51
binary, by letters, 51, 52
by words, 55

Coding delays in, 49
devices, 26, 27
by letters, 51–54
binary, 51
and numbers, 54
ternary, 54
problem of, 30
sequential, 30–49
and capacity of channel, 37, 38
with one symbol per length, 36, 37
with symbols of equal length, 34, 35
of two different lengths, 35, 36
and value of information, 296
by words, 54
alphabetic, 58
binary, 55
Communication, electrical, negentropy cost of, 294
negentropy principle applied to, 259–266
Complementarity, Bohr's principle of, 229
Complexions, 120, 152
number of, 120, 121
and entropy, 120, 166
as a function of energy, 121, 122, 123
continuity of, 122
a maximum, 121
Computation, program of, for differentiation, 285, 286
for integration, 283–285
linear invariant, 275, 276
reversible, 270, 272
organization of, 267, 296
resonant frequency of, 283
stability of, 280, 281–283
transfer function of, 277, 284, 285
poles of, 280, 281, 282
Computing, 1
errors and approximations in, and loss of information, 268
problem of, 267–286
relation of to translation and coding, 267, 268, 295
and value of information, 296
Computing machine, 267–274, 295
of Babbage, 268, 269
in a circuit, 279, 280
transfer function for, 279
as a circuit element, 273–275
Computing machine
compared to a transmission channel, 268
input and output for, 267, 270, 275
Fourier components of, 270
matrix relating, 270, 271, 276
redundancy in, 270
spectra for, 271, 277
transfer function for, 277–281
as a mathematical element, 269–272
negentropy cost of operation, 268
operating on sampled signals, 269–279
processes but does not create information, 267, 268, 271, 278
reversible and conservation of information, 268
Conditional information, 19, 21, 22
Conformal mapping, 281
Conjunction in symbolic logic, 298
Connectives in symbolic logic, 298
Constraints, 8, 9, 11, 20, 21, 23, 38
problems with different types of, 147
Content measure of information, 300
Control device containing computers and ordinary circuits, 278
system with computing device, 273
Convolution, 112
Correlation, 21
coding based on, 58
cross, 104
and joint events, 21
in language, 22
none and random events, 132, 138, 141, 292
and redundancy, 22, 61
Correspondence principle, 229
Cost, and coding, 44
in energy of nuclear experimentation, 236
in negentropy of developing a plate, 198
of an experiment, 203
of information, 184, 197, 209, 218, 254, 257, 260, 264
increases with reliability, 195, 215
of interferometric measurements, 210–213
of a measurement, 235
of an observation, 184, 188–190, 194, 223, 228, 230

Cost, in negentropy
of operation of computing machine, 268
total, 195
of transmission of information, 294
of writing, printing and communication, 294
of a symbol, 30
Coupling, of observer and observed, 229–232, 235
between ordered motion and thermal agitation, 148
between signal and cable, 255
strong, between a particle and surrounding medium, 136
Cross-correlation, 104
Cross referencing, 73–75
Crystal lattices, analysis of by neutrons, 105
by X-rays, 103, 105, 111, 112
periodicity of, 105
thermal agitation in, 124
Current(s), measurement of, 128
random, 137–139, 141–151
impossibility of rectification of, 148–151
Cut-off frequency, 221, 227, 239
by an ideal low pass filter, 104

D

Damping, viscous, coefficient of, 135, 136
and increase of entropy, 115, 195
noise due to, 146, 147
Debye-Scherrer method, 111
Decoding, 27
delays in, 49
and value of information, 296
Degradation of energy, 114, 116, 119, 148, 196
in amplifying devices, 233
Kelvin's principle of, 116, 119, 154
Degree(s) of freedom, active, 219
number of, 96, 110, 226, 246, 256
finite, 102, 222, 245
of a message, 93
thermal excitation of, 175
average kinetic energy per, 147
Demodulation of a signal, 89
Demon, Maxwell's, 162–183, 184, 188
entropy decrease achieved by, 170
and the negentropy principle of information, 162–183
observation by in a thermostat, 163
methods available to, 164
operation of as conversion of information into negentropy, 163, 168–175
efficiency of, 171, 176, 189
pressure and temperature, 168
and uncertainty principle, 163
use of negentropy by, 164
Desampling, 286
a filtering process, 275
Descartes' rule, 50
Difference equation, linear, 31, 49
in sequential coding, 31
characteristic equation of, 32, 33, 35, 37
roots of, 33
solutions of, 31
dominant term of, 33, 34, 38
instability of, 33
oscillating terms of, 33, 34
stability of, 33, 35, 36, 37
absolute, 33, 36, 37
relative, 33, 36, 37
Diffraction, 207
Digits, binary, 2, 261
Digrams, 59, 60
Dirichlet's kernel, 112
Disjunction in symbolic logic, 298
Disorder and lack of information, measured by entropy, 160
Disordered agitation, 129
motion and thermal agitation, 125
Dissipation, 116
of energy, 185, 187, 195, 259
as heat, 148, 196, 234
devices to reduce, 196, 208, 209, 213, 228
mechanism for, 255
Distances, measurement of, 204–216, 234
efficiency of, 209, 210
with high accuracy, 206–208, 212, 213
frequencies, 206–208

Distances, measurement of
with an interferometer, 210–213, 228
cost of in negentropy, 210–213
with low accuracy, 204–206, 211, 212
frequencies, 204–206
number of quanta required for, 211
small, 210–216
Distribution of message points, 251–254
of energy, most probable, 121
frequency, of noise due to thermal emf's, 141–144
Gaussian, 140
random, 251
of symbols, asymptotic, 40, 43
average, 43
most probable, 38, 41, 43
for maximum information, 39–43
Distributions, coincidence of average and most probable, 44
Duration, average per letter, 51, 52
nominal, 174
of a signal, 30
and band width, 29, 87, 88
of symbols, 29, 31
total of a message, 29

E

Efficiency, of the demon's operation, 171, 176, 189
of observation, 212, 228
dependence on accuracy and reliability, 209, 210
of self correcting and self checking codes, 67
thermal, 118
Electric circuit, noise in and thermal agitation, 125, 137–139, 141–151
Electromagnetic fields, uncertainty in measurement of, 243, 244
Emission, average rate of, 134
completely random, 133
Energy, complexions, number of, a function of, 121, 122, 123
content, total of a system, 116
cost of nuclear experimentation, 236
degradation of, 114, 116, 119, 148, 196
in amplifying processes, 233
Kelvin's principle of, 116, 119, 154
Energy,
per degree of freedom, average kinetic, 147
dissipation of, 185, 187, 259
by damping, 195
devices to reduce, 196, 208, 209, 213, 228
as heat, 148, 196, 234
fluctuations, 122–127, 257, 258
magnitude of, 127
and frequency, relation between, 120
grade of, and negentropy, 114, 116, 154
levels, probabilities of for a quantized oscillator, 124
of a low frequency oscillator, average kinetic, 123, 124, 146
total, 124, 125, 246
and momentum, relation between, 235
most probable distribution of, 121
noise, average, 247–254
most probable value of, 249
of a quantized oscillator, average kinetic, 125, 186
coincidence of median and average values, 189
distinction between average and most probable values, 125, 126
median, 186, 188
required for an observation, 196, 212, 213, 214, 234
thermal, and accuracy of measurements, 126
and work done by random forces, 136
Engines, thermal, 117, 118, 167
work done by, 118
Entropy, 3, 27, 114, 116
decrease of, achieved by demon, 170
and information, 152, 153
definition of, 115, 122
a dimensionless number, 118
and disorder, 160
high and stability, 159
of an ideal monatomic gas, 156
increase of, 115, 158, 166, 175, 179, 185, 188, 192, 193, 196, 201, 209, 214, 222, 232, 234
and information, 190, 209
and loss of information, 157–159

Entropy, increase and measurement, 168, 185, 209
interferometric, 210–213
minimum for an observation, 184, 185, 194, 198–201
of given reliability, 197
during an observation, 184, 211
per observation, 184, 190
and information, connection between, 3, 114, 152–161, 176, 177, 190, 293
bound, 153
difference of, 204
low and instability, 159
a measure of lack of information, 160, 293
negative (see Negentropy), 114
related to probability, 119
Shannon's definition of, 161
statistical interpretation of, 119–122
of a system defined by reversible transformations, 116, 118
units, 3, 30, 288, 293
Equivalence in symbolic logic, 298
Error, absolute, 202
comparative, 202
relation to accuracy, 218
correcting codes, 62–70
correction and redundancy, 61, 62
detecting codes, 62–70
per digit in a code, 67, 68
probability of greater than 50%, 295
and reliability, 194, 295
and value, 295
proportional, 202
and range of variation, 242
relative, 202
Errors, average in time and frequency, 91
experimental and information, 202, 203
and loss of information, 260, 268
of observation and reliability, 184, 295
and information in a physical law, 290
probability of in a code, 67, 68
due to thermal agitation, 187, 194
rounding off of, 132
and loss of information, 272
Euclidean geometry, limits of, 235, 236
space, 233
Experiments, non-perturbing, 230, 231

F

Factually true, or logically indeterminate, 298
False, logically, 298
Feedback, amplifier with, 279
transfer function for, 280
capacity of a channel with, 296
Fejer's kernel, 112
Field of apparatus, 220
electromagnetic, uncertainty in measurements on, 243, 244
of observation, 194
and information, 203, 289
and negentropy cost, 203, 223
Figure of merit of a code, 68
in evaluation of information, 297
Filing, 71–75
cells, optimum size of, 71, 73, 74, 75
with cross referencing, 71, 73–75
with miscellaneous cell, 71, 72, 73, 75
Filter, band-pass, 105
for desampling, design of, 286
ideal low-pass, 105
cut-off by, 104
transfer function of, 104
Filtering, for desampling, 275, 286
and selection of information, 297
First law of thermodynamics, 114
Fluctuation, average square, 133, 134
Fluctuations, 125–127, 179
of energy, 122–127, 257, 258
and accuracy of measurement, 126
magnitude of, 127
in information, 178
observations due to, 189
random, and Carnot's principle, 155
thermal and reliability, 187, 194, 204, 209, 295
Focus in a wave guide, 220–226
Forces, average square of, 136, 147
random, 135, 148
work done by and thermal energy, 136
Fourier coefficients, intensities of, 111, 112
phases of, 111, 112
and sampled values, 96
Fourier components, 270
and points of reciprocal lattice, 109
number of, 110

Fourier integrals, 83, 99, 104, 277
Fourier method, 78–97, 245
  and Laplace transform, 278
Fourier series, 78–86, 99
  complex, 78, 96, 101, 103
  containing a finite number of terms, 94
  convergence of, 80
  of a discontinuous function, 81, 83
  and method of finite intervals, 78
  successive approximations of, 82
  triple, 105–112
Fourier spectrum(s), finite, 200
  of particular functions, 86
Frequencies, cable for transmission of continuous range of, 143
  cut-off of higher, 104
  finite range of, 87
  high, 221, 227
    experiments using, 196–198
    for high accuracy, 206–208, 209, 212
    observations using, 206–208
      number of quanta required for, 211
    quantum limitations at, 147
    results for, 147, 193, 195, 227
  low, 246
    conditions for, 250
    for low accuracy, 204–206
    observations using, 204–206
      number of quanta required for, 211
    results for, 147, 195, 196, 227
    simultaneous observations at, 127, 190–194, 196
Frequency, average error in, 91
  cut-off, 221, 227, 239
  distribution of noise due to thermal emf's, 141–144
  and energy, relation between, 120
  high, oscillator, and cost of an observation, 188–190
    fluctuations in energy of, 127
  limit, same in all directions, 108, 109
    different in different directions, 107–109
  low, oscillator, 194
    average kinetic energy of, 123, 124, 146
    average total energy of, 124, 125, 146
    fluctuations in energy of, 127
Frequency, of occurrence, of letters, 5, 52
    of words, 24, 44–47
  resonant of a program of computation, 283
  and time, symmetry in, 84, 85
    uncertainty relation for, 89, 93, 218
  upper, 87
Function, autocorrelation, 101, 102
    Wiener's, 112
  with discontinuities, Fourier series of, 81, 83
  with a finite band width, 87, 100
  impulse, 98
    of Linvill, 274
    of Shannon, 273, 274
  periodic, 94
  proper "m", 300
  pulse, 95
  range of variation of in a physical law, 289, 290
    reduced by advance knowledge, 292
  single message, 94, 97, 99
  transfer for an amplifier, 280, 281
    for a computer, 277, 284, 285
      in a circuit, 279
    of a filter, 104
    poles of, 280, 281, 282
      and instability, 281
  transformation, 103, 104
  transformed, 103
Functions, Gabor's sine and cosine message, 100
  inverse, 85
  orthogonal, 247
  spectrums of, 86

G

Gabor's discussion of Szilard's problem, 179–182, 223
  formula, 257, 258
  information cells, 99–101, 245
  machine, 180
  sine and cosine message functions, 100
Gas, diffusion and loss of information, 158, 159
  ideal monatomic, entropy of, 156
Gaussian distribution, 140
  noise, 250

Gaussian pulse, 85
spectrum, 85
Gibbs' formula, 122–124
phenomenon, 80
Hartley-Tuller-Shannon formula, 248–257, 258
Heat, 115
energy dissipated as, 148, 196, 234
engine, 117–118, 167
well informed, 176–179
work done by, 118
exchange of between two bodies, 121
flow, 115
and work, interchange of, 118
Heavy nuclei, use of for measurement, 236–238
High-pass system, 87
Human processes beyond scope of information theory, 287
Hyperspace, representation of signals and noise in, 246–254
Hypersphere, plane section of, 250
volume of, 247

I

Impedance, characteristic, 143, 144
Implication in symbolic logic, 298
Impulse(s), of force, average square of, 136
function, 98
of Linvill, 274
of Shannon, 273, 274
random, theory of, 132–134, 141, 142
Individual or noun, 298
Indeterminate, logically, or factual, 298
Information, absolute, 265, 266
value of greater than relative value of, 297
average per letter, 5, 8, 25
per symbol, 6–8, 11, 39
with correlation between symbols, 22, 23
bound, 152, 156, 158
and negentropy, 153, 154, 155
cells, Gabor's, 99–101, 245
various ways of selecting, 100
conditional, 19, 21, 22
contained in a blueprint, 287
in a living organism, 289
Information, contained in a message, 22, 27
in a numerical table, 291–293
in a physical law, 289–291
in a wiring diagram, 287–289
converted to negentropy, 163, 164, 168–175, 184
dead, 261
decreased by constraint, 8, 9, 11, 20, 21, 23
definition of, 1, 202, 290
distributed, 266
distribution for maximum, 39–43
duration of validity of, 160, 189
and entropy, connection between, 3, 114, 152–161, 176, 177, 293
and experimental errors, 202, 203
and field of observation, 203, 289
fluctuations in, 178
free, 152, 154
and negentropy, 155
as a function of accuracy, 199, 203, 218, 228, 289, 290
lack of and disorder, 160
measured by entropy, 293
live, 259
loss of, by errors and approximations, 260, 268, 272
in gas diffusion, 158, 159
and increase of entropy, 157–159
a maximum for equal a priori probabilities, 14–17
measure of, 1, 3, 11, 301
in bits, 2, 30, 288, 293
content, 300
in entropy units, 3, 30, 288, 293
by state descriptions, 299–301
metrical, 291
multiplication of, 260
negentropy, changed into 154, 164, 176, 184, 257, 261, 263
cost of, 184, 197, 209, 218, 254, 257, 260, 264
equivalent of 168, 189, 190, 257
very small, 288, 293, 294
negentropy principle of, 152–161, 219, 233, 288, 293
a generalization of Carnot's principle, 153–156, 228, 293

Information, negentropy principle of, applied to a channel with noise, 254–257
to communication, 259–266
in general physics, 184–201
and Maxwell's demon, 162–183
in telecommunications, 245–258
new, 265
and role of computing machine, 267, 268, 271, 278
and observation, 202–228
and organization, 287–289
positions for in an error detecting code, 63, 65
properties of, 12–17
rate of emission of, 28
of flow of, 28, 255
maximum average and capacity, 30, 40
ratio of to cost in negentropy, 209
recorded, 260
selection of according to a figure of merit, 297
selective, 291
semantic, 297–301
statistical definition of, 1, 267
consequences of, 291
stored, 261
structural, 291
theory, connection with quantum mechanics, 233, 243
problems beyond the scope of, 294
and thermodynamics, 114, 190, 293
transmission of, 259
negentropy cost of, 294
used by demon to decrease entropy, 163–166
value of, 294–297
and computing, coding and translation, 296
human, 9, 10
negative, 10
relative less than absolute, 297
and reliability, 295
Input data for computing machine, 267, 275
Fourier components of, 270
Fourier integrals for, 277
matrix of, to output, 270, 271, 276
Input matrix of,
inverse of, 271
redundancy in, 270
spectrum, 271, 277
ratio of output spectrum to, 277
Instability, of a program of computation, 281–283
of a system and low entropy, 159
Integral(s), Fourier, 83, 99, 104, 172
methods of approximation of, 284, 285
sine, 81
Interaction between observer and observed, 230, 232
Interferometer, measurements of length with, 210–213, 228, 234
negentropy cost of, 210–213
Interval(s),
sampling, 98, 105
and band width, 280
time, measurement of, 217–219
Irreversible coding device, 27
process, 27, 116, 268
accompanies an observation, 184, 231, 232
applications of thermodynamics to, 147

J

Joint events, 17–20
and correlation, 21

K

Kelvin's principle of degradation of energy, 116, 119, 154
Kernel(s), Dirichlet's, 112
Fejer's, 112
for linear transformations, 112

L

Lagrange's identity, 95, 173
Language, matching with channel, 30
redundancy content of, 24, 26
Laplace transform and Fourier method, 278
Lattice, analysis of, by neutrons, 105
by X-rays, 103, 105, 111, 112
face-centered cubic, 110
fundamental cell of, 106, 110, 112
hexagonal type, 110

Lattice, periodicity of, 105
  reciprocal, 106, 107, 108
    cell of, 106
    points of and Fourier components, 109
    spherical boundary in, 110
  rectangular, 106
    of sampling points, 109
  thermal agitation in, 124
Length, characteristic, 207, 232, 234
  measurement of, 204–216, 234
    efficiency of, 209, 210
    with high accuracy, 206–208, 212, 213
      frequencies, 206–208
    with an interferometer, 210–213, 228
      cost of in negentropy, 210–213
    with low accuracy, 204–206, 211, 212
      frequencies, 204–206
    number of quanta required for, 211
    small, 210–216
  minimum and quantum theory, 236
Letter, bits per, 5, 25
  information per, 5, 8
Letters, blocks, complexes, or groups of, 22, 23, 24
    code for, binary, 52
      ternary, 53
    coding based on, 58
  coding by, 54
  and numbers, coding by, 54
  probability of occurrence of, 5, 52
Linear mathematical program, 270, 272, 275
Linear transformations, 103
  pulses as kernels for, 112
Linvill's impulse function, 274
Living organism, information contained in, 289
  need of for negentropy, 116
Logic, symbolic, notation of, 298
Locus in Q plane of unit circle in z plane, 282, 286
  interior of, 282
Logically, false, 298
  indeterminate or factual, 298
  true, 298
Low-pass filter, ideal, 105
    cut-off by, 104
  system, 87

M

Macroscopic variables, 120, 153
Maelzel, chess player of, 269
Matching characteristic impedance, 44
  code with a channel, 38
  language with channel, 30
  problem, 44
    solution of, 47
Matrix, of input to output, 270, 271, 276
  inverse of, 271
Maxwell's Demon, 162–183, 184, 188
  entropy decrease achieved by 170
  and the negentropy principle of information, 162–183
  observation by in a thermostat, 163
    methods available to, 164
  operation of as conversion of information to negentropy, 163, 168–175
    efficiency of, 171, 176, 189
  pressure and temperature, 168
  and uncertainty principle, 163
  use of negentropy by, 164
Measure, content, of information, 300
  function, proper, 300
  of information, 1, 3, 11, 301
    by state descriptions, 299–301
  of state description, 299
Measurement, accuracy of, 184, 202–219
    limitations of, 232–236
    ultimate, 128
    unlimited, impossibility of, 125
  cost of in negentropy, 235
    minimum, 188, 194
  of current, 128
  efficiency of, 209, 210
  and entropy increase, 168
  high accuracy, total energy required, 196–198, 208, 212, 213
  of length, 204–216, 234
    efficiency of, 209, 210
    with high accuracy, 206–208, 212, 213
      frequencies, 206–208
    with an interferometer, 210–213, 228
      cost of in negentropy, 210–213
    with low accuracy, 204–206, 211, 212
      frequencies, 204–206
Measurement, of length, number of quanta required for, 211

Measurement, of length, small, 210–216
of momentum, 241–243
of position with a microscope, 219–228
reliability of, 184, 187
of time intervals, 217–219
Measurements, field, uncertainty in, 243, 244
Measuring device, coupled with system under observation, 230, 232
Memory device(s), 58
magnetic, and spin distribution, 160
and rate of attenuation, 160
Message, degrees of freedom of, 93
function(s), Gabor's sine and cosine, 100
single, 94, 97, 99
information content of, 22, 27
points, distribution of, 251–254
total duration of, 29
Messages, number of distinct, 6, 7, 8
of given total duration, 29, 31, 33
or less, 33, 34
Microscope, measurement of position with, 219–228
number of photons required for, 241
time definition in, 240, 241
and uncertainty relations, 238–241
observation with, 234, 244
Microscopic effect, conversion to a macroscopic effect, 198, 233
variables, 120
Minimum length and quantum theory, 236
Molecules, number of in a living organism, 289
observation of, 162, 188
Momentum and energy, relation between, 235
as a function of wave length, 235
measurement of, 241–243
Monogrammer, 59, 60
Motion, Brownian, 134–137, 138, 148, 185
displacement in, 147
and perpetuum mobile of second kind, 162
and thermal agitation, 125, 128, 134–137
ordered, coupled with thermal agitation, 148
random, 135

N

Negation in symbolic logic, 298
Negentropy, 114
changed into information, 154, 164, 176, 184, 257, 261, 263
cost of developing a photographic plate, 198
of an experiment, 203
increases with reliability, 195, 215
of information, 184, 197, 209, 218, 254, 257, 260, 264
of measurement, 235
interferometric, 210–213
of an observation, 184, 188–190, 194, 223, 228, 230
of operating a computing machine, 268
ratio of information to, 209
total, 195
of transmission of information, 294
of writing, printing, and communication, 294
equivalent of information, 168, 189, 190, 257
very small, 288, 293, 294
a measure of grade of energy, 114, 116, 154
required for an observation, 170–176
minimum, 184, 196–201
sources of, 116, 185
structural, 288, 289
of a system and its potential for work, 116
use of by living organisms, 116
by Maxwell's demon, 164
of a wiring diagram, 288
Negentropy principle of information, 152–161, 219, 233, 288, 293
applied to a channel with noise, 254–257
to communication, 259–266
in general physics, 184–201
a generalization of Carnot's principle, 153–156, 228, 293
and Maxwell's demon, 162–183
in telecommunications, 245–258
Noise, capacity of a channel with, 69, 247–258

Noise, due to damping, 146–148
in electric circuits and thermal agitation, 125, 137–139, 141–151
energy, average, 247–254
most probable value, 249
frequency distribution of, 141–144
power, 245–248, 254–258
in resistors, 143, 144
and signals, beats between, 257, 258
representation in hyperspace, 246–254
in tubes, 132–134
Noun or individual, 298
Nuclear experimentation, cost in energy, 236
Numerical table, information contained in, 291–293
Nyquist's formula, 141–144, 146
generalizations of, 146, 147
method, 143, 144

O

Observation, effect of thermal fluctuations on, 126
efficiency of, 212, 228
dependency on accuracy and reliability, 209, 210
energy required for, 196, 234
errors in and reliability, 184, 295
field of, and information, 203, 223, 289–291
with high frequencies, 188–190, 206–208, 211
and information, 202–228
and irreversibility, 184, 231, 232
with low frequencies, 204–206, 211
with a microscope, 219–228, 234, 244
negentropy required for, 170–176, 184, 188–190, 194, 211, 223, 228, 230
dependence on reliability, 195, 197
minimum, 184, 188, 196–201
number of quanta required for, 181, 211
on an oscillator, 185–190
system of, 190–194
photographic method of, 197
physical limits of, 229–244
reliability of, 184, 187, 188, 189
and value, 295
Observation,
spurious, probability of, 189, 191, 194, 212
uncertainty of, and information, 203
Organism, living, information contained in, 289
need for negentropy, 116
Organization and information, 287–289
Oscillator(s), harmonic, fluctuations in energy of, 127
high frequency, and cost of observation, 188–190
low frequency, 194
average energy of, 123, 124, 125, 146
quantized, 124, 125, 126, 185–190
average energy of, 125, 186
coincidence of average and median energies, 189
distinction between average and most probable energies, 125, 126
median energy of, 186–188
probabilities of energy levels, 124
system of, energy fluctuations of, 127
observations on, 190–194
negentropy cost of, 195, 196
Output data, 267, 270, 275
Fourier integral for, 277
matrix from input to, 270, 271, 276
inverse of, 271
redundancy in, 270
spectrum, 271, 277
ratio of, to input spectrum, 277
Overdetermination, 153, 154

P

Parity check, 62, 66
Parseval relation, 80, 85, 174
Pascal's triangle, 129
Perpetual motion, impossibility of, 117, 162
Phases of oscillating terms, 102, 103
Phonemes, 4, 30, 44
Photographic method of observation, 197, 198
Photons, number required for observation, 211
with microscope, 241–243

Physical law, information contained in, 289–291
limits of observation, 229–244
theory of information, 293
Physics, relation between classical and quantum, 229–233
Planck formula, 125
Planck-Boltzmann formula, 120, 122, 166
Planck's constant and the negentropy of information, 168, 233
and the uncertainty principle, 89, 229
Position, measurement of with a microscope, 219–228
Predicate or adjective, 298
Printing, 263, 264
negentropy cost of, 294
Probabilities in the random walk, 130, 139
of energy levels for a quantized oscillator, 124
of quantum states, 186
Probability, absolute logical, 300
of a complexion, 123, 249
conditional, 21
density, 90
distribution, Gaussian, 140
and entropy, connection between, 119
of error per digit of a code, 67, 68
due to thermal agitation, 187, 194, 251
and reliability and value, 295
of occurrence of letters, 5, 52
of words, 24, 44, 45
of a spurious observation, 189, 191, 194, 212
of a state description, 299
Program of computation, for differentiation, 285, 286
for integration, 283–285
linear invariant, 275, 276
reversible, 270, 272
organization of, 267, 296
resonant frequency of, 283
stability of, 280, 281–283
transfer function of, 277, 284, 285
poles of, 280, 281, 282
Proper "*m*" function, 300
Pulse function, 95
Gaussian, 85
length and band width, 87
Pulse function,
rectangular, 85
spectrum of, 85, 141, 142
symmetrical, 85
system, 105
technique, 83
triangular, 85
Pulses, attenuation of a system of, 160
as kernels for linear transformations, 112
Linvill, 274
of radiation, rectangular, succession of, 172, 198
random, spectrum of, 141
rounded, succession of, 174
Shannon, 273, 274
yielding transfer functions, 104

Q

Quantized oscillator, 124, 125, 126, 185–190
average energy of, 125, 186
and most probable energy, distinction between, 125, 126
coincidence of average and median energies, 189
median energy, 186–188
probabilities of energy levels of, 124
Quantum effect, a typical, 127
limitations at high frequencies, 147
mechanics and information theory, connection between, 233, 243
number, average, 125, 186
coincidence of average and median, 189
median, 186, 188
state(s), most probable, 125
probabilities of, 186

R

Radiation, black body, and high frequencies, 190, 193
and Maxwell's demon, 162–168, 188
and Planck's formula, 125
pulses of, succession of, 172, 198
Radioactive transformations, application of random walk to, 132
Random currents, impossibility of rectification of, 137–139, 141–151

Random, emission, 132–134
events and lack of correlation, 132, 138, 141, 292
fluctuations, and Carnot's principle, 155
forces, work done by, and thermal energy, 136
impulses, theory of, 132–134, 141, 142
motion, 135
numbers, table of, 291, 292
oscillations, kinetic energy of, 128
succession of rectangular pulses, spectrum of, 141
walk, 129–132, 133, 134, 137, 139
applications of, 132–140
probabilities in, 130, 139
Range of a sentence, 299
of variation of a function in a physical law, 290
reduced by advance knowledge, 292
of variables in a physical law, 289, 290
Reading, 260, 261–263
negentropy lost in, 262, 263
Realizability of an operation by a computer, 283
Reciprocal lattice, 106, 107, 108
cell of, 106
points of and Fourier components, 109
spherical boundary in, 110
Reciprocal vectors, 106
Rectangular pulse(s), 85
spectrum of, 85, 141, 142
of a random succession of, 141
Rectangular spectrum, 85
Rectification of random currents, impossibility of, 148–151
Rectifier, characteristic curve of, 148, 149, 150
thermal agitation in, 148–151, 162
Redundancy, 21–27, 28, 265, 270, 295
content of English language, 26
and correlation, 22
definition of, 24
prediction, and error correction, 61, 62
and detection of errors, 24, 62
Reliability and accuracy, distinction between, 194, 203
efficiency of an observation as a function of, 209, 210
Reliability,
high, 194–196, 204, 212, 242
of a negative reading, 190
negentropy cost as a function of, 195, 197, 215
of an observation, 184, 187, 188, 189, 295
and probability of error, 194, 295
and thermal fluctuations, 187, 194, 204, 209, 295
and value of information, 295
Reproducibility of an observation, 230
Resistor, noise in, 143, 144
Resolving power, 207, 226
and uncertainty of observation, 203
Reversible coding device, 27
process, 27, 117
transformations, 184
and total entropy of a system, 116, 118

S

Sampled data, at a given time, computing from, 275, 276
values, 95, 102, 245
and Fourier coefficients, 96
Sampling interval, 98, 105
and band width, 200
Sampling method, 95, 245
and computing machine, 269–279
in three dimensions, 105–112
Shannon's, 97–99, 105, 245, 252
applied to computing machines, 273–275
Sampling points, 98, 102
number of, 95, 96, 97, 110
Sampling procedures, 78, 102, 109
Schwarz' inequality, 92, 113
Second law of thermodynamics, 114, 148, 165, 166, 189
and Maxwell's demon, 162, 164
valid on the average, 189
Semantic information, 297–301
Sequence of symbols, unconstrained, 31, 38
Sequential coding, 30–49
and capacity of a channel, 37, 38
with one symbol per length, 36, 37
with symbols of equal length, 34, 35
of two different lengths, 35, 36

Shannon-Hartley-Tuller formula, 248–257, 258
Shannon's formula, 5, 6, 7, 8
Shannon's impulse function, 273, 274
Shannon's sampling method, 97–99, 105, 245, 252
applied to computing machines, 273–275
Shot effect, 132–134
Signal, checking, 62
coupling with cable, 255
demodulation of, 89
duration of, 30
points in hyperspace, 246–254
Signals, analysis of, 78–113
binary, 62
length of and band width, 29, 87, 88
number per elementary cell for maximum efficiency, 75–77
and thermal noise, representation in hyperspace, 246–254
beats between, 257, 258
Simpson's rules, 285
Sine integral, 81
Spectrum, Fourier, for particular functions, 86
Gaussian, 85
input and output, 271, 277
ratio of, 277
of a random succession of rectangular pulses, 141
rectangular, 85
of a rectangular pulse, 85, 141, 142
symmetrical, 85
Spin distribution and magnetic memory devices, 160
Spring valve as a Maxwell demon, 162
Stability and high entropy, 159
of a program of computation, 280, 281–283
State description(s), 299
equally probable, 301
measure of, 299
probability of, 299
Statistical definition of information, 1, 267
consequences of, 291
discussions, examples of in thermodynamics, 121–123
Stirling's formula, 6, 39, 139
Structure, negentropy of, 288, 289
Sum, checking, 66
Symbol, average information per, 6–8, 11, 39
with correlation between symbols, 22, 23
cost of, 30
Symbolic logic, notation of, 298
Symbols, 30
with different lengths, 41–44
two, 35, 36
distribution of, most probable, 38, 40, 41, 43
durations of, 29, 30, 31
of equal length, 34, 39
groups of, all of equal length, 49
independent, 29, 31
sequences of, unconstrained, 31, 38
Szilard's machine, 177
Szilard's problem, 176–179
Gabor's discussion of, 179–182

T

Telecommunication(s), 1, 87, 105
and information theory, 293
and the negentropy principle of information, 245–258
and rate of attenuation of signals, 160
Telephone network, information contained in, 288
Television, 61, 87, 93
Temperature, absolute (Kelvin), 115, 122, 184
low, and high accuracy, measurement at, 212, 213
Tetragrams, 60
Thermal agitation, 123–129
and Brownian motion, 125, 128, 134–137
coupled with ordered motion, 148
in a crystal, 124
and disordered motion, 125
in an electric circuit, 137–139, 141–151
at high frequencies, 147
energy of, 123
and work done by random forces, 136
errors due to, probability of, 187, 194
noise due to, 125, 138
in a rectifier, 148–151, 163

Thermal agitation,
and reliability, 187, 194, 204, 209, 295
Thermal conduction and loss of negentropy, 116
Thermal efficiency, 118
Thermal emf, noise due to, frequency distribution of, 141–144
Thermal energy and accuracy of measurements, 126
and work done by random forces, 136
Thermal engines, 117, 118, 167
work done by, 118
Thermal fluctuations and reliability, 187, 194, 204, 209, 295
Thermal noise, analysis of, 141–151
in an electric circuit, 137–139, 141–151
and signals, representation in hyperspace, 246–254
Thermodynamic cycles, 117
Thermodynamic units, 3, 30, 288, 293
Thermodynamics, 114–127
applications to irreversible processes, 147
first law of, 114
and information theory, 114, 190
second law of, 114, 148, 165, 166
and Maxwell's demon, 162, 164
valid on the average, 189
use of statistical considerations in, 121–123
Thermostat, 122, 123, 191, 192, 193, 196
Thought processes, exclusion of from information theory, 155, 260, 267, 287
Time, average error in, 91
delays in computing, 286
and frequency, symmetry in, 84, 85
uncertainty relation for, 89, 93, 218
with many photons, 238
modified, 240
intervals, measurement of, 217–219
Transducers, 28
Transfer function, and amplification, 281
for an amplifier, 280
for a computer, 277, 284, 285
in a circuit, 279
of a filter, 104
poles of, 280, 281, 282
Transfer function, poles of,
and instability, 281
Transformations, irreversible, 115, 184
linear and filters, 103–105
radioactive, application of random walk to, 132
reversible, 184
linear, 103
pulses as kernels for, 112
matrix of, from input to output, 270, 271, 276
and total entropy of a system, 116, 118
Translating, and computing, 268
and value of information, 296
Transmission of information, 259, 260
negentropy cost of, 294
Trapezoidal rule, 284
Trigrams, 59, 60
True, logically, 298
Tube, electron, 217
noise in, 132
Tuller-Hartley-Shannon formula, 248–257, 258

U

Uncertainty, in field measurements, 243, 244
of an observation and information, 203
principle, 89, 90, 229–244, 235, 236
and Maxwell's demon, 163
and negentropy principle of information, 168
independent of one another, 233
relation for time and frequency, 89, 93, 218
with many photons, 238
modified, 240
relations and observation with a microscope, 238–244
Units, entropy, 3, 30, 288, 293
Unit systems, 2, 288, 293

V

Value of information, 294–297
human, 9, 10
negative, 10
relative less than absolute, 297

Value of information,
and reliability, 295
and translation, coding and computing, 296
Variables, macroscopic, 120, 153
microscopic, 120
Variation, range of a function in a physical law, 290
reduced by advance knowledge of, 292
of variables in a physical law, 289, 290
Velocity, group and phase, 221
Vibrations, similarity of electrical and mechanical, 137–139, 146
thermal, in a crystal, 124
Viscous damping, coefficient of, 135, 136
and increase of entropy, 115
and noise, 146, 147
Viscous resistance and coupling between ordered motion and thermal agitation, 148
Vocabulary, total number of words in, 24, 46

W

Walk, radom, 129–132, 133, 134, 137, 139
applications of, 132–140
probabilities in, 130, 139
Wave guide, focus in, 220–226
Wavelength, momentum as a function of, 235
Wiener-Khintchine formula, 101, 102
Wiener's autocorrelation function, 112
Wiring diagram, information contained in, 287–289
in bits, 288
in entropy units, 288
Word frequency, 44, 45
as a function of word order, 24, 46
Mandelbrot's law for, 45
Zipf's law for, 46
Word order, 24, 45
Word rank, 45
Word statistics, 24, 44
problems of, 44–47
Words, coding by, 54
alphabetic, 58
binary, 55
frequency of occurrence of, 24, 44, 45
total number of, 24, 46
Work, 116
done by random forces, and thermal energy, 136
thermal engines, 118
and heat, interchange of, 118
potential and negentropy content of a system, 116
Writing, 260, 261, 263
negentropy cost of, 294